TROUT UNLIMITED'S
GUIDE TO

AMERICA'S
100
BEST
TROUT
STREAMS

TROUT UNLIMITED'S GUIDE TO

AMERICA'S 100 BEST TROUT STREAMS

Updated and Revised

John Ross

THE LYONS PRESS
Guilford, Connecticut
An imprint of The Globe Pequot Press

The Lyons Press is an imprint of The Globe Pequot Press.

10 9 8 7 6 5 4 3 2 1

Printed in the United States of America

Library of Congress Cataloging-in-Publication Data

Ross, John, 1946–
  Trout Unlimited's guide to America's 100 best trout streams / John Ross.—Updated
and rev.
    p. cm.
  Includes bibliographical references and index.
  ISBN 1-59228-585-6 (trade paper)
  1. Trout fishing—United States—Guidebooks.   I. Trout Unlimited. II. Title. II. Title:
Guide to America's 100 best trout streams.
SH688.U67 2005
799.17'57'0973--dc22

                                                              2005006084

To every adult who teaches a child to fish for trout.

Trout Unlimited has emerged from the foothills of the conservation community and taken on the mountains where public policy is made. Western waters, eastern brook trout, acid rain, and mine seepage—TU has rolled up its sleeves and is slugging it out in the chambers of government and regulatory agencies where pressing issues of coldwater conservation are decided.

Reestablishment of once-native and wild species, restoration of habitat, and abatement of pollution are the three conservation initiatives highest on most TUer's agendas. But the future of trout and salmon fishing depends not only on the union of good science and good policy, but on whether or not the next half century will foster a cadre of activists who'll continue the fight for clear cold water and the fish that swim therein. Without a new army of coldwater conservationists, gains made since the beginning of TU will erode and wash away.

Coldwater conservationists are made, not born. The first step is to take a kid fishing. Plant the seed. Nurture it with kids days, first cast and scout programs, and summer trout camps. In this way, the future of trout fishing in America will be assured.

CONTENTS

ACKNOWLEDGMENTS

Like an old brown trout, I'm content to lie in my hole and pick off morsels that drift down my lane. This happy state of affairs existed until the first edition of this book was published in 1999. Marcia Woolman, then president of the Rapidan chapter of TU, spotted the little dimple I made in the current. She invited me to give a talk on the new book at a chapter meeting. Had I an option? I was asked to buy a packet of raffle tickets for a cane rod made by her husband, Hank. It was only $25. How could I refuse? You know what happened next, of course. I won the durn rod, a wonderful seven-and-a-half-foot 4-weight that's perfect for trout anywhere in the East, and Marcia set the hook.

Now, how could I turn down the chapter's requests to edit the newsletter, to photograph and write up Rapidan's fishing show, youth days, camps for kids, stream sampling, and habitat improvement? Marcia moved on to vice presidency of the Virginia Council. She and Frank Deviney, council chair, had conceived and implemented a strategic planning process. Never shy about providing advice, I was soon in over my waders. I began representing the council in regional and national meetings and working with other chapters in the state.

So along with the hands-on experience I have gained from my first involvement with Trout Unlimited as a member of the Win Cres chapter in Winona, Minnesota, through the Rapidan chapter and Virginia Council, I'd become engaged in the program and policy side of TU. I'm grateful to Marcia for grabbing my suspenders and hauling me into the fray.

Scores of TU members have graciously provided information for this book. I hope they'll accept my collective thanks. Their willingness to share is one of TU's greatest strengths. I'm doubly grateful to TU's national staff, particularly Duncan Blair, Steve Moyer, T. Grand, Beth Duris, and Kenny Mendez for their unfailing good counsel and support. I have benefited deeply from Charles Gauvin's leadership as TU president and from the cadre of exemplary volunteer leaders that he has gathered in support of coldwater conservation. In addition, my appreciation goes to my former editor at *Sports Afield*, Jay Cassell, now of The Lyons Press, and his colleague Lisa Purcell, whose good cheer and infinite patience have made this a much better book.

John Ross, Chair
Virginia Council Trout Unlimited
Upperville, Virginia
2005

FOREWORD

As I began thinking about what would be an appropriate message to include in a book about America's 100 best trout streams, the very notion of 100 great trout streams suddenly struck me like a thunderbolt. One hundred "best" trout streams and scores of other great ones that did not make the "best" list. That is truly something for which we should be thankful.

There remain a good number of untrammeled, pristine places in the United States, and some of them are among the locations featured in this book. But this book's unwritten subtitle is really stewardship and restoration. More than a few of the streams selected as among the best are places that, but for human intervention, could have become or remained among the worst. I am pleased to say that Trout Unlimited's volunteers and staff have had a major role in that intervention and have, for almost 50 years, befriended, protected, and restored many of the 100 best and helped many other quality streams.

Although there are legitimate concerns about urbanization and the loss of public access in some places, in many areas there is greater opportunity to find quality trout fishing today than existed 20 or 30 years ago. Without investment in such protection and restoration, it is difficult to imagine that a number of the waters featured in this book—the Kennebec and the Little Juniata come most readily to mind—would have qualified.

In addition to improvements in water quality, better trout management—much of it the result of Trout Unlimited persuasion—has benefited a number of the streams in this book. It's difficult to argue with the results of Montana's or Pennsylvania's wild trout programs, and it's great to see even some of the most hatchery-dependent states kicking some of the habit and focusing more on habitat.

In recent years, Trout Unlimited's stewardship and restoration focus has expanded to include maintaining sufficient flows in a number of the 100 best. Recent initiatives in drought response management have benefited the perennially stressed Big Hole. There is more water in the Madison and a number of other Montana rivers thanks to water leases our staff has developed with ranchers. The legendary Gunnison's roaring flow is one major step closer to preservation thanks to our Colorado Water Project staff's deft lawyering. With new sources of program support, we are now turning our attention eastward and securing more fish-friendly flows for such great rivers as the Delaware and the Housatonic.

Yet, much as we want to congratulate ourselves on having produced a national largesse of quality angling opportunity, we should ponder for a moment the fate of our native coldwater fisheries. Here, things are far different. Of the 30 recognized native trout and salmon species and sub-species, 25 are either extinct, are sufficiently threatened or endangered to require special protection, or are of special concern to scientists and fish managers. Try as we might, we cannot reengineer evolution. Our success in creating all the great opportunities we have today for catching wild fish that are not indigenous to their habitats—browns everywhere in the U.S.; rainbows everywhere outside the Pacific coast drainages; brookies west of the Mississippi)—can never compensate for the loss of our natural heritage. We need to preserve as much as we can of our natural and our angling heritage; they're both important.

So, as we head off to enjoy the 100 best and the scores of our nation's other great trout and salmon streams, let's remember that being a complete angler requires more than mere skill with a rod and a reel, that for each moment we enjoy, we should also give back in equal or greater measure to the land, the water, and the fish themselves.

Charles F. Gauvin,
President
Trout Unlimited
Arlington, Virginia, 2005

INTRODUCTION

Rods on pegs, waders hung, pop-tops popped, we've all sat around gnawing on the old bone: "What's the best trout stream?" Since starting this gig in the late 1990s, I've snagged my backcasts in brush along a bunch of streams throughout the country. But I still couldn't begin to tell you which one is the best. So, in picking the streams for this book, we asked TU members to offer their choices based on the quality of the fishing. They considered populations of trout, wild and stocked; public access; scenic beauty; and whether TU chapters have had a hand in improving the fishery. More than 1,000 members cast their votes.

Are the 100 streams they picked really the "best"? Hard to say. Fishing is such a matter of individual tastes. What's best for me may not be best for you. Anybody who's seen me cast a fly knows that long lines and I are utter strangers. I much prefer intimate waters that I can read, as opposed to those whose personae are hidden by heavy flows. Casting blind bores me. I'll sit for half an hour watching a pool before I'll wet a fly. I'd rather work a fish I can see or a lie that holds promise than cast blindly into whatever fate there may be. My pace is slow, boringly methodical. Naturally, I like big fish as well as the next fellow. The older I get, the more my fly is floated by waters that see fewer anglers. A modicum of solitude during the act of fishing is important to me, perhaps because I'm embarrassed by my slovenly ways (though not so much as to improve them), but more so because fishing is, for me, a contemplative sport.

The 100 streams profiled here represent an incredible array of trout and salmon fishing opportunities, the most diverse and most accessible of those in any nation on earth. True fact. Just after ice-out, streamers provoke slashing strikes from ravenous landlocked salmon on Grand Lake Stream. A hike into the wilds of upper Kern River will introduce you to the most brilliantly colored wild rainbows on earth. Teeny tiny nymphs fished between the ruts of the Guadalupe's limestone beds will connect with four-pound rainbows. Brookies rise eagerly when lady's slippers bloom along the Rapidan. Spring creeks like the Letort demand infinite skill, while all you gotta do on Alaska's Russian is be present to win. Fish with flies, spinners, treble-hooked lures, or bait. Most of the streams provide at least some access for fans of virtually any sport-fishing tackle.

Most of the trout stream guides on bookshelves today are written by fly fishers for their colleagues. They do so, not for money, Lord knows, but because they really enjoy sharing information with others of like mind. I do not know of a richer trove of information for any individual sport than books on fly fishing. Spin and bait anglers can take advantage of all this knowledge. Not only do regional guides—and there are several listed in the chapters in this book—provide accurate where-to-go, what-to-use, and how-to information, but you'll also find scores of titles on fly-tying, tackle-craft, and technique. And there are those marvelous little volumes of essays—a literary pool as deep as the Yellowstone is long—that live on our bedside tables and shorten our nocturnal wanderings.

How to Use This Guide

In this book you'll find the broad-brush profile of America's most popular trout waters. Each write-up sets forth the basics and provides a bit of context that distinguishes one stream from another. The information contained is but a scant introduction. For greater depth, check out the regional guides, talk with staff at tackle shops, read the most current state regulations, and surf the Web. Best of all, look up the closest TU chapter and give its president a call: you may just find yourself a guide.

Each profile opens with a few basic facts; this is the briefest of shorthand.

Location: Where the river flows.

Short take: A description, in 25 words or less, of why the stream is worth visiting with a rod and reel.

Type of stream: General character of the water, but it may change from spring creek to freestone to tailwater over the length of its run.

Angling methods: Most streams are open to use of spinning, casting, or fly-fishing tackle. Bait and lures may be used, but often streams include mileage that's specially regulated for one technique or another. And this changes from year to year. Read current state regulations carefully.

Species: The range of trout and salmon that inhabit a stream differs depending on where you fish it. Great brown trout rivers may have a few native brookies in their headwaters. Listed in this book are the species you're most likely to catch in each stream.

Access: On some rivers, such as the Alagnak, none of the water can be reached without a long boat trip or fly-in. It's difficult to access, to say the least. Other rivers are so easy, you can park, rig your rod, and be fishing in less than five minutes.

Season: Some rivers are open for fishing all year but only fish well during specific periods. Others have closed seasons. Fishing is permitted year-round on many rivers in this book, but technique and creel limits may vary. Check current fishing regulations before you buy a license.

Supporting services: The closest places to find supplies and services that you'll need on a fishing vacation.

Handicapped access: On the Beaverkill and Willowemoc in the Catskills, Project Access has created a number of ramps and platforms where wheelchair-bound anglers can fish successfully. On other streams, physically challenged anglers may find that boat launching areas offer a place to fish. Just how accessible a river is depends on the nature of the physical impairment. Tackle shop owners and state fisheries personnel are excellent sources of information and advice.

Closest TU chapter: With nearly 150,000 members and close to 500 chapters, TU is a vast network of anglers who are committed to coldwater fishing.

Many of the profiles contain the name of a nearby chapter, but because presidents of the chapters change with some frequency, I did not include addresses. Those, along with phone numbers and addresses, are readily available on TU's Web site: www.tu.org. If you're thinking about fishing one of the streams in this book, call the local TU chapter for first-hand, up-to-date, and accurate information.

Along with each profile is a map that provides general directions to each stream and its best waters. At the close of each chapter is a list of sources: **Gearing up** and **Accommodations,** listing fly and tackle shops, chambers of commerce, visitor centers, and the like that will provide further information about each of the areas; and **Books** that will assist you in finding answers to your questions before you make a trek to fish one or another of these streams. Check with the publishers; revised editions and new titles appear almost daily.

LOCATOR MAP

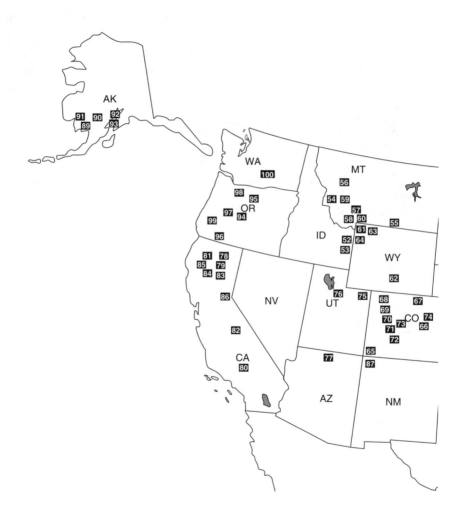

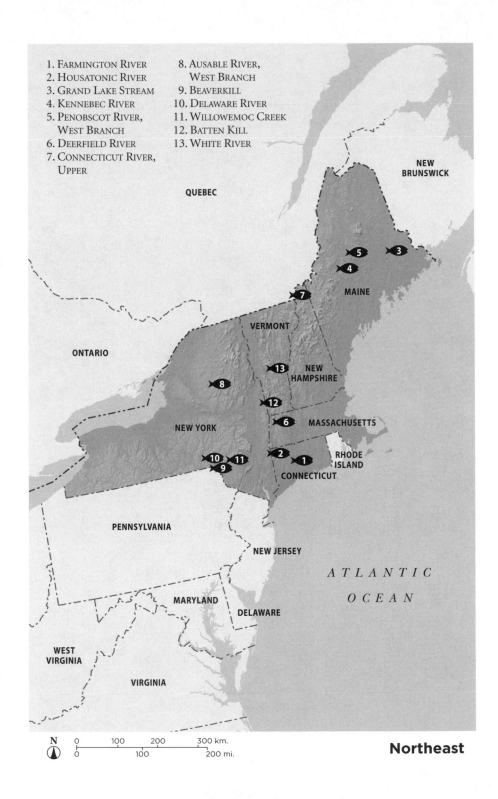

1. FARMINGTON RIVER
2. HOUSATONIC RIVER
3. GRAND LAKE STREAM
4. KENNEBEC RIVER
5. PENOBSCOT RIVER,
   WEST BRANCH
6. DEERFIELD RIVER
7. CONNECTICUT RIVER,
   UPPER
8. AUSABLE RIVER,
   WEST BRANCH
9. BEAVERKILL
10. DELAWARE RIVER
11. WILLOWEMOC CREEK
12. BATTEN KILL
13. WHITE RIVER

NEW BRUNSWICK

QUEBEC

MAINE

ONTARIO

VERMONT

NEW HAMPSHIRE

NEW YORK

MASSACHUSETTS

RHODE ISLAND

CONNECTICUT

PENNSYLVANIA

NEW JERSEY

ATLANTIC OCEAN

MARYLAND

DELAWARE

WEST VIRGINIA

VIRGINIA

N

0   100   200   300 km.
0   100   200 mi.

Northeast

NORTHEAST

Connecticut

Maine

Massachusetts

New Hampshire

New York

Vermont

1 FARMINGTON RIVER

Location: Central Connecticut.
Short take: A trio of trout rivers in one.
Type of stream: Tailwater.
Angling methods: Fly, spin, bait.
Species: Rainbow, brown.
Access: Easy.
Season: Year-round.
Supporting services: New Hartford.
Handicapped access: Yes.
Closest TU chapter: Farmington Valley.

ISSUING FROM THE BASE OF GOODWIN DAM clear as ether, the Farmington enters a set of pocket-water stretches that canoeists describe as class I and II rapids. For more than 22 miles, the river runs south-southeast through rustic and historic country and a bevy of small towns. One of the state's two premier trout rivers, the Farmington is blessed with reasonably stable flows and excellent populations of holdover browns and rainbows. The Farmington has been added to Connecticut's experimental adult Atlantic salmon stocking program, as well. The presence of three state forests—Peoples, Tunxis, American Legion on the east—ensures ample access. Canoe launch sites are numerous along the entire route. And a fishing pier with wheelchair facilities is located on the east side of the river in Pleasant Valley, about half a mile south of the Route 318 bridge.

The Still River—the middle of three so named in Connecticut—enters the Farmington from the west below Riverton. Silt-rich in spate, this tributary and others along the route add sediment that settles and provides improved habitat for caddisflies, mayflies, and stoneflies. Olives, blue quills, and quill gordons come off with the wildflowers of April and last, as the blossoms do, into late May. Sulphurs hatch sporadically from mid-May deep into June. Slate drakes make their appearance in July and continue until frosts add color to maples and beech on valley floors and white birch on the higher hills.

While the upper river is managed for trophy trout first, and then smallmouth, a run of about 3.5 miles from a mile upstream of the Route 318 bridge down to the Route 219 bridge is set aside as a catch-and-release area. Only barbless hooks may be used. Below the upper of the bridges, the river braids, flowing around a number of tear-shaped islands. Some of the channels sink to near dryness in the height of summer, but when the river is high, these side streams with their slower currents may harbor larger fish. While some natural reproduction occurs in the river, browns and rainbows are either stocked or holdovers. Still, any fish in the 14-inch-plus range is fun. This run is open year-round.

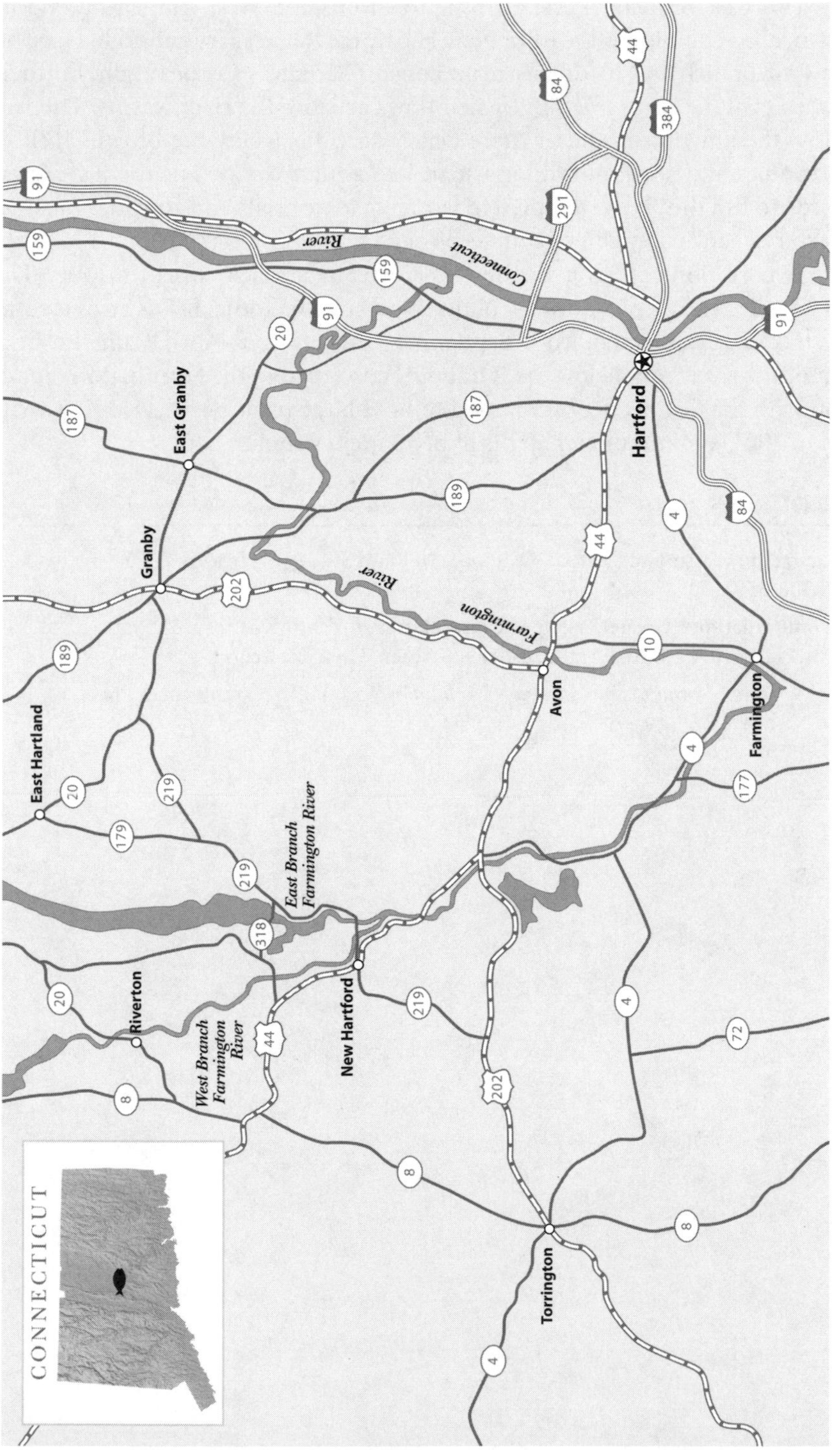

Farmington River

CONNECTICUT

Hartford

East Granby

Granby

East Hartland

Avon

Farmington

Riverton

New Hartford

Torrington

Connecticut *River*

Farmington *River*

West Branch
Farmington
River

East Branch
Farmington River

N

0   5   10   15 km.
0   5   10 mi.

The East Branch of the Farmington joins the West Branch at Puddle Town, about a mile southeast of New Hartford. Releases from Saville Dam on the East Branch and its downstream cousin, Richard's Corner Dam, do their best to cool the main river. But when flows are low, the river warms. The run below the junction is one of those classic sections where big browns lurk in dark holes and smallmouth bass soar, like aquatic hawks, in the fast water. Were I to fish this, I'd be tempted to work big terrestrials and streamers against overhung banks. I might, of course, be dead wrong.

Two sections of river farther downstream are also worth a look. The three-mile reach from Lower Collinsville Dam to Route 177 is managed as catch-and-release water from September through mid-April. And the final run of the river from below the Rainbow Dam canal to the Farmington's junction with the Connecticut is reputed to hold large trout. As this is being written in 2004, a minimum length limit of 15 inches applies here.

RESOURCES

Gearing up: Classic and Custom Fly Shop, 190 Main St., New Hartford, CT 06057; 860-738-3597.

Accommodations: Greater Hartford Convention and Visitor's Bureau, 31 Pratt St., 4th Floor, Hartford, CT 06103; 860-728-6789; www.enjoyhartford.com.

Books: *Trout Streams of Southern New England* by Tom Fuller, Countryman Press.

2 Housatonic River

Location: Western Connecticut.
Short take: New agreements guarantee natural flows, better habitat, more trout, and smallmouth.
Type of stream: Tailwater.
Angling methods: Fly, spin, bait.
Species: Rainbow, brown.
Access: Easy.
Season: Year-round.
Supporting services: West Cromwell.
Handicapped access: No.
Closest TU chapter: Northwest Connecticut.

CONNECTICUT MAY BE THE BEST LEAST-KNOWN trout fishery in the East. When I'm pounding up the interstates north out of New York bound for the angling delights of Vermont, Maine, or New Hampshire, I seldom give streams of the Nutmeg State more than a passing thought. My mistake. This neighbor to more than a quarter of the nation's population is surprisingly rich with cold waters that provide excellent fishing. Efforts by the Connecticut Council of Trout Unlimited in partnership with the Housatonic Coalition and Connecticut Department of Environmental Protection have resulted in the restoration and guarantee of natural flows in the river. Central to this landmark conservation victory is the requirement that the Falls Village and Bulls Bridge project be operated as "run-of-river." These facilities historically have been operated as "peaking" facilities, where water was stored during low-demand times of day, and released when the demand for electricity was highest. These operations produced daily fluctuations in river flows that impaired the health of the river.

Though the Housy rises in the Berkshires, and its southwest branch is something of an early-season fishery, the river comes into its own about nine miles south of the Massachusetts border where U.S. Route 7 and State Route 112 cross below Falls Village. Here, the river channel begins to constrict into a narrow valley that runs for 10.4 miles down to Cornwall Bridge. This mileage contains the famed Housatonic Trout Management Area and an excellent state park, Housatonic Meadows, with very good camping facilities. The Warren Turnpike follows the east side of the river and US 7, the west.

Open year-round, this stretch is strictly catch-and-release. Plagued with warm flows in summer, from June 15 to August 31, angling within 100-foot tributaries is forbidden where posted. A three-mile section, from the top of Housatonic Meadows at a pool called the Meat Hole downstream to Route 4 at Cornwall Bridge, is set aside for fly fishing. Access is excellent from both sides

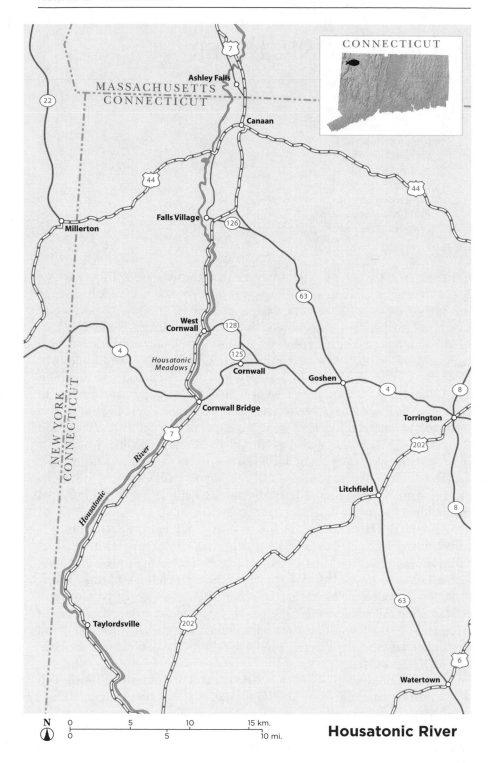

Housatonic River

To some anglers, the Connecticut's Housatonic River resembles a Western stream.

of the river, though the road along the east bank carries you to such famous runs as Push 'em Up Pool, the Doctor's Hole, and the Elms. To the south are Garbage (natural, not human flotsam), Horse, Carse Brook, Cellar, Rainbow Run, and the list continues.

In the mileage well above the covered bridge at West Cornwall, the bottom is unconsolidated sediment, ideal green drake habitat. In profusion, these big mayflies hatch in mid- to late May. Up from the old bridge, as the valley begins to narrow, the Housy gains momentum. Swift runs, riffles, and pools characterize this stretch. Easily wadable during low flows, the Housy can come up in a hurry. A wading staff is good insurance, as is keeping an eye on a marker rock on the bank.

Browns, generally in the 10-inch to 15-inch class, constitute the bulk of the fishery, though rainbows up to 18 inches are also encountered. When it comes to flies that produce consistently, the Blue-Winged Olive is hard to beat from late March through October. Late May brings light cahills, and June starts the terrestrial season, which lasts into late fall. Slate drakes debut in June. Caddis, such a staple on other streams, are limited to May and mid-June on the Housy.

About a dozen miles downstream from Cornwall Bridge, a small dam near Bulls Bridge impounds the Housy. For three miles downstream, catch-and-release regulations apply to trout as well as to smallmouth and large-mouth bass. Unlike most trout management waters, bait fishing is permitted, logic being, I guess, that if you can't eat the fish anyway, what's the difference how you catch them?

RESOURCES

Gearing up: Housatonic River Outfitters, Rte. 128 at the Bridge, W. Cornwall, CT 06796; 860-672-1010; www.dryflies.com.

Accommodations: Northwest Connecticut Chamber of Commerce, P.O. Box 59, 333 Kennedy Dr., Torrington, CT; 860-482-6586; www.northwestchamber.org.

Books: *Great Rivers—Great Hatches* by Charles Meck and Greg Hoover, Stackpole Books.

Trout Streams of Southern New England by Tom Fuller, Countryman Press.

3 GRAND LAKE STREAM

Location: Eastern Maine.
Short take: Shortest, sweetest salmon river you'll ever fish.
Type of stream: Freestone, tailwater.
Angling methods: Fly.
Species: Landlocked salmon, brook.
Access: Easy.
Season: April through mid-October.
Supporting services: Grand Lake Stream.
Handicapped access: None on the stream, but a pier above the dam provides wheelchair-bound anglers a reasonable chance of hooking a landlocked salmon in the first two weeks of October.
Closest TU chapter: Sunkhaze Stream.

THINK OF IT. THREE AND A HALF MILES of gravel-bottom runs punctuated by a 10-foot fall, a number of clattering rapids, occasional pools, and the rocky point where Curt Goudy of American Sportsman fame would fish all day. Grand Lake Stream is that happy run that connects West Grand Lake to Big Lake. Following the stream's north bank runs Water Street, and scores of paths lead down to the river. Beginning in mid-April and lasting until the end of May, feeding landlocked salmon fill West Grand Lake. They return in September when heart-shaped leaves of birch turn to gold and your breath frosts in the morning air. Summer warms the water, and salmon head for the depths of the lake. But brookies lurk in the shade, and they're willing customers for dry and wet mayfly, stonefly, and caddis patterns. Streamers, of course, always produce.

Spring melt swells Grand Lake Stream, and weighted ties and sinking lines are the order of the day. While it's tempting to want to work eddies behind boulders, salmon often hold in quieter water near the bank. A stealthy approach can pay dividends. Fish near water first, and thoroughly. Leaders need be neither long nor fine. Some Downeasters say that three feet is plenty. In April, smelt patterns in sizes 4 to 8 are most productive: Ghosts, Red & White, Joe's Smelt, Sanborn, Barnes Special, One Post, and Putts Favorite. This early in the season, the typical drill is to cast across, throw a mend, and work the fly as slowly as you dare among the cobble and occasional boulders where fish lie. Since water temperatures may be in the 40s, early-season fish may not be overly aggressive with their take.

With the warming and lowering of the river, salmon become increasingly active, but more discriminating. Fewer are the hookups on streamers fished deep. Instead, toss the usual nymphs: Prince, Hare's Ear, Pheasant Tail, Red Squirrel, and Black Stonefly. Fill your box with sizes 4 to 12 and you'll be set. Try, too, a tandem rig with a #16 or #18 Brassie; 18 inches behind a bead-head

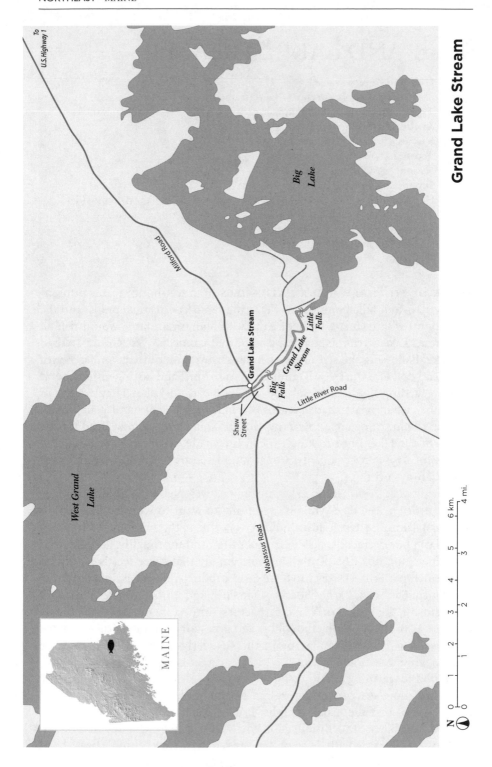

Grand Lake Stream

Landlocked salmon in the three-pound class draw anglers to Grand Lake Stream.

pattern proves productive. Dull days in late May foster those early hatches of mayflies. Dark Hendricksons and Blue-Winged Olives generate strikes. Let the sun shine for a few days, and stoneflies appear.

Depending on water temperature and volume, salmon begin drifting down into Big Lake in late May. After the second week of June, they've pretty much left the river. Brookies, which have played second fiddle to landlockeds all spring, take center stage. Though not as large as those in the Kennebago/ Rangeley Lakes system, they're ready and willing to eat a well-presented fly. Adams are always effective, as are all varieties of caddis (don't overlook smallish little black caddis). After the Fourth of July, terrestrials, particularly ants, but also beetles and grasshoppers, fill trout gullets. Throughout the summer, Wulffs and Stimulators are effective. Ties with Yellow or Orange Parachutes are easiest to see against the dark tannin, white foam–flecked waters.

With the first chill days of late August, salmon move back into the river. Water, then, is low and clear, and you can easily sight fish. But, if you can see them, they can see you. They're apt to be spooky. You may take them on Yellow Sallies or larger dries than those used for brookies, which, by the way, are turning more aggressive as they begin their spawn. The general season closes at the end of September, but catch-and-release fishing continues until mid-October. Among the patterns recommended by the Pine Tree Store is #6 lead shot, which, when propelled by a deftly mounted 20-gauge side-by-side, has been known to catch a pa'tridge.

A timeless patina lays over the village. Generations of anglers have made their ways here, first up from Boston by train, and then by boat or wagon from the nearest railhead. Every run carries a name and a legend: Upham's Corner, Hatchery Pool (easy access and apt to be crowded), and The Wall, where first come is likely to be first served. Goudy's Point, Evening Pool, The Glide, Cable Point, Big Falls, Little Falls, and The Meadow are productive beats in mid- to late season. Paths lace both sides of the river. Public access is clearly marked, but it never hurts to ask permission if there's even a hint of doubt in your mind.

RESOURCES

Gearing up: Pine Tree Store, Grand Lake Stream, ME 04637; 207-796-5027.

Accommodations: Weatherby's, Box 69, Grand Lake Stream, ME 04637; 207-796-5558; www.weatherbys.com.

Books: *Fishing Maine* by Tom Seymour, Falcon Press.

4 Kennebec River

Location: Central Maine.
Short take: Try the super salmonoid slam—browns, 'bows, brookies, and landlockeds—all in a single day! Only 5-weights need apply.
Type of stream: Freestone with many dams.
Angling methods: Fly, spin, bait.
Species: Brook, brown, rainbow, landlocked salmon, smallmouth.
Access: Easy.
Season: April through mid-October.
Supporting services: Waterville, the Forks.
Handicapped access: No.
Closest TU chapters: Kennebec Valley, Somerset.

FROM ITS HEADWATERS AT THE OUTFLOW of Moosehead Lake to Fort Popham on the Gulf of Maine, the Kennebec River flows for 230 miles, draining about 5,870 square miles, or about 20 percent of the state of Maine. Breaching of Edwards Dam in 1999, a landmark victory for TU, opened an additional 17 miles of river to migrating anadromous species: striped bass, shade, alewives, sea-run brown trout, and, it's hoped, Atlantic salmon. First about Atlantic salmon. Maine law expressly prohibits angling for Atlantic salmon. One needn't worry much about that on the Kennebec, for the odds of hooking one are slightly worse than winning a zillion bucks in the lottery. Save your Spey rods and blue charms for Canada's Maritimes.

In the main, the Kennebec is a smallmouth river with populations of landlocked salmon (same genus and species—*Salmo salar*—as Atlantic salmon but generally lacking the reddish spots or blotches found on anadromous Atlantics) and rainbow, brown, and brook trout where flows are cool year-round and well oxygenated. Three areas of this long river are of particular interest to trout anglers, though trout may be found throughout the river.

Affectionately known to Mainers as the East Outlet, outflow from Moosehead Lake to Indian Pond is one of the top landlocked salmon and brook trout fisheries in the state. An unimproved farm road rides along the north bank and an angler's path traces the south. Fishing begins at the dam just upstream from the railroad trestle. If flows are below 2,000 cubic feet per second, the section is wadable. Any higher and you'll have to canoe it or fish from a drift-boat. If you wade, bring and use a wading staff. You'll need it. Water fluctuates rapidly and without warning, so an inflatable life preserver may be the best insurance you'll ever buy. Beach Pool consistently yields excellent fish, which is why it's generally well populated with anglers. Push upstream or down to Ledge Falls, a class III rapid. The run below is as well known for its brook trout as it is for its landlocked salmon. The West Outlet, below Rockford, is much slower and more of a smallmouth than a salmon or trout fishery. Still, it's

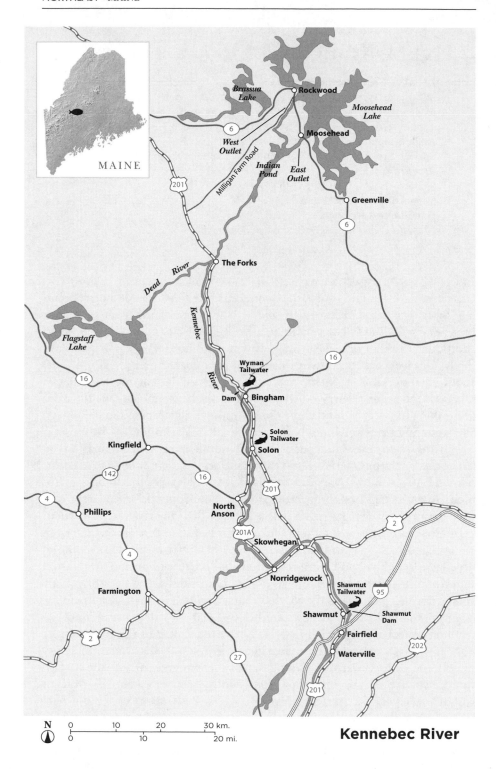

MAINE

N

0   10   20   30 km.
0   10   20 mi.

Kennebec River

worth a shot in May and late September. Also worthy of attention is the head of the gorge below Indian Pond, accessible from Chase Stream Road coming in from the northwest.

The Wyman Dam tailwater, two miles north of Bingham, carries one of the few wild populations of rainbow trout in the state. There's no wading immediately below the dam—banks are too steep—but a canoe launched in town will carry you upstream with little effort. Coldwater releases from the dam and Austin Stream sustain this fishery. Because it's the nursery for spawning 'bows, Austin Stream is closed to spring fishing. Peak demand for electricity triggers Wyman Dam's generators. In summer, when Bostonians turn on their air conditioners at 8:00 a.m., river flows climb from 2,000 to 5,000 cubic feet per second. Rising water turns off the fish. But daylight comes early to central Maine. In late June, you can be fishing shortly after 4:00 a.m. and be off the river by the time the water rises. By mid-July, the water has warmed to such a degree that angling senselessly stresses the trout. It's best to avoid this section until September.

The same holds true, more or less, on the six miles from Wilson Dam in Solon down to North Anson. Unspoiled by development and chock-full of browns and brookies with rainbows and landlocks as well, it's no wonder that Sean McCormick, former Kennebec Valley TU chapter president and member of TU's National Leadership Council, is so enamored of this float. If you want to try the Kennebec Slam!—brookie, brown, 'bow, and landlocked salmon—you'll start on this stretch targeting landlocks and brook trout. Those caught and released, you'll make haste for a shrimp salad sandwich at the Big G deli in Winslow before chasing your brown and rainbow below Shawmut. If you're dead set on wading, dash down to the mile below Shawmut Dam. Here, the river's width ranges between 200 and 300 yards and it's shallow enough to wade comfortably. Browns and rainbows, with a few smallies mixed in, cavort in the flats upstream from the Interstate 95 bridge north of Waterville. There's no better place on the river to cast to rising trout.

As for patterns for the Kennebec, Mike Holt of Fly Fishing Only, a trout shop in Fairfield, just upstream from Waterville, puts it this way: "There's nothing unusual about the hatches on the Kennebec." Blue-Winged Olives are the staple flies on the river. Hatches begin in April and continue sporadically—generally in periods of heavy cloud cover—into October. Little black stoneflies, best fished as #12 to #16 nymphs, appear in May and continue throughout the season. Tan caddis, quill gordons and hendricksons begin coming off in June and July brings little black caddis and some hendricksons. March browns, yellow stones, and light cahills finally make it in late July. "While mayflies get all the press on the Kennebec," says Mike, "caddis is king!" and there are even some tan caddis in September. Woolly Buggers, Gold-Ribbed Hare's Ears, Zug Bugs, Tellicos, Black and Brown Stones, as well as Mickey Finns and Black Ghosts all belong in an angler's fly box. Spin fishers will find inch-and-a-half crankbaits, Mepps, and Panther Martins all to be good bets where legal. Most anglers arrive over-rodded for the Kennebec. A nine-foot-six is more than adequate. A sink tip line will pay big dividends in spring. Spin fishers will find ultra-light gear hard to beat.

Two other sections ought not be overlooked, according to Bob Mallard of Kennebec River Outfitters. The easily wadable two miles below the dams at Madison offer superb angling for browns, especially during June's stonefly hatch. Also, a shallow gorge below the twin dams in Skowhegan channels the river over brawly riffles and produces good browns as well. Best fishing here tends to come with the olive hatch in the fall.

RESOURCES

Gearing up: Aardvark Outfitters, 108 Fairbanks Rd., Farmington, ME 04938; 207-278-3330; www.aardvarkoutfitters.com.

Fly Fishing Only, 230 Main St., Fairfield, ME 04937; 207-453-6242; www.maineflyfishing.com.

Kennebec River Outfitters, Rte. 201, Madison, ME 04950; 207-474-2500; www.kennebecriveroutfitters.com.

Accommodations: Mid-Maine Chamber of Commerce, 1 Post Office Sq., Waterville, ME 04901; 207-873-3315; www.midmainechamber.com.

Books: *Fishing Maine* by Tom Seymour, Falcon Press.

5 PENOBSCOT RIVER, WEST BRANCH

Location: Central Maine, near Baxter State Park.
Short take: West Branch's the name and salmon's the game.
Type of stream: Freestone, tailwater.
Angling methods: Fly, spin
Species: Landlocked salmon, brook.
Access: Easy to awful.
Season: April through September.
Supporting services: Millinocket.
Handicapped access: No.
Closest TU chapter: Sunkhaze Stream.

PRETTY PRESUMPTUOUS TO DEFINE A RIVER AS "the best" (though it didn't seem to stop us, did it?), but when one thinks of landlocked salmon in Maine, it's the West Branch of the Penobscot that comes to mind. Rising at the top of Seboomook Lake, north and west of Moosehead, the West Branch of the Penobscot flows first northeast then southeast in a 60-mile arc before issuing forth from Ripogenus Dam. The dam backs water up for nearly 30 miles, establishing a haven for smelt, some landlocked salmon, and brook trout. In spring, when flood gates open wide, and later, in summer, when generators at McKay Station arc churning, tons of the two- to three-inch food fish are flushed into the most popular section of the West Branch. Added to those dumped in from atop are millions more that migrate upstream from the Pemadumcook/Ambajejus Lake system below. Wither goeth the smelt goeth also landlocked salmon.

And wither goeth landlocked salmon follow hordes of anglers, hell bent on bending hell out of their rods. Goodly numbers make tracks for the West Branch of the Penobscot. Not only can one expect three, four, or more hookups per day, but also good road stretches all the way from Ripogenus Dam to Interstate 95. Golden Road—a private paper company toll road—follows the valley of the West Branch. The upper 11.5 miles of the tailwater from the dam down to Abol Bridge is probably the best-known stretch of the river. Steep and difficult to descend, Rip Gorge carries the river for its first mile below the dam. Pools in the gorge hold nice numbers of very good fish. Why not? They get first crack at the steady stream of chum coursing out of the penstocks. If you want to fish this water, hire a guide who'll show you the way.

Most anglers intent on fishing the uppermost section park where Telos Road crosses the river about a mile and a half below the dam. While SUVs may be bunched up like cattle in a feedlot, their passengers will be fairly evenly spread out on the stream. During the spring, enterprising fly fishers eschew

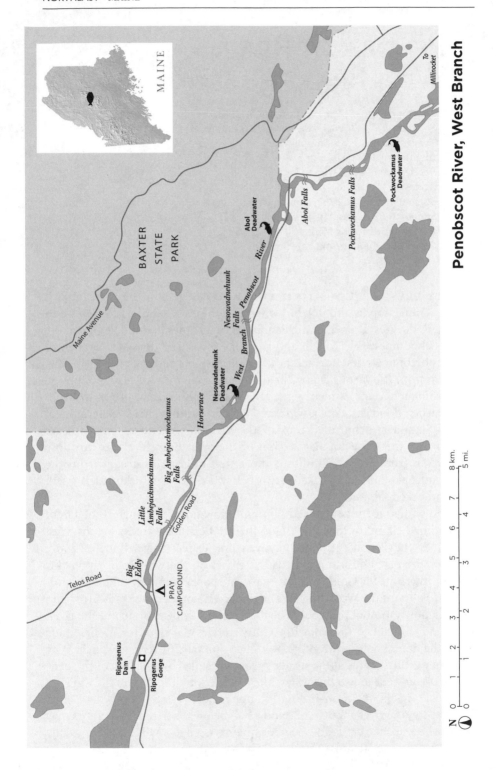

Penobscot River, West Branch

MAINE

BAXTER
STATE
PARK

Maine Avenue

To
Millinocket

Pockwockamus
Deadwater

Abol Falls

Pockwockamus Falls

Abol
Deadwater

Penobscot River

Nesowadnehunk
Falls

West Branch

Nesowadnehunk
Deadwater

Horserace

Big Ambejackmockamus
Falls

Little
Ambejackmockamus
Falls

Golden Road

Big
Eddy

Telos Road

PRAY
CAMPGROUND

Ripogenus
Dam

Ripogenus
Gorge

N

0   1   2   3   4   5   6   7   8 km.
0   1   2   3   4   5 mi.

traditional smelt ties, preferring floating dead smelt patterns. Cast 'em upstream, let 'em drift with the current, twitch 'em once in a while as if in spasm. Landlockeds will smash them . . . and your tackle too if you're sleeping at the switch. Below the gorge, the river widens into Big Eddy, and then tightens into a torrent that races through heavy rapids, swirling backwaters, and bouldery runs. A number of paths lead to the river in these, the 10 miles between Telos and Abol bridges. While it may be tempting to launch a canoe and take off downstream, it ain't, pardon my patois, such a good idea. Two sets of falls, Little and then Big Ambejackmockamus, are waiting to kick you around, and then there's the Horserace. The best way to get a sense of this run is to spring for a licensed guide with a driftboat or reinforced raft. When you wade, don't forget your wading staff.

Below the Horserace, the river pools up in the Nesowadnehunk Deadwater, which isn't dead early in the season. Then salmon and trout abound in its upper end. Downstream of this long flat, the river gains speed and hustles through a series of pools and runs. The Abol Deadwater, also a misnomer, marks the end of the best section of the West Branch, though there's some trout and salmon action all the way down to Lake Ambajejus. While landlockeds fought in the West Branch may be smaller than those of yore—a two-and-a-half pounder is typical—their numbers seem to be greater, reports Dan Legere of Maine Guide Fly Shop in Greenville, who guides on this section of the river.

In addition to smelt patterns already mentioned, nymphs are always productive. Hatches begin in late May, about the time when fishing gets really good. Fill your boxes with Red Quills and Hendricksons. By the end of June, you may also see some Green Drakes. Caddis, too, are a staple of these fish, so stock up on varying hues in sizes 12 to 16 and don't overlook caddis larvae and pupae as well. Big water this is. A nine-foot 6-weight is the order of the day. Current regulations mandate fly fishing from August 15 through September 30 from Telos Bridge down to Debsconeag Falls. Otherwise spinning gear with single-hook, artificial lures are perfectly legit.

RESOURCES

Gearing up: Maine Guide Fly Shop, P.O. Box 1202, Main St., Greenville, ME 04441; 207-695-2266; www.maineguideflyshop.com.

Accommodations: Katahdin Area Chamber of Commerce, 1029 Central St., Millinocket, ME 04462; 207-732-4443; www.mainerec.com/millhome.

Books: *Fishing Maine* by Tom Seymour, Falcon Press.

6 DEERFIELD RIVER

Location: Northwestern Massachusetts.
Short take: Where fly fishers and floaters are friends.
Type of stream: Tailwater.
Angling methods: Fly, spin.
Species: Brown, rainbow, occasional brook.
Access: Easy to moderate.
Season: Year-round.
Supporting services: Charlemont.
Handicapped access: Limited.
Closest TU chapter: Deerfield/Millers.

HERE'S THE DEAL. THE WATER WAS OFF when you entered the Deerfield. Fish were rising on the other side. So across you waded. There turned out to be good browns in the 14- to 16-inch range. You casted to the one rising at the bottom of the pod. On the fifth cast, he took. Your 5-weight bowed nicely, but cognizant of the imperative not to overstress these trout, you brought him in quickly and released him with a flick of your forceps. The other fish were still working. You thought you'd pick off another one, and you did. And one more. This one was the best of the lot—16 to 17 inches. You moved toward shore where the water was slower, and landed her. It was then that you realized the river was rising rapidly. The prospect of a mile's hike up to the Tunnel Road bridge was not appealing. Just then, a flotilla of rafts from Crab Apple rounded the bend. You hailed them and one of the guides oared his way over. "Want a ride?" he asked.

Now it doesn't always happen like this, but guides from Crab Apple White Water and other licensed rafting companies, whose gaily colored watercraft bob along when flows are high, have asked their guides to assist stranded anglers should the need arise. All this is a sort of mutual coexistence on a river that runs through a charming valley wilderness not much more than a couple hours' drive for 20 million Americans. A decade ago, TU and other conservation organizations negotiated minimum flows from hydrodams. Flows are timed to suit the needs of commercial rafting operations, and the river can rise a couple of feet in minutes. Typically, a slug of water is released in mid-morning. Rafts and kayaks ride the bulge over sections of class III rapids. Levels return to normal by mid-afternoon. Fluctuations of flow don't seem to bother trout much, but anglers must pay attention. Wading staffs and inflatable vests can be lifesavers.

Cooler and no longer subject to scouring floods, the tailwater provides excellent habitat for stocked 'bows and browns. While typical trout run in the 12-inch to 14-inch range, holdovers of more than 18 inches are reasonably frequent. You're more apt to find them in two catch-and-release runs, each of

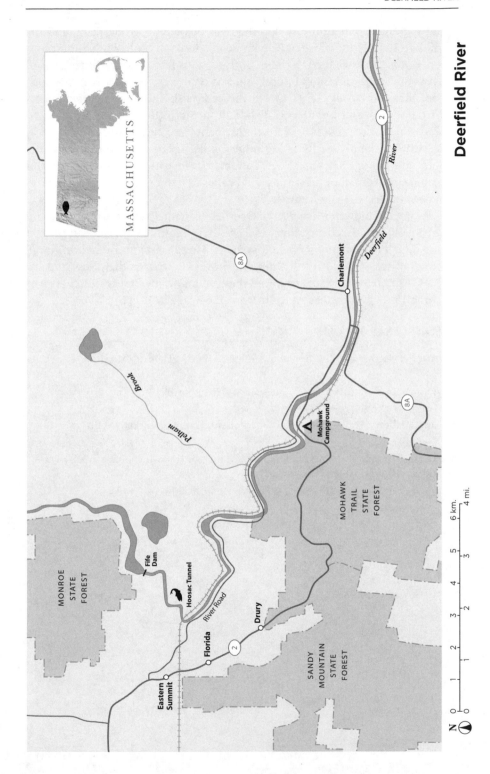

Deerfield River

MASSACHUSETTS

about two miles. The first picks up the river below Fife Brook Dam, and the second, from the confluence of Pelham Brook down to Mohawk Campground where Route 2 crosses the Deerfield. Both sections feature longish stretches of pocket water with occasional pools and sets of rapids. The upper catch-and-release area, says Walt Geryk of Northeast Flyfishing Guide Service, seems to be holding greater numbers of fish than formerly. Browns run in the two-pound range and rainbows of 18 to 22 inches are caught "every couple of days." Known mainly for its caddis, Blue Quills, Tricos, Light Cahills, and the ubiquitous Adams also produce. You may fare better with nymphs and streamers. And grasshoppers, ants, and beetles cast under overhanging vegetation turn the trick in late summer.

Though a coldwater fishery, the Deerfield can't help but warm in July and August. Walt advises clients, then, to leave their light rods at home and use at least 5-weight, and better, 6-weight systems. He suggests fluorocarbon tippet material of four-pound test. Landing fish quickly stresses them less and increases their chances of survival. And that, we know, increases your chance of catching 18-inchers instead of fresh-from-the-truck stockers.

RESOURCES

Gearing up: Northeast Flyfishing Guide Service, 38 Elm St., Hatfield, MA 01038; 413-247-5579.

Housatonic River Outfitters, 684 South Main St., Great Barrington, MA 01230; 413-528-8811; www.dryflies.com.

Accommodations: Oxbow Resort, Route 2, Mohawk Trail, Charlemont, MA 01339; 413-625-6011.

Books: *Anglers Guide to Trout Fishing in Massachusetts* by Brian Tucholke, ed., Massachusetts/Rhode Island Chapter TU.

Trout Streams of Southern New England by Tom Fuller, Countryman Press.

7 Connecticut River, Upper

Location: Northern New Hampshire.
Short take: Two times two is tremendous—and the rest isn't bad.
Type of stream: Tailwater.
Angling methods: Fly, spin.
Species: Landlocked salmon, brown, brook, rainbow.
Access: Easy to moderate.
Season: January 1 through mid-October.
Supporting services: Pittsburg.
Handicapped access: No.
Closest TU chapter: Contact the state council of TU.

RISING IN A POND THAT'S GRANDLY CALLED the Fourth Connecticut Lake, but in reality is but a few acres in size, if that, the Connecticut River runs from a click south of New Hampshire's border with Quebec to Long Island Sound at Old Lyme. The upper reaches of the river, those farthest from the press of urbanization, are as bucolic and tranquil as the lower river is fraught with hustle and bustle. Reaching this neck of woods requires a half-day's trek from Boston and double that from New York City. Worth the drive it is, and there's no other way to get there.

The New Hampshire Fish and Game Department has created two special-regulations sections on the uppermost run of the Connecticut. From Second Connecticut Lake down to First Connecticut Lake, a distance of about two miles, is catch-and-release, artificial-lure water. Below First Connecticut Lake down to Lake Francis, the river is managed for trophy trout. You'll only find brookies and landlocked salmon in the upper catch-and-release water, but rainbows, brookies, browns, and landlocked salmon run the lower two miles plus of flowing water.

Come ice-out—late April or early May—smelt begin running up from the lakes and landlocked salmon chase 'em. Heavy runoff from melting snow clears this section fairly early and mayflies begin hatching in, well, May. Blue-Winged Olives and emerger patterns are staples. So are caddis. John Howe of Tall Timber Lodge finds Soft Hackle Wets very effective. Bead Head Pheasant Tails also produce consistently. Traditional smelt-like streamers fished with a sink tip line draw lots of strikes.

Mainly pocket water, which pools intermittently and occasionally gathers itself in a fast run, both sections of upper river are fairly easy to fish. Bring a wading staff and lots of bug dope. Some don head nets to escape biting black flies, and others fire up cigars. If—no, when—you fish these two sections, pay particular attention to the mouths of tributaries such as Dry, Smith, and Big brooks. Typically cooler than the main river in summer, these thin streams draw fish to them like magnets.

Connecticut River, Upper

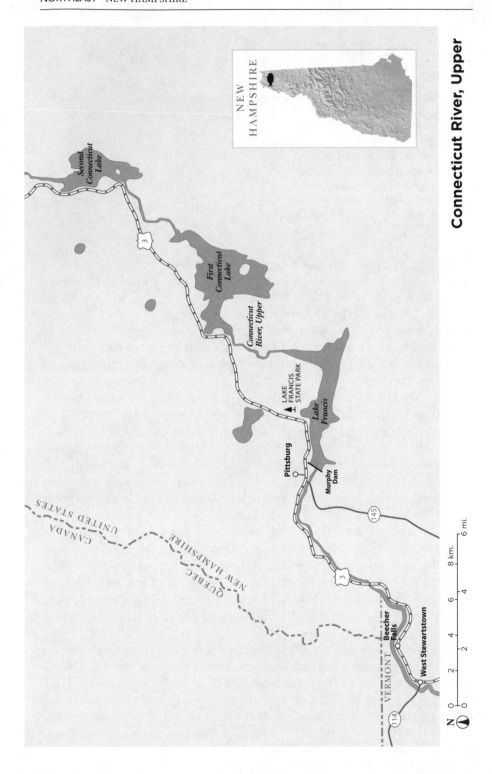

From June into September, the Upper Connecticut is primarily trout water. Almost any pattern from size 12 to size 16 produces. And the river will, of course, be more crowded. It's not as if this mileage is undiscovered. But crowds thin in late August and September. Leaves color up. There's a crispness in the air that tells of coming frost. Brookies, browns, and salmon move up from Lake Francis into the trophy trout section. Salmon and brook trout do the same into the catch-and-release zone upstream of First Connecticut Lake. The fishing gets better and better with falling temperatures. Don't be distracted by white, chalk-like dribbles on the fading green flora at your feet. It's only bird poop. After all, who cares about the migrating woodcock that settled in last night? I do! Hand me the 20-gauge and fetch me that Brittany pup.

RESOURCES

Gearing up: Lopstick Lodge and Outfitters, First Connecticut Lake, Pittsburg, NH 03592; 800-558-6659.

Tall Timber Lodge, 231 Beach Rd., Pittsburg, NH 03592; 800-835-6343.

8 AUSABLE RIVER, WEST BRANCH

Location: Northeastern New York, in the Adirondacks.
Short take: Big stocked trout and stunning scenery.
Type of stream: Freestone.
Angling methods: Fly, spin.
Species: Brown, brook, rainbow.
Access: Easy.
Season: Year-round.
Supporting services: Wilmington, Lake Placid.
Handicapped access: Yes.
Closest TU chapter: Lake Champlain.

AROUND ANGULAR BLACK BOULDERS COURSE the dark and foaming waters of the West Branch of the Ausable River. This is New York's quintessential Adirondack stream, the same way the Beaverkill and Willowemoc are best known among the Catskill's many fine trout waters. A pair of lazy meadow streams (the easternmost is born on the northwest flank of Mount Marcy) coalesce in the Mount Van Hoevenberg State Recreation area. They slip along the shoulder of Route 73, slide under the highway at its junction with County Highway 21 (Riverside Drive), which dogs its course for the next four miles or so to the intersection with Route 86. From the point where Holcomb Pond outlet enters the stream downstream to 2.2 miles below Monument Falls, and again from the bridge to the base of Little White Face Mountain down to where Route 86 crosses the river at the Flume, fishing the West Branch is governed by artificials-only, catch-and-release regulations.

From the Flume, a chute-like set of heavy rapids, the West Branch boils into a pool that bears the name of author and guide Fran Betters. Betters is largely responsible for the establishment of the catch-and-release segments of the river. He'll tell you to use a fly of his own design—the Ausable Wulff—to catch fish on top in this big-fish pool. Other anglers fish nymphs and streamers. After this pool, the river tails out into a small lake backed up by a little dam in the town. Physically challenged anglers can fish the river from the park along the small lake in the village of Wilmington. The two miles of pocket water below town are among Betters' favorite haunts.

Famous for green drakes and golden stones that come off from mid- to late June, hatches progress from hendricksons and caddis in May through sulphurs and olives and Tricos in July to slate drakes in September. While every season, browns and rainbows in the 20-inch plus range are caught and released on dries, the larger percentage of behemoths fall for nymphs and bugger-like streamers of one persuasion or another. Take your choice. Snowmelt clears the river in late May, generally well before the drake hatches. September and October, with their showy displays of brilliant foliage, are among the best

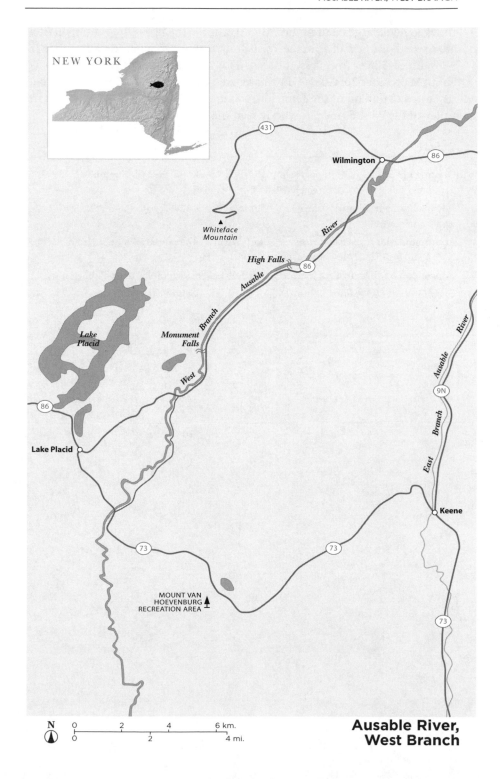

NEW YORK

431

Wilmington

86

Whiteface
Mountain

High Falls

86

River

Ausable

Monument
Falls

Branch

Lake
Placid

West

86

Lake Placid

Ausable

River

9N

East

Branch

Keene

73

73

73

MOUNT VAN
HOEVENBURG
RECREATION AREA

N

| 0 | 2 | 4 | 6 km. |
| 0 | | 2 | 4 mi. |

**Ausable River,
West Branch**

times to hook large trout in the river. Except for the upper special-regulations area, which is open all year, the West Branch closes to angling on October 15. Now, unless I miss my guess, the season for ruffed grouse opens in these parts about September 20. Guess I'd be hard pressed to think of another venue better suited to pursuit of the game bird of kings and pre-spawn browns than the valley of the West Branch. Anybody seen that Brittany?

RESOURCES

Gearing up: Ausable River Sports Shop, P.O. Box 448, Route 86, Wilmington, NY 12997; 518-946-1250; www.ausableriversportshop.

Adirondack Sport Shop, P.O. Box 125, Wilmington, NY 12997; 518-946-2605; www.ausablewulff.com.

Accommodations: Lake Placid/Essex County Visitor's Bureau, 216 Main St., Lake Placid, NY 12946; 518-523-2445; www.lakeplacid.com.

Books: *Ausable River* by Paul Mariner, River Journal Series, Frank Amato Publications.

Good Fishing in the Adirondacks by Dennis April, ed., Backcountry Publications.

9 BEAVERKILL

Location: Southeastern New York, in the southern Catskills.
Short take: Although it's the most studied trout stream in the East, the fishing's still good!
Type of stream: Freestone.
Angling methods: Fly, spin.
Species: Brown, brook, rainbow.
Access: Easy.
Season: Year-round.
Supporting services: Roscoe.
Handicapped access: Excellent.
Closest TU chapter: Beamoc.

WIFE KATIE AND I, ON A TOUR of America's fishing lodges for another book, pulled into the Beaverkill Valley Inn across the road and a little downstream from Joan Wulff's fly-fishing school. August was the month, and this reach of the river, about a mile upstream of Lew Beach, was running low. After being assured by the chef that he'd feed me should I return after dark—one does not want to miss dinner here—I rigged my 3-weight and set off across the croquet court toward the trees that line the river. I reached it where it bends hard against the narrow macadam road—County Highway 54—that traces the Beaverkill's course.

Blocks of riprap shored up the road. Beneath them flowed a deep pool. I crouched in the brush, lest my silhouette against the evening sky spook the wild browns. They had been fished, I assumed, by scores of anglers before me. Rises, steadily along the far rocky bank, broke the surface's sheen. I eased down to the tail of the pool and targeted the closest rising fish. Five minutes later, the fish, an 11-inch brown, chunky and dark, darted back for the boulders from which my Slate Drake had lured him. In the quarter of mile of stream I fished that night, I could do no wrong. We live for such moments, for they come so seldom.

Beloved is the way many anglers think of the Beaverkill. So much of America's fly-fishing traditions is rooted in its gentle 44-mile course draining the southwestern corner of the Catskills. The upper half of the river flows through a valley that once bustled with the rickety clack of horse-drawn mowers cutting hay that a decade earlier fell to man-swung scythes. The fields are still now. It is as if the land itself has paused. Beyond the fringe of trees, the river runs apace, still the way Sparse Grey Hackle would have known it, as Lee Wulff would have viewed it as he side-slipped in for a landing in his Super Cub, as the Darbees and the Dettees did when they tested their fly patterns on the river's wild browns and rainbows. You can still buy their flies.

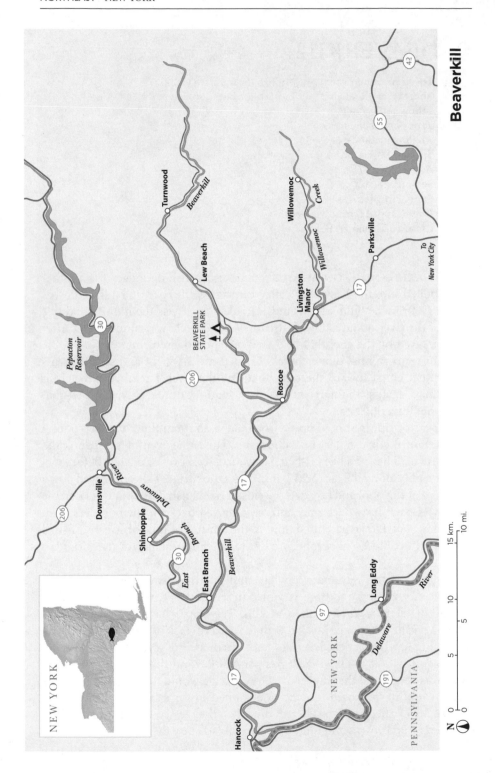

Beaverkill

The Beaverkill offers anglers classic American dry-fly fishing.

The uppermost two miles of the Beaverkill flow through the Balsam Lake Mountain Forest and along the boundary of Big Indian Forest, and are therefore accessible. Trout are small, delightful, and readily take almost any small dry—use an Adams or a Little Tan Caddis of #12 or #14. You can hike to the upper water from Round Pond trailhead, but the river below is almost exclusively private. Students at the Wulff School of Fly Fishing and guests at the Beaverkill Valley Inn have access to a mile or so of outstanding pocket water.

Beaverkill State Park downstream from Lew Beach and the 2.5 miles from the Route 206 bridge down to the famed Junction Pool downstream from Roscoe provide public access to the upper river. Pressure is heavy throughout the summer and on weekends, spring, and fall. Mid-week fishing, if you can swing it, is the answer. Hendrickson and green drake hatches in May and terrestrials from mid- to late summer turn the trick on browns to 18 inches. Most measure a foot or so.

The lower stretch of the river below Roscoe is much larger than the upper because the Willowemoc enters at the Junction Pool. From there downstream to its confluence with the East Branch of the Delaware is some of the most celebrated trout water in America. To say that it's easily accessible is an understatement: Route 17—the Southern Tier Expressway from New York City to Binghamton—runs along the river's course. Parking spots are ample and most of the water can be fished with lure or bait, whichever is your choice. Two runs are set aside as no-kill, artificials-only sections. The first is the 2.5 miles from the Sullivan County line downstream to an old railroad trestle. The second runs from one mile upstream of the iron bridge near the confluence of Horton Brook to 1.6 miles below. The lower section of the Beaverkill warms quickly in summer. From July 1 through August 31, the mileage from the iron bridge at Horton down to the next Route 17 overpass is closed to all angling.

In 1994, TU initiated a pilot economic impact study of the Beaverkill and its major tributary, the Willowemoc, which comes in at Roscoe. That study showed that trout-related tourism is a major component of the redevelopment of this rugged countryside where lumbering and agriculture no longer support local communities. Data gave impetus to additional extensive studies of factors affecting the quality of the fishery and steps required to sustain it. In many ways, the Beaverkill resembles many of the other Eastern trout rivers. Continually threatened by streamside real estate development, the vagaries of drought and flood, and growing numbers of anglers, the Beaverkill watershed has become a model of public and private collaboration. Since the first TU study, numerous bank stabilization and other habitat improvement projects have been completed. The river also benefits from ongoing creel surveys and water-quality monitoring, mostly on the river's critical tributaries. In many areas, the river has been reconnected to its historic floodplain, reducing flooding and improving habitat. But of greatest importance is the increased awareness of non-angling residents and visitors to the value of the Beaverkill to the region. This appreciation has laid the foundation for informed decision-making regarding real estate development, point-source pollution, flood response, and stream closures to protect the health of the trout. Thanks to this unusual partnership between New York's Department of Environmental Conservation, private foundations, Orvis, TU, and hosts of volunteers, America's most hallowed dry-fly fishery will be there for anglers for generations to come.

RESOURCES

Gearing up: Beaverkill Angler, P.O. Box 198, Roscoe, NY 12776; 607-498-5194; www.beaverkillangler.com.

Catskill Flies, Roscoe, NY 12776; 607-498-6146; www.catskillflies.com.

Of special interest: Catskill Fly Fishing Center and Museum, 1031 Old Rte. 17, P.O. Box 1295, Livingston Manor, NY 12758; 914-439-4810; www.cffcm.org.

Accommodations: Roscoe-Rockland Chamber of Commerce, P.O. Box 443, Roscoe, NY 12776; 607-498-6055; www.roscoeny.org.

Livingston Manor Chamber of Commerce, P.O. Box 122, Livingston Manor, NY 12758; 914-439-4859; livingstonmanor.org.

Books: *The Beaverkill: The History of a River and Its People* by Ed Van Put, Lyons Press.

Fly Fishing the Beaverkill by Eric Peper and Gary LaFontaine, Lyons Press.

Good Fishing in the Catskills by Jim Capossela, Countryman Press.

10 Delaware River

Location: South-central New York, northeast Pennsylvania.
Short take: The easternmost Western river in the U.S.
Type of stream: Tailwater.
Angling methods: Fly, spin.
Species: Rainbow, brown.
Access: Moderate.
Season: April 1 through October 15.
Supporting services: Hancock.
Handicapped access: No.
Closest TU chapter: Al Hazzard (Binghamton).

FROM CANNONSVILLE DAM DOWNSTREAM TO HANCOCK, where the East Branch comes in and on to Lordville, some say that no waters in the East offer trout as rich a diet. Every major species and many of the subspecies of caddis, mayfly, and stonefly found in the East hatch on this river. Small fish are abundant as well—minnows, shad, and the fry of spawning trout. Rainbow, brown, and brook trout roam the river, migrating from the deeper waters of the main stem up into the branches and feeder streams to spawn. Primarily a brown trout river, the West Branch sees its share of large 'bows when the main stem below Hancock warms in midsummer. Though only two hours from metro New York and three from Boston, many who fish the 20 miles plus of the West Branch liken it to the Madison and other great Western streams.

Below Deposit, the West Branch enters a modest valley. Its bed is largely glacial cobble, though outcrops of country rock cause some rapids and deep pools. Here and there, the stream braids around islands, the tails of which often create still waters where trout sip. Like trout anywhere, these trout like cover and holds where they can lie in slow water, darting out to snatch a morsel drifting by in heavier current. The most common mistake made by many who fish the West Branch is heading into the main river without fishing banks and side currents first. Those who fish the river thoughtfully, catch more and larger fish.

In the main, the West Branch is easily wadable from numerous public access points maintained by New York and Pennsylvania. A number of outfitters and guides float anglers down the river in driftboats. Though flows are heavier in spring, the river is generally manageable for those who prefer to wade. Even when the river is running high and handsome, trout will be found in side channels. They don't want to battle the current any more than you do. Many anglers head for the artificials-only section that runs from the Route 17 bridge in Deposit downstream for two miles.

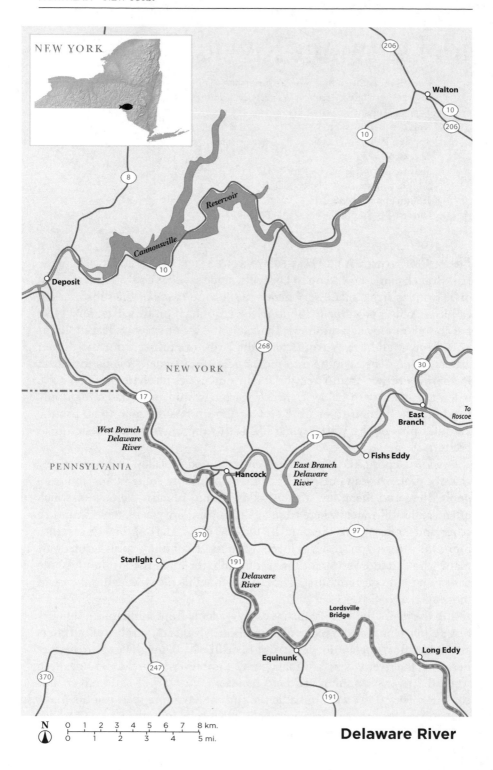

NEW YORK

Walton

Reservoir

Cannonsville

Deposit

NEW YORK

East
Branch

To
Roscoe

West Branch
Delaware
River

PENNSYLVANIA

Fishs Eddy

Hancock

East Branch
Delaware
River

Starlight

Delaware
River

Lordsville
Bridge

Long Eddy

Equinunk

N
0 1 2 3 4 5 6 7 8 km.
0 1 2 3 4 5 mi.

Delaware River

As you stand there flicking Sulphurs to that brown sipping at the tail of the island, it's difficult to keep in mind that you're standing in the midst of a war zone. But that's where you are. To quench the thirst of its residents, New York City laid claim to the Delaware's water early in the 1950s. Two reservoirs—Cannonsville on the West Branch and Pepacton on the East Branch—were constructed in the 1960s. Minimum flows were part of the deal, but only enough to flush away effluent from towns downstream. Both are bottom-draw dams, and their releases cooled what had been a pair of rivers that warm like the lower Beaverkill, which is closed to angling in July and August to avoid stressing trout.

New York and Pennsylvania had been stocking the West Branch with rainbows and browns, which augmented a natural trout population that had found its way into the river, thanks to well-meaning anglers. Their plan was to expand the river's fish population—smallmouth, shad, walleye, and stripped bass—with a few trout that'd bend their dainty cane rods. With the coming of cold-water flows, the trout flourished, as they're wont to do in tailwater fisheries as far south as Texas. Everybody along the river congratulated themselves on their good fortune. Employment from timber and agriculture was plummeting, and the blossoming trout population held out the prospects of attracting tourists. In the late 1980s, New York City's demand for water soared. Flows in the river fell to a few tens of cubic feet per second. Fish eggs and insect larvae dried when exposed. At other times, the river roared during spawning periods, and redds were scoured clean. There was neither rhyme nor reason to the cycle. Enter TU.

Taking the Henry's Fork Foundation as a model, TU created an office in the southern Catskills to explore solutions to flow issues on the branches of the Delaware and the Neverskink, the river where Theodore Gordon pioneered dry-fly fishing in America. TU's approach was holistic, meaning that solutions are about more than trout fishing. Economic development, pollution, needs of cities with legal claims on water, as well as the welfare of the trout themselves were considered. A landmark economic impact study by TU in 1994 on the Beamoc watershed proved beyond any doubt that trout brought tourists who brought new dollars to the financially beleaguered region. So what conditions would create a sustainable population of trout, large enough and numerous enough to draw anglers from throughout the East? Further, how can the entire watershed be managed so that balance is maintained among the diverse and competing demands on it? The answers can only be found in good science and continuing collaboration with stakeholders. The effort continues, led by TU's Catskill coordinator working in close partnership with the Delaware River Watershed Committee of the New York State Council and the Hazzard Chapter in Binghamton, about 20 miles west of the river. Stay tuned!

RESOURCES

Gearing up: Ultimate Flyfishing Store, 159 E. Front St., Hancock, NY 13783; 607-637-4296; www.ultimateflyfishing.com.

Accommodations: Hancock Area Chamber of Commerce, P.O. Box 525, Hancock, NY 13783; 607-637-4756; www.hancockareachamber.com.

Books: *Mid-Atlantic Budget Angler* by Ann McIntosh, Stackpole Books, 1998.

11 WILLOWEMOC CREEK

Location: Southeastern New York, in the southern Catskills.
Short take: As fine an intimate stream as you'll encounter near New York City.
Type of stream: Freestone.
Angling methods: Fly, spin.
Species: Brown, rainbow, brook.
Access: Easy.
Season: Year-round.
Supporting services: Roscoe, Livingston Manor.
Handicapped access: Ample.
Closest TU chapter: Beamoc.

AMONG THE FAMED TROUT STREAMS OF THE SOUTHWESTERN CATSKILLS is the Willowemoc. I think of it as smaller and more intimate water than its more famous sibling, the Beaverkill, or the West and East branches of the Delaware, both tailwaters. With more ample public access than the Beaverkill, angling pressure is more evenly distributed. You're less apt to feel crowded, though tracks in the mud from parking accesses to the stream will show you that somebody's been here before. I don't let that worry me much. Trout live for but two purposes: to eat and to breed. While they may be dissuaded from either by commotion nearby, they'll generally return to their duties as soon as the stream settles down.

In its upper reaches, the Willowemoc is a brook trout stream. Vivacious as only a brookie can be, they lie in wait in every tiny pocket, darting swiftly to grab lunch before it passes. Fishing the shaded runs above the stream's namesake hamlet always raises this question: Is the better strategy a long rod to dapple waters impossible to reach with a cast? Or is a short 3-weight, easy to work beneath streamside brush, the right choice? Let me know when you find the answer. Access to some of this water is limited, but between Fir Brook (itself a reasonable small fishery for brookies and some browns), which comes in from the southeast, and Butternut, which joins the Willowemoc from the north about a mile and a half upstream, the state controls much of the river.

At the confluence of Mongaup Creek just up from Debruce, the Willowemoc Valley opens. A number of public easements provide access to the stream. Flowing under Route 17, the creek enters the little town of Livingston Manor and runs past the Catskill Fly Fishing Center and Museum. Project Access, a non-profit group dedicated to providing facilities from which physically challenged anglers can fish, has created a number of such sites on both the Beaverkill and the Willowemoc. Two are located near the bridge, which enters the Center.

And the Center itself is well worth a visit. Here you'll meet the nineteenth-century pioneers of American dry-fly angling: Theodore Gordon, Uncle Thad

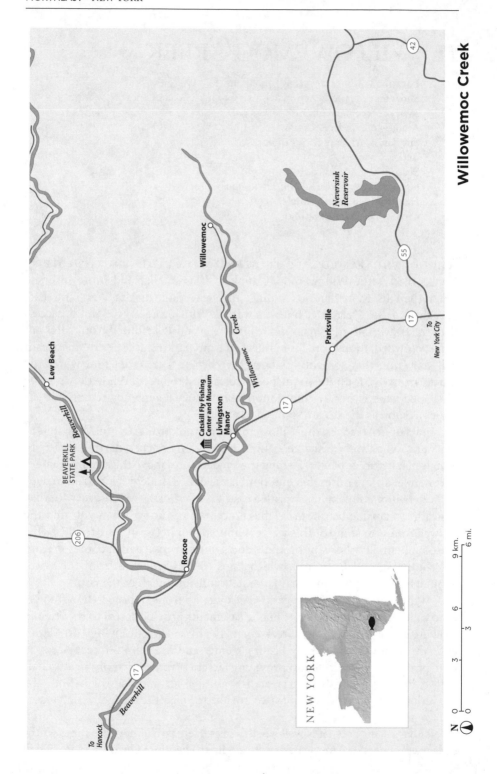

Willowemoc Creek

Norris, Edward R. Hewitt, and George LaBranche. You'll run into, as well, the second generation—those anglers of the 1920s and 1930s like Ray Bergman, Hiram Leonard, Roy Steenrood, and Sparse Grey Hackle whose wife, Louise, knew him first as Alfred W. Miller. There you'll find Lee Wulff's prototype fishing vest and displays of the region's legendary fly tyers—Wulff, Walt and Winne Dette, and Harry and Elsie Darbee. Along with the museum, the Center offers an extensive array of programs on casting, tying, and rod-building and environmental education for adults and children. And, of particular interest, is a mile of the prime, catch-and-release Willowemoc.

Below Livingston Manor, the Willowemoc assumes its adult configuration, coursing through gravel runs and over rocky ledges through patches of forest and much meadow. Route 17 shadows the river for most of the mileage to Roscoe where it flows into the Beaverkill. Known for its great hendrickson and march brown hatches in May and the green drakes of June, the lower river warms by July, and wise anglers opt to fish nearby tailwaters.

RESOURCES

Gearing Up: Beaverkill Angler, P.O. Box 198, Roscoe, NY 12776; 607-498-5194; www.beaverkillangler.com.

Catskill Flies, Roscoe, NY 12776; 607-498-6146; www.catskillflies.com.

Of special interest: Catskill Fly Fishing Center and Museum, 1031 Old Rte. 17, P.O. Box 1295, Livingston Manor, NY 12758; 914-439-4810; www.cffcm.org.

Accommodations: Roscoe-Rockland Chamber of Commerce, P.O. Box 443, Roscoe, NY 12776; 607-498-6055; www.roscoeny.org.

Livingston Manor Chamber of Commerce, P.O. Box 122, Livingston Manor, NY 12758; 914-439-4859; livingstonmanor.org.

Books: *Good Fishing in the Catskills* by Jim Capossela, Countryman Press, 1992.

12 BATTEN KILL

Location: Western Vermont, eastern New York.
Short take: More and better brookies, but fewer, though larger, browns.
Type of stream: Freestone.
Angling methods: Fly, spin, bait.
Species: Brown, rainbow, brook.
Access: Moderate.
Season: Mid-April through mid-October.
Supporting services: Manchester.
Handicapped access: No.
Closest TU chapters: Clearwater, (NY), Batten Kill (Vermont).

WITH ITS NAME EMBOSSED ON MORE ANGLING and travel gear than that of any other stream in the country, the Batten Kill is known throughout the world as one of America's premier trout streams. Sometimes reputation lags behind reality, and as of this writing, the Batten Kill is not the river it once was. In the 1990s, the brown trout population began to sag. Today, it's estimated to be less than half of what it was. Vermont Department of Fish and Wildlife—with a $10,000 grant from TU's Coldwater Conservation fund—has undertaken extensive studies of habitat, aquatic life, and water quality. A program to educate streamside landowners on the benefits of buffer zones has been funded by Embrace A Stream. Despite the research, conservation, and education efforts, no single cause, no set of reasons for the decline has emerged. Some blame the fall-off on growing numbers of mergansers and great blue herons, which have insatiable appetites for trout. As yet, no studies suggest that either of these fish-eating birds prefer browns to brook trout.

Though browns are fewer, those caught tend to be larger than before. Brown trout in the 16-inch class are not uncommon. Anglers are catching greater numbers of brook trout, and they tend as well to be larger than previously. As of this writing, brook trout average about 10 inches. Don't get your hopes up, however, cautions long-time guide Peter Basta. Though brookies are more gullible than browns, the Batten Kill's fairly gentle gradient and general absence of large structure from Manchester Center to Arlington, where the river bends west toward New York, means lots of long slow runs. Batten Kill brookies have plenty of time to inspect a fly, and they take it. Long, fine tippets of 6X, delicate patterns, and deft presentations are the keys to success on the storied runs of this river. Use Blue Quills early in April when the trees along the river first blush green. Black caddis begin then, too. Hatches march along with hendricksons and red quills in May and light cahills, as well, that continue into August. Among the better hatches, though, are Baetis that come off in the fall. That's the best time to visit these waters.

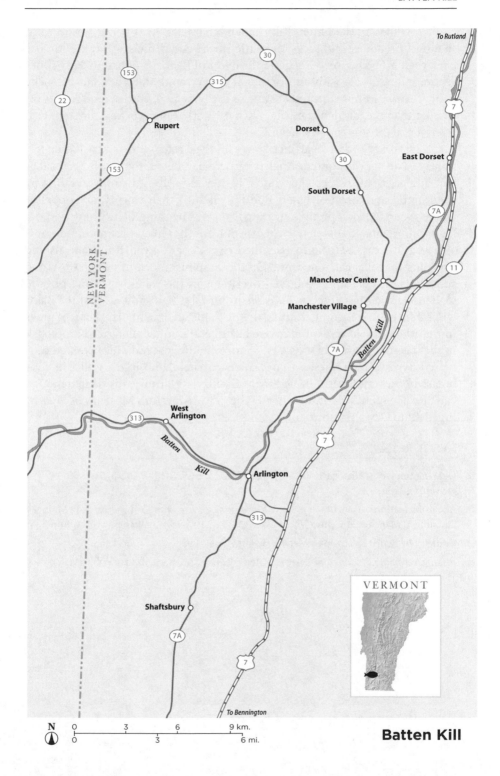

To Rutland

22

153

315

30

7

Rupert

Dorset

East Dorset

153

30

7A

South Dorset

11

Manchester Center

Manchester Village

7A

Batten Kill

NEW YORK
VERMONT

West
Arlington

313

*Batten
Kill*

7

Arlington

313

7

VERMONT

Shaftsbury

7A

7

To Bennington

N

0   3   6   9 km.

0   3   6 mi.

Batten Kill

At Arlington, the Batten Kill changes character. As it bends westward, it shallows, broadens, and picks up a little steam. An artificials-only section has been established between Rochester Bridge and Benedict Crossing. Easy riffles separate long pools with an occasional rocky rapid and undercut or rocky bank. Browns in this run, and the one to the New York border, tend to be a bit smaller than the few denizens who lie in the dark waters above Arlington. Fish the river all the way to the state line.

New Yorkers insist on artificial lures on their catch-and-release Batten Kill mileage. Not so, Vermonters. Anglers can use bait here if they wish. Seems that bait anglers want to keep their catch. If they're prohibited from so doing by state statute and threat of a hefty fine, they'll dunk their worms and corn elsewhere. Sounds like a pretty savvy way to avoid banning bait fishing with its higher mortality; 'bout what you'd expect from the Green Mountain Boys.

As is the case with so many famed rivers, there is much more to fishing this river than just catching trout. On those August mornings when the rising sun turns to sepia mists collected overnight in the valley, one can't be sure Ogden Pleissner hasn't set up his easel around the bend. You wait for the Baldwin steam engine to come chuffing up the grade and the matched pair of grays to pull the carriage across the covered bridge. It's not at all hard to drop back to the days of Charles F. Orvis' first factory-made cane rods, his patented ventilated fly reel, linen lines, cat-gut leaders carried damp in the wallet in your breast pocket, and wet flies tied by Mary Orvis Marbury, his daughter. One can't escape such apparitions after a visit to the American Museum of Flyfishing, next to Orvis' flagship store.

RESOURCES

Gearing up: Orvis, Historic Route 7A, Manchester, VT 05254; 802-362-3750; www.orvis.com.

Accommodations: Manchester and the Mountains Chamber of Commerce, 5046 Main St., Suite 1, Manchester Center, VT 05255; 802-362-2100; www.manchestervermont.net.

Books: *The Batten Kill* by John Merwin, Lyons Press, 1993.

Fishing Vermont's Streams and Lakes by Peter F. Cammann, Backcountry Publications, 1992.

13 WHITE RIVER

Location: East-central Vermont.
Short take: September's secret: rapacious trout, riotous color, scant pressure.
Type of stream: Freestone.
Angling methods: Fly, spin, bait.
Species: Rainbow, brook, brown.
Access: Easy.
Season: Year-round from Bethel downstream.
Supporting services: White River Junction and along the river.
Handicapped access: No.
Closest TU chapter: White River Watershed.

WHEN THE LATEST SET OF GLACIERS PUSHED THROUGH CENTRAL VERMONT, they rounded mountain tops, rasping smooth the passes between them and filling the valleys below with rounded gravels. There's no lovelier run of this terrain than the upper valley of the White River. Rising in Granville Notch between a pair of 3,000-foot peaks, Alder Meadow Brook tumbles nearly 700 feet until it slows at the head of a narrow valley. Here, a thin mountain stream joins it from the west. The stream is the White River, born of rivulets spawned on the flank of Battell Mountain and augmented with flows from Patterson and Clark brooks. Plunge pools hold small brook trout and rainbows and see scant pressure when compared with the more popular sections of the river farther south. This is water for fans of tight lines, short and precise casts, and crouching behind boulders lest the fish in the pool above be spooked.

From Granville to Stockbridge, the White ambles down a narrow valley, here bending against one bank, there undercutting another. Each bend holds a pool and the pools carry surprisingly nice brook trout and rainbows. They're seldom fished. Typically a quarter mile separates each bend, often the best water is something of a walk from Route 100, which runs along the river, and few anglers are willing to make that much effort. Those who do, find solitude even at the peak of Vermont's tourist seasons.

At Stockbridge, the White picks up the waters of the Tweed River. Brook trout are fewer and rainbows more prevalent. The valley begins to close in on the White where Blackmer Boulevard and Morse Road cross Route 107 at the hamlet once known as Riverside. Here, where the White changes course and heads to the northeast, it passes through something of a narrows. Downstream, the gradient relaxes again. But now the White has matured and become quite popular. Special regulations—artificial lures and catch-and-release for trout smaller than 18 inches—apply in the three-mile run from Lillieville Brook to Cleveland Brook, which comes in from the south about a mile upstream from Bethel. Route 107 shadows the river on the south and

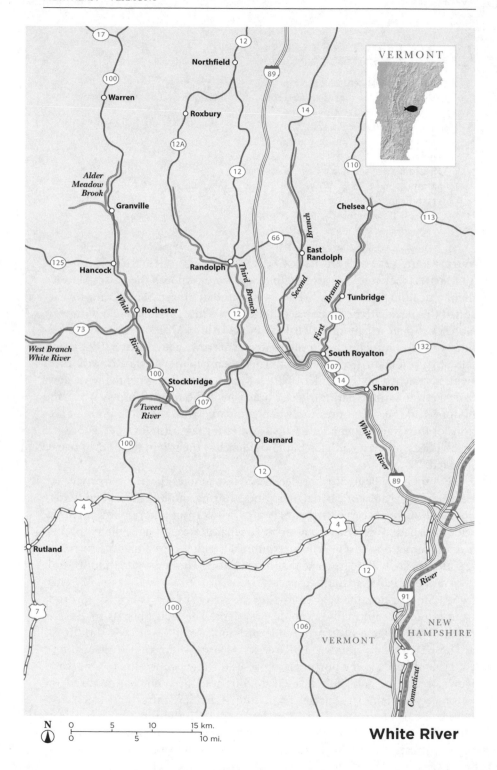

White River

River Street, accessible after crossing the bridge at Gaysville or from Bethel, runs along the north bank.

From Bethel to Sharon, the White becomes wider and deeper. Ledge rock floors many pools, at times too deep to wade. Drifting this section of river with a guide like Brad Yoder, a former TU chapter president and maestro of Trout on the Fly in South Royalton, is probably the best way to fish the river. Those insisting on wading should consider Third Branch, which joins the White at Bethel; Second Branch, which comes in at Royalton (fish this above North Randolph); and First Branch, at South Royalton. Each offers good fishing for browns and rainbows with fewer folks than on the main stem's special-regs run. And that's not all. Each is also crossed by covered bridges, the perfect backdrop for that "I'm fishing in Vermont" photo you'll e-mail back to your buddies stuck toiling in the office. Though the lower mileage of the White from Sharon to the mouth at White River Junction is open and shallow in spots, its deeper holes harbor browns of three to six pounds and smallmouth to match. Anglers whose aesthetics are not offended by tossing Rubber Leg Woolly Buggers often find that the big brown they thought they hooked is actually a somersaulting smallie hell-bent on busting their tackle. Otherwise, day in and day out, the most reliable patterns on the White are the typical run of caddis, mayflies, and large stoneflies found in everyone's box. Blue-Winged Olives are productive in April and May and again in September and October. Midges can be effective throughout the season, and terrestrials, of course, draw good strikes from mid-summer until the leaves turn.

Mid- to late September, that's when I'd head for the White. I'd set aside three or four days; to plan fewer would be to risk heartbreak. I'd begin in the headwaters tossing BWOs on a seven-and-a-half-foot 4-weight, probably cane. The next day would find me probing bend pools below Granville. I'd fish these on weekend days when tourists might fill the more popular run from Stockbridge to Bethel. That, I'd work on Monday with dries. Tuesday I'd set aside for the mileage from Royalton to Sharon and below, switching from cane to graphite and from dries to that damned ugly rubber-leg rig so productive on big fish. That evening, I'd make the short drive across the Green Mountains to Manchester, where I'd hole up in the old and lovely Equinox Hotel. The following morning would find me on the Batten Kill. Now there, my friend, is the perfect fall fishing vacation.

RESOURCES

Gearing up: Trout on the Fly, 344 Hidden Ridge Rd., S. Royalton, VT 05068; 802-457-9498; www.troutonthefly.com.

Accommodations: Upper Valley Chamber of Commerce, P.O. Box 697, White River Junction, VT 05001; 802-295-6200.

Mid-Atlantic

14. BIG GUNPOWDER
    FALLS RIVER
15. POTOMAC RIVER,
    NORTH BRANCH
16. SAVAGE RIVER
17. CEDAR RUN
18. FISHING CREEK
19. KETTLE CREEK

20. LETORT SPRING RUN
21. LITTLE JUNIATA RIVER
22. PENNS CREEK
23. SLATE RUN
24. SPRUCE CREEK
25. CRANBERRY RIVER
26. SENECA CREEK

N

0   100   200   300 mi.

0   100   200   300   400 km.

MID-ATLANTIC

MARYLAND

PENNSYLVANIA

VIRGINIA

WEST VIRGINIA

14 BIG GUNPOWDER FALLS RIVER

Location: Northeastern Maryland.
Short take: Seclusion and selective trout 30 minutes from Baltimore.
Type of stream: Tailwater.
Angling methods: Fly, spin, bait.
Species: Brown.
Access: Easy.
Season: Year-round.
Supporting services: Tackle shops, accommodations.
Handicapped access: Yes.
Closest TU chapter: Maryland Chapter.

CITIES AND TROUT DO NOT COEXIST PEACEFULLY. The search for wild trout and even a semblance of solitude carries anglers far from the metropolises of the East. Yet there's one stream, Big Gunpowder Falls River, that's just off Interstate 83 and within two hours of Baltimore, Washington, D.C., and Philadelphia. You might say it's the home river for more than eight million Americans. Now that conjures up visions of long theme park–like lines of anglers, snaking through bucolic countryside, waiting their turns to cast into a pool where a trout may deign to rise. Nothing could be further from the truth.

In 1986, the Maryland Chapter of Trout Unlimited and the Maryland Department of Natural Resources negotiated minimum flows on the Gunpowder below Prettyboy Dam. After stockings of fertilized eggs and fingerlings and adult rainbows and browns, the first natural reproduction of browns was seen in 1989 and rainbows in 1991. Given the fairly unusual arrangement of intakes at depths of 17, 55, and 100 feet in the lake, outflows from the dam normally can be managed to maintain optimum temperatures of about 56 degrees for trout in the river below. Even during hurricanes, when most rivers in this region turn the color of mud, the narrow and shallow Gunpowder will cloud and then clear after three or four days.

As a result, the Big Gunpowder has become the East's premier metropolitan wild trout fishery. The first 7.2 miles from the plunge pool at the base of the dam are managed as artificials-only, catch-and-release water. The next 4.2 miles, down to Corbett Bridge is also wild trout water, but anglers may use any tackle and keep two trout per day. Another 6.1 miles below Corbett Bridge is stocked with rainbows and five fish per day, any tackle regs apply.

It had been hoped that rainbows would reproduce in the river as well as browns. That didn't prove to be the case. While you may catch 'bows anywhere in the wild trout waters, reproduction has only been documented in the 1.2 miles immediately downstream from Prettyboy Dam. The remaining 10 miles of the river is brown trout water. Most fish run in the 10-inch to 12-inch range, according to Theaux Le Gardeau who operates Back Water Angler, the

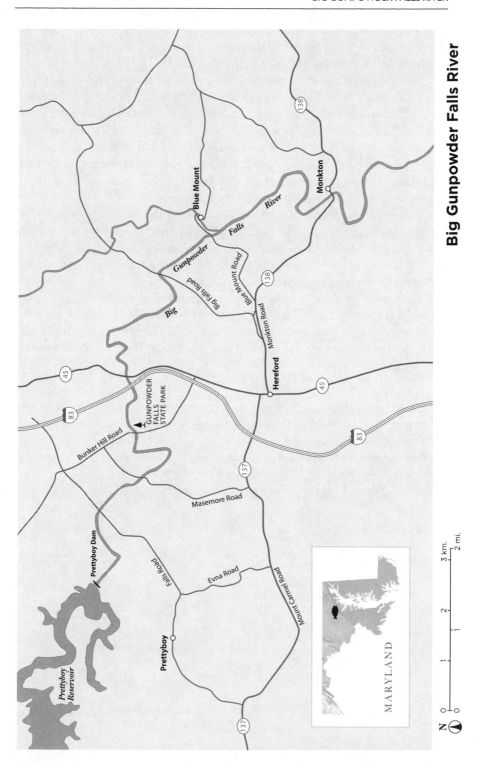

Big Gunpowder Falls River

quintessential fly shop in Monkton, a couple of miles from the best runs of the river. Browns of 14 inches or so, however, are caught and released regularly, and a few bruisers in the 16- to 20-inch range are hooked each year.

Big Gunpowder is open year-round. Fishers of dries will throw Midges and Little Black Stoneflies from January into March. April brings mayflies: Hendricksons, Blue and Red Quills, and March Browns. May adds Sulphurs and Caddis to the mix and June brings the first consistent action on terrestrials and Blue-Winged Olives. Olives, Caddis, and various terrestrials continue deep into Maryland's long and gentle fall. May, as it is everywhere in the East, is probably the most active time on the river. Hatches and anglers arrive in force. But there's no real downtime on the Gunpowder.

Except for the boulder, swirl, pool nature of the first mile or so below Prettyboy Dam, the bed of the river is mainly cobble with long riffles ending in pools that shallow into riffles again. Rangers in Big Gunpowder Falls State Park, through which much of the upper catch-and-release section flows, do not remove timber that falls into the stream. Currents eat out the gravels downstream from these deadfalls, creating marvelous pockets where larger fish lie. As is true in many rivers, an angler who probes such lies and undercut banks with nymphs and streamers will connect with larger fish. Trails running along the river from the dam to the parking access at Big Falls Road provide easy access.

RESOURCES

Gearing up: Backwater Angler, 538 Monkton Rd., Monkton, MD 21111; 410-329-6821; www.backwaterangler.com.

Accommodations: Baltimore County Conference and Visitors Bureau, P.O. Box 5426, Lutherville, MD 21094–5426; 410-296-4886; www.visitbacomd.com.

Books: *Mid-Atlantic Budget Angler* by Ann McIntosh, Stackpole Books.

15 POTOMAC RIVER, NORTH BRANCH

Location: West Virginia/Maryland border.
Short take: What tailwater produced the state record brown, brookie, and cutthroat?
Type of stream: Freestone, tailwater.
Angling methods: Fly, spin.
Species: Brook, brown, cutthroat, rainbow.
Access: Easy to moderate.
Season: Year-round.
Supporting services: Oakland.
Handicapped access: No.
Closest TU chapter: Youghioghney.

ANGLERS FROM PITTSBURGH TO BALTIMORE AND SOUTH TO HAMPTON ROADS make tracks for this little appendix of wooded highlands at the western end of Maryland's panhandle. There, in a 30-mile radius, are found two of the streams—the North Fork of the Potomac and the Savage River—voted among America's 100 Best (whether they are or not is up to you!) and one also-ran, the Youghioghney. Tailwaters all three, each has its champions, which is what keeps the debate interesting.

Of them, though, the North Fork is the most interesting. From its origin in the spring beneath the Fairfax Stone down to its confluence with the South Branch, the North Branch forms the border between Maryland and West Virginia. If you divide the river into an 18.5-mile headwaters section, a run of about 9 miles of tailwater immediately below Jennings Randolph Dam, and another 20 miles or so that grades from superb trout water to runs unparalleled for smallmouth, the North Fork offers all the strokes for angling folks. The first 0.38 mile below the dam is set aside for natural propagation and for catch-and-release angling. Next comes the mile-long run at the head of the Barnum Whitewater Area, which flows past the 40-acre park that Mineral County leases along an abandoned railroad grade. Access is very easy and anglers may keep their catches up to the limit set by West Virginia or Maryland.

Fly fishers are attracted to the 3.9 miles of river that begins with the famed Blue Hole and ends at where Piney Swamp Run comes in from the West Virginia side. Rainbows, browns, brook trout, fine spotted Yellowstone cutthroat, and golden trout are all stocked, and heavily, in this section. There's some hope that natural reproduction will take hold, and with a new water-release policy in place at Jennings Randolph Dam, the potential is improving. In the main, you'll catch and release rainbows of 12 inches or so, and browns that are a little bit bigger. Occasionally, anglers land leviathans. As this was being

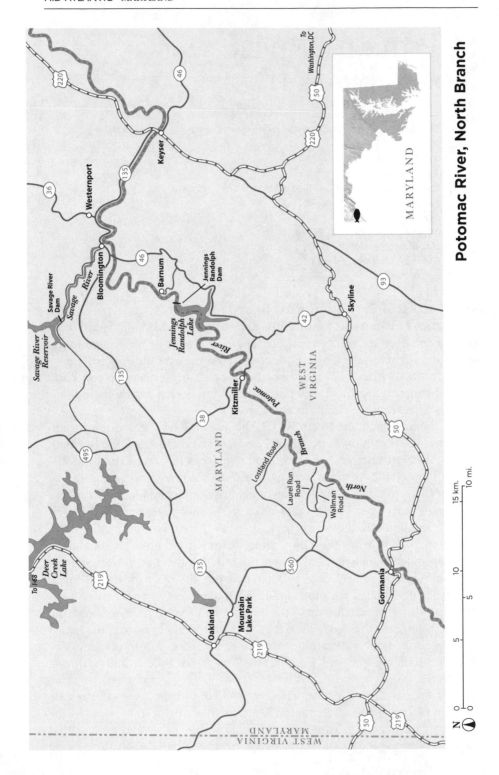

Potomac River, North Branch

written, the current Maryland record brookie (6 pounds, 2 ounces), brown (18 pounds, 3 ounces), and cutthroat (7 pounds, 9 ounces) have been taken from the North Branch.

Stimulators and caddis are probably the most effective dries day in and day out, but the river sees its share of hatches usually found in the region. Immediately following stockings, anglers who throw three-inch bicolored streamers or Clousers stand a pretty good chance of hooking a trophy of 18 inches or more. While the abandoned railroad grade follows the river, wading in many places is nothing short of treacherous. Class II and class III rapids punctuate this section, making floating challenging for novice boaters. Those who wade should wear studded shoes and flotation suspenders on their waders. William Heresniak, of Eastern Trophies Fly Fishing, guides extensively on this water. He suggests a wading staff and whistle, as well.

The upper 18.5 miles of river above Jennings Randolph is catch-and-keep water. The first 12 miles upstream of the impoundment, and the 952-acre lake itself, receive annual stockings of browns and rainbows. But the 7.5 miles of river that forms the southeastern boundary of Potomac-Garrett State Forest is managed under a delayed harvest concept. During the first nine months of the year—January through September—this mileage is strictly artificials only and catch-and-release. For the balance of the year, standard regulations apply. That there are trout at all in this run of the river, and downstream of Jennings Randolph as well, is due to the placement of "dosers," Rube Goldbergesque contraptions that deposit measured quantities of crushed limestone rock into what had been one of the region's streams most plagued by acid mine drainage.

Access to the delayed harvest area is extremely limited: Lostland Run Road, Laurel Run Road, and the Audley Riley Road to Wallman. Anglers who walk a mile up or down from the parking areas find themselves in an utterly wild country of ledge rock pools and gravel runs. Maryland DNR takes special pride in stocking this mileage. They borrow a truck fitted with railroad wheels, mount their aerated stock tank on the back, and run the rails along the eastern side of the river depositing fish as they go.

RESOURCES

Gearing up: Spring Creek Outfitters, 208 N. Second St., Oakland, MD 21550; 301-334-4023; www.springcreekoutfitter.com.

Accommodations: Garrett County Chamber of Commerce, 15 Visitors Center Dr., McHenry, MD 21541; 301-387-4386; www.garrettchamber.com.

Books: *Mid-Atlantic Budget Angler* by Ann McIntosh, Stackpole Books.

16 SAVAGE RIVER

Location: Western Maryland.
Short take: A little tailwater that fishes big below the dam.
Type of stream: Freestone, tailwater.
Angling methods: Fly, spin.
Species: Brown, brook, and a few rainbow.
Access: Easy down low, difficult above the lake.
Season: Year-round.
Supporting services: Oakland.
Handicapped access: Not formally.
Closest TU chapter: Youghioghney.

ONLY FOUR MILES LONG AND FOLLOWED BY A ROAD for its entire length, the tailwater has to be one of the most accessible trout fisheries in the Mid-Atlantic states. It's also one of the very best. When the water from the dam is running in the neighborhood of 50 to 60 cubic feet per second, wading is easy. Browns of 11 inches and brookies in the 8-inch range fall to the usual lineup of spring and fall flies. The best time to fish this section, says long-tenured guide Harold Harsh of Spring Creek Outfitters in nearby Oakland, is mid-May and again in October.

That there's a trout fishery here at all is something of an accident. In 1952 when Savage Reservoir Dam—constructed largely to supply water to the downstream community and pulp plant—was completed, the outflow was sort of forgotten. Then, in the early 1980s, Maryland DNR discovered that brook trout were reproducing naturally in the deeply shaded pocket water and pools. By the end of the decade, the Savage was earning something of a reputation for wild trout, and in 1991 stocking ended. Recent studies of the river show that browns make up about 60 percent of the stream's population and brook trout, the balance. An occasional rainbow may wander in from the North Branch of the Potomac, which the Savage joins at Bloomington.

At first glance, when you turn up Savage River Road from Route 135, the locale seems pretty uninviting. It's tempting to do a U-turn and head back for the North Branch. Push on. Soon the road veers away from the river, and except for one more short patch of houses, it blooms into a marvelous little tailwater. Large angular boulders pave the bottoms of pools deep enough to provide challenging wading even at minimum flows. The blocks have broken off the ledges that cross the river, channeling its waters into foaming chutes. In between the ledges are long glides and a few pocket-water riffles. Above Allegany Bridge, 3.5 miles from the mouth of the Savage, runs a mile and a quarter of fly-fishing-only, catch-and-release water right to the base of the dam.

Biggest mistake, Harsh says, is for anglers to concentrate on the big deep pools. More fish, and more *bigger* fish, are hooked in pocket water immediately

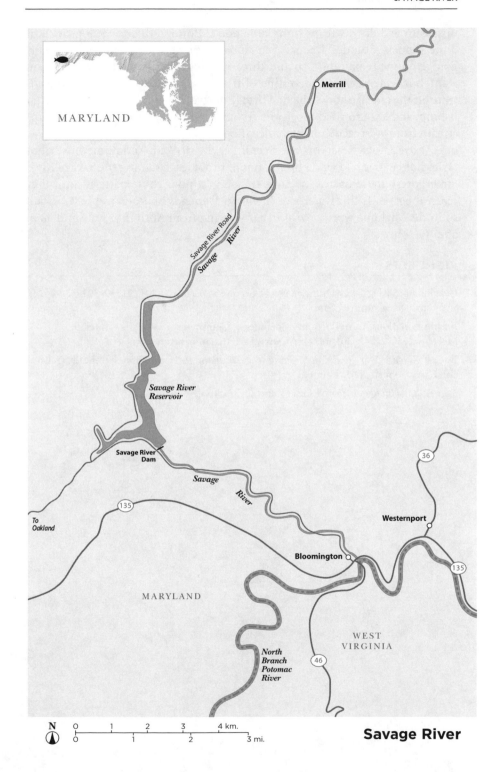

MARYLAND

Merrill

Savage River Road

Savage River

Savage River
Reservoir

Savage River
Dam

To
Oakland

135

Savage

River

36

Westernport

135

Bloomington

MARYLAND

North
Branch
Potomac
River

46

WEST
VIRGINIA

N

| 0 | 1 | 2 | 3 | 4 km. |
| 0 | 1 | 2 | 3 mi. |

Savage River

upstream and downstream from large pools. Bottom, due to algal growth, is quite slippery. Studded waders aren't a bad idea. Downstream from Allegany Bridge, in the remaining two and three-quarter miles, toss any artificial you want, but remember: no harvesting of trout is allowed. Most anglers concentrate on the mileage above the first bridge upstream from Bloomington. Better fishing, and less crowded too, is often found below the bridge in the area upstream from Westvaco's maintenance shop.

Above Savage Reservoir, the river is heavily stocked. And numerous tributaries hold native and wild populations of brookies. Draining the Savage River State Forest, these narrow streams trickle in a pool-chute pattern until they reach the river. Is this water worth a look? Depends on how deeply you want solitude. Might be worth a visit in early spring from April into June and later, after October 1.

RESOURCES

Gearing up: Spring Creek Outfitter, 208 N. Second St., Oakland, MD 21550; 301-334-4023; www.springcreekoutfitter.com.

Accommodations: Garrett County Chamber of Commerce, 15 Visitors Center Dr., McHenry, MD 21541; 301-387-4386; www.garrettchamber.com.

Books: *Guide to Maryland Trout Fishing: The Catch and Release Streams* by Charlie Gelso and Larry Coburn, K&D Limited.

Mid-Atlantic Budget Angler by Ann McIntosh, Stackpole Books.

17 CEDAR RUN

Location: North-central Pennsylvania.
Short take: Maybe a little easier to fish than Slate Run . . . but maybe not!
Type of stream: Freestone.
Angling methods: Fly.
Species: Brown, brook.
Access: Moderate.
Season: Year-round.
Supporting services: Slate Run.
Handicapped access: No.
Closest TU chapter: Contact the state council of TU.
Closest TU chapter: Northwest Connecticut.

ON THE SOUTHWEST EDGE OF TIOGA STATE FOREST, good things run in sevens—as in miles. Seven miles of Cedar Run, which enters Pine Creek, at— you guessed it—Cedar Run, is classified by the Pennsylvania Fish and Boat Commission as Trophy Trout water. Seven miles of Slate Run is Heritage Trout water (fly fishing only and catch-and-release). Separating these two superb fisheries is about, yep, seven miles of Pine Creek. Big water with long pools and broad riffles, Pine Creek can be fun for fans of long casts to stocked trout that are not particularly wary. Encroach on the lie of a Pine Creek brown, and he'll move 10 or 15 yards away. Get too close to one in Cedar Run, and he's outta here . . . more than likely spooking everything else in the pool as well.

Cedar Run is seldom wider than 30 feet, but contains pools that may be shadier and deeper than those on Slate Run. Boughs of fir and thin limbs of streamside bushes overhang much of the best water. This is one place where stealth and side-arm casting—not much more than two or three feet over the surface of the water—pay off big time. And by big time, I mean browns that have been known to reach 22 inches and five to six pounds. You won't entice them by casting your shadow on the floor of the pool, sending vibrations through the water as you wade, or splatting your line onto the surface. A 4-weight, of seven and a half or eight feet, is ideal. The lower water and the higher the sun in the sky, the longer and finer a leader you need.

As on Slate, hatches are heavy and diverse. Charles R. Meck, in *Trout Streams and Hatches of Pennsylvania,* talks of fishing in one day three hatches in succession. First came blue quills, then quill gordons, and lastly, the hendricksons. Each hatch lasted an hour or so. Late May brings out the olives, gray foxes, and march browns. Brown, green, and slate drakes emerge toward evening. When water temperatures rise and levels fall, terrestrials, particularly ants, can be extremely effective. Don't overlook tan or black caddis.

Were it not for Buck Run, which joins this stream from the west above Leetonia and marks the top of the Trophy Trout water, Cedar would likely

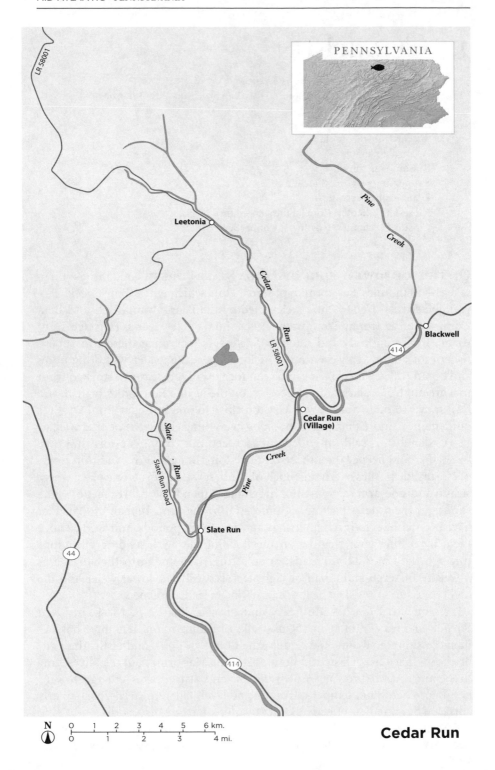

PENNSYLVANIA

LR 58001

Leetonia

Pine Creek

Cedar Run

LR 58001

Blackwell

414

Cedar Run
(Village)

Slate Run

Pine Creek

Slate Run Road

Slate Run

44

114

N
0 1 2 3 4 5 6 km.
0 1 2 3 4 mi.

Cedar Run

warm too much to hold onto its trout in July and August. Not only is Buck Run worth pursuing for smaller browns and brook trout, but also so are Fahnstock and Mine Hole runs that come in below Leetonia from the northeast. And like Slate Run, the lower pools of Cedar Run pick up pods of browns and rainbows that move up from the warming Pine Creek below. Access to Cedar Run is generally easier. It's not that its valley walls are less steep. The river road—LR 58001—shadows the stream like a good cornerback, leaving little bank for anglers to descend before reaching the water. Because of its easier access, Cedar Run is more apt to attract anglers than its downstream sibling.

RESOURCES

Gearing up and accommodations: Wolf's General Store and Slate Run Tackle Shop, P.O. Box 1, Slate Run, PA 17769; 570-753-8551; www.slaterun.com.

Books: *Trout Streams and Hatches* by Charles R. Meck, Backcountry Publications.

Trout Streams of Pennsylvania by Dwight Landis, Hempstead-Lyndell.

18 FISHING CREEK

Location: North-central Pennsylvania.
Short take: The best Fishing Creek in Pennsy.
Type of stream: Limestone.
Angling methods: Fly, spin.
Species: Brown, brook.
Access: Moderate.
Season: Year-round.
Supporting services: Lock Haven.
Handicapped access: No.
Closest TU chapter: Lock Haven.

GOOD ROADS PROVIDE REASONABLE ACCESS TO SOME 25 miles of fishable water that look for all the world like a freestone stream. You'll find no more beautiful run of first-class trout water than the five miles of Fishing Creek that courses through the Narrows, a cleft in the plunging and folded rocks of Big Mountain south of Lock Haven. Flanked by 14-inch minimum, two-fish-per-day Trophy Trout regs, the 0.9 mile upstream and 2.1 miles below the middle 2-mile run of Fishing Creek is strictly catch-and-release. Easily reached from Interstate 80, and incredibly well known throughout the Mid-Atlantic states and open year-round, the Narrows sees very heavy fishing pressure. Stubbornly boorish behavior by anglers who feel that fishing is their divine right has forced many landowners in the Narrows to post their property against fishing on Sunday.

How terribly sad. This stream, according to Charles R. Meck in *Trout Streams and Hatches of Pennsylvania*, compares with Henry's Fork for the density and diversity of its hatches. Hendricksons, quill gordons, and blue quills are coming off when Pennsylvania's trout season officially opens in mid-April. Black caddis appear a few days later, only to be joined by march browns and light cahills. The green drake hatch is relatively short here, a week or so at Memorial Day, but, in June, slate drakes kick in and reproduce all the way into October. Caddis are excellent into the fall, as well.

Hatches are particularly rich because the limestones flooring Sugar Valley underlie the Fishing Creek flowage. Rising near Green Gap, Fishing Creek slides southwestward between Nittany and Big Mountain through Loganton to Tylersville, where large springs add to the river's flow. These springs feed the state hatchery, the effluent from which had been polluting downstream runs. An agreement reached in 2001 limits the poundage of fish produced at the hatchery and reduces the amount of water from the springs that can be diverted to hatchery use.

After emerging from the Narrows, upstream from Lamar, Fishing Creek cuts to the northeast across another broad limestone valley before punching

Fishing Creek

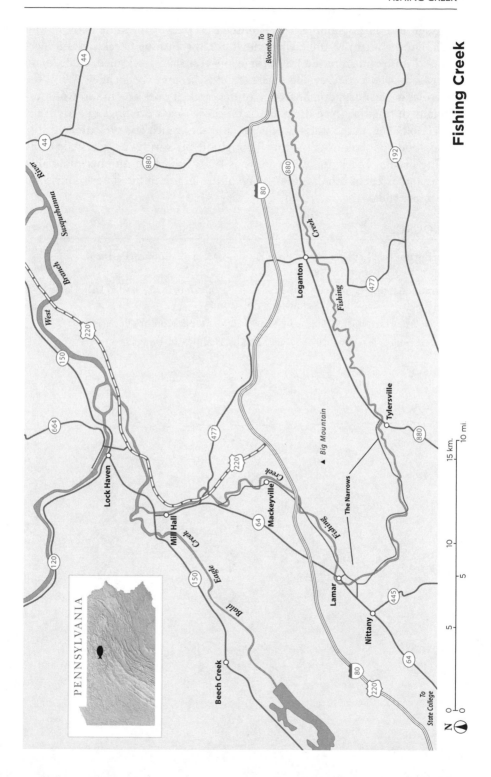

through Bald Eagle Mountain and joining the creek by the same name at Mill Hall. During warm weather, when flows are low, Fishing Creek slides underground upstream from the I-80 bridge and resurfaces—cleaned, cooled, and refreshed—above Mackeyville, where it almost seems to begin anew. While the Narrows is the most popular section of the creek, it does become crowded, especially during the green drake hatch on those lovely evenings in early June.

Look, then, at the water downstream. It sees much less pressure and sustains good populations of browns. Though the big springs at Tylersville really define Fishing Creek, the water above is kept frigid by a number of smaller seeps and excellent brook trout—some of the largest in the state—flourish in the upper end of the watershed.

RESOURCES

Gearing up: The Feathered Hook Inn & Fly Shop, Main St., Coburn, PA 16832; 814-349-8757; www.thefeatheredhook.com.

Accommodations: Clinton County Economic Partnership, 212 N. Jay St., Lock Haven, PA 17745; 570-748-5782; www.clintoncountyinfo.com.

Books: *Trout Streams and Hatches* by Charles R. Meck, Backcountry Publications.

Trout Streams of Pennsylvania by Dwight Landis, Hempstead-Lyndell.

19 KETTLE CREEK

Location: North-central Pennsylvania.
Short take: A stream in recovery, with excellent fishing in its upper reaches.
Type of stream: Freestone.
Angling methods: Fly.
Species: Brown, brook.
Access: Easy.
Season: Year-round.
Supporting services: Renovo.
Handicapped access: Yes.
Closest TU chapter: Allegheny Mountain Chapter, God's Country.

HOW DIFFICULT IT IS, WHILE CASTING A TAN CADDIS to a brown rising along boulders the color of weathered bronze near Oleona on Kettle Creek, to remember that warm flows and acid drainage have severely plagued this river. Instead, your head is turned by the dimpling rise form, steady in the gathering evening. While this mileage is stocked by the commonwealth, there is still a reasonable chance that the fish may be stream-bred or, if not, a holdover. The fish rises once more. You see its nose. You allow the concentric circles to dissipate and then you cast. The fly settles 10 feet above where it should be holding. The drift is good.

Kettle Creek was highly regarded by Keystone State anglers but the host of habitat problems that beset this small river have finally come home to roost. That this stream and its trout may, in the end, enjoy a bright future is due in large measure to the efforts of the Kettle Creek Watershed Association, the Allegheny Mountain Chapter, and the Pennsylvania Council of Trout Unlimited. In 1999, severely polluted with acid mine drainage, Kettle Creek became the third of TU's Home Rivers Initiatives. The goals of the project were four: assess the condition of the watershed, address acid mine drainage on the lower reaches, improve habitat for trout on the middle and upper reaches, and strengthen public awareness and action to protect the watershed through the development of the watershed association. In pursuit of these objectives, TU and the association has implemented a model acid mine drainage abatement program, helped establish the wild brook trout restoration program on the upper 28.3 miles of the watershed, and conducted numerous habitat rehabilitation projects in the river. For this work, the association and TU have received the Pennsylvania Governor's Award for Watershed Stewardship. With all that it has accomplished and learned in the Kettle Creek project, TU is now expanding its efforts to other tributaries of the Susquehanna's West Branch.

The most popular section of Kettle Creek ambles along through a narrow, sometimes grassy, sometimes shady valley shared with Route 144. In the midst of this, Pennsylvania has established a delayed-harvest, fly-fishing-only section.

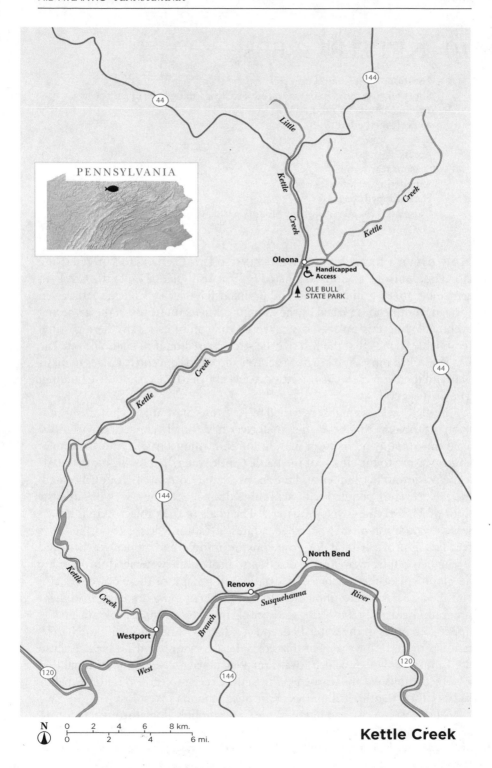

PENNSYLVANIA

Oleona

Handicapped Access

OLE BULL STATE PARK

North Bend

Renovo

Westport

Susquehanna River

West Branch

Little Kettle Creek

Kettle Creek

N

0   2   4   6   8 km.

0   2   4   6 mi.

Kettle Creek

The special-regs water begins 500 feet downstream of the uppermost Route 144 bridge and runs upstream for 1.7 miles. The water here is easily read. Not the least difficult to wade, pockets that will hold fish are obvious. You can see deep water and seams in the pools where fish will hold. It's always productive to work the riffles, and casts need not be as precise as on smaller streams. On this water, a novice can be as successful as a nimrod. You'll find all the usual central Pennsylvania hatches here.

Few trout streams in Penn's woods accommodate physically challenged anglers. But, at Ole Bull State Park, provisions have been made from the dam impounding the swimming area downstream to a ford. This water is heavily stocked and open to children as well. Below the confluence of Cross Fork, the river warms rapidly as the sun climbs towards its zenith and then basks until the nights of mid-August take on a chill. Though trout can be caught when river temperatures reach the 70s, it's heartbreaking to release them knowing they're likely to expire. Use your digital thermometer, the one God gave you. If the Kettle is tepid, cross the highland to Slate or Cedar Run.

RESOURCES

Gearing up: Kettle Creek Tackle Shop, HCR 62, Box 140, Renovo, Pa 17764; 570-923-1416.

Wolf's General Store and Slate Run Tackle Shop, P.O. Box 1, Slate Run, PA 17769; 570-753-8551; www.slaterun.com.

Books: *Trout Streams and Hatches* by Charles R. Meck, Backcountry Publications.

Trout Streams of Pennsylvania by Dwight Landis, Hempstead-Lyndell.

20 LETORT SPRING RUN

Location: South-central Pennsylvania.
Short take: Quintessential chalk stream filled with hulking browns with attitudes to match their sizes.
Type of stream: Limestone spring creek.
Angling methods: Fly, spin.
Species: Brown.
Access: Easy.
Season: Mid-April through February.
Supporting services: Carlisle, Boiling Springs.
Handicapped access: Yes.
Closest TU chapter: Cumberland Valley.

IF THE WILLOWEMOC, BEAVERKILL, AND NEVERSINK IN THE CATSKILLS were the classrooms where American dry-fly fishing was hatched, graduate courses were taught down in the Keystone State on the Letort. Charlie Fox, Vince Marinaro, Ed Koch, and Ed Shenk ran the lab. Crouched back from the bank of this tiny stream—seldom more than two dozen feet across—they observed in detail the behavior of browns that grew big beneath the aelodea and cresses. While mayflies and caddis and various crustacea constitute a large portion of their diet, big browns want as much protein as they can get every time they open their mouths. Ants, beetles, grasshoppers, and jassids are easy targets from June on. Patiently watching the stream, they learned to differentiate one kind of rise from another. They learned which insects trout took, and those that they let float by. The patterns they developed elegantly represented naturals. Their use of precisely tapered leaders and tippets to deliver the fly with just the right amount of splash forms the core of our knowledge of terrestrial fishing. A savvy angler simply cannot fish the meadows of the Letort between the railroad trestle and Bonny Brook Quarry without the thought that Vince and the boys are keeping an eye on those browns.

The waters from the railroad bridge at the south end of the Borough of Carlisle's Letort Park upstream for one and a half miles rank right up there with Silver Creek in Idaho as the most challenging wild trout stream in the United States. The browns here have no lake or big river to migrate into as they do elsewhere. They stay put and they come to know their lies with ultimate intimacy. Says Dusty Weidner of Coldspring Angler in Carlisle, a careless footfall, any wading, and dragging floats will spook these browns as surely as sunrise. Successful anglers scout the stream from a distance, target a working trout, move into position, and then kneel waiting for the fish to resume its feeding pattern. If there's a signature hatch on the Letort, it would have to be sulphurs and early black stoneflies that come off at dark from early May into June. You'll also find tiny blue-winged olives in early spring and late fall.

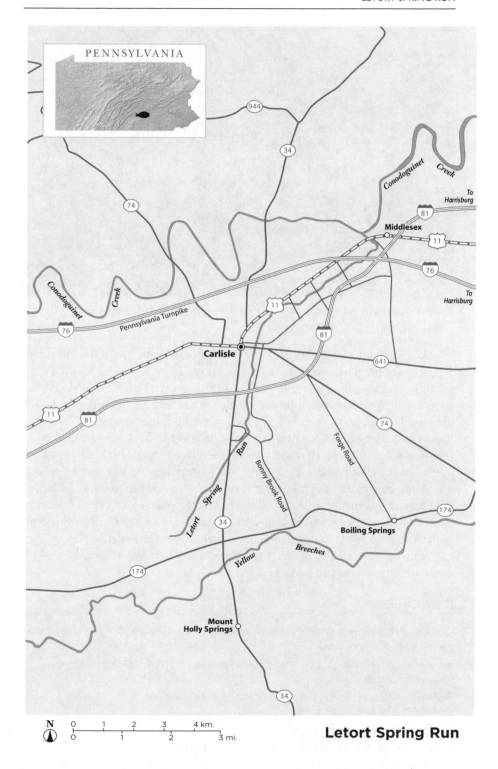

Letort Spring Run

Tiny insects and large fish make the Letort Spring Run a perfect brown trout laboratory.

Access, thanks to TUers over the years, is excellent. The mile and a half upstream of the park is designated for Heritage Trophy Angling by the Pennsylvania Fish and Boat Commission and thus reserved for catch-and-release fly fishing. Upstream, you'll find some fast water and shade at Bonny Brook Quarry. The farther up you fish, the more prevalent the beds of cress and the more challenging the water. At a small wooden bridge, the Letort forks and becomes smaller still. The Heritage water is the place to start. Park at the park or at the small pullout where TU has erected monuments to Fox and Marinaro.

After leaving Letort Park, the river flows through the town and Carlisle Barracks, site of the Army War College. Below the post, it enters private lands, some of which are open to angling. Often a gentle knock at a landowner's door is all that's required to gain permission to fish. Don't overlook this run, though its trout are fewer and smaller than those cressy stretches upstream. With more structure, runs and pools become more clearly defined.

RESOURCES

Gearing up: Cold Spring Anglers, 419 E. High St., Suite A, Carlisle, PA 17013; 717-245-2646; www.coldspringangler.com.

Yellow Breeches Outfitters, 2 First St., Boiling Springs, PA 17007: 717-258-6752; www.yellowbreeches.com.

Accommodations: Greater Carlisle Area Chamber of Commerce, 212 N. Hanover St., Carlisle PA 17014; 717-243-4515.

Books: *Trout Streams and Hatches* by Charles R. Meck, Backcountry Publications.

Trout Streams of Pennsylvania by Dwight Landis, Hempstead-Lyndell.

21 LITTLE JUNIATA RIVER

Location: North-central Pennsylvania.
Short take: A truly cool place to fish.
Type of stream: Limestone/freestone.
Angling methods: Fly, spin.
Species: Brown, rainbow.
Access: Easy and ample.
Season: Year-round.
Supporting services: Tyrone, Huntingdon.
Handicapped access: No.
Closest TU chapter: Blair County.

ONE OF THE KEYSTONE STATE'S LARGER TROUT RIVERS, the Little Juniata rises on the flanks of the Alleghany Highlands above Bellwood, flows northeast toward Tyrone along Interstate 99, junctions there with Bald Eagle Creek, and then breaks to the southwest toward Huntingdon. The river here is primarily a warm-water stream—with the exception of a 0.75-mile delayed-harvest area from Bellwood to Fostoria—holding few trout but some reasonable-sized smallmouth.

Springs near Grier School change all that. Here, plumes of lime-rich water of consistent mid-50s temperature enter the Little J, the first of scores of such springs and cold-water seeps that condition its flows for the next 13.5 miles down to where Frankstown Branch of the Juniata enters from the southwest. On the bar between the two, according to veteran biologist and angling guru Joe McMullen, you can cast for browns to the north and smallies to the south.

Increased alkalinity fosters plenteous populations of mayflies and caddis and sets the stage for an abundance of minnows and crawfish. Countless riffles chatter over angular cobbles before the river spreads into broad pools, some deep and others shallow. The entire run is shaded. Primarily brown trout water, you'll find a few rainbows and maybe an occasional brook trout fugitive from private stockings of tributaries.

There is no "best" run of this river. It's all good, according to Allan Bright, long-time guide, fly shop owner, and lodge operator in Spruce Creek. A number of roads track the river from the bridge at Ironton down to Spruce Creek. Below the junction of this famous stream, access is a matter of shank's mare. Spring Ridge Club privately controls the well-known 1.3-mile Espy mileage. You have to be a member of the club or a guest to enter the water to fish it. Below the Espy farm, the Little J flows through a narrow gorge of two miles. The gorge is part of Rothrock State Forest. Anglers park at the mouth of the gorge above Barree and hike up an abandoned woods road to fish lovely runs and deep pools.

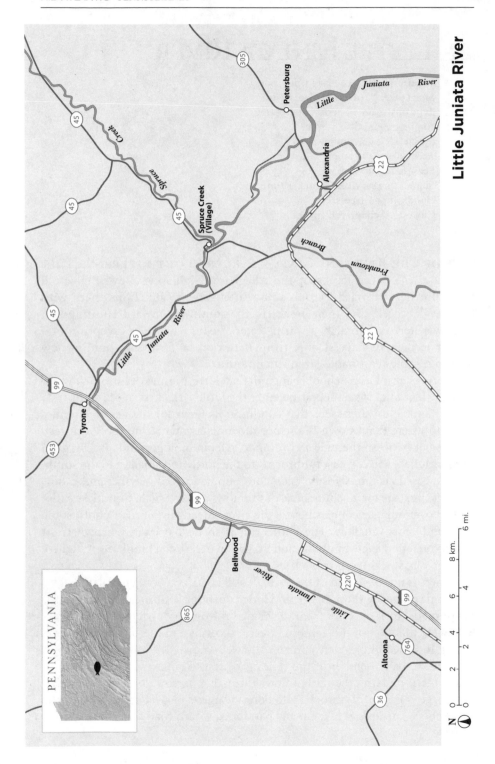

Little Juniata River

The Little Juniata has all the hatches, easier access, and as much charm as its more exclusive cousin, Spruce Creek.

The Little Juniata has seen its share of challenges. Pollution from paper mills kept its waters as brown and frothy as root beer into the 1970s. A chemical spill in the early 1990s decimated aquatic insects. But periodic floods flushed the river and returned it to health. Currently, the Espy mileage is the subject of a landmark legal case to determine whether rivers deemed "navigable" in the 1700s and early 1800s—when rafts floated pig iron and timber downstream on spring floods—should continue to be accessible to anyone below the average high-water mark. This is a classic case of who owns the water and the fish therein. With the exception of the gorge through Rothrock State Forest, all of the land on either side of the Little J is privately held. Wise anglers will stop at Spruce Creek Outfitters or the Spring Ridge Club to determine where they can legally enter the river.

Fishing on the Little J is a year-round affair. Action begins in February when spikes in water temperature—even from 34 to 38 degrees Fahrenheit—trigger mid-day midge hatches. In May, sulphurs, slate drakes, and cahills prevail. Green drakes blossom below the Route 45 bridge in Spruce Creek well into June. As summer runs its course anglers tossing ants, crickets, and beetles beneath overhanging brush along rocky banks connect, as do those fishing dead-drifted Bead Head Prince, Hare's Ear, or Pheasant Tails in riffles. In mid-August, the early evening white mayfly hatch is as heavy and productive as it is on the Yellow Breeches at Boiling Springs. Chucking crayfish patterns or Ugly Woolly Buggers with a 6-weight can pay off with larger than average browns. Bright and others who love the river fish cautiously during the brown spawn from mid-October into November. Hooking a hen then causes her to jettison her eggs, and her progeny is lost. Bright avoids spawning areas. "When they are on their redds," he says, "we'll let them have a cigarette and a glass of wine!" They deserve a break.

RESOURCES

Gearing up: Spruce Creek Outfitters, Route 45, P.O. Box 36, Spruce Creek, PA 16683; 814-632-3071; www.sprucecreekoutfitters.org.

Spring Ridge Club, Route 45, P.O. Box 88, Spruce Creek, PA 16683; 814-632-5827; www.springridgeclub.com.

Accommodations: Huntingdon County Visitors Bureau, R.D. 1, Box 222-A Seven Points Rd., Hesston, PA 16647; 814-658-0060 or 1-88-Raystown; www.raystown.org.

Books: *Trout Streams and Hatches* by Charles R. Meck, Backcountry Publications.

22 PENNS CREEK

Location: North-central Pennsylvania.
Short take: Lots of browns for any angler.
Type of stream: Limestone/freestone.
Angling methods: Fly, spin.
Species: Brown, rainbow.
Access: Easy and ample.
Season: Year-round.
Supporting services: State College.
Handicapped access: No.
Closest TU chapters: Penns Creek, Raymond B. Winter.

THAT PENNS CREEK IS CONSIDERED BY SOME as the Keystone State's premier limestone trout fishery is as much an accident of geology as the result of generations of hard work by dedicated anglers, TUers among them. The creek issues forth from Penn's Cave, a tourist attraction east of State College on PA Route 192. The cave's owner has dammed the stream at the mouth of the cave to allow patrons to tour the cavern by boat. Below the dam, Penns Creek is a fee fishery, currently leased to the Spring Ridge Club in Spruce Creek.

Penns becomes public at the Village of Spring Mills where PA Route 45 crosses. From Spring Mills to Coburn, a distance of about six miles, the Pennsylvania Fish and Boating Commission classifies the creek as approved trout waters, meaning that it can be stocked. From the bridge through the village and downstream to where Penns Creek Road crosses it, this stream offers angling that's often overlooked. From that bridge, though, down to the old milldam just above Coburn, it's sluggish and worthy of little attention.

At Coburn begins Penns Creek's main event. From this tiny town, which boasts an excellent fly shop, Penns is cooled by spring-fed Elk and Pine creeks. Like a shot of adrenaline, these flows reinvigorate trout and the hatches on which they feed. At the same time, Penns begins to enter a seven-mile rift in the crumpled-up ridges. Gradient increases. Broad riffles tail into deep pools and swirl around big boulders tumbled long ago into the stream. No longer a creek per se, with the added flows of the Elk and the Pine, Penns becomes a small river. An abandoned railroad grade turned foot trail/bike path follows the course through the hills, and a mile's walk in from either end will take you to waters that see only modest pressure. The road to Ingleby provides vehicular access to the center of this stretch, which is managed as Trophy Trout water by the commonwealth.

Below Poe Paddy Campground, rules for fishing become catch-and-release for the next four miles. This is the most remote of the sections of Penns Creek. The railroad grade follows the river, and like most walk-in sections, the

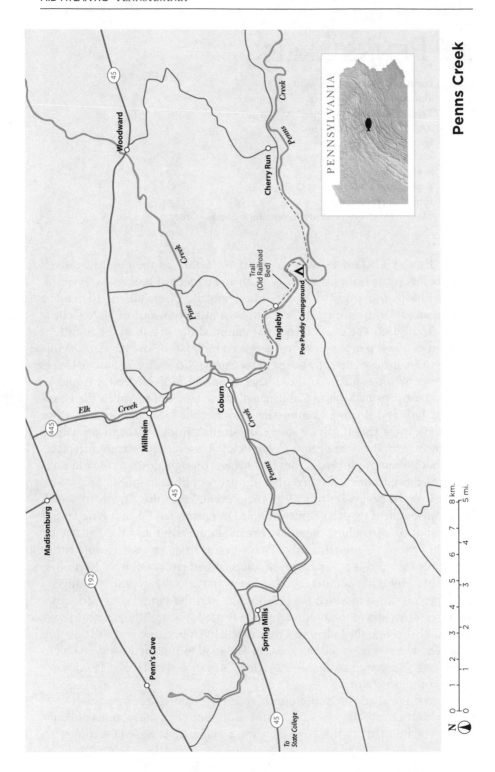

Penns Creek

PENNSYLVANIA

Anglers flock to Penns Creek in early June for the emergence of the green drakes.

use it sees decreases with distance from the gates at the top or just above where Cherry Run enters west of the village of Weikert.

The hatch of green drakes occurring around Memorial Day and lasting through the first week in June sees the heaviest use of Penns Creek. These big mayflies—*Ephemera guttulata*—are called shad flies locally (because the hatch coincides to some degree with the spring run of shad in the large rivers of the Mid-Atlantic states), and they attract platoons of anglers from throughout the East. Though of a different genus and species as those found in the West, the green drake hatch is as important on Penns Creek as it is on Henry's Fork in Idaho and on the Metolius in Oregon. On Penns Creek, the heaviest hatches of green drakes may not be the best time to fish big dry Spinners or Duns. Fish may have a difficult time selecting the artificial. But after the primary hatch has passed, sporadic emergences will occur and trout seem to take imitations more readily. Green drake nymphs are also very productive. This hatch often begins late in the day and continues into the night. Some of the best fishing is found after dark. Caddisflies, particularly grannon caddis, are also very productive in mid- to late April, as are the sulphurs of May and June.

Together with Pine Creek, and the shorter Elk, its tributary, the Penns Creek drainage makes up the longest run of wild trout water in Pennsylvania. Several years ago, a coalition involving Penns Valley Conservation Association and TU's local chapters beat back a plan to quarry limestone below the water table, which could have upset the delicate ecological balance of the stream.

The Conservation Association has also been very aggressive in working with farmers to fence cattle out of the creek. At the moment, at least, the future for trout in Penns Creek looks very bright.

RESOURCES

Gearing up: The Feathered Hook Inn & Fly Shop, Main St., Coburn, PA 16832; 814-349-8757; www.thefeatheredhook.com.

Flyfishers Paradise, 2603 E. College Ave., State College, PA 16801; 814-234-4189; www.flyfishersparadise.com.

Accommodations: Central Pennsylvania Convention and Visitors Bureau, 1402 S. Atherton St., State College, PA 16801; 800-358-5466; www.visitpennstate.org.

Books: *Penn's Creek* by Daniel Shields, River Journal Series, Frank Amato Publications.

Trout Streams and Hatches by Charles R. Meck, Backcountry Publications.

Trout Streams of Pennsylvania by Dwight Landis, Hempstead-Lyndell.

23 SLATE RUN

Location: North-central Pennsylvania.
Short take: Toughest stream you'll ever love to fish.
Type of stream: Freestone.
Angling methods: Fly.
Species: Brown, brook.
Access: Not easy.
Season: Year-round.
Supportin services: Slate Run.
Handicapped access: No.
Closest TU chapter: Contact the state council of TU.

LATER ON YOU'LL SEE ME WRITING ABOUT ANOTHER PISCATORIAL
TRILOGY—Henry's Fork, the Madison, and the Yellowstone—that rises in the
calderas where Wyoming, Montana, and Idaho meet. There's one here, too, on
the high Allegheny Plateau—Slate Run, Cedar Run, and Kettle Creek. Much
smaller, of course, than those out West, these three streams in north-central
Pennsylvania comprise a destination well worth a week's visit. Of the three,
Slate Run is classified a Heritage Trout Area by the Pennsylvania Boat and Fish
Commission, and thus, as of this writing, is restricted to fly fishing only. Here
you'll find stunning angling for wild browns and smaller brookies in their
headwaters.

Francis and Cushman brooks meet seven miles from the mouth of Slate
Run and drop 500 feet before entering Pine Creek at the hamlet where maestro
Tom Finkbiner holds forth in his eclectic deli cum fly-fishing emporium. The
first two miles upstream from the village follow a narrow valley of pools,
pocket water, and a few riffles. Just downstream from where Manor Fork comes
in from the west, Slate Run Road pulls up from the stream. A little track continues north to its confluence. The valley tightens further and becomes more difficult to reach. The angling improves, simply due to lack of pressure.

Hatches on this stream are abundant. Assuming normal spring run-off
has flushed through the river in March, you'll encounter blizzards of blue
quills in April; a medley of grey foxes, march browns, sulphurs, and olives in
early May; and then the drakes—brown, green, and slate in late May and early
June. Slate drakes continue to hatch into September. Caddisflies are also very
much in evidence with the October caddis ending the season on a high note.
As flows decline on these highland streams in July and August, they warm, but
not as much as Pine Creek. Big browns move up from the larger stream into
the lower reaches of Slate Run and provide an excellent nighttime fishery.
While browns are the main event, brook trout are also prevalent, and especially so in Francis and Cushman brooks. An 11-inch brook trout is not unusual, though they tend to run between six and eight inches.

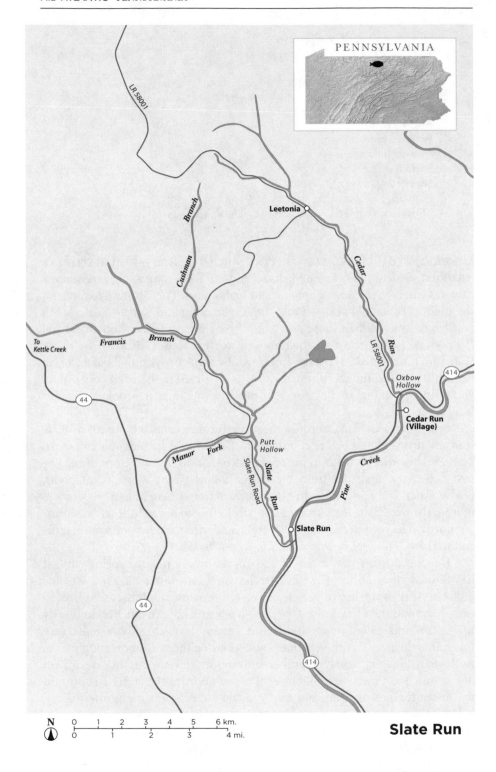

PENNSYLVANIA

LR 58001

Leetonia

Branch

Cushman

Cedar

To
Kettle Creek

Francis   Branch

LR 58001

Run

Oxbow
Hollow

414

44

Cedar Run
(Village)

Manor   Fork

Putt
Hollow

Slate Run Road

Slate   Run

Creek

Pine

Slate Run

44

414

N

0 1 2 3 4 5 6 km.
0   1   2   3   4 mi.

Slate Run

Fishing Slate Run is not easy, says Finkbiner. When an angler enters his shop and drops a reference to fishing the Madison, Finkbiner immediately thinks "greenhorn" and knows that most likely the nimrod will find Slate Run frustrating. His advice is straightforward: Before wetting a fly, walk a mile of the stream. Develop a mental sense of how pocket water and pools fit together. Sit on a bluff or cliff and watch the creek. More and better fish are taken from pockets than big pools. Return to where you started your scout and begin to fish there. Work each pocket with two to three good casts. Pay attention to little projections of the run's namesake rock. Think of them as natural lunker structures because that's what they are.

RESOURCES

Gearing up and accommodations: Wolf's General Store and Slate Run Tackle Shop, P.O. Box 1, Slate Run, PA 17769; 570-753-8551; www.slaterun.com.

Books: *Trout Streams and Hatches* by Charles R. Meck, Backcountry Publications.

Trout Streams of Pennsylvania by Dwight Landis, Hempstead-Lyndell.

24 SPRUCE CREEK

Location: Central Pennsylvania.
Short take: Water to suit every wallet, even this reporter's thin purse.
Type of stream: Limestone.
Angling methods: Fly, spin.
Species: Brown, rainbow.
Access: Limited.
Season: Year-round.
Supporting services: Spruce Creek, Huntingdon.
Handicapped access: No.
Closest TU chapter: Blair County.

LOCAL ANGLERS KNEW A GOOD THING WHEN THEY HAD IT. A drive along PA Route 45 upstream from the village of Spruce Creek shows a crop of summer cabins spread along the floodplain. Most date from the 1950s when affluent WWII vets purchased little plots and built bungalows along the water they loved to fish. Soon though, the cabins thin as the Spruce Creek valley climbs to the northeast. The 10-mile route through the hamlets of Colerain, Franklinville, Seven Stars, and Graysville to Spruce Creek's headwaters near Pennsylvania Furnace, an early-nineteenth-century iron bloomery and one of a half dozen in the area, is charming. The valley is floored with limestone and numerous springs and seeps cool the water and raise its alkalinity, creating a near-perfect environment for aquatic insects.

Browns and rainbows thrive in these waters. Action begins in March with a small olive hatch. Then comes the fabulous hatch of grannon caddis in late April. Late May brings heavy sulphurs and the renowned hatch of drakes (both green and slate) around Memorial Day. Tricos come off in August. As May verges on full-blown summer, don't overlook traditional terrestrials, especially ants, beetles, and crickets. Single, barbless hook hardware can be used in the 0.6-mile public-access section owned and managed by Pennsylvania State University and named for legendary fly-fishing educator George Harvey.

Located about a mile upstream from Spruce Creek's confluence with the Little Juniata, the Harvey section is managed as catch-and-release trout water by the Pennsylvania Fish and Boating Commission. Here, Spruce divides into two channels. The western is narrow, seldom wider than 10 feet. Tendrils of shrub kiss the surface and leafy canopy shades the water. Often overlooked, the knee-deep runs of the west channel hold respectable trout. The better fishing, and relatively easier, is found in the pools and chute-like rapids of the eastern channel. This is wild Spruce Creek fishing at a fee all of us can afford.

The remaining mileage is open to public access, albeit for a range of fees. As this edition went to press, the half-mile section immediately above the bridge to Camp Espy Farms could be accessed for a few tens of dollars, a very

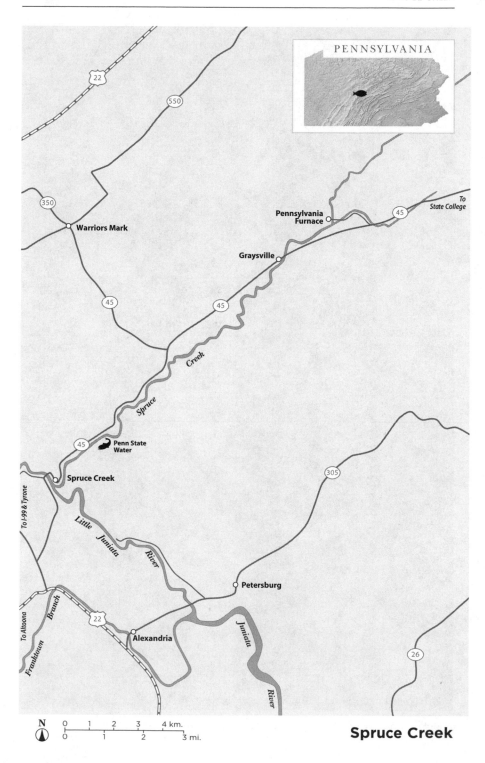

PENNSYLVANIA

22
550
350
Warriors Mark
Pennsylvania Furnace
45
To State College
Graysville
45
45
Creek
Spruce
45
Penn State Water
305
Spruce Creek
To I-99 & Tyrone
Little Juniata River
Petersburg
To Altoona
Frankstown Branch
22
Alexandria
Juniata
26
Juniata River

N

| 0 | 1 | 2 | 3 | 4 km. |
| 0 | | 1 | 2 | 3 mi. |

Spruce Creek

Multiple hatches draw anglers to Spruce Creek, where browns and rainbows thrive.

reasonable tariff compared to the hundreds of dollars charged to fish water leased from local landowners. It must be remembered that landowners set policies for accessing their waters, and that the fees for fishing Spruce Creek's private runs are not in the least out of line with what one pays for a day in a driftboat on Henry's Fork or a run up the Colorado at Lees Ferry. You'll find a number of comfortable bed-and-breakfasts in the Spruce Creek valley, as well as private clubs that cater to anglers. Other accommodations can be found in Huntingdon, 10 miles to the southeast, or in State College, about 30 miles to the northeast.

RESOURCES

Gearing up: Spruce Creek Outfitters, Route 45, P.O. Box 36, Spruce Creek, PA 16683; 814-632-3071; www.sprucecreekoutfitters.org.

Spring Ridge Club, Route 45, P.O. Box 88, Spruce Creek, PA 16683; 814-632-5827; www.springridgeclub.com.

Accommodations: Huntingdon County Visitors Bureau, R.D. 1, Box 222-A Seven Points Rd., Hesston, PA 16647; 814-658-0060 or 1-888-Raystown; www.raystown.org.

Books: *Trout Streams and Hatches* by Charles R. Meck, Backcountry Publications.

Trout Streams of Pennsylvania by Dwight Landis, Hempstead-Lyndell.

25 CRANBERRY RIVER

Location: Central West Virginia.
Short take: A marvelous example of how a once-sterile stream can be restored to a prominent trout fishery.
Type of stream: Freestone.
Angling methods: Fly, spin.
Species: Brook, brown, rainbow.
Access: Moderate.
Season: Year-round.
Supporting services: Richwood.
Handicapped access: Yes.
Closest TU chapter: Kanawha.

THROUGH THE LARGEST FEDERALLY MANDATED WILDERNESS in the East flow the North and Dogway forks of West Virginia's Cranberry River. Rising in the Cranberry Glades—a post-glacial bog with flora similar to that of Canadian muskeg—between Black Mountain and Blue Knob, the river flows through a 35,864-acre wilderness area inaccessible save by foot, bike, or horse and wagon.

The upper reaches of North, South, and Dogway forks are brook trout country. Faintly tinged with tannin reminiscent of New England streams, the waters are thin and dark and overhung by laurel and rhododendron. Their pinkish white blooms, first the laurel and then the rhodies, coincide with the best angling on these stretches. When flows are low and warm, a condition exacerbated by recent drier years, brook trout are best left undisturbed. In spring and early summer, angling can be stupendous. A good brookie runs 10 to 12 inches and feeds as eagerly as brook trout do in sparse waters. All of Dogway Fork is restricted to fly fishing only. Catch-and-release rules apply to the Cranberry from the confluence of the Dogway 4.3 miles upstream to where the South Fork comes in, and then on the North Fork above the junction for another quarter mile to the liming station.

It is these liming stations, installed after intense advocacy by the West Virginia Council of Trout Unlimited, that have been instrumental in the reclamation of the Cranberry from the ravages of acid deposition. In the East, highlands above 3,000 feet are particularly threatened by acidic rain, fogs, and snows. The elevation where Dogway Fork joins the Cranberry is about 2,950 feet. By the mid-1980s, acid deposition had nearly eliminated aquatic insects from the upper reaches of the watershed and brook trout were all but eradicated. Though admittedly a band-aid approach, liming of the upper Cranberry has restored populations of wild brook trout.

Below the junction, the river becomes a rainbow and brown trout fishery. It is diligently stocked by the West Virginia Department of Natural Resources and,

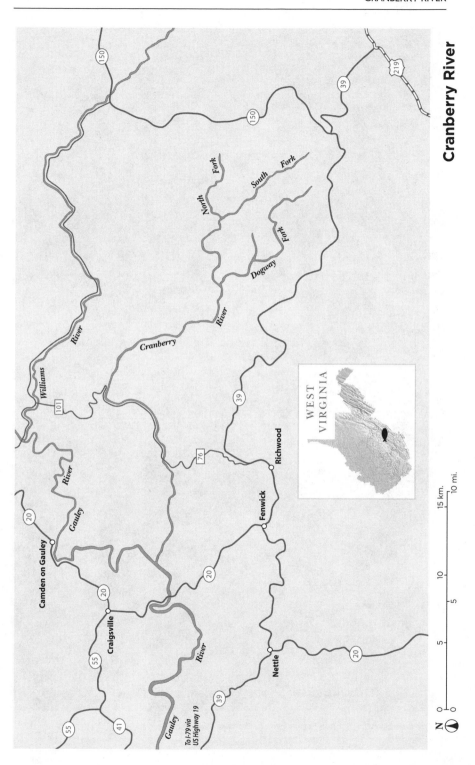

Cranberry River

A nice Cranberry brown falls to a patiently presented Woolly Bugger.

in the popular catch-and-release section from Woodbine picnic area 1.2 miles downstream to Camp Splinter, by the Kanawha Chapter of TU. At Woodbine, 300 yards are reserved for children and those who are modestly physically impaired but no wheelchair access is available. Here, rainbows and browns of 16 inches are not all that rare, but low, clear flows make midday fishing an exercise in persistence or frustration. Better summer angling occurs early or late.

Oak Myers, a middle-school teacher who's guided on the Cranberry for more than a dozen years, says that hatches are becoming more prolific. Among the best are the little black stoneflies that come off in March. They're followed by blue-winged olives, blue quills, and quill gordons, and caddis ranging from little blacks to grannons. Light cahills come off just before dusk in June and early July. There's also something of a green drake and slate drake hatch, but trout don't key on these the way they do in Pennsylvania's famed limestone streams. Nor do Cranberry trout seem to be as turned on by terrestrials as those on other waters. That said, Myers admits that tiny black ants are often the pattern du jour.

Stripped nearly bare by loggers who moved into the region in the late 1800s (the nearby town of Richwood—as in "rich" and "wood"—was created by Cherry River Boom and Lumber Company in 1901), the forest is webbed by abandoned woods roads. Beds of narrow-gauge railroads run alongside the Cranberry and its tributaries. Long pools, often floored with sandstone bedrock, are interrupted by runs through courses of angular boulders under which great browns and rainbows hide. Wading is not difficult during periods of normal flow.

Many anglers ride mountain bikes on gated forest services roads to reach more isolated stretches of the river. Some anglers walk. Many hike to streamside Adirondack shelters, available on a first-come-first-served basis. Others take advantage of Myers' mule cart. He'll haul your dunnage—tents, cots, tables, food chests, gas grills, etc.—in a wagon pulled by a matched team. He can set up your camp, guide your fishing, and sling your hash. Or he can shake your hand, swing aboard the cart, and promise to pick you up in a few days or in a week, whatever your druthers. Come some fine mid-week in May, don't look for me anywhere else.

RESOURCES

Gearing up: Cranberry Wilderness Outfitters Inc., Box 263, Fenwick, WV 26202, 304-846-6805; wvoutfitters.com.

Accommodations: Richwood Convention and Visitor's Bureau, 1 E. Main St., Richwood, VA 26261; 304-846-6790; www.richwoodwv.com.

Books: *Flyfisher's Guide to the Virginias: Including West Virginia's Best Fly Waters* by David Hart, Wilderness Adventures Press.

Mid-Atlantic Budget Angler by Ann McIntosh, Stackpole Books.

26 SENECA CREEK

Location: Eastern West Virginia.
Short take: The size of the brookies is astounding, but head for the upper end.
Type of stream: Freestone.
Angling methods: Fly, spin, bait.
Species: Brook, rainbow.
Access: Long, but not difficult.
Season: Year-round.
Supporting services: Seneca Rocks.
Handicapped access: No.
Closest TU chapter: Contact the state council of TU.

TROUT STREAMS ARE LIKE PEOPLE. Some, upon first meeting, you feel you've known your whole life. They wear their personalities on their sleeves, like the Little River in the Great Smokies, the middle run of the Madison, and the Beaverkill. Other rivers are more taciturn. To know them and know them well is not an easy process. Seneca Creek is one such stream.

Joining the North Fork of the South Branch of the Potomac River at the foot of Seneca Rocks, that climber's paradise in West Virginia, Seneca Creek struck me as a fairly typical foothills stream. Its course here is wideish and scoured by flash floods that roar down the valley. The narrow floodplain carries a hodge-podge of settlement from backyards to highway maintenance sheds to the smallish pastures of shirttail farms whose owners work in Elkins, 30 miles farther west. "How could this be one of America's 100 best?" I wondered as I drove along U.S. Route 33, which shadows the creek up the valley.

About two and a half miles west of Seneca Rocks, the creek turns abruptly south. White's Run Road, County Route 33/3, follows the stream so closely that you could almost cast from your car. The famous mileage of Seneca Creek begins at the confluence of White's Run. A locked barrier stops further travel by auto. Anglers who fish the lower section park here. Popular destinations are the pools below Seneca Falls, three miles upstream.

An old railroad grade serves as a road to a node of private land all but surrounded by the Monongahela National Forest. There's about two miles of fishable stream in the forest below the private parcel. The mile of water inside the private property can be fished, but it's courteous to ask permission of anyone found at the camp along the trail.

When fishing with guide Eric Owens one dry October, we were scanning the creek from the trail 20 feet above it when Eric gasped: "Look at that!" in sotto voce. "Wow!"

Wow, indeed! The tip of quivering Eric's 5-weight pointed at a huge trout lying above a flat sheet of rock. To its left was a patch of undisturbed gravel. A female brookie of 15 to 18 inches, we guessed she was. By her side finned a

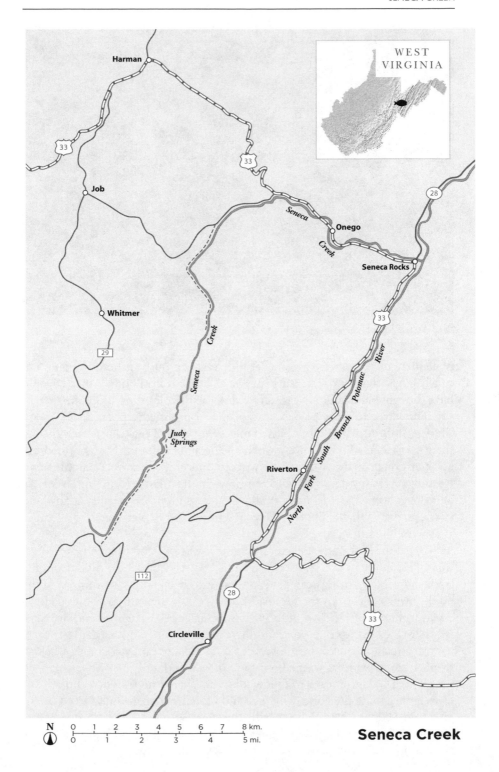

WEST VIRGINIA

Harman

Job

Whitmer

29

33

33

28

Seneca

Onego

Creek

Seneca Rocks

33

Seneca

Creek

Judy
Springs

Riverton

North Fork

South Branch

Potomac River

112

28

33

Circleville

N

| 0 | 1 | 2 | 3 | 4 | 5 | 6 | 7 | 8 km. |
| 0 | | 1 | | 2 | | 3 | | 4 | 5 mi. |

Seneca Creek

Seneca Creek holds brookies as well as rainbows.

male of 10 to 12 inches. Two smaller brookies nervously cruised the pool not much larger than a king-sized bed. She floated so immobilely that I would have thought her a large sucker were it not for the coloration of her fins.

The lower mileage of Seneca can be astounding. Reports TUer David Thorne from nearby Elkins: "I had one experience a few years back fishing the lower reaches in early May when all the stars apparently were lined up. Most any fly probably would have worked, but grey foxes were hatching and I caught probably 15 to 20 wild rainbows better than a foot, and at least a half dozen were 15 to 16 inches. All were taken on dries, mostly Adams and Para-Adams!" On the Seneca, May and June, and September and October are the months.

To get the best of the Seneca, forgo the lower run and hike in from Forest Road 112, about 15 miles west of US 33 near Circleville. Three miles from the trailhead is Judy Springs campsite, a small grassy meadow. Trout hold in the pool downstream from the footbridge that brings the camp's namesake trail down from the east. Below Judy Springs, Seneca Creek narrows and deepens. It is here the best water begins, and there's six miles of it to fish. A mile or so below the camp, Seneca drops over a 14-foot fall and enters a gorge. A hellish tropical storm in 1985 washed out the railroad bed and the bridges planked over by the CCC that used to follow this run. There's no trail now, but an angler can negotiate the gorge with care and patience. According to trout biologist Tom Oldham, who'd been with the West Virginia Division of Natural Resources for 26 years, wild rainbows of 16 to 18 inches can be found in the section below the campsite. Makes the walk worth taking, no?

RESOURCES

Gearing up: Bring what you need.

Accommodations: Pendleton County Chamber of Commerce, P.O. Box 737, Franklin, WV 26807; 304-358-3884; www.visitpendleton.com.

Books: *Flyfisher's Guide to the Virginias: Including West Virginia's Best Fly Waters* by David Hart, Wilderness Adventures Press.

Mid-Atlantic Budget Angler by Ann McIntosh, Stackpole Books.

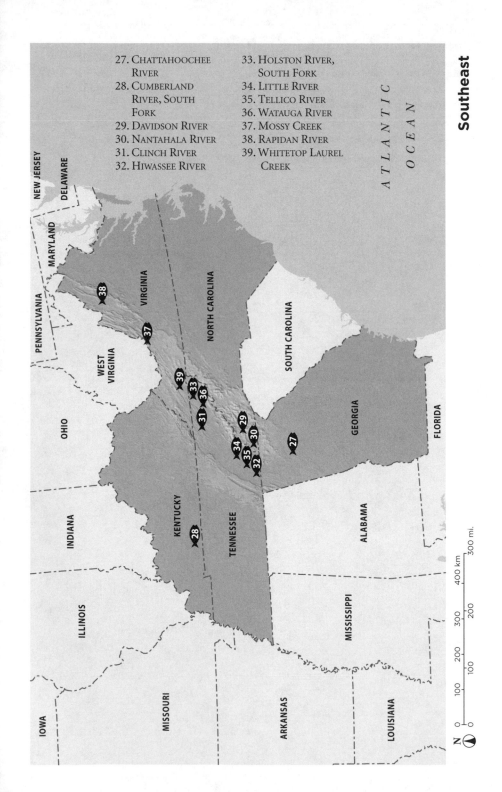

Southeast

27. CHATTAHOOCHEE RIVER
28. CUMBERLAND RIVER, SOUTH FORK
29. DAVIDSON RIVER
30. NANTAHALA RIVER
31. CLINCH RIVER
32. HIWASSEE RIVER
33. HOLSTON RIVER, SOUTH FORK
34. LITTLE RIVER
35. TELLICO RIVER
36. WATAUGA RIVER
37. MOSSY CREEK
38. RAPIDAN RIVER
39. WHITETOP LAUREL CREEK

SOUTHEAST

GEORGIA

KENTUCKY

NORTH CAROLINA

TENNESSEE

VIRGINIA

27 CHATTAHOOCHEE RIVER

Location: Northern Georgia.
Short take: Atlanta's Central Park with trout.
Type of stream: Tailwater.
Angling methods: Fly, spin, bait.
Species: Brown, rainbow.
Access: Easy to moderate.
Season: Year-round.
Supporting services: Atlanta, Norcross.
Handicapped access: Yes.
Closest TU chapters: Tailwater, Upper Chattahoochee.

EVERYBODY THINKS OF PISCATORIAL PRESIDENT JIMMY CARTER fishing with flies up on Spruce Creek in Pennsylvania. But his angling interests also lay closer to home. When he signed the legislation in 1978 creating the Chattahoochee River National Recreation Area that runs from Buford Dam near Gainesville 48 miles south to Peach Tree Creek in downtown Atlanta, he had this to say: "It's a rare occasion when within the city limits of one of our major cities, one can find pure water and trout and free canoeing and rapids and the seclusion of the Earth the way God made it. But the Chattahoochee River is this kind of place."

Rare indeed! Metropolitan Atlanta is among, if not the, most rapidly growing urban areas in the Southeast. Tendrils of development spread northeast along Interstate 85 and its spur Interstate 985 toward Gainesville and Lake Lanier, the most heavily used Corps of Engineers lake in the county. Shopping malls, industrial parks, and instant residential developments cover in pavement thousands of new acres each year. Sediment from construction and hot-water runoff from thundershower rains that fall on vast parking lots and suburban streets threaten the viability of the "Hooch," as it's called by anglers who love it. Trout Unlimited has played a key role in its preservation by advocating for more stringent enforcement of riverside buffer zones and related environmental laws. Applying these laws is proving vital to mitigating the pollution that threatens the river.

Their love is not misplaced for the Chattahoochee. In the midst of the hassle of urban development, it provides a source of tranquility. Chris Scalley, of River Through Atlanta Guide Service, thinks of the river as the region's Central Park. As a former denizen of Manhattan, I can tell you he's not wrong. Cool through the hottest summer and warm enough for good winter hatches, the Hooch is a kind of miraculous trout fishery. An extensive survey of macroinvertebrates confirms year-round hatches of olives and midges. Stoneflies come off from January into July, and caddisflies blossom from March through June. You can get a firsthand look at patterns that work on the Hooch from

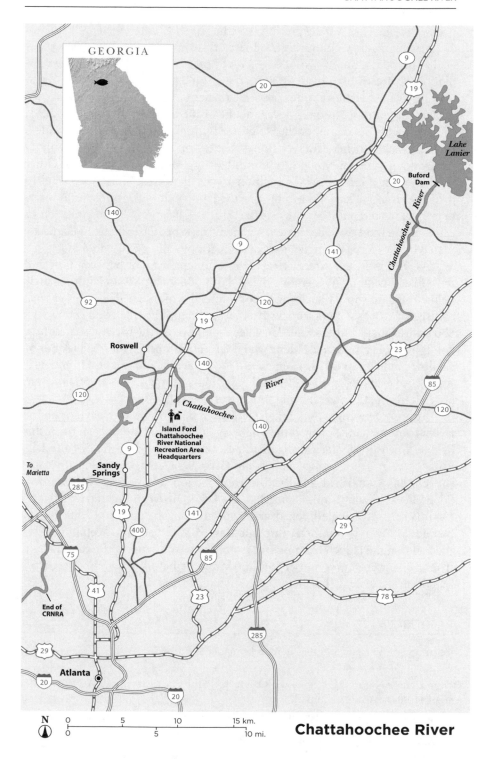

Chattahoochee River

Chattahoochee Flies, a DVD produced by the Upper Chattahoochee Chapter of TU in conjunction with Orvis. Add terrestrials, scuds, crayfish, sowbugs, as well as myriad minnows. Trout have a lot to eat here. Estimates place the population of stream-bred trout at 30 percent. You'll find more browns closer to Buford Dam and more 'bows closer to Atlanta. The Georgia state record brown—8 pounds, 7 ounces—was caught in the Hooch in November, 2001.

Access to the Chattahoochee tailwater is ample and more is being added. In the Chattahoochee River National Recreation Area and city and county parks along the river, you'll find more than two dozen parking areas. Other publicly owned land provides additional walk-in access. Those who want to drift the river will have no trouble picking launch and take-out sites. A number of guides and outfitters provide float tips and liveries will rent you a raft or canoe if you want to do it yourself. A generation schedule for Buford Dam, operated by the Corps of Engineers, can be heard by calling 770-945-1466.

As with most tailwaters, releases move downstream at between four and five miles per hour. Waders on the shoal at Bowman's Island immediately below the dam should head for high ground the moment their marker rock vanishes. (What's a marker rock? It's that rock atop of which you've placed a $50 bill weighted with a stone. You'll keep your eye on the rock no matter how good the fishing, trust me!) Many who float the river beach on small islands or shallow sandbars and wade from there. Good wadable water is also found near Jones Bridge and Island Ford. The shoals below Morgan Falls Dam, however, are rich in aquatic insect life and thus attract most fly fishers.

Approved personal flotation devices must be worn by anyone in or on the river from the dam down to the Highway 20 bridge. The mileage from this bridge down to Medlock Bridge Park, essentially the upper half of the tailwater, is set aside for artificial lures only. Georgia's Department of Natural Resources has established a delayed-harvest section of five miles from where Sope Creek flows in from the north to the US 41 bridge in northwest Atlanta. On this run, only single-hooked, artificial lures may be used and all fish must be released from November 1 through May 14. Also useful to keep in mind is the fact that the Hooch from Buford Dam down to Atlanta is closed to fishing from 30 minutes after sunset until 30 minutes before dawn. So much for matching late evening hatches.

RESOURCES

Gearing up: Fish Hawk, 279 Buckhead Ave., Atlanta, GA 30305; 404-237-3473; www.thefishhawk.com.

Orvis Company Store, 3255 Peachtree Rd. NE, Buckhead Square, Atlanta, GA 30305; 404-841-0093; www.orvis.com.

Orvis Company Store, 5161 Peachtree Pkwy. NW, Suite 630, Norcross, GA 30092; 770-798-9983; www.orvis.com.

Information: Chattahoochee River National Recreation Area, 1978 Island Ford Pkwy., Atlanta, GA 30350; 687-538-1200; www.nps.gov/cha.

Accommodations: Atlanta Convention and Visitors Bureau, 233 Peachtree St. NE, Suite 100, Atlanta, GA 30303; 800-285-2682; www.atlanta.net/atlantanet.

Books: *Chattahoochee Flies*, DVD, Upper Chattahoochee Chapter, Trout Unlimited.

Tailwater Trout in the South by Jimmy Jacobs, Backcountry Publications.

Trout Streams of Southern Appalachia by Jimmy Jacobs, Backcountry Publications.

28 CUMBERLAND RIVER, SOUTH FORK

Location: South-central Kentucky.
Short take: Gargantuan browns in a largely unknown river.
Type of stream: Tailwater.
Angling methods: Fly, spin.
Species: Brown, rainbow.
Access: Limited.
Season: Year-round.
Supporting services: Brukesville.
Handicapped access: No.
Closest TU chapter: Contact the state council of TU.

LONG AND BROAD AND MEAN, the Cumberland River below Wolf Creek Dam in south-central Kentucky is well on its way to becoming the best chance for trophy rainbows and browns in the Southeast and, possibly, the nation. The Kentucky record brown of 21 pounds fell to a crankbait tossed by Thomas Malone in 2000, and the state's largest rainbow, a 14-pound, 6-ounce fish, was caught in this tailwater a generation earlier in 1972. In case you're curious, the state record lake trout, a mere five-pounder plus, also came from these waters.

After blasting out of the Corps of Engineers dam, icy waters from the bottom of Lake Cumberland create a coldwater plume that extends some 65 miles, nearly to the Tennessee state line. According to river guide Ken Glenn, when the dam's generators are not running, shoals near islands provide good opportunities for wading anglers. But he's quick to issue a caveat: When the generators come on, the river can rise *six to eight feet*! Heedless anglers can be swept to their deaths. The Corps posts a daily 24-hour generating schedule on a telephone recording (270-343-0153). If, for instance, the report says generation will begin at 9:00 a.m. Central Time, you can bet the surge of water will travel downstream at a rate of roughly four miles per hour. Thus, if you're fishing 10 miles below, the water should begin to come up around 11:30. While this is a reasonable rule of thumb, don't bet your life on it!

Now here's where things get dicey. Those who know the river best maintain that big trout are turned on by increasing flows. More food, they contend, is washed into the river, and increased depths mean greater cover from predators. Being trout, they'll not burn up calories by hanging in heavy current but seek softer water behind obstructions or along the bank. The most successful anglers use their own boats or hire a guide, like Ken, who has a 20-foot jetboat that allows him access to water he knows holds fish, whether the river is running full or not.

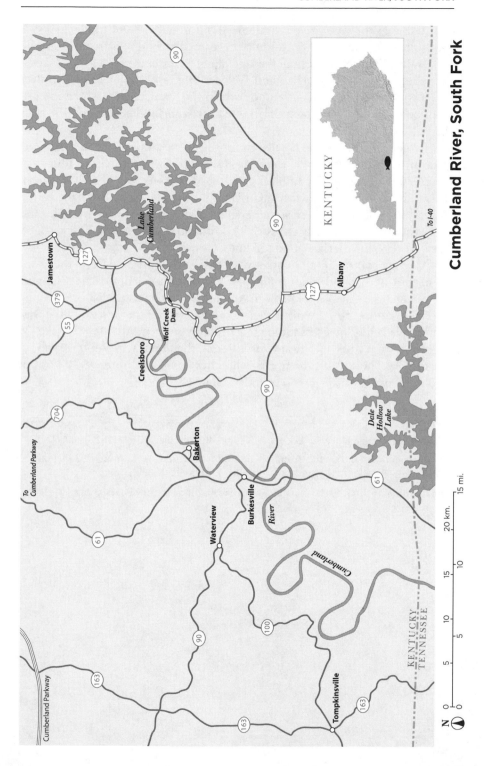

Cumberland River, South Fork

KENTUCKY

To I-40

Jamestown

127

379

55

Lake Cumberland

90

Creelsboro

Wolf Creek Dam

Albany

127

90

704

To Cumberland Parkway

Bakerton

90

Dale Hollow Lake

Waterview

Burkesville

River

61

61

Cumberland Parkway

163

90

100

Cumberland

15

20 km.

15 mi.

Tompkinsville

163

163

KENTUCKY
TENNESSEE

N

0 5 10
0 5 10 15

Access to the river is very limited. About a half mile of public access is available at the Kendall Recreation Area immediately downstream from the dam. Other than that, nearly all the land along the river is privately held. Local gear shops such as Strange Bait and Tackle in Burkesville may be able to steer you toward wadable stretches of the river. In the main, anglers who don't fish from boats end up bank-bound. No one time seems to be better on the river than others.

Large plugs and spinners account for the greatest number of big fish. Anglers of the fly, however, will catch their share of fish on three- to four-inch Clousers, the Chicago Fly (a black bead-head sparsely tied Woolly Bugger), or Deceivers. Were I to fly fish this river, I'd bring along an 8-weight with a sinking line for hurling big streamers and a soft 5-weight for nymphs and occasional dries (primarily terrestrials). My spinning rig would be a six-foot, light-action rod with six-pound test line.

Much of south-central Kentucky is floored with limestone, and the channel of the Cumberland winds gently past bluffs of the calcium-rich rock, similar to sections of the White River in Arkansas. Gentle pastureland rolls along the river's course. Few are the towns or bridges or major roads along the way. Burkesville is headquarters for anglers heading up from Atlanta who take US 127 north from Interstate 40 at Crossville and then Kentucky Route 90 west to Burkesville. Those from the north will either come south on US 127 out of Lexington or pick up Route 90 from Interstate 65.

RESOURCES

Gearing up: Strange Bait and Tackle, 849 S. Main, Burkesville, KY 42717; 270-864-2248.

Accommodations: Burkesville-Cumberland County Chamber of Commerce, P.O. Box 312, Burkesville, KY 42717; 270-864-5890; www.burkesville.com/chamber.

Books: *Tailwater Trout in the South* by Jimmy Jacobs, Backcountry Publications.

29 DAVIDSON RIVER

Location: Western North Carolina.
Short take: Easy access, big wild trout, but they're wise.
Type of stream: Freestone.
Angling methods: Fly, spin.
Species: Brown, rainbow, brook.
Access: Easy.
Season: Year-round.
Supporting services: Asheville, Brevard.
Handicapped access: No.
Closest TU chapter: Pisgah.

IN THE SUMMER OF 2004, A PAIR OF HURRICANES boiled up the southern Appalachians, turning trout streams into seething currents the color of bittersweet chocolate. But on the Davidson, as on other rivers at the base of Blue Ridge, the hellish flooding may have been a blessing. Heavy flows blasted tons of clayish mud from gravel beds where browns and rainbows spawn. Thus refreshed, the beds may play host to more redds, and natural propagation could spike upward. And there's nothing that gladdens a TUer's heart like wild fish.

Stocked with browns and rainbows from Avery Creek down to its confluence with the French Broad, the mileage upstream to its headwaters on the flanks of Chestnut, Rich, and Pilot mountains—particularly the run upstream and down from the Pisgah Forest fish hatchery on the forest service road—is more popular with fly fishers. Not only do current regs specify fly fishing only, but the run is also renowned for midge hatches throughout the year. According to Warren Spahr at Davidson River Outfitters, the quintessential fly shop on the Davidson where U.S. Route 276 joins U.S. Route 64 at Ecusta, fish are "so particular that they know who tied the fly!" Leaders of 12 feet or more and tapering to 6X to 7X, and tiny #22 to #24 droppers—either pupae if there's a midge hatch in the fall or emergers in spring—hold the secret of success. While the Davidson sees most of the same hatches found on western Carolina mountain waters, ant patterns produce most consistently day in and day out during the summer.

Nowhere in the catch-and-release area is the river wider than 50 to 60 feet. Bottoms are a combination of horizontal ledge rock and alluvial cobbles. Here and there, the Davidson runs hard against a cliff creating deep pools where bigger browns tend to hole up. The floods of 2004 and accompanying winds toppled numerous trees into the stream, a challenge for casting but additional cover for trophy trout. Paved and gravel roads stalk the river along most of its length. On other than weekdays in midwinter, you can bet on encountering other anglers here. Good manners demand bypassing water any closer than

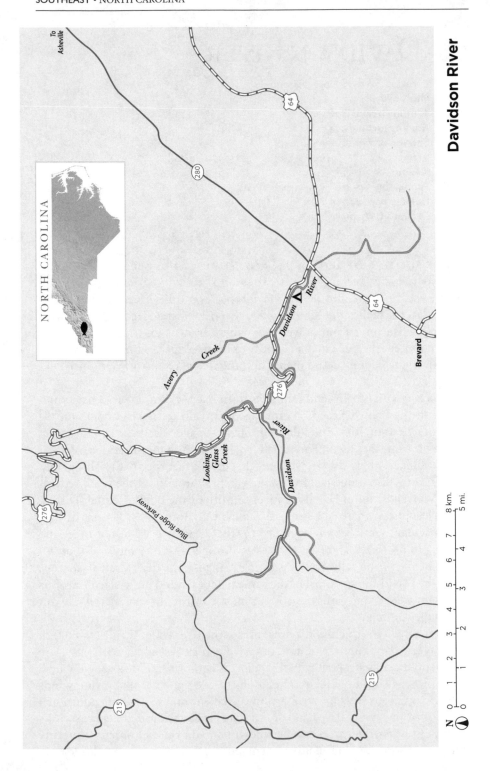

two-casts distance from another fisherman. If you're dead set on fishing water occupied by another angler, sit and watch and learn from his or her mistakes.

If you've come to fish the Davidson, don't pass up the Looking Glass below the falls. These waters abound with 6- to 10-inch rainbows, thanks to TU's feeding program. Seldom wider than 25 feet and often no more than 10, Looking Glass Creek can be fished with fly or spinner, but few anglers do so. Guess they're not much interested in the prospect of bumping into wild 'bows up to 14 inches. The Davidson and its principal tributaries—Looking Glass and Avery creeks—fish best during March and April and late September and October, prime months on southern Appalachian waters.

As is the case with all freestone streams in the southern Appalachians, the Davidson is prone to low flows in late summer and early fall. Because of its deeply shaded course, the river seems to resist the warming that plagues other similar waters in the region. Its trout move into holes where there's oxygenated current. Woolly Buggers and sculpin patterns, worked through backwaters and eddies, consistently take fish when the river is flowing high, wide, and handsome. This is one of those rivers where there is, truly, no bad time to fish.

RESOURCES

Gearing up: Davidson River Outfitters, 4 Pisgah Hwy., Pisgah Forest, NC 28768; 828-877-4181; www.DavidsonFlyFishing.com.

Accommodations: Brevard/Transylvania Chamber of Commerce, 35 W. Main St., Brevard, NC 28712; 800-648-4523; www.visitwaterfalls.com.

Books: *Trout Streams of Southern Appalachia* by Jimmy Jacobs, Backcountry Press.

30 NANTAHALA RIVER

Location: Southwestern North Carolina.
Short take: Kayaks and rafts own the river, but the fish care not one whit.
Type of stream: Tailwater.
Angling methods: Fly, spin.
Species: Rainbow, brown.
Access: Easy.
Season: Year-round.
Supporting services: Cherokee, Bryson City.
Handicapped access: No.
Closest TU chapter: Carolina Headwaters.

THE MOUNTAINS OF WESTERN NORTH CAROLINA ARE STILL one of those locales where contour lines are close together, as Horace Kephart would say, and people are not. A century ago, Kephart, bibliographer turned mountain man, retreated to the deep valleys beneath old Smoky in a desperate attempt to salvage his life. In the process, he penned *Our Southern Highlanders*, perhaps the best chronicle of life in the narrow coves where brook trout teem in streams shaded by mountain laurel whose blooms explode in May and June. The Cherokee called such places *nantahala*—land of the noonday sun.

Kephart would be amazed that you can still find bright streams at the base of steep-sided ridges like the Nantahala above the USFS Standing Indian campground at Whiteoak Bottoms where Kimsey Creek comes in from the south. In the seven miles upstream, you'll find browns and rainbows, offspring from now-discontinued stockings, and a few brookies that may or may not be native. Two strains of eastern brook trout are found in the South. The Southern Appalachian brookies were identified by Steve Moore and his fisheries colleagues in the Great Smoky Mountain National Park. But stocking of many mountain streams, particularly in the 1940s and 1950s, was pretty much an ad hoc affair, so some northern-strain brookies may have been mixed in. A forest service road shadows the upper reaches of the Nan up to Mooney Falls, but it turns into a trail a mile or so farther up. Northwest of U.S. Route 64, the Rainbow Springs Road follows the river down toward Nantahala Lake. Some of the land along this run is private and may be posted. When the road begins its climb up and around Fire Gap Ridge, a side road continues a ways down the Nan toward the lake.

Essentially, the Nantahala below the dam is termed "hatchery supported trout water" by the North Carolina Wildlife Resource Commission. From Whiteoak Creek down to the outflow of the dam's powerhouse delayed harvest rules apply. At the powerhouse, the personality of the Nantahala changes dramatically. No longer a dewatered mountain river course subject to the vagaries of flows from dams on Whiteoak and Dicks creeks, here the Nan

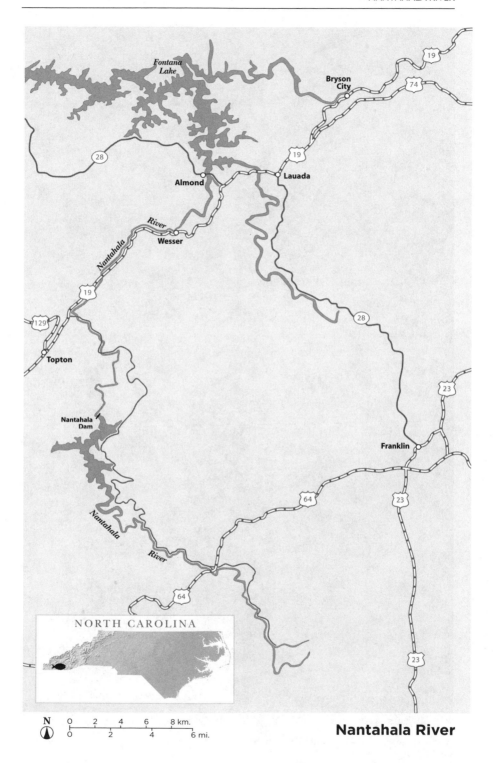

NORTH CAROLINA

Nantahala River

As one of the most popular whitewater runs in the Southeast, the Nantahala River demands that anglers get an early start.

becomes a wild mountain tailwater, beloved by legions of rafters. Reach this stunning run of cataracts and foaming pools after 10:00 a.m. on a summer's day, and you'll see scores of lavender and yellow kayaks and dozens of fat rubber rafts racing through the rapids. The kayakers are serious on this championship water. They ride the reverse eddies to have another run through the chutes. Rafters are the opposite. They shriek as their elongated donuts tip precariously over roostertails and splash each other where the water is dull and flat. It's enough to send a dedicated trouter to the relative sanity of a fish-for-fee pond, but don't let yourself be turned off. The trout aren't; why should you?

The 'bows and browns of the Nan's lower eight miles have seen it all and on every summer day. They're used to people. And that's the first of the Nantahala's big secrets. When the river is "on," it flows bank full and trout look for refuges, those little lies in eddies behind logs and boulders and along the bank. Anglers who work the edges and cast flies, spinners, or bait upstream will be rewarded by some very nice fish—20-inch browns and 'bows are not at all unusual. And every once in a while, some lucky fisher hauls out a four- or five-pounder. If you don't mind the rafter's clamor, fishing through the day can be productive. But angling is really better morning and evenings, before and after flotillas of happy vacationers have passed.

And if you're seeking a really big brown, wait until dark settles into the gorge and roll-cast big dries to likely-looking pockets or work streamers deep through glassy runs. The gorge is littered with huge blocks of rock, the product of construction of rail and auto roads among most of its course. Wading can be dicey. Expect to splash and dash. Forgo a wading staff at your peril. Spend an hour or two before nightfall thoroughly scouting the area you plan to fish.

If you're traveling into this area, you owe it to yourself to spend a week. Along with the Nan, you'll want to fish the Deep, Hazel, Forney, and Oconoluftee creeks that drain the southeastern slopes of the Great Smokies. Time your trip to coincide with the blossoming of, first, mountain laurel and, later, rhododendron or just after fall color has hit its peak in early November. That's when the biggest of the browns are on the move.

RESOURCES

Gearing up: Fly Shop & Fishing Guide Service, P.O. Box 2396, Cherokee, NC 28719; 828-497-1555; www.cssflyfishing.com.

Accommodations: Swain County Chamber of Commerce, P.O. Box 509, Bryson City, NC 28713; 800-585-4497; www.greatsmokies.com.

Books: *Tailwater Trout in the South* by Jimmy Jacobs, Backcountry Publications.

31 CLINCH RIVER

Location: East Tennessee.
Short take: Lunker browns and good rainbows lurk in still waters.
Type of stream: Tailwater.
Angling methods: Fly, spin, bait.
Species: Brown, rainbow.
Access: Moderate.
Season: Year-round.
Supporting services: Knoxville.
Handicapped access: Yes.
Closest TU chapter: Clinch River.

AS A FRY, I WAS TRANSPLANTED TO KNOXVILLE in the mid-1950s. On those sweltering airless August afternoons when even the normally stiff leaves of sycamores along the creek in our backyard hung limp, Mom and Dad would pack my brothers and me off to picnic in the park along the Clinch River below Norris Dam. We'd arrive about six, just as the generators came on and the river began to brawl. Soon a delicious coolness welled up from the river. Moisture in the air condensed. Tendrils of fog swirled around our ankles as we ran to the catch fly balls Dad hit with his bat.

A decade later, my elder brother and I, now volunteers with the Tennessee Archaeology Society, labored to record Indian settlements that would be flooded by the new dam at Melton Hill and lost to the construction of the steam plant at Bull Run. I pushed a long-handled shovel, clearing 10-foot-by-10-foot squares of the sandy loaming soil of the plow zone. When the digging was done, we'd slip our creels over our shoulders, pick up our ultralights, and wade V-shaped fish traps casting Mepps or drifting worms or salmon eggs for stocked 'bows. We always caught enough for dinner.

The Clinch is the oldest of the quartet of east Tennessee's trout tailwaters. Created with the closure of Norris Dam in 1936, the Clinch was first stocked with rainbows in the late 1930s. Some held over, but put-and-take fishing was the norm on this river. The problem was that water drawn from the depths of Norris Lake lacked oxygen sufficient to sustain a healthy trout fishery. Also, TVA practiced a feast-or-famine flow regimen. Either the river was scoured by raging releases or starved with niggardly flows in summer to maintain a recreational pool for boaters in the lake above the dam. In 1984, a low, regulating weir was installed about a mile below Norris Dam to help maintain a minimum flow of 200 fps in the river. Baffles were added to the turbines to suck air into the water, adding the dissolved oxygen so vital to a healthy trout population. TU worked closely with TVA and the Tennessee Wildlife Resources Agency in this reservoir release improvement effort.

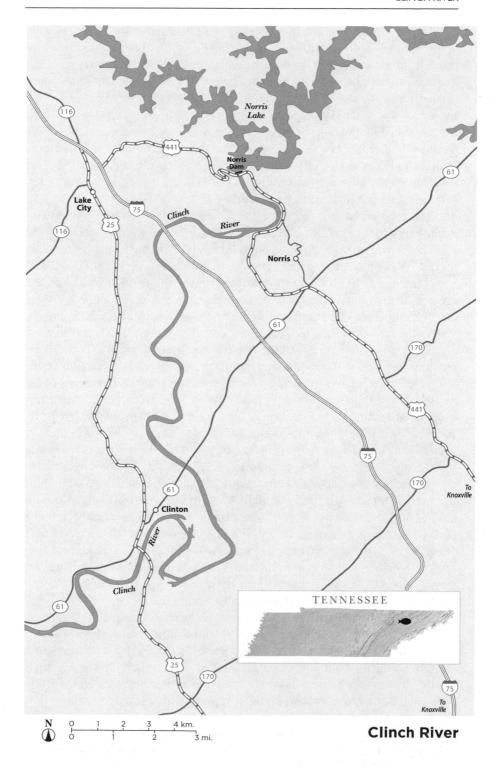

Clinch River

Like the long-gone but deeply lamented Little Tennessee River tailwater below Chilhowee Dam in the pre–Tellico Lake era, the Clinch is earning a reputation for trout that are, indeed, trophies. In 1988, Greg Ensor pulled the Tennessee record brown, a 28-pound, 12-ounce beauty, from two miles below the dam near the weir. John Thurman, Clinch River chapter member and retired biologist with TVA, reports examining a 38-inch, 32-pound brown he discovered while floating the river. The fish was in the final states of natural death so Thurman was able to shepherd it to shore and take its measurements. (Nefarious members of other angling organizations might have considered hooking a #24 midge in this behemoth's jaw and making tracks for the closest certified scale, but not a dedicated TUer!)

The most significant change to the tailwater fishery has been the notable decline in sulphur mayflies (*Ephemerella invaria* is the primary species in the Clinch). During the late 1980s through the mid-1990s, the Clinch featured an incredible sulphur emergence beginning in early April and lasting well into June. The mayfly hatch has been greatly diminished since 1998, and biologists are not sure what has happened. A severe drought during the period 1999 to 2001 accompanied by a number of significant floods that added significant volumes of sediment to the river may be the culprits, but this is only speculation.

Thurman, who has studied the river professionally as well as fished it extensively, believes that mayflies and caddis constitute a small fraction of the annual diet of Clinch trout. Midges, he says, make up about 70 percent of the annual diet of the average trout; blackfly larvae, 20 percent; and scuds, sowbugs, mayflies, and caddis the remaining 10 percent. Many anglers err in restricting their fishing to riffles in pursuit of good trout. Good fishing can be found in the long and oh-so-slowly flowing pools when the water is moving at its 200 cubic feet per second minimum. A 6X tippet of 12 feet or longer tied to a strike indicator or #16 Attractor from which a #18 or smaller Midge Pupa has been dropped, is the best method for catching a wild 14- to 20-inch rainbow or brown during low flow. Cast upstream. Given the clarity of the water, casts of 50-plus feet are required. Stealth is de rigueur. Size-18 to size-20 dark (olive, brown, black, or red) Midge Pupae, size-16 Olive/Gray Scuds and size-16 Gray Sowbugs will fool enough fish to keep a day very interesting. There are ample numbers of wild (either stream born or stocked as fry or fingerlings) 14- to 16-inch fish, and 20-inchers are fairly common.

When generators are running, the river is generally unwadable. Floating it in a classic jon boat, canoe, or driftboat—and fishing hardware on spinning gear—is the best way to catch big trout. Some fly fishers throw big streamers from boats during high flows, but it is a lot of work. When the water is high, floating in a tube is dangerous and not recommended; however, a tube works well when the river is at minimum flow. At present, no special regulations govern trout fishing on the Clinch.

The Clinch is a half-hour car ride north of Knoxville. Access to the river is easy around boat launch ramps and bridges and on the Norris Dam Reservation, which extends downstream from Norris Dam about two miles. Most of the bank downstream from the TVA property is privately owned. TU's Clinch River Chapter is working to restore streamside habitat and build relationships with landowners. With the Great Smoky Mountains, about an hour to the South, and Knoxville with its two interstates (I-40 and I-75) in between, the Clinch is a very convenient tailwater.

RESOURCES

Gearing up: Clinch River Outfitters, located one mile east of I-75; 865-494-0972.

Accommodations: Anderson County Tourist Council, P.O. Box 147, Clinton TN 37717; 800-524-3620; www.yallcome.org.

Books: *Tailwater Trout in the South* by Jimmy Jacobs, Backcountry Publications.

32 HIWASSEE RIVER

Location: Southeast Tennessee.
Short take: Tailwater as broad as its browns.
Type of stream: Tailwater.
Angling methods: Fly, spin.
Species: Brown, rainbow.
Access: Easy.
Season: Year-round.
Supporting services: Reliance, Chattanooga.
Handicapped access: Possible.
Closest TU chapter: Hiwassee.

WHERE DO HUNDREDS OF RESIDENTS OF METROPOLITAN ATLANTA take their fly rods in pursuit of browns and rainbows? They head up U.S. Route 411, turn right on Tennessee State Route 30, and make a beeline for Reliance on the Hiwassee River, one of the finest tailwater fisheries in east Tennessee. Let there be no mistake: the Hiwassee is the biggest, most scenic, and the most uniformly wadable of east Tennessee's famed trout tailwater quartet. Further, the 10.5 miles or so from the US 411 bridge where the river emerges from the foothills to the mouth of Apalachia Dam's powerhouse penstock has a reputation for large brown trout.

Below the powerhouse portals—with "Apalachia" spelled with one less "p" than usual—the Hiwassee spreads across a river channel that, at times, comes close to a quarter mile in width. The river clatters over low transverse ledges and bars of small, round river rock. Riffles that result aerate the flows, adding oxygen. That's the good news. Bad news is that the river seems to lack small gravels favored by browns for spawning. In addition, in winter, as the Tennessee Valley Authority draws the four reservoirs upstream down to provide flood protection capacity for the runoffs of typically rainy springs, extended high flows wash eggs from the few redds. The flow regimen is again an issue in late summer and early fall, typically dry in these climes. The TVA, the Tennessee Wildlife Resources Agency, and Trout Unlimited are working out a balance that will ensure pulses of amply cold water through the trout fishery while preserving levels to satisfy the desires of landowners on the lakes behind the dams. What all of this means for anglers is this: the Hiwassee is stocked water but with good numbers of holdover browns and rainbows.

From Apalachia powerhouse to Patty Bridge, regulations now mandate a minimum size of 14 inches for browns. TRWA has designated the mileage from the L&N Railroad bridge above the hamlet of Reliance to the U.S. Forest Service parking area at Big Bend as a Quality Trout Fishing Area, which means that all trout smaller than 14 inches must be released unharmed and that use of bait in any form is prohibited. Anglers using small plugs, and spinners are

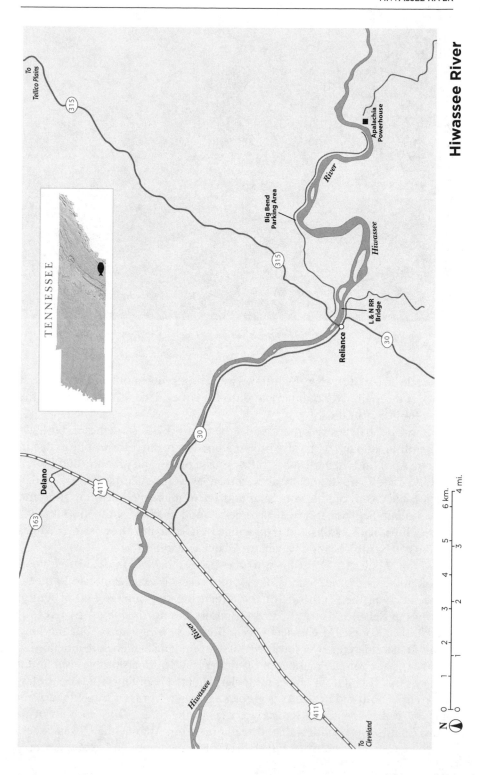

Hiwassee River

Big fish and great wading make the Hiwassee River one of Tennessee's premier trout tailwaters.

especially successful when high flows move big browns out of their lairs in holes of the main river channel and onto the riffley flats. Big streamers do the same for fishers of the fly.

Hiwassee hatches are prolific and varied. Early black stoneflies and midges come off in January, with early brown stoneflies making their appearance in March. April finds hendricksons, blue-winged olives, and grannon and brown caddis. Caddis are abundant all summer. May produces sulphurs, golden stones, and cream caddis. Isonychias and Tricos make their debut in June and hold up into September, which also sees a good hatch of white mayflies. Fall brings little black caddis and blue-winged olives again. Dropper rigs with a #16 to #20 Nymph below a Parachute Adams is standard fare.

From Apalachia Dam down to the US 411 bridge, the Hiwassee flows through the Cherokee National Forest and access is excellent. State Route 30 runs up along the south side of the river from the campground at Quinn Springs to Reliance. Forest Road 108 follows the north side of the river for much of its course. At Childers Creek, the road swings north, but the John Muir Trail follows the river for three miles around big bend before junctioning again with the road. A number of outfitters run driftboats on the river and it can be easily fished from canoes by anglers adept at handling rapids up to class II. Walk-in and wading access is ample. Parking permits of three dollars per day are available at many self-service sites in the forest. Only an hour or so from Chattanooga and less than three hours from Atlanta, the Hiwassee sees its share of fishing pressure, but the river is big enough and access is ample enough so that one never need feel too crowded. Accommodations are available in Cleveland, a small city some 25 miles west of the river on Interstate 75.

RESOURCES

Gearing up: Hiwassee Outfitters, P.O. Box 62, Reliance, TN 37369; 800-338-8133; www.hiwasseeoutfitters.com.

Accommodations: Cleveland/Bradley County Chamber of Commerce, P.O. Box 2275, Cleveland, TN 37320; 423-472-6587; www.clevelandchamber.com.

Books: *Tailwater Trout in the South* by Jimmy Jacobs, Backcountry Publications.

33 HOLSTON RIVER, SOUTH FORK

Location: Northeast Tennessee.
Short take: Wild browns take root in this oxygen-rich tailwater.
Type of stream: Tailwater.
Angling methods: Fly, spin.
Species: Brown, rainbow.
Access: Easy.
Season: Year-round.
Supporting services: Johnson City, Abingdon.
Handicapped access: Yes.
Closest TU chapter: Overmountain.

WHEN YOU TALK TO TUERS ABOUT TAILWATER TROUT in Tennessee, the South Fork of the Holston River is the stream that immediately comes to tongue. Begun in 1942, not completed until 1950 because of World War II, South Holston Dam created a tailwater fishery where cold water had not existed before. There was then much that was unknown about creating viable trout habitat from water that once held sunnies, rock bass, and catfish. It turned out that water from the bottom-draw dams lacked the dissolved oxygen trout need to thrive. In 1991, a set of weirs with a drop of about 7.5 feet was added at Osceola Island. The weirs oxygenate releases and, because they create a sort of mini-impoundment afterbay, they also help ensure minimum flows when the dam's turbines are not generating.

Improved water quality and more consistent flows facilitated spawning of browns, the dominant species, in the South Holston tailwater. And unlike other tailwaters, particularly the Watauga, the South Fork Holston is floored in spots with gravels over which browns are more likely to spawn. To encourage reproduction, the Tennessee Wildlife Resources Agency changed the fishing regulations for the river downstream from the dam to the bridge carrying State Highway 37 across at Bluff City. First, no trout between 16 and 22 inches can be kept, although regulations permit harvesting of seven fish per day. Of those, only one can exceed 22 inches in length. To promote spawning, two areas are closed to fishing from November 1 through January 31: from Bottom Creek down to Hickory Tree Bridge, and from the top of the first island above Webb Road Bridge down to the top of the first island below Weaver Pike Bridge. The combined benefit of the aerating weirs, slot limit, and closed fishing over active redds is paying off with larger populations of naturally reproducing browns. Local TU chapters were the first to champion these initiatives and are ever vigilant in their monitoring of the river.

Though trout populations are growing and access to the river is relatively easy, success on the South Holston is not a sure thing. When compared to the Watauga, about 45 minutes to the east, South Holston trout seem more

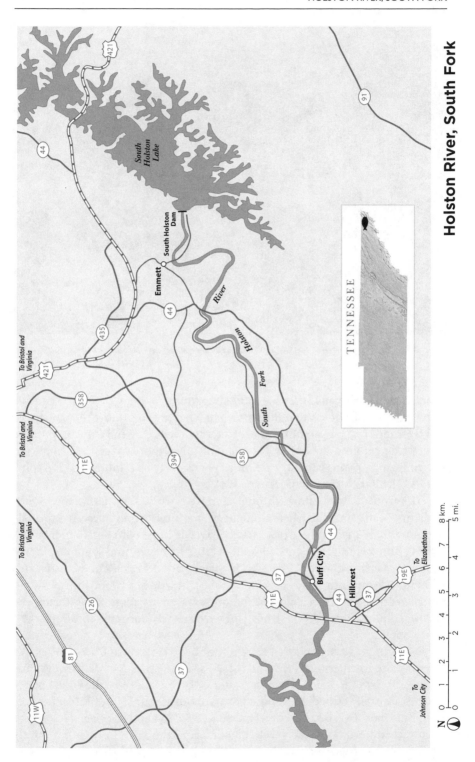

Holston River, South Fork

Weirs add life-giving oxygen to the Holston River, another superb east Tennessee tailwater.

finicky. Perhaps because they see more fly patterns per day than their cousins to the east, or maybe it's that the natural hatches are so prolific than an artificial fly stands out like a moonshiner at a temperance ball, but for whatever the reason the gentle waters of the South Holston require a very well-matched hatch. Rising browns can be every bit as persnickety as rainbows taking spinners on the Ranch section of Henry's Fork.

If a trout tailwater flows through a more bucolic setting than the South Holston, I can't imagine where it might be. Serious farming deserted the valley more than a generation past. Yet the river is lined with small after-hours farms, with fields neatly tended and weathered barns, and a smattering of modern riverfront homes. Preceded by black caddis in March, the usual run of hendricksons and olives follow. Sliding beneath hardwood-tufted ridges where redbud and then dogwood blooms, the trout come alive during the spring sulphur hatch. Terrestrials work from early summer into fall when more olives appear.

Most anglers take their first look at the South Holston at Osceola Park. It's a great place to enter the river. And there's a fishing pier for handicapped anglers just below the weirs. When the water is "off," as they say, the river's upper reaches are easily waded. Minimum flow is about 100 to 150 cubic feet per second. But when TVA is generating (call 800-238-2264 and use river code #01 to check schedules), flows can reach 2,800 cfs and the bottom becomes utterly impossible to negotiate. That's when the river is best floated by driftboat, canoe, or raft. Cast spinners or spoons or crawlers weighted with non-toxic shot. Fly fishers willing to heave sinking lines with large weighted streamers and nymphs also find success. Bigger fish generally become more active during periods of high flow.

While the river is well served by a number of secondary roads—both gravel and paved—along the 14 miles of its best fishing water, public access is limited. Routes 44, 358, and 37 bridge the stream at sites progressively farther downstream from the dam. A maze of farm roads and lanes lead toward the stream: all you need do is follow your nose. Yet, the bulk of land is held privately. Some owners will grant permission to fish when asked. Others charge a small fee for parking and access.

Upper east Tennessee includes a number of fine trout waters—particularly the nearby Watauga River tailwater, the Elk River, and Stony Creek—making the region a good destination for traveling anglers. Also worth exploring are the spring-fed headwaters of the South Holston, about an hour's drive north of Bristol, east of Marion, Virginia. At the Virginia Department of Game and Inland Fisheries Buller Hatchery, the river skips from the mouth of a four-mile gorge known by locals for its excellent populations of wild rainbows. A gravel road, open to foot traffic, runs along the river and a mile's walk upstream takes you to the best water. The run along the northwest edge of the hatchery is known for huge rainbows—mostly "retired" breeding stock—that eagerly and often indiscriminately take nymphs and dries. This is, of course, catch-and-release water, and these fine fish should be brought quickly to net and returned so they'll live to take your fly on the morrow.

RESOURCES

Gearing up: Virginia Creeper Fly Shop, 16501 JEB Stuart Hwy., Abingdon, VA 24211; 276-628-3826; www.vcflyshop.com.

Accommodations: Bristol Chamber of Commerce, P.O. Box 519, Bristol, VA/TN 24203; 423-989-4850; www.bristolchamber.org.

Books: *Tailwater Trout in the South* by Jimmy Jacobs, Backcountry Publications.

Tennessee Trout Waters by Ian Rutter, Frank Amato Publications.

34 LITTLE RIVER

Location: Southeastern Tennessee, in the Great Smoky Mountains National Park.
Short take: Followed by a highway for much of its length, this is still one fine trout stream.
Type of stream: Freestone.
Angling methods: Fly, spin.
Species: Brown, rainbow, brook.
Access: Easy.
Season: Year-round.
Supporting services: Gatlinburg, Townsend.
Handicapped access: Yes, at Townsend.
Closest TU chapters: Little River, Great Smoky.

NEXT TIME YOU DRIVE THE ROAD ALONG THE LITTLE RIVER in the Great Smoky Mountain National Park, think of yourself as a nimrod riding a high-roofed L&N coach behind the Baldwin chuffing through the gorge headed for Elkmont. Stumps and broken logs clutter the banks of the river, left there by raging floods that have scoured the streambed bare. At Elkmont, once the bustling main yard of the Colonel Townsend's Little River Railroad and Lumber Company, you switch to the open observation car coupled behind the tender of an offset Shay. The three vertical pistons of this mountain workhorse create a sound as different from the driving rods of the Baldwin as the view in 1925 was as different from today. Timber has been stripped from the ridges. Slash, the limbs and tops that have no value, lie helter-skelter on the steep slopes like jackstraws thrown down by a mad child. In the lower valleys, the first feathery green fronds of new hemlock and pine are just sprouting like they did in Yellowstone after the 1988 fire.

That it's taken only 70 years to heal many of the wounds of the exploitation of the Elkmont drainage is something of a marvel to me. Never will we see the primeval stands of hemlock and poplar, but the slopes are lush with deep forest and pregnant with blooms of laurel, azalea, and rhododendron, each in their season. Streams run clear again, and trout—browns, rainbows, and brookies of native Southern Appalachian strain—teem in the reaches of the Little River. To angle here is to fish in the rumpled bed of mountain history, natural and human intertwined.

Most folks meet the Little River where it leaves the park at Townsend. It's broad with waters from the West Prong that joins the east at the Y, and here you'll find smallmouth and browns and occasional rainbows. The road to Cades Cove, through which Abrams Creek flows before reaching the good fishing water above Abrams Falls, runs up along the West Prong. Not far, the Middle Prong comes in from the south shadowed by the road to Tremont,

Little River

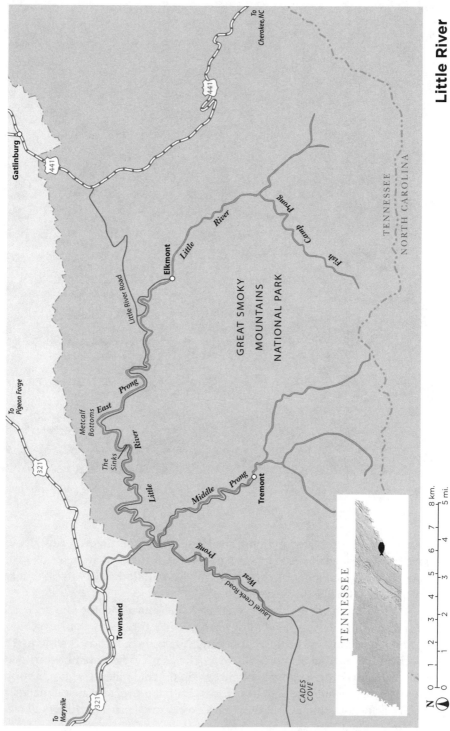

Followed by highway for much of its length, the Little River is nonetheless one fine trout stream.

once a logging yard like Elkmont. The West Prong continues. A tiny stream now, it's all but overlooked by visiting anglers who are not aware of its eager wild rainbows. Rainbows predominate in the Middle Prong as well, but its larger waters also hold some very respectable browns.

If you want to fish the history of the park, hie yourself up the four-mile trail from Elkmont to the junction of Fish Camp Prong. It's an easy walk of a couple of hours, pleasant in the early morning. You're looking for Southern Appalachian brook trout, a genetically distinctive species first identified by park fisheries biologist Steve Moore. They're here in the cold waters that tumble from chutes to pool about large boulders. Release them immediately as you marvel at their brilliant color. Fishing your way back down, you'll pick up native rainbows, generally smallish, but with backs as dark as a night sky. Rainbows were first stocked in 1910 and have been competing with brookies for habitat ever since.

Below Elkmont, the East Prong becomes a mature trout stream where pools are wide, and many deeper than you are tall. Stretches of pocket water burble along between dark runs often located hard against the bed of the highway née railroad. Exiting the Elkmont basin, the East Prong turns west and broadens at Metcalf Bottoms. Here, and in the mileage down to the Sinks, the largest plunge pool on this prong, large browns stack up to spawn in the fall. Large streamers and nymphs take fish that are twice as long as those brought to net in spring and summer.

Because it is so accessible to the main east–west highway through the park—you can see rising trout from your car window if you dare take your eyes from the winding road—the East Prong fills with swimmers and, when water is high, kayakers in summer. It's a cloud with something of a silver lining. The fishing is lousy when folks play in the river, but the trout do become somewhat acclimated to the presence of people. If you want solitude, head for the backcountry section of the West Prong—a small stream that's followed by the road into Cades Cove but veers sharply south.

Since the early 1990s, TU and the Great Smoky Mountains National Park have enjoyed a model partnership. Two chapters—Great Smoky Mountains and Little River—provide hundreds of hours of manpower to monitor water quality and advocate for reductions in emissions from fossil fuel–burning power plants and automobiles. While the Tennessee Valley Authority, with its coal-fired steam plants, ranks high among sources of acid particulates that strangle the park's spruce fir forests, the local effects of vehicle exhausts are equally villainous. So severe is the damage from acid deposition, the highest waters of the Smokies are barren of trout, even the intensely pH-tolerant Southern Appalachian brook trout. Nowhere in the Appalachians is the threat posed by acid rain more clearly drawn. As in the 1920s, when visionary conservationists waged the war to wrest the Smokies from the loggers, it's up to TU and others of similar stripe to save the Smokies again.

RESOURCES

Gearing up: Little River Outfitters, 7807 E. Lamar Alexander Pkwy., P.O. Box 505, Townsend, TN 37882; 423-448-9459.

Smoky Mountain Anglers, Brookside Village, Hwy. 321 N, P.O. Box 241, Gatlinburg, TN 37738; 423-436-8746.

Accommodations: Townsend Area Visitor's Bureau, 7906 E. Lamar Alexander Pkwy., Townsend, TN 37882; 800-525-6834; www.smokymountains.org.

Gatlinburg Department of Tourism, 234 Airport Rd., Gatlinburg, TN 37738; 800-267-7088; www.gatlinburgtennessee.com.

Books: *Fly-Fishing Guide to the Great Smoky Mountains* by Don Kirk, Menasha Ridge Press.

35 TELLICO RIVER

Location: Central Tennessee.
Short take: A put-and-take river that everybody loves, including die-hard native trout addicts.
Type of stream: Freestone.
Angling methods: Fly, spin.
Species: Brook, brown, rainbow.
Access: Easy.
Season: Year-round.
Supporting services: Tellico Plains.
Handicapped access: Yes.
Closest TU chapter: Clinch River.

IF YOU'VE EVER WONDERED ABOUT WHAT CAN HAPPEN to a trout stream surrounded by a heavily used national forest and one inside a national park, all you need do is compare the Tellico in the Cherokee/Nantahala National Forests and Little River in the Great Smokies. Given two days' hard rain, the Tellico River will turn as muddy as milky coffee. Under the same conditions, the Little River takes on the color of coffee too, but coffee from which the grounds have yet to settle. In a day, the Little River will be running sweet again. Sometimes it takes the Tellico a week to turn clear. The reason? The upper reaches of the Tellico's watershed is a favored playground of the ATV crowd. Throttles full open, ATVs roar, their knobby tires chewing through the thin veneer of ground cover and churning the thin soils of these clear-cut slopes into dust. Downpours sluice fine powders into myriad headwater streams—streams where wild brook trout struggle to survive—that dump the slurry into the Tellico. Were it not for the national park, the Little River would surely get the same treatment. I'm being overly hard on the Tellico, I know. Its stewards, including the U.S. Forest Service, Tennessee Wildlife Resources Agency, and Trout Unlimited, are working diligently with off-road vehicle recreation interests to accommodate this exciting sport without further damage to the watershed. Some progress has been made and surely more will follow.

TWRA manages the Tellico River as a put-and-take fishery. From March 15 through September 15, the river is heavily stocked (and closed to fishing) on Thursdays and Fridays. You'll need a daily permit ($3.50) to fish it or its sister river, Citico Creek downstream from the forks, during the summer. Though extremely popular with the catch-and-keep crowd, the Tellico is big enough and long enough for you to find water that nobody else is on. My best advice is to fish the main stem of the Tellico in October and November or February. The river is legendary for its gargantuan holdover browns.

And while the Tellico itself gets a little silty and fills with bait fishers in summer, its main tributaries—the Bald and North rivers—provide stellar

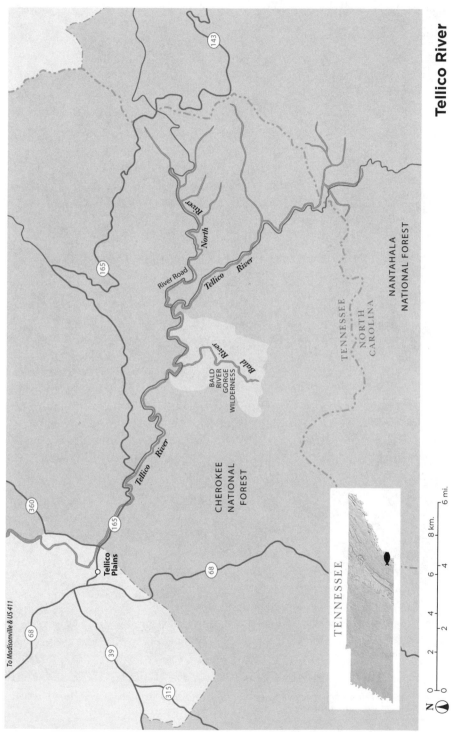

Tellico River

143

Expect to find stellar small-stream angling activity for wild browns, rainbows, and brook trout on the Tellico River's main tributaries.

small-stream dry-fly activity for wild browns, rainbows, and brook trout. The North River flows through a classic mountain valley, and it's not hard to imagine where hardy mountaineers sited their cabins and cleared their pastures. The stream—never wider than 50 feet—steps its way down a few ledges and falls, but mainly runs from pocket to pocket, cutting against one bank in bends. Here, you'll find deeper pools. Along the way, you'll see wooden shelters that TU sunk into the stream to provide cover for wild trout. These trout are not choosy. Attractor patterns work well, as do ants in summer.

While the North River is shadowed by a road for most of its length, the Bald River runs close to pavement for only a mile. Above the 120-foot Bald River Falls, the river has been cutting its way through a gorge. A foot trail follows its upstream course, which is characterized by plunge pools and chutes and riffles. Above the gorge, the stream opens up a little, but the climb is no less rigorous. Relatively few anglers venture in very far. Thus, the trout are more apt to welcome your offering.

As you work your way up either the Bald or North rivers, slip off the trail and fish some of the side streams. These are the favored haunts of Southern Appalachian brook trout, as pretty as the bluets that blossom along the banks. Return these gems carefully to their waters. They are the true treasures of the Tellico.

RESOURCES

Gearing up: Telliquah Outfitters, 1659 Cherohala Skyway, Tellico Plains, TN 37385; 423-253-3087; www.telliquahoutfitters.com.

Accommodations: Monroe County Chamber of Commerce, 520 Cook St., Ste. A, Madisonville, TN 37354; 423-442-4588; www.monroecountychamber.org.

Books: *Tennessee Trout Waters* by Ian Rutter, Frank Amato Publications.

36 WATAUGA RIVER

Location: Northeast Tennessee.
Short take: Excellent tailwater for browns and rainbows.
Type of stream: Tailwater.
Angling methods: Fly, spin.
Species: Brook, brown, rainbow.
Access: Easy.
Season: Year-round.
Supporting services: Johnson City.
Handicapped access: Yes.
Closest TU chapter: Overmountain.

GRADUATING FROM HIGH SCHOOL WITH WHAT WAS CHARITABLY DESCRIBED as a "high D" average, I enrolled in East Tennessee State in Johnson City, the only college that would take me. One other factor influenced my choice: my older brother, Sam, had enrolled too. He'd rented an apartment with two beds and a kitchen. We could fry our trout. Neither he nor I realized at the time that we were about to drop into the best trout fishing the Volunteer State had to offer. That was in the mid-1960s. It's still true today. The Watauga below TVA's Wilbur Dam was then, and is now, one hell of a fine trout river.

In those days I carried my tackle—#10 hooks, split shot, barrel sinkers, a plastic hook box containing three or four Squirrel-Tail Gold Mepps, and a pair of needle-nosed pliers—in the inside pockets of an army surplus gas mask bag. I preferred Pautzke's Balls of Fire but would settle for small green cans of Kounty Kist corn that I opened with the blade of my scout knife. With proceeds from cutting weeds, I'd bought a Mitchell 308, spooled it with four-pound test Trilene, and mounted it on a five-foot light-action rod. Our favorite hole lay beneath Bee Cliffs. We'd rig up, cast out, prop the rod up with some rocks, open a beer, and wait for a bite. If the river was on, we'd move up to the lake and set up shop. Seldom did we fail to produce dinner. Half a dozen years later, with college and a stab at newspapering behind me, I fished the Watauga behind Elizabethton and lost some of the largest browns I've ever seen. Fishing in the Watauga then ended above the rayon plants because pollution had killed the river below.

Not so today for nearly 20 miles from the base of Wilbur Dam to the headwaters of Boone Lake. The Watauga is now a first-class trout fishery. The upper half of the river slips through a short and very narrow gorge in the western foothills of Iron Mountain, skips past Bee Cliff, and enters a series of islands and braids just above the old bridge pillars at the store in Siam. There, the river picks up a little western flavor, due largely to a few islands separated by cobbly runs. Winding gently, here hard against a hillside and there sprawling through meadows, the Watauga rounds a low mountain and bends back to

Watauga River

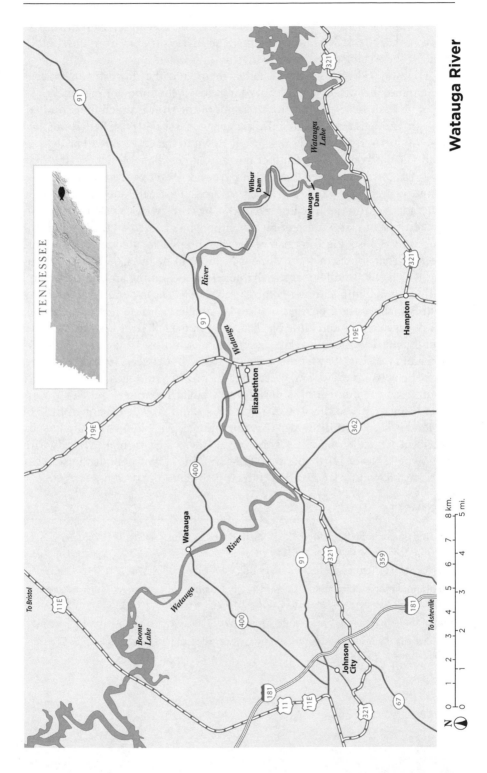

the west, picking up the water from Stoney Creek flowing in from the north. From Stoney Creek down to where the Doe River comes in from the south is some of the Watauga's most productive wading waters.

Highway 19E crosses the Watauga there, and the downstream mileage runs on past the former rayon plants, long closed, for another nine miles or so to Boone Lake. Access to the lower reaches of the river is much more limited. Though the Tennessee Wildlife Resource Agency has designated about two miles of the river, from Smallings Bridge down to the CSX railroad bridges, as Quality Trout Water—two fish per day and larger than 14 inches—the only walk-in access is via River Ridge Campground. Water in front of the camp-ground is deep, but when the river is off, runs upstream and down provide stellar angling. You can monitor river flows by checking TVA's web site.

According to Jason Reep of Elizabethton who's guided on the Watauga for a dozen years or so, the lower half of the river holds a greater variety of aquatic insects. He attributes this to sediment brought in by the Doe River, particu-larly, which often muddies at the slightest rain. Beginning around Easter and continuing well into summer is the caddis hatch. They're grannoms and big. Upstream above the Doe, flies tend to be smaller. Until terrestrial time, fish Blue-Winged Olives and Little Black Caddis. In the fall, large browns move up from Boone Lake, augmenting other browns, brook trout, and rainbows stocked in the river. The typical Watauga fish runs between 10 and 12 inches, but behemoth rainbows and, occasionally, browns are taken in the Quality Trout section. A number of guides from Virginia, Tennessee, and North Car-olina bring clients to the Watauga, but it's seldom crowded. Though little of the land is posted on the upper run, one storekeeper told me that anglers, fly fishers in particular, have not gone out of their ways to make friends with landowners. Never hurts to swap "Howdys" and a word about the weather with the folks whose land you want to cross to get to the stream.

RESOURCES

Gearing up: Mahoney Outfitters, 2513 North Roan St., Johnson City, TN 37601; 423-282-8889; www.mahoneysports.com.

The Fly Shop of Tennessee, 102 Willmary Rd., Johnson City, TN 37601; 423-928-2007.

Accommodations: Elizabethton-Carter County Chamber of Commerce Tourism Council, P.O. Box 190, Eizabethton, TN 37644; 423-547-385; www.tourelizabethton.com.

Books: *Tailwater Trout in the South* by Jimmy Jacobs, Backcountry Publications.

Tailwaters of the Southern Appalachians by C. Richards and J. Krause, Antekeier & Krause Publications.

37 Mossy Creek

Location: Northwestern Virginia, in the Shenandoah Valley.
Short take: The Letort's poorer cousin.
Type of stream: Spring creek.
Angling methods: Fly.
Species: Brown, brook.
Access: Easy.
Season: Year-round.
Supporting services: Harrisonburg.
Handicapped access: No.
Closest TU chapter: Massanutten.

THE CUMBERLAND VALLEY, FLOORED IN PARTS BY CARBONATE ROCKS, gives birth to a number of stellar trout streams in Pennsylvania—the Letort, Big Spring, and Falling Spring immediately come to mind. The same geology swings southwest of the Blue Ridge in Virginia. A number of fine little trout streams issue from springs. Most of them are small. Some sustain populations of wild trout. Few are open to the public. The most well known of those with public access is Mossy Creek, about 20 miles south of Harrisonburg and a little southwest of Bridgewater.

Mossy Creek may not look like much at first glance. Seldom more than 15 feet in width, it wanders through pasture bottomland, meandering as it wants, carving a bank here, and dumping a little clay there. Most anglers prefer the mileage above the iron bridge behind the Mossy Creek Presbyterian Church. The downstream section flows through open pasture with few distinctive features other than those created by deadfalls and woody debris in the creek on the lower half mile or so. The remainder of this section contains wavy beds of aquatic weed and cress that thicken significantly as spring warms into summer. In addition, undercut banks provide some cover for browns.

The upper reach contains more drop, and short stretches of riffles are present, if infrequent. Immediately upstream from the iron bridge, Mossy runs for about a quarter mile through a series of deep but narrow pools hedged with outcrop. The top of this run is intensely shaded and comparatively deep. Anglers adept at casting fat streamers under overhanging branches frequently feel a tremendous tug and then hear a snap—the sound of tippet parting. Above the shaded water, the creek shallows and braids, thanks largely to reduced gradient and banks broken down by cattle. Most fish taken in this section fall into the 8- to 11-inch range. Among them, however, you may catch a brook trout, product of a stocking in times past.

One more section of Mossy is worth mention. A concrete bridge carries Country Route 809—the link between VA Route 42 and County 747 known as the Mossy Creek Road—over the stream. Remains of an abandoned milldam

Mossy Creek

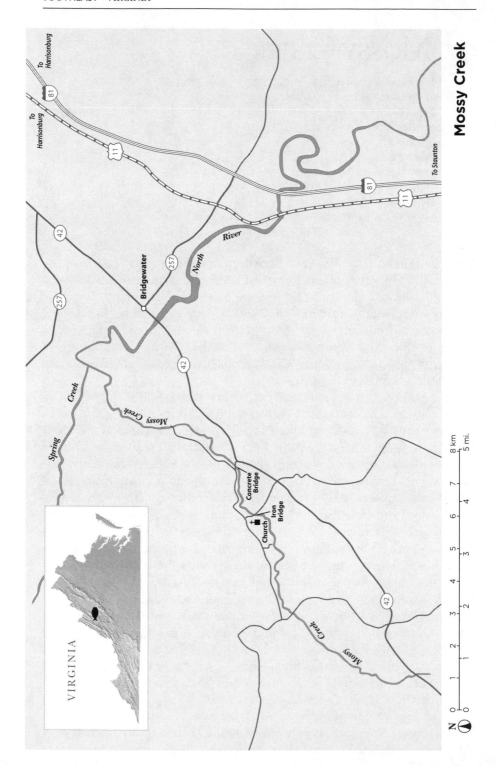

Even with its challenges, Mossy Creek provides plenty of trout action.

create a series of deep, intricate, and incredibly difficult-to-fish pools less than 100 yards from the road. Publicly accessible water continues for about a quarter mile downstream to the Augusta-Rockingham county line. Young forest canopy shades the stream here, banks are overgrown, and—because wading is verboten (anglers must not enter the water)—casting is extremely challenging. To their loss, few anglers take the time to fish this.

Mossy Creek regulars like Bob Cramer, who's guided on the stream for more than a dozen years, note general decline in the rich abundance of mayflies for which it's been renowned. In the 1970s, TU members took the lead in developing relationships with local landowners that resulted in the installation of electric fences, the creation of stiles, and access to a narrow corridor of private property along Mossy's banks. While access is still available (one needs a signed permit free from the nearby Verona office of the Virginia Department of Game and Inland Fisheries, which can be obtained by mail), as of this writing fencing is in disrepair, allowing cattle to water in the stream at will. Increased sedimentation may be the prime culprit in the decline of Mossy's famed mayfly hatches. TU, VDGIF, and landowners have formed a new coalition to restore the quality of this fishery.

Make no mistake, though. While Mossy may have its challenges, it's still one fine trout stream. It's open all year, and there's no other water where the chances of tagging a great spring creek brown come as early as the first mild weekend in February. Terrestrial fishing is excellent throughout the summer and well into fall. Ants, by the way, seem to outfish hoppers. The usual run of drys produce on Mossy, and she or he who can place a fly hard against the bank *and* engineer a drift-free float catch the most fish. Classed Trophy Trout Water by VDGIF, anglers are allowed to creel one trout per day as long as it's 20 inches or longer.

RESOURCES

Gearing up: Blue Ridge Angler, 1756 S. Main St., Harrisonburg, VA 22801; 540-574-3474; www.blueridgeangler.com.

Mossy Creek Fly Fishing, 2035 E. Main St., Ste. 71A, Harrisonburg, VA 22801; 540-434-2444, www.mossycreekflyfishing.com.

Accommodations: Anderson County Tourist Council, P.O. Box 147, Clinton, TN 37717; 800-524-3620; www.yallcome.org.

Harrison-Rockingham Chamber of Commerce, 800 Country Club Rd., Harrisonburg, VA 22801; 540-434-3862; www.hr-chamber.org.

Books: *Tailwater Trout in the South* by Jimmy Jacobs, Backcountry Publications.

Virginia Trout Streams by Harry Slone, Countryman Press.

38 RAPIDAN RIVER

Location: Central Virginia.
Short take: Eager brookies, a gentle trail, lots of anglers.
Type of stream: Freestone.
Angling methods: Fly.
Species: Brook.
Access: Easy.
Season: All year.
Supporting services: Madison.
Handicapped access: No.
Closest TU chapter: Rapidan.

NAMESAKE RIVER OF MY HOME TU CHAPTER, the Rapidan is the most popular of a score of freestone streams that rise high on the eastern flank of the Blue Ridge and tumble from chute to pool through riffle to pool to boulder-bound chute again. As the Roaring Twenties were going bust, trout-fishing President Herbert Hoover sought respite in a cluster of cabins arrayed in a glade below Big Rock Falls on the Rapidan. Why there? Aside from its convenience to Washington, the Rapidan benefits from an accident of geology: its headwaters are underlain by the Catoctin Formation, a dark-green metamorphosed basalt. Shenandoah National Park fisheries biologists explain that basalts, when weathered, add alkaline minerals to stream flows, which buffer acidity and encourage aquatic insect populations.

New to a neighborhood and want to find the best of a set of mountain trout streams? Hie thyself to the nearest library. Check out the state's geologic map. Look for mountain creeks flowing over limestones, basalts, or granites. Avoid those where the rock is predominantly shale or sandstone. But so much for the geology, now to the fishing.

In 1995 and 1996, a pair of hurricanes pillaged the stream. Heavy oaks and hemlocks, uprooted by the raging torrent, were smashed to splinters by tumbling boulders loosened from the steep mountainside. Rock and log, coursing down the channel, blasted bridges off their iron beams and scoured the channel bare. Receding waters left the river littered with tree trunks and flotsam, providing shade and cover for the stocks of brook trout that somehow survived the deluge. Remarkably resilient these brook trout are. Despite continuing flooding, they remain numerous and eager.

Above Camp Hoover on Mill Prong, you'll find fish in every plunge pool. Casting, due to overhanging vegetation, is difficult. Best success comes from dappling a #14 or #16 Attractor in the foam and letting it ride as drag free as you can. For a mile and a half, from Camp Hoover to the boundary of the Rapidan Wildlife Management Area, the stream picks its way through a series of tiny pools, fed by rushing sluices. Though followed by the road to the camp,

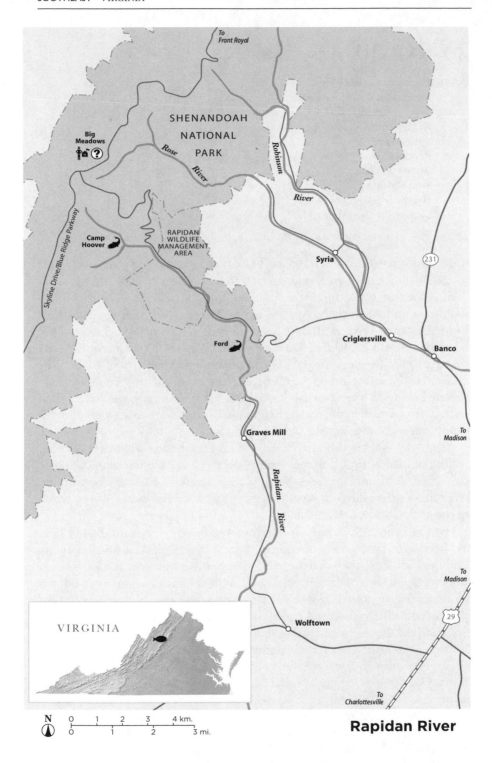

Rapidan River

You'll find jewel-like native trout in the history-rich Rapidan River.

a locked gate bars the way. Thus, angling pressure is diminished. Fish each pool, and a trout or two will come to you. They won't be big, but they are plentiful and willing.

Below the gate, the stream, of course, sees more pressure. This is a favorite spot for weekend campers in virtually every season of the year. The stream widens, pools deepen, and runs of pocket water appear. Among my friends who fish the Rapidan, there are those who maintain that once a pool's been fished, it'll be no good for two or three hours. My experience has been quite the contrary. Left undisturbed for 20 minutes, fish return to their feeding stations and go back to work. The best and most popular section of the Rapidan flows from the group of private cabins that once housed President Hoover's Marine guards down to the ford on the old washed-out road down to Graves Mill. Most anglers drive in from Criglersville, cross a low gap on Chapman Mountain, drop down into the Rapidan, and park in pullouts to fish. Here, the mountain road joins the one, now closed, coming up from Graves Mill. Excellent angling is available to those willing to hike the three miles or so down to where the river breaks free of its mountain valley and then fish their ways up stream. Wild raspberries have overgrown edges of the lower trail along the river. They ripen in late June.

On the mountain section of the river, only fly fishing is allowed. Ant patterns and a local favorite, the Mr. Rapidan, invented by Harry Murray, are generally successful in sizes of #16 and smaller. You'll also find the usual mayflies and caddis. Small nymphs also are effective, and they're best fished as droppers under a parachute dry. Every once in a while, one brookie will nail your indicator fly while another takes your dropper. Open all year, the Rapidan fishes best from late March into early July. Conscientious anglers avoid August because of low flows and are very careful when fishing in late September and October to avoid redds where big females (you'll be blown away by their size) are busy in spawn.

RESOURCES

Gearing up: Murray's Fly Shop, P.O. Box 156, Edinburg, VA 22824; 540-984-4212; www.murraysflyshop.com.

Accommodations: Madison County Chamber of Commerce, 110A N. Main St.,

P.O. Box 373, Madison, VA 22727; 540-948-4455; www.madison-va.com.

Books: *Trout Fishing in Shenandoah National Park* by Harry Murray, Shenandoah Publishing.

Virginia's Trout Streams by Harry Slone, Countryman Press.

Virginia Blue-Ribbon Streams by Harry Murray, Frank Amato Publications.

39 WHITETOP LAUREL CREEK

Location: Southwest Virginia.
Short take: Plunge pools, shaded runs, clear water, and steep gradients. Two-mile walk into artificials-only section.
Type of stream: Freestone.
Angling methods: Fly, spin.
Species: Brown, rainbow.
Access: Easy.
Season: Year-round.
Supporting services: Lodging in Damascus.
Handicapped access: No.
Closest TU chapter: Overmountain.

WHITETOP LAUREL IS OFTEN CONSIDERED VIRGINIA'S premier wild trout stream. That may be true. For more than 20 miles, first as a trickle forming north of the rounded crest of Mount Rodgers and growing into the small river that cuts through the old lumber town of Damascus, the waters of Whitetop Laurel two-step over ledges, through cataracts, down chutes, and into pools the depth of which would surprise you, were you to attempt to wade in to free the snagged weighted Bugger with which you were prospecting for 20-inch browns.

They're there, a few of them, big browns that have survived stockings and grown fat on wild rainbows that seem to proliferate like rabbits in these insect-rich flows. A typical Whitetop 'bow will run about 10 inches, but it's as game as a smallmouth and almost as fat. When water temperatures climb into the 40s with the coming of spring in late March, rainbows become much more active. Blue Quills, March Browns, Light Cahills, or a Parachute Adams—all #14 to #16—will provoke strikes. At this time of year, 'bows just aren't overly persnickety. Wild rainbows of a foot or so and brown occasionally reaching 20 inches and more fin gently in dozens of dark and shady pools of this easily accessed freestone creek. As spring progresses into summer, sulphurs and caddis become dominant, with the latter continuing sporadically into fall. As it the case everywhere, terrestrials, particularly black ants, become the most effective pattern in late July.

Special regulations govern most of Whitetop Laurel. Artificial lures and a 12-inch minimum are required for the two miles upstream from the junction of Straight Creek to the boundary of the Jefferson National Forest below the hamlet of Taylors Valley. A short stretch through the cluster of white frame houses—there are no services here—is put-and-take water. Then special regulations resume for the mileage from the first bridge up to the headwaters and including the first mile of Green Cove Creek above its confluence with Whitetop Laurel.

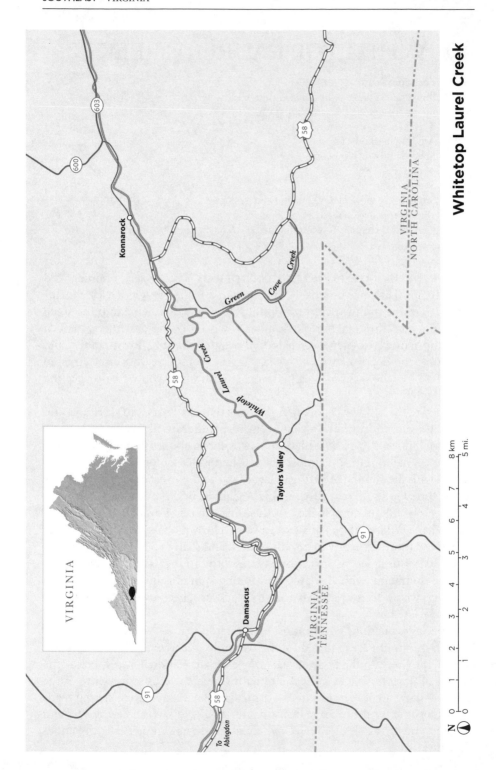

Whitetop Laurel Creek

The grade that once carried chuffing steam engines of the Virginia-Carolina Railroad, later the Abingdon Branch of the Norfolk and Western, follows the course of the river from Damascus to Konnarock. Fondly remembered as the Virginia Creeper, because of the slow pace of trains ascending and descending the steep grade, the railroad ceased operations in 1977. The roadbed became a well-cindered trail maintained by a local civic organization. Numerous bridges cross the creek. Increasingly, anglers eager to outdistance the shank's mare crowd, ride mountain bikes into more remote sections of the stream.

Easily accessible from Interstate 81 at Abingdon, Virginia, via U.S. Route 58, Whitetop Laurel offers a safety valve for anglers caught by heavy generation on the nearby South Holston and Watauga tailwaters in Tennessee. How long that may last is in question. Whitetop Laurel will be sorely threatened by the Virginia Department of Highway's ambitious plan to straighten and widen US 58, which runs nearly alongside the stream for much of its course. TU and other organizations have expressed deep concern that VDOT's construction practices will result in heavy sedimentation of the creek. If you want to experience Whitetop Laurel in its prime, make plans to fish it soon, for years will be required before the creek recovers from the ravages of highway construction.

RESOURCES

Gearing up: Virginia Creeper Flyshop, 16501 JEB Stuart Hwy., Abingdon, VA 24211; 540-628-3826; www.vcflyshop.com.

Accommodations: Washington County Chamber of Commerce, 179 E. Main St., Abingdon, VA 24210; 276-628-8141; www.washingtonvachamber.org.

Books: *Virginia Blue-Ribbon Streams* by Harry Murray, Frank Amato Publications.

Virginia Trout Streams by Harry Slone, Countryman Press.

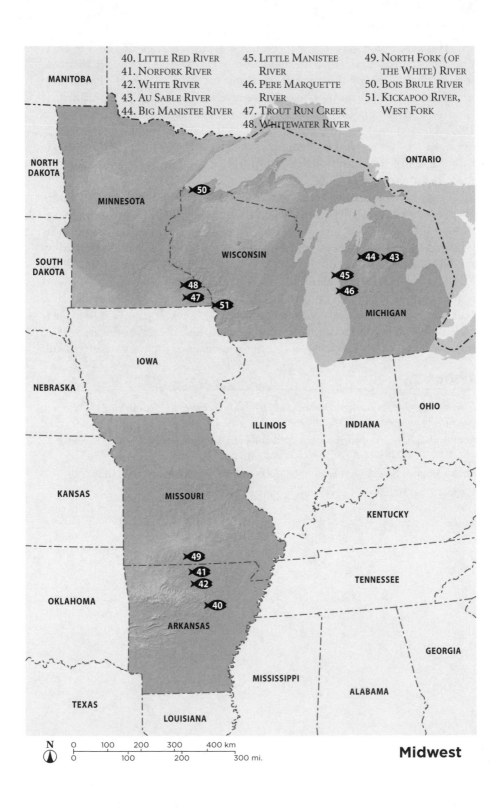

40. LITTLE RED RIVER
41. NORFORK RIVER
42. WHITE RIVER
43. AU SABLE RIVER
44. BIG MANISTEE RIVER
45. LITTLE MANISTEE RIVER
46. PERE MARQUETTE RIVER
47. TROUT RUN CREEK
48. WHITEWATER RIVER
49. NORTH FORK (OF THE WHITE) RIVER
50. BOIS BRULE RIVER
51. KICKAPOO RIVER, WEST FORK

Midwest

MIDWEST

ARKANSAS

MICHIGAN

MINNESOTA

MISSOURI

WISCONSIN

40 LITTLE RED RIVER

Location: Central Arkansas.
Short take: Lookin' for a record-book brown? Stop here.
Type of stream: Tailwater.
Angling methods: Any.
Species: Brown, rainbow, cutthroat, brook.
Access: Easy.
Season: Year-round.
Supporting services: Heber Springs.
Handicapped access: No.
Closest TU chapter: Central Arkansas.

WARM LOW-PRESSURE CELLS HEAVY WITH MOISTURE, welling up from the Gulf of Mexico and pushed eastward by ridges of high pressure dipping south from Canada, dump torrential rains on the highlands of the Ozark plateau. To control flooding, the Army Corps of Engineers began construction in the 1940s of a series of dams on the White River and its tributaries—the North Fork of the White and the Little Red River. Underlying the gently undulating fields and forests of mixed hardwoods are thinly bedded limestones, riddled with caves and solution channels. Tailwaters that issued forth from the new dams and the alkaline-rich groundwater seeping into river channels created the most fertile set of tailwater trout fisheries in America.

The southernmost of the trio is the Little Red River flowing from beneath Greers Ferry Dam, three miles northeast of Heber. Not far downstream, below Sugarloaf Mountain near Barnett access, Rip Collins saw a huge brown cruising in the greenish water and flipped a $\frac{1}{32}$-ounce Olive Marabou Jig in its direction with his ultralight spooled with four-pound test line. The jig resembled a sculpin, favorite fodder of browns that go native in these waters. The leviathan struck. Collins struck back and after a tussle, the duration and difficulty of which grows with age, brought it to boat. Kept alive for a day before reaching a certified scale, the fish weighed in at 40 pounds, 4 ounces, the world-record brown as this is being written.

Tempted to think of this gargantuan brown as a fluke? Don't. Browns of 20 pounds plus have been taken with enough regularity to earn little more than a polite "good fish" from seasoned anglers of the Little Red. Browns have not been stocked in the Little Red since the early 1980s. And there's more than one note to this unpretentious-looking waterway. Until Greg Corkin landed a 4-pound, 12-ounce brook trout in the Norfork below Norfork Dam in 2000, the previous state record brookie—just 8 ounces lighter—had come from the Little Red. Rainbows of four or five pounds rarely raise an eyebrow and earn newcomers who brag a condescending smile from locals who know the river.

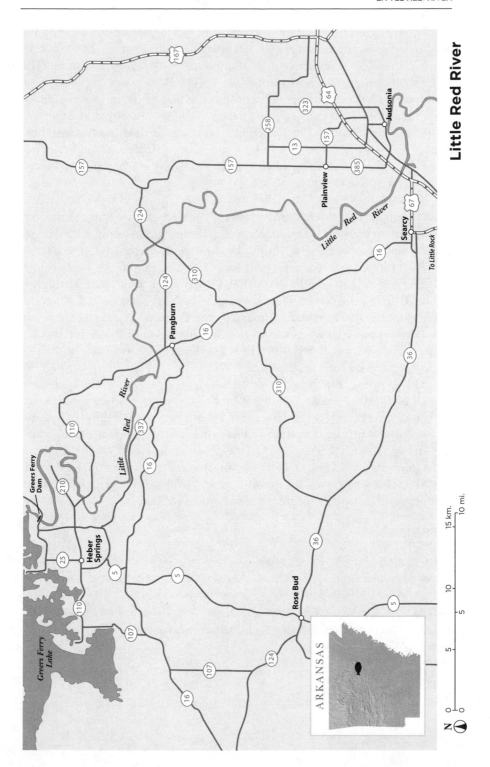

Little Red River

While natural propagation does occur in fall for browns and spring for rainbows, the river receives annual stockings of more than 435,000 trout. In all, the Little Red offers more than 30 miles of first-class trout fishing. The mileage immediately downstream from Greers Ferry Dam contains large boulders, but below, the river deepens into the first of its long, glassy pools. What follows is a seemingly endless progression of shoals, ledges, and pools as the river ambles beneath limestone bluffs or winds through pastureland bottoms. The Arkansas Game and Fish Commission maintains a number of access points along the trout water. Otherwise, banks are privately held and require permission to fish.

Narrower in channel than its cousins, the White and the North Fork, when Greers Ferry's generators are running, the river can rise four to nine feet. Floating when the river is raging in jon or drift boat is less popular on the Little Red than on other rivers. Those who do dare its currents tend to anchor above submerged structure and drift bait or cast lures into the holds below. Swift current swamps carelessly anchored boats every year, often with tragic results. Better and safer angling occurs after the surge has passed when the river begins to fall. Flows are controlled by the Corps of Engineers, and while schedules are posted, they change regularly. This is one of those rivers where anglers who have not fished it before are well served by investing in the services of a guide for their first outing.

Bait, spinning, and fly tackle are used with great success on the Little Red. Creel limits vary by species and should be checked when you buy your license. Caddis in spring, midges and terrestrials in summer, and nymphs year-round all work well. At times of low flow in late summer, long, delicate tippets and tiny emergers are all that's need to do the job on rising trout. While the river is open to angling year-round, conservation-minded anglers forgo angling for those huge browns during the spawn-in from October into January. No sense, they argue, in jeopardizing future generations of wild trout.

RESOURCES

Gearing up: Ozark Angler, Heber Springs, AR 72543; 501-362-3597; www.ozrkangler.com.

Accommodations: Heber Springs Chamber of Commerce, 1001 W. Main St., Heber Springs, AR 72543, 501-362-2444; www.heber-springs.com.

Books: *Ozarks Blue-Ribbon Trout Streams* by Danny Hicks, Frank Amato Publications. *Tailwater Trout in the South* by Jimmy Jacobs, Backcountry Publications.

41 NORFORK RIVER

Location: Central Arkansas.
Short take: Short but oh so sweet.
Type of stream: Tailwater.
Angling methods: Any.
Species: Brown, rainbow, cutthroat, brook.
Access: Easy.
Season: Year-round
Supporting services: Mountain Home
Handicapped access: Yes.
Closest TU chapter: Central Arkansas.

LESS THAN FIVE MILES IN LENGTH, the North Fork River tailwater below Norfork Dam produces some of the largest trout in the country. Technically, it's the North Fork of the White River, but locals call it the "Norfork River," after the dam, and to differentiate it from Missouri's North Fork of the White. Once or twice each decade, the Norfork yields a brown in the 30-pound range, rainbows of 15 pounds or more, and cutthroats and brookies of 3 pounds plus. The current Arkansas record brook trout, a 4-pound, 12-ounce beauty, was hauled in by Greg Corkin in 2000. Fish grow like weeds—in some documented cases, more than 7 inches per year—in this ultrarich coldwater bouillabaisse of suds, sow bugs, and sculpins.

With only two generators, releases from Norfork Dam do not produce as heavy a surge as encountered on the White and Little Red rivers. Yet, high flows can sweep down the entire tailwater in an hour or less. Prudent anglers move to higher ground the moment they notice an increase in current. That said, the Norfork fishes very well when roaring high, wide, and handsome. Most effective are big streamers or nymphs—white if shad are being sucked through the turbines—fished with full sinking lines on 7- or 8-weight systems. Generally speaking, you'll need a boat for this, but the action can be nonstop and only slows a little during winter. This is probably the best way of hooking a brown or 'bow of double-digit weight. Numerous guides offer float trips in Mackenzie as well as traditional White River jon boats.

When generators are off or only one is running, the Norfork can be waded. Quarry State Park and River Ridge provide public access to shoals and riffles. Paid access is also available at numerous trout docks. Nymphing is the name of the game on the Norfork. Use a small non-toxic split shot to keep your fly bouncing and drag-free just off the bottom. Strike indicators are essential for consistent hookups. Fly fishers favor the catch-and-release run from Otter Creek to 100 yards above River Ridge, where a handicapped-access pier is available.

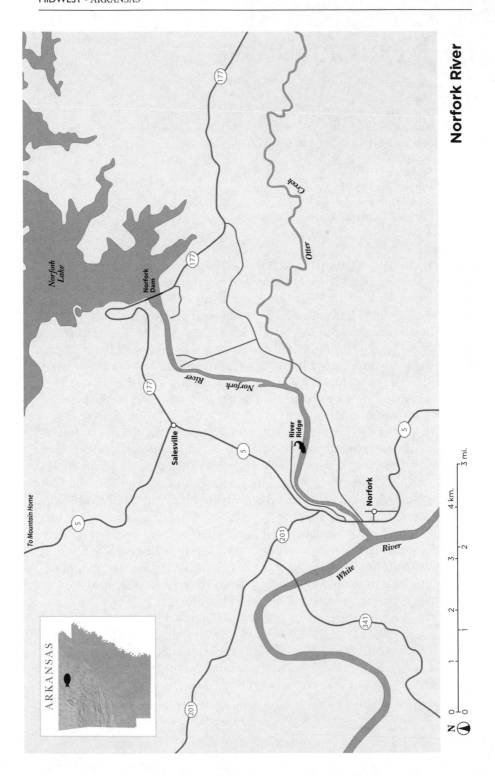

Norfork River

RESOURCES

Gearing up: Blue Ribbon Fly Shop, 343 Hwy. 5 S, Mountain Home, AR 72653; 870-425-0447; www.mthnhome.net/brf.

Accommodations: Mountain Home Area Chamber of Commerce, Hwy. 412/62 E, P.O. Box 488, Mountain Home, AR 72654-0488; 870-425-5111; www.mtnhomechamber.com.

Books: *Home Waters* by Joseph Monninger, Broadway Books.

Ozarks Blue-Ribbon Trout Streams by Danny Hicks, Frank Amato Publications.

Tailwater Trout in the South by Jimmy Jacobs, Backcountry Publications.

42 WHITE RIVER

Location: North-central Arkansas.
Short take: The best trout river in the Midwest, and maybe the United States.
Type of stream: Tailwater.
Angling methods: Fly, spin, cast.
Species: Brown, cutthroat, rainbow, brook.
Access: Easy to moderate.
Season: Year-round.
Supporting services: Mountain Home.
Handicapped access: No.
Closest TU chapter: Central Arkansas.

RISING IN THE OZARK HIGHLANDS OF NORTHWEST ARKANSAS and southwest Missouri, the White River is, perhaps, the longest and best series of tailwater trout fisheries in the United States. Adding up the 10 miles below Beaver Dam, more than 20 miles below Table Rock Lake and Lake Taneycomo at Branson, the 44 miles downstream from Bull Shoals Dam, and the cold-water plume that extends another 57 miles below the junction of the North Fork and the White at Norfork, and you've got a lot of trout water to cover. In addition, most of this water is open year-round. If that weren't enough, factor in springs and falls that begin early and stay late and winters so gentle that folks from up north hardly notice 'em. Finally, there are trout. Millions are stocked annually. Tens of thousands, primarily browns but also rainbows, spawn every year. Growth rates—five to seven inches per season—are nothing short of phenomenal. People in these parts measure their trout with scales, not rulers.

Time was when the White was the quintessential smallmouth fishery. You floated in narrow, blunt-ended, flat-bottomed jon boats casting crawdads from level-wind reels mounted on the first fiberglass rods, a product of World War II technology. But with the war came the need for electric power and the demand for flood control and the construction by the Army Corps of Engineers of the series of dams in the White River watershed. Cold water was an unintended consequence. Experiments proved the rivers satisfactory for trout stocking. Those initial fish were the harbinger of what's grown into a trout tourism industry worth hundreds of millions annually to the heretofore agrarian and economically depressed economy.

Jimmy Jacobs, in his fine book *Tailwater Trout of the South,* says everything about the White River is "big." Below Bull Shoals Dam, the river runs wider than two football fields. When all eight generators are "pulling," the tan-green currents rise into lower limbs of bank-side trees and swirl with a meanness that had better discourage anglers who value their futures. But when flows are

White River

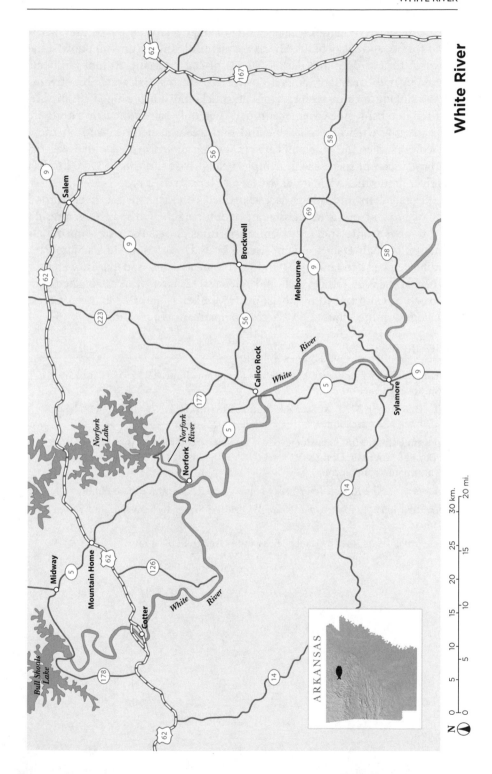

reasonable, the river glides sedately along through a tableau of pastures, hardwood forests, and rocky bluffs. Shoals are plentiful. Riffles run into pools, some of which turn as deep and dark as stands of cedar. Classic 20-foot jon boats pushed by outboards ferry anglers down river. During high water, big streamers and sinking lines are required, though chuck-and-duck fishing with streamers fired into bank-side cover take trout. When only half of the dam's units are generating, fish tend to collect behind midstream structures. And on those blessed days when the generators are off, wading anglers armed with 5-weights will have excellent success with nymphs below strike indicators. Were I to fish this river in summer when it's down, I'd give terrestrials a try.

TU members and others have expressed concern that the river's brood stock of brown trout is needlessly targeted during the fall spawn. As a result, the Arkansas Game and Fish Commission has closed the run immediately below Bull Shoals Dam to the upstream boundary of Bull Shoals State Park from November 1 to January 31 and set it aside as catch-and-release water for the rest of the year. Other catch-and-release areas have been established near the town of Cotter at Rim Shoals; from Monkey Island to Moccasin Creek; and from near the Mount Olive Access to upstream of Jack's Resort.

RESOURCES

Gearing up: Blue Ribbon Flies, 1343 Hwy. 5, Mountain Home, AR 72653; 870-425-0447; www.mthnhome.net/brf/.

White River Angler, 577 E. Millsap Rd., Suite 3, Fayetteville, AR 72703; 479-442-2193; www.whiteriverangler.com.

Accommodations: Mountain Home Area Chamber of Commerce, Hwy. 412/62, P.O. Box 488 Mountain Home, AR 72653-0488; 870-425-5111 or 800-822-3536; www.mtnhomechamber.com.

Books: *Ozarks Blue-Ribbon Trout Streams* by Danny Hicks, Frank Amato Publications.

Ozark Trout Tales: A Fishing Guide for the White River System by Steve Wright, White River Chronicle.

River Journal: White River by Danny Hicks, Frank Amato Publications.

43 AU SABLE RIVER

Location: Michigan, northern lower peninsula.
Short take: TU's home waters—need we say more?
Type of stream: Freestone.
Angling methods: Fly, spin.
Species: Brown, rainbow, brook.
Access: Easy.
Season: Year-round.
Supporting services: Grayling, Mio.
Handicapped access: Yes.
Closest TU chapters: Challenge Martuch, Mason, Mershon.

AT HIS COTTAGE, THE BARBLESS HOOK, one July afternoon in 1959, George Griffith hosted 14 fishing pals who shared his passion for the Au Sable and saw what would happen if planting hatchery fish continued as the preferred method of restoring trout to suitable streams. He also knew well the threats to trout streams. The Au Sable, which flowed past his cottage, often ran chocolate with suspended sediment. Indiscriminate logging accelerated erosion. Real estate and industrial developments were gobbling up wetlands vital to the nourishment of the river. He knew as well, that without the clout of a large organization with a clear mission—and the money to back it up—anglers acting in small groups would never develop the muscle to affect public policy. That, after all, is the key to long-term conservation.

That afternoon, George and his cronies laid out the framework of Trout Unlimited. They sought to fashion an organization that would do for coldwater fisheries what Ducks Unlimited, begun 25 years earlier, was accomplishing for waterfowl and wetlands. What success their vision has achieved! In virtually every state with naturally occurring trout water or tailwaters that will sustain trout, conservation efforts now include plans to improve wild trout reproduction. I'm convinced that, were it not in part for the energy of Trout Unlimited, the National Park Service might not have abandoned its stocking policies in favor of encouraging natural reproduction. Movements to restore cutthroat fisheries in the West and brook trout in the East can be traced to George's door. These gentlemen brought forth a revolution, and nowhere is the battle more telling than on the stream that flows past the Barbless Hook's front stoop.

Several TU chapters devote hundreds of hours to active stewardship of the Au Sable, TU's home waters. They've been tireless in their work to stabilize sand banks that threaten to erode and dump suffocating sediments into the river. They have focused public attention on the need to regulate slant drilling for natural gas under the Mason Tract, a parcel with nearly a mile of frontage

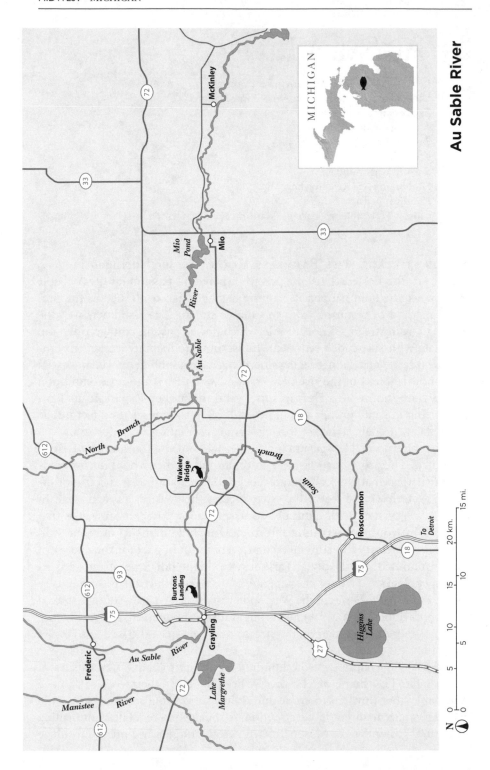

Au Sable River

on the South Branch of the Au Sable. And they are indefatigable in pursuing their education programs for youth, the most critical conservation issue faced by TU.

Flowing from the center of Michigan east-southeast to Lake Huron, the Au Sable drains a 90-mile east–west-running corridor that ranges between 10 and 30 miles in width. During its 129-mile course, the river drops about 650 feet, a modest gradient for the river's 129-mile length. Termed "river of sand" by early explorers, the Au Sable flows over unconsolidated sediments with no ledges of bedrock. While the bottom is generally firm on the upper end, bars of sand shift with high water creating new shoals and pools where there were none earlier. Banks on the river are equally unstable, especially those that have been stripped of forest and other cover. Most rehabilitation efforts attempt to forestall bank degradation through the emplacement of woody debris.

The main stem of the Au Sable rises in springs just west of Interstate 75 and northwest of the town of Grayling. Wild brookies, browns, and rainbows are found in the headwaters. After cutting through the town, gathering water from the confluence with its East Branch and ducking under the highway, the river takes the shape that will sustain it through the Holy Water—eight miles of fly-fishing-only, no-kill angling that begins at Burton's Landing and continues to Wakeley Bridge. Riffling over a gravel and sand bottom, tufted with waving strands of aquatic grasses, the river here is quite wadable and fish hold in easily seen lies. Seducing them to strike is another matter. Early in the year, Hendricksons garner the most interest from anglers. Later, in May, come the Sulphurs. Near the middle of this section is Rusty Gate's famed Au Sable Lodge. Bridges provide good access for waders. And there are ample launching points for those who choose to fish this section from those wonderful narrow wooden three-man boats named for the river.

Hexigenia limbata, also called the Michigan caddisfly, is the signature hatch of the river's next run from Wakeley Bridge to Mio Pond. From late May into mid-June, nymphal forms will prove successful if fished late in the day and into the evening. Duns emerge in June and early July, and fishing for hoggish browns in the dark of night is as challenging as it is exciting. The famed Au Sable brown drake hatch is a precursor to the Hex. Then the river is in its prime. Below Mio Pond Dam to McKinley Bridge, anglers are permitted only two trout and each must exceed 15 inches. They may be taken only by artificial means. Here the river requires great patience to wade safely, though McKinley Road leads to many access points that allow some wading and bank fishing.

The South Branch, particularly the fly-fishing-only, no-kill section of four miles below Chase Bridge, and the North Branch (flies only from Sheep Ranch Access above the town of Lovells to its mouth) are worth considering if the main stem is too crowded. You'll find more brookies on the North Branch and some dandy browns as well.

RESOURCES

Gearing up: Bob Linsenman's Au Sable Angler, 56A Richard Dr., Mio, MI 48647; 989-826-8500; www.ausableangler.com.

Gates Au Sable Lodge and Flyshop, 471 Stephan Bridge Rd., Grayling, MI 49738; 517-348-8462; www.gateslodge.com.

Accommodations: Grayling Regional Chamber of Commerce, P.O. Box 406, Grayling, MI 49738; 800-937-8837; www.grayling-mi.com.

Books: *Au Sable River* by Bob Linsenman, River Journal Series, Frank Amato Publications.

Au Sable River Guide by John J. P. Long, ed., Challenge Chapter TU.

Flyfisher's Guide to Michigan by Jim Bedford, Wilderness Adventure Press.

Michigan Blue-Ribbon Fly Fishing Guide by Bob Linsenman, Frank Amato Publications.

Michigan Trout Streams by Bob Linsenman and Steve Nevala, Backcountry Publications.

44 Big Manistee River

Location: West-central Michigan.
Short take: Where guides go on their days off.
Type of stream: Spring-fed freestone.
Angling methods: Fly, spin.
Species: Brook, brown, steelhead, salmon.
Access: Easy.
Season: Year-round.
Supporting services: Grayling.
Handicapped access: Yes.
Closest TU chapters: Adams, Pine, West Michigan.

WHERE DO MICHIGAN'S GUIDES GO TO GET FAR from the madding crowd? The Big Manistee—only where they fish it, it ain't big. The Upper Manistee is a jewel of a trout stream, tremendously overshadowed by the Au Sable, which rises to the east on the same plain. Once, fishery historians thought that the native range of brook trout in Michigan extended no farther south than the Boardman River, but an 1869 article in the *Manistee Times* carries a report of an angler catching a "mess" of "speckled brook trout" in Pine Creek, a tributary of the Manistee.

Linsenman and Nevala describe the uppermost run of the river above Mancelona Bridge on County Route 38 as having the sandy bottom of a Montana spring creek, but the land on either side is boggy. Narrow and studded with downed logs and bank-side brush, this is fine brook trout water and home to a few browns as well. By the time the Manistee reaches the former lumbering community of Deward, it has broadened with inflows from springs and small creeks and has taken on the trappings of a mature trout river. You'll find more gravel in the bottom, a few riffles, and better casting. Mayflies, stoneflies, and caddis are all present.

For the next 14.5 miles, from Deward to the bridge carrying M 72 across the river, the Manistee becomes more interesting. It now ranges in width from 30 to 50 feet, and the gradient of the stream steepens with a few riffles but more long runs. Undercut banks and fallen trees provide cover for browns, which increasingly dominate trout populations. Though some canoeists launch this far upstream, anglers mostly have these runs to themselves. Cameron Bridge marks the bottom of the upper third of this mileage and is a popular access point for anglers as well as canoeists. The fish don't seem bothered by the latter. The Manistee deepens here and begins, occasionally, to braid. The section between Cameron and the County Route 612 bridge is possibly the best of the Upper Manistee. Downstream from CR 612, a popular campground fills the stream with swimmers and tubers and canoes, forcing anglers who seek solitude to fish early in the season or after Labor Day or

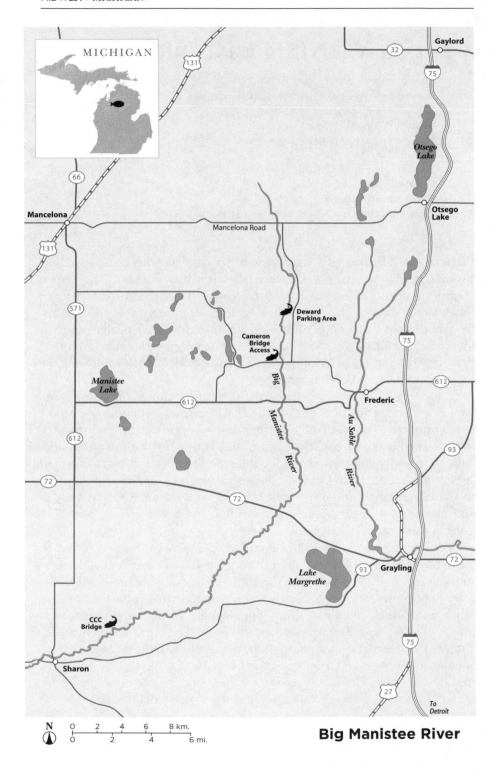

MICHIGAN

Gaylord

Otsego
Lake

Otsego
Lake

Mancelona

Mancelona Road

Deward
Parking Area

Cameron
Bridge
Access

Manistee
Lake

Frederic

Big

Manistee
River

Au Sable
River

Lake
Margrethe

Grayling

CCC
Bridge

Sharon

To
Detroit

N

| 0 | 2 | 4 | 6 | 8 km. |

| 0 | 2 | 4 | 6 mi. |

Big Manistee River

restrict their presence to early morning or late afternoon. The season on the Manistee from its headwaters to the M 72 bridge extends from the last Saturday in April through September 30.

From the M 72 bridge downstream to the Civilian Conservation Corps bridge on Sunset Trail Road, the Manistee is restricted to fly fishing only and is open to year-round angling, though possession of fish is only permitted during the regular season. This is a favorite with guides because of its prolific hatches and sizable stocks of big browns and brook trout. From sandy tracks and streamside roads, access to this section is ample. Though private land borders the river, anglers do have the right to wade the streambed and to leave it to avoid obstacles. This is, however, not a point to be argued. Below the CCC bridge, the Manistee again falls under Michigan's general regulations, and quality trout fishing declines below Sharon where County Route 571 crosses. But don't overlook this run, for it holds large browns with steelhead below Tippy Dam.

RESOURCES

Gearing up: The Fly Factory & Ray's Canoeing, 200 Ingham, P.O. Box 709, Grayling, MI 49738; 989-348-5844; www.troutbums.com.

Gates Au Sable Lodge and Flyshop, 471 Stephan Bridge Rd., Grayling, MI 49738; 517-348-8462; www. www.gateslodge.com.

Accommodations: Grayling Regional Chamber of Commerce, P.O. Box 406, Grayling, MI 49738; 800-937-8837; www.grayling-mi.com.

Books: *Flyfishers Guide to Michigan* by Jim Bedford, Wilderness Adventure Press.

The Manistee River Guide Book by John J. P. Long, ed., Challenge Chapter, TU.

Michigan Blue-Ribbon Fly Fishing Guide by Bob Linsenman, Frank Amato Publications.

Michigan Trout Streams by Bob Linsenman and Steve Nevala, Back Country Publications.

45 LITTLE MANISTEE RIVER

Location: West-central Michigan.
Short take: Small river with big salmon, steelhead, and wonderful brookies.
Type of stream: Freestone.
Angling methods: Fly, spin.
Species: Steelhead, chinook, rainbow, brown, brook.
Access: Moderate.
Season: Varies with section; check regulations.
Supporting services: Wellston and Irons.
Handicapped access: No.
Closest TU chapters: Adams, Pine River, West Michigan.

FOR MORE THAN 40 MILES, THE LITTLE MANISTEE cuts northwest across west-central Michigan's scrubby pine barrens. Not nearly so famed as the Au Sable or Pere Marquette, the Little Manistee in many ways has more to offer, but only if you're an advocate of the "less is more" theory of life. Never very wide or particularly deep (be careful where you wade, though), this charming black-water river explodes with spring and fall steelhead and salmon—cohos, pink, and Atlantic—that burst into the river like fireworks on the Fourth of July. You'll find aggressive rainbows and shy browns, and up in the headwaters around Luther, rapacious brookies.

The upper river rises in swamps near Luther east of Route 37 and glides over a sandy bottom through alders so thick they sometimes form a tight canopy over the stream. This is where you'll find the brookies, lurking in little pools. Brightly spotted browns hold here too, and some will surprise your rod. Below the Route 37 bridge, the river becomes easier to fish. It widens to 30 feet or so and offers a firm bottom. The mileage from Spencer Bridge to Johnson's Bridge marks seven miles of fly-fishing-only water, and most of it is private. Michigan DNR provides access below Spencer Bridge, and if you stay in the river, leaving only to avoid downed trees, you won't trespass. Scores of sandy two-lane tracks, too informal to be called roads, though some have seen gravel, wander close the river's channel. Hunting cabins have become more numerous due to increasing populations of grouse and deer. Pull-offs provide clues to access.

The Little Manistee contains more riffles and shoals than the upper and most popular runs of its longer brother. In the area of the Udell Hills, the river cuts through moraines left by retreating continental glaciers 12,000 years ago. Its pace quickens through gravelly runs. Current, never heavy here save during spring runoff or summer spate (which triggers strikes from holding steelhead, by the way), pushes against cobble banks and carves hides where browns or steelies lie here in the dark choosing their fare *à la carte*. You'll know the difference when one strikes your weighted streamer. The best of this water flows

160

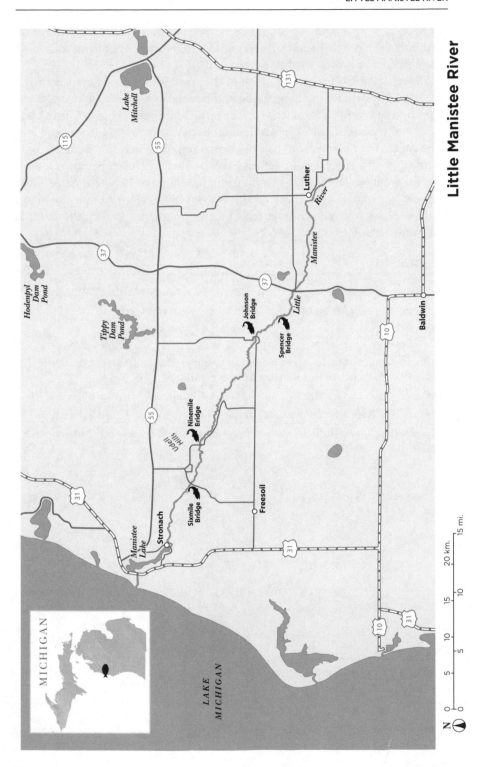

Little Manistee River

between Ninemile and Sixmile bridges. Below, the river slows and at Old Stronach Bridge, Michigan DNR runs a fish weir where eggs from migrating steelhead and salmon are collected for incubation.

Special regulations govern much of the river. Prudence suggests getting a copy of DNR's current angling guide and having a knowledgeable angler explain it to you. Targetable hatches on the Little Manistee begin with little black stoneflies in March, caddis in April, and olives and Isonychia from June into September. The best times to fish the river vary, of course. For salmon, come in July and early August; for steelhead, fish in April or November and December; for trout, work the Hex hatch during late June. In between, chase those wise old browns the same way you'd hunt a trophy buck: hike a mile down to a likely pool, set yourself down with back against a tree, and watch the water as afternoon fades into dusk.

RESOURCES

Gearing up: Baldwin Bait and Tackle, 9331 S. M-37, Baldwin MI 49304; 877-422-5946.

Ed's Sport Shop, 712 Michigan Ave., Baldwin MI 49304; 231/745-4974.

Schmidt Outfitters, 918 Seaman Rd., Wellston, MI 49689; 888-221-9056; www.schmidtoutfitters.com.

Accommodations: Manistee Area Chamber of Commerce, 11 Cypress St., Manistee MI 49660; 800-288-2286; www.manisteeareachamber.com.

Books: *Flyfisher's Guide to Michigan* by Jim Bedford, Wilderness Adventure Press.

Michigan Blue-Ribbon Fly Fishing Guide by Bob Linsenman, Frank Amato Publications.

Michigan Trout Streams by Bob Linsenman and Steve Nevala, Backcountry Publications.

46 PERE MARQUETTE RIVER

Location: Northwest Michigan.
Short take: Famous steelhead, salmon, and brown trout river.
Type of stream: Freestone.
Angling methods: Fly, spin.
Species: Brown, rainbow, steelhead, salmon.
Access: Moderate.
Season: Year-round.
Supporting services: Tackle shops, guides, accommodations.
Handicapped access: Yes.
Closest TU chapters: Mid-Michigan, Muskegon-White River, Schrems
West Michigan.

THAT THE PERE MARQUETTE DESERVES TO RANK among America's 100
best trout streams, there can be no argument. Its 38-mile fishable length, beginning in the boggy kettles of Manistee National Forest south and east of
Baldwin, contains wonderful trout, and in their season, steelhead and salmon.
The upper river is made up of the Middle Branch and the Little South Branch.
The Middle Branch becomes fishable at the Rosa Road Bridge, and runs more
or less north-northwest for 18 miles to Gleason's Landing. Downstream from
Gleason's and all the way to Lake Michigan—a distance of about 20 miles—
the river is big, grows increasingly deep, and holds browns the sizes of which
never fail to surprise anglers from Idaho and Montana.

The Middle Branch, east of the Route 37 bridge offers fine angling for
browns. In this section the river is narrow, averaging about 20 feet, and shallow—seldom more than three feet deep. Water chatters happily down gravel
riffles in places and in others flows like glass over sandy bottoms. Overhanging
brush provides shade and shelter, as do a number of undercut banks, for very
nice browns. Hendricksons, BWOs, Sulphurs, Gray and Brown Drakes, and
Caddis each have their turn into July when deftly delivered. Hoppers, sized #14
or #16, or #18 Ants provoke strikes. About the middle of this stretch, the Little
South Branch joins the Middle Branch and the Pere Marquette is born.

The Little South Branch comes in at the Route 37 bridge, which marks the
beginning of an eight-mile run of flies-only, catch-and-release, year-round
water. One look at paths trodden into the sandy loam tells you that the popularity of this section cannot be overstated. Bottomed with gravel, but occasionally slippery clay and shifting sand, the river twists as if scratching an itch. Each
tight bend contains a cut-bank pool, usually overhung with brush. Blow-
downs and deadfalls deflecting the current prove marvelous hides for browns.
Halfway through the fly-fishing mileage, above the Green Cottage, the Big
South Branch adds its water, doubling the river's flow. Downstream from the
Cottage, you'll want to use caution or engage a guide (or friend) with a boat.

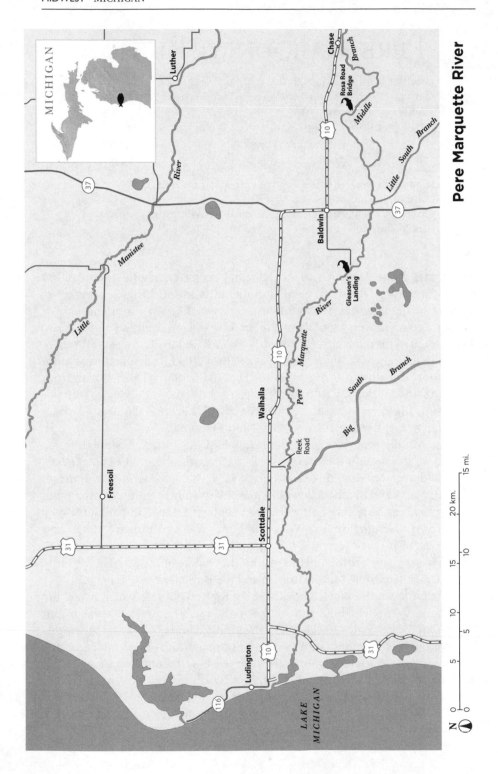

Pere Marquette River

This lower section of the fly-fishing-only water has a distinct Western feel—deep pools, wide flats, sharply powerful runs—about it. Nymphs and streamers are the order of the day here. Fish Black Stonefly, Woolly Buggers, almost-black Hare's Ears, dark Clousers, yellow and black Marabou Muddlers. Large drys also pay off in June: *Hexigenia limbata* and Brown and Gray Drakes. Fly boxes should also contain Adams, Elkhair Caddis, Boercher's Drake, and Lime Trude.

The Pere Marquette reaches maturity below Gleason's Landing, the western limit of the fly-fishing-only water. Though open all year (possession season runs from the last Saturday in April through September 30), any tackle may be used. Just before snow begins to melt in March, the runs near Gleason's are at their lowest and clearest and attract numbers of steelhead. Steelies and salmon seem to use the river throughout the year with the possible exception of June, when you'll just have to contend with lunker browns. All standard egg and streamer patterns will seduce the anadromous visitors, it's more a question of what you'd prefer to lose when a 10-pounder runs beneath the logjam. The farther downstream you fish, the more challenging the wading becomes. Yet prospecting carefully those sandy tracks that lead toward the river will reveal occasional shallows, which can be safely waded. Most anglers, however, float this section and cast to trout holding by the scores of sunken logs along the banks.

As is the case with most of central Michigan's trout streams, these rivers flow across glacial outwash plains. Usually bedrock is deeply buried by layers of gravel, sands, and clays. After the glaciers melted, the land resembled high arid arctic steppes and massive dust storms distributed fine silt called "loess" across the surface. These sandy soils are easily eroded, hence work by the Michigan Council of Trout Unlimited, Michigan's Department of Natural Resources, and a host of federal and state agencies to deploy woody debris in an effort to stabilize banks.

RESOURCES

Gearing up: Baldwin Bait and Tackle, 9331 S. M-37, Baldwin, MI 49304; 877-422-5946.

Ed's Sport Shop, 712 Michigan Ave., Baldwin, MI 49304; 231-745-4974.

Pere Marquette Lodge, 8841 S. M-37, Baldwin, MI 49304; 231-745-3972; www.pmlodge.com.

Schmidt's Outfitters, 918 Seaman Rd., Wellston, MI 49689; 888-221-9056; www.schmidtoutfitters.com.

Accommodations: Lake County Chamber of Commerce, 911 Michigan Ave., P.O. Box 130, Baldwin, MI 49304; 616-745-4331; lakecountymichigan.com.

Books: *Flyfishers Guide to Michigan* by Jim Bedford, Wilderness Adventure Press.

Pere Marquette River by Matt Supinski, River Journal Series, Frank Amato Publications.

Pere Marquette River Guide by John J. P. Long, ed. Challenge Chapter TU.

Michigan Blue-Ribbon Fly Fishing Guide by Bob Linsenman, Frank Amato Publications.

Michigan Trout Streams by Bob Linsenman and Steve Nevala, Backcountry Publications.

47 TROUT RUN CREEK

Location: Southeast Minnesota.
Short take: New slot limit promises more big trout.
Type of stream: Spring-fed freestone.
Angling methods: Fly, spin.
Species: Brown, brook.
Access: Easy.
Season: April through September.
Supporting services: Lanesboro, Rochester.
Handicapped access: No.
Closest TU chapters: Hiawatha, Win Cres.

IF THERE EXISTS IN THE UNITED STATES a more bucolic trout fishery than southeastern Minnesota, I'd be hard pressed to tell you where it is. Splayed and laid flat, the hands of the Great Plains reach eastward toward the Mississippi River, but they never quite grasp it. On the back of each finger sit neatly tended dairy farms interspersed with those growing corn soybeans. Between each lies a valley, deeply cut in thinly bedded limestones. Precipitation seeps down through thick soil, rich and dark as chocolate fudge frosting, into cracks and cavities in the carbonate rocks and emerges as springs where impervious sandstone floors the valley. Had it not been for a slight rise in the topography, epochs of continental glaciation would have filled these valleys with unconsolidated boulders and sand and clay and cobble called "drift" by geologists. Instead, the topographic high forces the glaciers to flow around this region, making it "driftless" and leaving the pre-glacial valleys intact.

Trout Run Creek is one of a score of these spring-fed jeweled veins fanning through this corner of Minnesota. The river rises on the prairie south of St. Charles and it flows almost due south for 13 miles to the Root River, itself a prime trout and smallmouth fishery. Access is easy and ample. Take the St. Charles exit from Interstate 90 and turn south on State Route 74. The first stream crossed by this road is the headwaters of Trout Run, but the stream does not reach really fishable size until the hamlet of Saratoga (you'll miss it if you blink). Most anglers consider Troy, where Winona County Road 6 comes in from the east, to be the top of the best mileage.

At Troy, take County Road 43 south. Trout Run flows west of the road but then loops back to the east and crosses under a bridge. The next road to the east drops down to the creek. Below the bridge is a heavily fished pool where you can watch small browns rise almost all day. Across the creek is one of the few surviving round barns in the region—designed so that a hay wagon could enter the upper level and offload its cargo on the floor above the livestock. Upstream, a thick patch of woods makes casting challenging, to say the least. But the canopy thins quickly as the stream crosses open pasture. Downstream, a

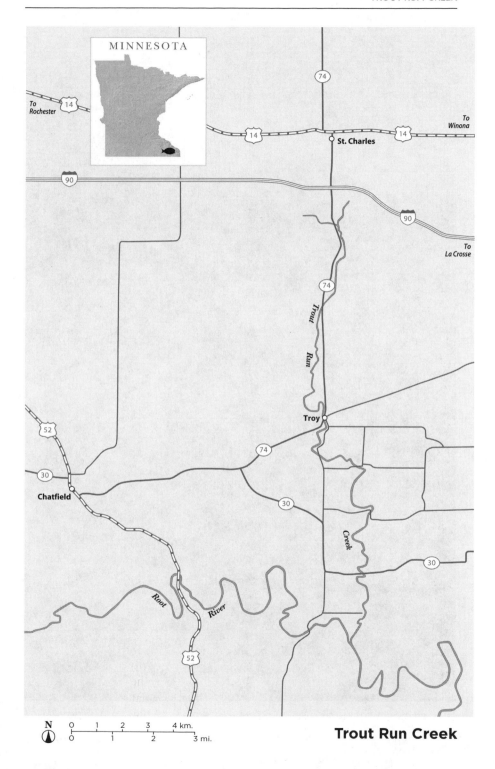

MINNESOTA

Trout Run Creek

N

0   1   2   3   4 km.
0   1   2   3 mi.

Trout Run is a small spring-fed creek with consistent flows, good pools and pockets, and surprising browns.

trail leads over a small knoll onto mileage that once flowed through a now defunct Boy Scout Camp.

At the boundary between Winona and Fillmore counties, CR 43 becomes County Road 11. The first intersection south of the county line takes you to a one-time vacation hamlet—Bide-a-Wee (yup!)—where a long green pool stretches north above the bridge and the pocket-water run below cuts through a brushy field. Banks in this section are frequently undercut and draped with vegetation. When the sun is on the water, you'll find fewer fish in the open. In summer, cast terrestrials upstream against the bank. CR 11 runs into State Route 30, and just south is another side road that takes you to the river. Making a sharp right-angled turn to the east, SR 30 drops down a hill and crosses below a low dam and picnic area at Bucksnort. The mileage above the little pond impounded by the dam is some of the best on the creek, as are the two miles or so downstream that eventually flow into the North Branch of the Root.

Long-time TUer Tom Dornack reports that olives and dark hendricksons come off by mid-April, followed by gray caddis late in the month, and then olive caddis. In late May, light hendricksons begin to hatch, grading into pseudocleons by the middle of June. With natural propagation of browns and brook trout in its uppermost runs, this creek is said to have populations between 2,000 and 5,000 fish per mile, making it one of the premier streams in the region. But many of its fish are on the small side. Slot limits will aid in producing greater numbers of big fish, but this stream would surely benefit if anglers kept and cooked a few of their smaller catches. Angling quality will also rise, thanks to stream improvements between the landmark red barn and Bide-a-Wee by the Hiawatha Chapter of TU.

RESOURCES

Gearing up: Gander Mountain, 1201 S. Broadway, Rochester, MN 55902; 507-289-4224; www.gandermountain.com.

Accommodations: Lanesboro Area Chamber of Commerce, P.O. Box 348, Lanesboro, MN 55949; 800-944-2670; www.lanesboro.com.

Books: *Fishing Minnesota* by Greg Breining, U. of Minnesota Press.

Wisconsin and Minnesota Trout Streams by Jim Humphrey and Bill Shogren, Backcountry Publications.

48 WHITEWATER RIVER

Location: Southeast Minnesota.
Short take: But it's dry cold—and the trout don't seem to mind.
Type of stream: Freestone.
Angling methods: Fly, spin.
Species: Brown, rainbow, brook.
Access: Easy.
Season: Year-round.
Supporting services: Rochester.
Handicapped access: No.
Closest TU chapter: Hiawatha, Win Cres,

IN 1985, THE WHITEWATER RIVER WAS IN SAD SHAPE. Intensive grazing had broken down its banks and sediment flooded into the stream with every freshet. It was an old story in this absolutely lovely basin framed with high, sparsely forested limestone ridges east of Rochester, home of the Mayo Clinic. Groundwater, seeping through limestone strata, was naturally rich in carbonates. And no doubt, the Whitewater and its tributaries once teemed with wild brook trout. But a century of abuse had stripped the watershed of its wild trout populations and robbed it of much of its forest as well.

It's hard to lay much blame on homesteading pioneers who entered the valley in the 1850s. Trying to wrest a living from the valley floor, they'd stripped it of its timber and burned its thick sod, and tilled its topsoil until it could stand no more. Massive floods blasted through the valley, leaving devastation and little hope of recovery. In 1919, the state acquired its first parcel in the valley and by 1931, after a petition from the Izaak Walton League in Rochester, began actively purchasing property to form what is now a 27,000-acre wildlife management area.

Thanks to a generation of conservation-minded TUers from the Hiawatha chapter in Rochester with an assist from Win Cres in Winona and Wa Hue in Red Wing and a plethora of local, regional, and state organizations, anglers have at their disposal more than 50 miles of first-class small-river fishing. And the work continues.

Three main branches—North, Middle, and South—and two tributaries—Trout Run and Beaver Creek—offer similar yet varied angling. Aside from the upper reaches of Middle and South branches, there are few rock outcrops in the stream itself. For the most part, the mileage consists of gravel runs and pools running along banks sparsely forested by cottonwoods and aspen. Cold springs feed the headwaters and seep into the branches at numerous points, giving birth to the most unusual aspect of the Whitewater fishery. Its open waters can be fished with barbless hook on a strict catch-and-release basis from New Year's Day until the end of March. Spring, in the form of midge hatches,

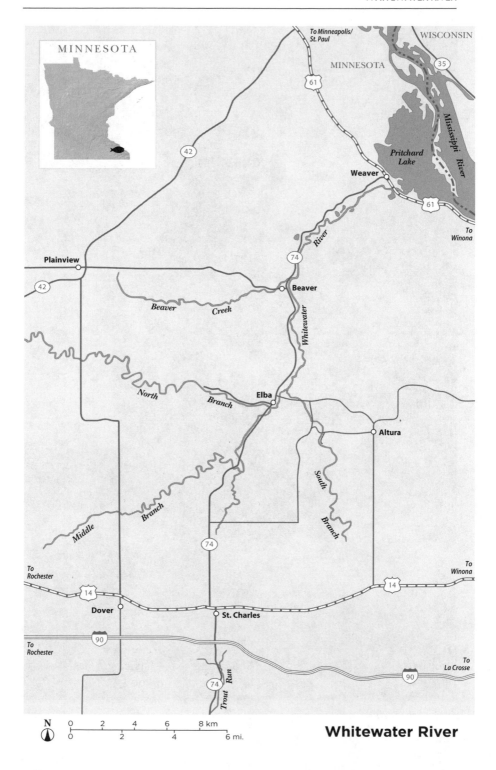

Whitewater River

Spring-fed, the Whitewater River offers a surprisingly good midwinter fishery.

comes early to southeast Minnesota, even if the temperature is hovering at zero degrees Fahrenheit. Typically from noon to 2:00 p.m. on even the coldest of sunny days without wind, you'll find a hatch. In pools, a nymph fished oh-so-slowly with a strike indictor will attract browns to 16 inches and longer. Dressed with fleece and five-mil neoprenes, anglers seem undeterred by the frigid temperatures. "But it's *dry* cold," they'll tell you if asked.

As of this writing, new regulations are going into effect for the North and Middle Branches of the Whitewater. A slot limit calling for the release of all trout between 12 inches and 16 inches now applies to 12.1 miles of the North Branch. And a 9.2-mile section of the Middle Branch becomes catch-and-release for all trout. In both branches, only artificial lures or flies may be used. Diehard fly fishers enjoy the challenge of angling in the little shady runs of Beaver Creek, a tributary to the North Branch, and Crow Spring Creek that flows into the top of the Middle Branch, but it's the complicated currents in the runs and pools of the South Branch that draw much of their attention. Fish shaded woods in deep summer or splash hoppers along grassy banks in the meadows. Numerous roads and trails crisscross the valley, and maps are readily available at the state park headquarters.

RESOURCES

Gearing up: Gander Mountain, 1201 S. Broadway, Rochester, MN 55902; 507-289-4224; www.gandermountain.com.

Accommodations: Winona Area Chamber of Commerce, 67 Main St., Winona, MN 55987; 507-452-2274; www.winonachamber.com.

Rochester Area Chamber of Commerce, 220 S. Broadway Suite 100, Rochester, MN 55904; 507-288-1122; www.rochesterchamber.com.

Books: *Fishing Minnesota* by Greg Breining, U. of Minnesota Press.

Wisconsin and Minnesota Trout Streams by Jim Humphrey and Bill Shogren, Backcountry Publications.

49 NORTH FORK (OF THE WHITE) RIVER

Location: South-central Missouri.
Short take: Big river, big browns, good rainbows.
Type of stream: Freestone.
Angling methods: Fly, spin.
Species: Brown, rainbow.
Access: Moderate.
Season: Year-round.
Supporting services: Tecumseh.
Handicapped access: No.
Closest TU chapter: Contact the state council of TU.

GLIDING THROUGH GENTLY ROLLING HILLS and unfettered by dams, the North Fork of the White River drains a swath of southernmost central Missouri before getting reined in by the headwaters of Norfork Lake. If you've scheduled a weekend chasing those behemoth browns of the White River below Bull Shoals Dam or you're holed up doing the country music thing in Branson and have played with the 'bows in the White downstream from Table Rock Lake, you owe it to yourself to take U.S. Route 160 east for an hour or so to the hamlet of Tecumseh, mouth of the North Fork's best trout water.

Tecumseh marks the lower boundary of 13.1 miles of special-regulation water so designated by the Missouri Department of Conservation. The 7.6 miles from Norfork Lake to Blair Bridge flows through a special trout management zone. Here anglers can harvest three fish per day with a minimum length limit of 15 inches. Above Blair Bridge, the size limit increases to 18 inches and one is all you can keep. Rainbows and browns predominate, with 'bows being more plentiful. They breed in the high-pH waters of the North Fork, while browns are stocked and grow large. Were it not for Double Springs (also known as Rainbow Springs), which pumps 82 million gallons of cold water into the North Fork, the river would be prime smallmouth water.

Small insects are not the main staple in the diet of these big trout, though tan caddis produce from May into October and late July and August mornings witness reasonably good Trico hatches. You'll find a few slate and golden drakes around from May into July, mixed in with first black and then yellow stoneflies. Blue-winged olives, hendricksons, and dark caddis come off in spring, and PMDs seem to do the number from mid-May into June. As seems to be the case on most Ozark trout rivers, nymphs and streamers take more big fish than dries. Hellgrammite and crayfish ties are phenomenally productive, as are the usual run of Dark Woolly Buggers and Bead Head Nymphs.

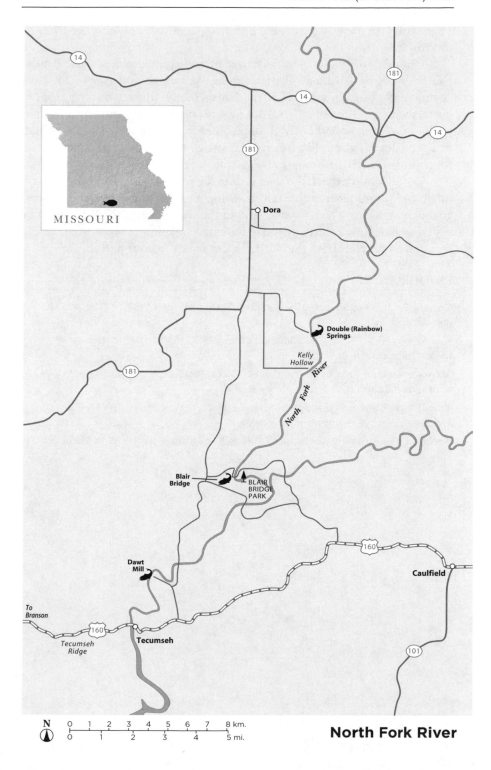

Dora

Double (Rainbow)
Springs

Kelly
Hollow

North Fork River

Blair
Bridge

BLAIR
BRIDGE
PARK

Dawt
Mill

Caulfield

To
Branson

Tecumseh
Ridge

Tecumseh

N

| 0 | 1 | 2 | 3 | 4 | 5 | 6 | 7 | 8 km. |

| 0 | 1 | 2 | 3 | 4 | 5 mi. |

North Fork River

These fish aren't overly particular. Effective patterns typically range from #8 to #16.

A number of points along the river provide public access: Blair Bridge, Dawt Mill, Kelly Ford, and Patrick Bridge. As long as you stay in the river channel, you can wade much of the North Fork without running afoul of owners who've posted their land. But a more enjoyable and productive plan is to float the river. Spend a day chasing 'bows from Rainbow Springs to Blair Bridge, a float of about five miles. Then switch to browns on the morrow on the mileage from Blair Bridge to Dawt Mill.

As one would expect, the river is popular with canoeists and they float it mightily in summer months. But in spring and fall, when the fishing is arguably best, they are largely gone. And in the winter, when the fishing can be superb, canoes are a rarity. If you're looking for solitude, serenity, and trout that make your reel sizzle, the North Fork may be just your potion.

RESOURCES

Gearing up: Bass Pro Shop, 1935 S. Campbell, Springfield, MO 65807; 417-887-7334; www.basspro.com.

Blue Ribbon Flies, 1343 Hwy. 5, Mountain Home, AR 72653; 870-425-0447; www.mtnhome.net/brf/.

Accommodations: River of Life Farm, Rte. 1, Box 4560, Dora, MO 65637; 417-261-7777; www.riveroflifefarm.com.

Twin Bridges Canoe and Campground, HC 64, Box 230, West Plains, MO 65775; 417-256-7507; www.twinbridgescanoe.com.

Books: *Fly Fishing for Trout in Missouri* by Chuck and Sharon Tryon, Ozark Mountain Fly Fishers.

50 BOIS BRULE RIVER

Location: Northwestern Wisconsin.
Short take: The "real" Brule with really big fish.
Type of stream: Freestone.
Angling methods: Fly, spin.
Species: Brook, brown, rainbow, chinook, coho.
Access: Moderate.
Season: March through mid-November.
Supporting services: Brule, Superior, Iron River.
Handicapped access: Yes.
Closest TU chapter: Wild Rivers.

FALL COMES EARLY TO THE BOIS BRULE, which drains into Lake Superior east of Duluth. Maples begin to color up in late August and birch leaves start to flutter gold after first frost early in September. By then, the fall run of steelhead is well underway and it will reach its peak before Columbus Day. They join chinook that began entering the river in July and streams of lake-run browns that began coming up at the same time. Coho are the last to arrive; their runs begin in late August. Add healthy populations of brookies, browns, and rainbows, and you'll know why this is the "river of presidents." Ulysses S. Grant was the first of a handful of American presidents that include Grover Cleveland, Calvin Coolidge, Herbert Hoover, and Dwight D. Eisenhower to fish the Bois Brule.

A river with a personality that's definitely split, the first 20 miles or so of the Bois Brule drains a bog of kettle ponds and scruffy forest of mixed alder, aspen, fir, and spruce. Ambling along the way a puppy might explore a new backyard, the river's imperceptible current picks up the flows of scores of unnamed springs and rivulets. Where it flows over beds of gravel, its waters glisten as if they were gold. Its depths are black as onyx. The dimple by the drowned spruce sweeper is a wild brookie. Regulations governing the mileage between County Highway S down to County Highway B allow anglers to retain only three fish per day—one rainbow of 26 inches or larger, two browns greater than 15 inches, up to three brookies at least 10 inches in length, and no more than three salmon no smaller than 12 inches. North or downstream of the Highway S bridge, the river widens, providing an excellent opportunity to float and fish with flies.

Canoeing is the most popular way to fish this run, which flows through Cedar Island Estate where President Coolidge came to fish. Though the Bois Brule State Forest protects the river, a corridor that stretches from its headwaters to Lake Superior, not all parcels are owned by the state. You'll float past many well-appointed cabins from the 1920s and the 1930s. The run down to the town of Brule resembles a Western meadow stream somewhat like the

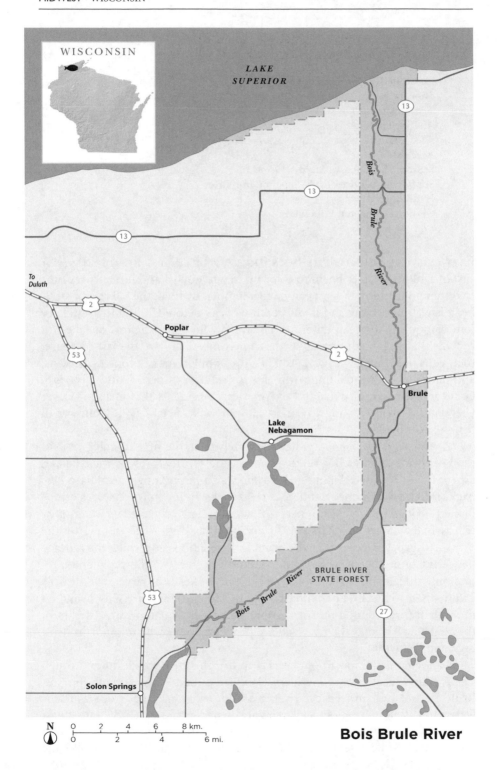

WISCONSIN

LAKE
SUPERIOR

13

Bois

Brule

River

13

To
Duluth

2

Poplar

53

2

Brule

Lake
Nebagamon

53

Bois Brule River

BRULE RIVER
STATE FOREST

27

Solon Springs

N

| 0 | 2 | 4 | 6 | 8 km. |
| 0 | | 2 | | 4 | | 6 mi. |

Bois Brule River

Railroad Ranch section of Henry's Fork. Below the Highway B bridge, limits become more generous, though only one rainbow with a minimum length of 26 inches may be kept.

To this point, about 40 percent of its length, the Bois Brule has dropped less than 100 feet, typical of a pine barrens stream. Below the Highway 2 bridge, all that is about to change. Down-cutting through the Copper Range, the river forges a course over ledges and gardens of angular boulders. Writhing rapids foam as they boil through chutes, spreading for a moment into choppy pools before hustling on again. Steelheaders and anglers seeking salmon and lake-run browns favor this superb pocket water. So that anglers may avail themselves of fall and spring runs, the season begins, here, on the first Saturday in March and concludes on November 15.

"Coasters," the appellation bestowed on Great Lake–run native brook trout, also frequent the Bois Brule. When hooked, they must be immediately released unharmed. Trout Unlimited, in collaboration with the Wisconsin Department of Natural Resources, Bad River Band of Lake Superior Chippewa, Red Cliff Band of Lake Superior Chippewa, and the U.S. Fish and Wildlife Service, is engaged in a massive campaign to understand the behaviors of these wildly gorgeous brookies and to restore their habitat. On the Bois Brule, the Brule River Sportsmen's Club has worked to create new spawning areas by adding gravel to reexpose spawning beds, by breaching beaver dams, and by adding streamside woody debris for cover. This initiative is a major component of TU's larger goal of conserving brook trout and their habitat throughout their native range in the upper Midwest and eastern United States.

RESOURCES

Gearing up: Brule River Classics, 6008 S. State Rte. 28, Brule, WI 54820; 715-372-8153; www.bruleriverclassics.com.

Accommodations: Superior/Douglas County Chamber of Commerce, 205 Belknap St., Superior, WI 54880; 715-394-7716; superiorwi.net.

Books: *Exploring Wisconsin Trout Streams* by Steve Born et al., U. of Wisconsin Press, 1997.

Flyfishers Guide to Wisconsin by John Motoviloff, Wilderness Adventure Press.

Wisconsin and Minnesota Trout Streams by Jim Humphrey and Bill Shogren, Backcountry Publications.

51 KICKAPOO RIVER, WEST FORK

Location: Southwestern Wisconsin.
Short take: Great browns in the most pastoral of settings.
Type of stream: Freestone spring creek.
Angling methods: Fly, spin.
Species: Brown, brook.
Access: Easy.
Season: March through September.
Supporting services: Coon Valley, LaCrosse.
Handicapped access: No.
Closest TU chapter: Coulee Region.

WHEN I HUNG MY HAT IN WINONA, I hooked up with a guy by the name of Dennis Graupe, who ran Spring Creek Angler in Coon Valley. What I knew about fly fishing then you could engrave on the point of a barbless fly. Dennis introduced me to angling in those marvelously gentle, though sometimes cantankerous spring creels that issue forth from the bases of limestone bluff–sided coulees. What wonderful streams they are. Grass overhangs the banks and drags in the water. Browns rise with regularity. At times we could count a dozen 8- to 12-inch browns finning at the head of a pool. Wisconsin's Department of Natural Resources had obtained easements along most of the best water. All you had to do was close gates behind you. Casting was never long nor difficult, though some precision—often more than I could muster then or now—was required to avoid spooking fish.

Among the streams we fished was the West Fork of the Kickapoo River. From its headwaters in the flat remnants of Wisconsin prairie on which sits the town of Cashton, the West Fork of the Kickapoo flows south-southeast for 24 miles before joining the main stem upstream from Readstown. From the headwaters 8.2 miles down to the bridge where State Highway 82 crosses, the river is termed a class I trout stream by Wisconsin DNR, meaning that it can sustain wild trout at or near its natural capacity. Below the bridge, the stream is a class II fishery. Some natural reproduction occurs in these waters and carry-over of adult fish is very good. From 1960 to 1998, brown trout were stocked in the West Fork, but in 1999, consistent with a revived interest in increasing populations of wild brook trout once native to the stream, only brookies were stocked.

In 1996, just as I was pulling up stakes and heading for new digs in Virginia, TU began the Kickapoo Watershed Project, the second after the Beaverkill of its Home Rivers Initiatives. Among the goals of the project was the identification of waters that could sustain brook trout, restoration of suitable habitat, increasing local support for river restoration, involving community members through monitoring and education projects, and tracing progress with an eye

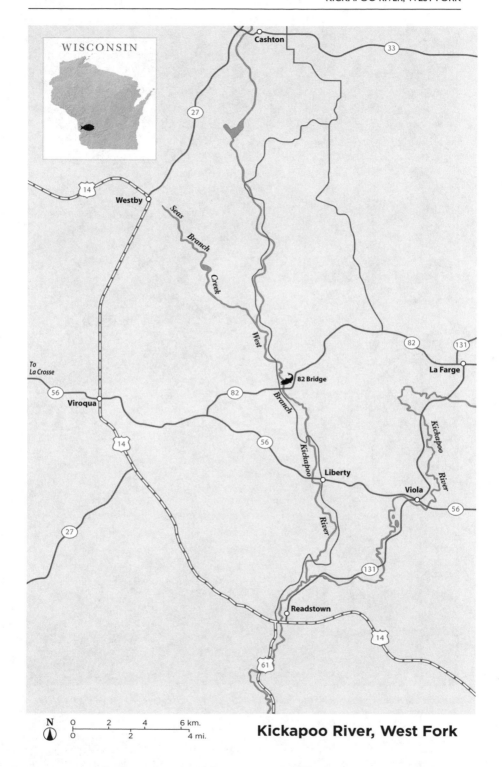

Kickapoo River, West Fork

A stealthy approach is essential if you intend to fool 16- to 18-inch browns on the West Fork of the Kickapoo.

to creating a model that could be applied in other watersheds, as appropriate, across the country. TUers from many local chapters including Coulee Region, Blackhawk in southern Wisconsin, and two suburban Chicago chapters—Lee Wulff and Gary Borger—pitched in with money, labor, or both. They joined forces with Roger Wildner Jr. and other members of the West Fork Sports Club, troops from Wisconsin DNR, and the county Land and Water Conservation offices to repair eroding banks and install overhead cover on many of the streams, including the West Fork. On the Seas Branch, a West Fork tributary where there is a bottom-draw dam, DNR implemented a plan to remove browns from the 11-acre Seas Branch Pond and upstream flows, and replace then with native brook trout transferred from another regional stream. Wild browns continue to flourish in many streams in the Kickapoo system, but native brook trout are expanding their range as conditions improve.

When I fished the West Fork, we caught browns of 10 to 14 inches. I'm told that browns of 16 inches are not all that unusual in the eight miles of catch-and-release water from the State Route 82 bridge upstream to the bridge at Bloomingdale. The stream here is fairly narrow, ranging from 15 to 30 feet in width. For the most part, it flows through grassy pasture past some structures that provide shade in areas otherwise terribly exposed to the sun. In other runs, banks are heavily brushed. In many spots, the river is easily wadable but, often, stealthy casting from the bank is more effective. Patience can bring anglers a few of those phenomenal days of a dozen fish no smaller than 12 inches.

Dry-fly fishing is great fun on this river, whether you're working March Browns in May, Sulphurs in June, Light Cahills, Yellow Sallies, or Caddis (Elkhair Caddis are good almost throughout the season). Terrestrials from July on are very important. Grasshoppers, beetles, crickets, and ants plopped right next to the bank will often draw strikes even on the stillest of days. Anglers seeking big fish throw Muskrats, Grey Woolly Buggers, and Muddlers as dark settles into the valley. Many of the streams that feed the West Fork are themselves excellent fisheries, and they provide a bit of a safety valve for the numbers of anglers who have discovered the main river. And, while the premier water is centered on the small hamlet of Avalanche, the mileage downstream from the Route 82 bridge holds some very big browns. The West Fork is bridged in more than a dozen places, and access from County Road S, which runs the course of the river, is more than ample.

RESOURCES

Gearing up: Spring Creek Anglers, P.O. Box 283, 219 Coon Valley, WI 54623; 608-452-3430.

Accommodations: Westby Area Chamber of Commerce, P.O. Box 94, 514 S. Main St., Suite D, Westby, WI 54667, 608-634-4011; www.westbywi.com.

Books: *Exploring Wisconsin Trout Streams* by Steve Born et al., U. of Wisconsin Press.

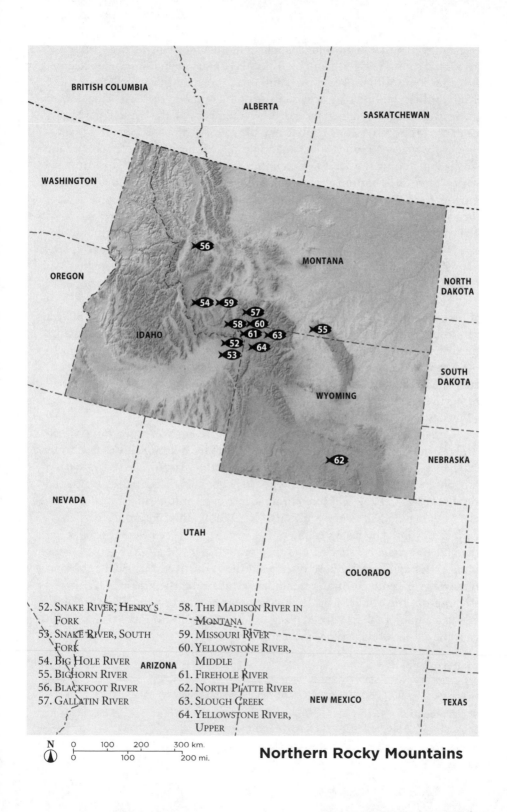

BRITISH COLUMBIA

ALBERTA

SASKATCHEWAN

WASHINGTON

OREGON

MONTANA

IDAHO

56

54 59

57

58 60

52 61 63

53 64

55

NORTH DAKOTA

SOUTH DAKOTA

WYOMING

62

NEBRASKA

NEVADA

UTAH

COLORADO

52. SNAKE RIVER, HENRY'S
    FORK
53. SNAKE RIVER, SOUTH
    FORK
54. BIG HOLE RIVER
55. BIGHORN RIVER
56. BLACKFOOT RIVER
57. GALLATIN RIVER

58. THE MADISON RIVER IN
    MONTANA
59. MISSOURI RIVER
60. YELLOWSTONE RIVER,
    MIDDLE
61. FIREHOLE RIVER
62. NORTH PLATTE RIVER
63. SLOUGH CREEK
64. YELLOWSTONE RIVER,
    UPPER

ARIZONA

NEW MEXICO

TEXAS

N

0   100   200   300 km.
0   100   200 mi.

Northern Rocky Mountains

NORTHERN ROCKY MOUNTAINS

IDAHO

MONTANA

WYOMING

52 SNAKE RIVER, HENRY'S FORK

Location: Eastern Idaho.
Short take: Ever popular, even when plagued by low flows, Henry's Fork is three rivers in one. Pick the stretch that matches your mood.
Type of stream: Freestone.
Angling methods: Fly, spin.
Species: Rainbow in upper reaches; brown and rainbow below Mesa Falls.
Access: Easy to moderate.
Season: Varies by section, check current Idaho regulations. Harriman Ranch, June 15 through November 30.
Supporting services: Last Chance.
Handicapped access: Yes, below Island Park Dam.
Closest TU chapters: Teton Valley, Upper Snake.

FOR MANY FLY FISHERS, HENRY'S FORK OF THE SNAKE IS MECCA. It's three rivers in one: roiling pocket water, a silken spring creek, miles of heavy riffles and runs—all home to brawny rainbows and browns. Pick the mileage that matches your mood. If #20s and gossamer tippets turn you on, hike the mile plus into Millionaire's Pool on the Railroad Ranch, pretend you're a Harriman or a Guggenheim and that you're a major shareholder in the Union Pacific, unlimber your Payne or Leonard, and cast gently to the bruiser sipping where grass from the bank drags in the water. If patience ain't your cup of tea, hustle your bod to the launch below Island Park Dam, climb aboard a rubber raft, chuck Bead Head Woolly Buggers, and pick 'bows from the Box Canyon's pockets.

Rising in a bowl framed by the Continental Divide's 10,000-foot peaks, Henry's Fork cuts across the crater of a dormant volcano before plunging over its rim some 180 feet to the flat prairie below. Drawing its first waters from half a dozen creeks that feed Henry's Lake, Henry's Fork isn't much more than a thin, little, and sometimes warm stream that wanders a dozen miles to the southeast before meeting up with frigid waters issuing from Big Springs. Most anglers overlook this run, but early in the season large rainbows cluster in the section between U.S. Route 20 and the lake. There's no fishing in Big Springs—its gravel channel is a prime nursery for the stream's rainbows, and any time of year you can see really huge 'bows cruising back and forth at the observation walkway over the spring. Below Big Springs, Henry's Fork becomes fishable. Though often crowded with tubers and swimmers, the section below Mack's Inn through Coffee Pot Rapids to McRae Bridge is easy to reach, regularly stocked, and a great place for beginners.

The main event, and most popular section of Henry's Fork, begins in the tailwater beneath Island Park Dam. Access here is easy, and nymphing when the water's off can be quite productive. Many anglers park at the access, make a few casts in the quarter-mile run below the dam, and then fish their way up

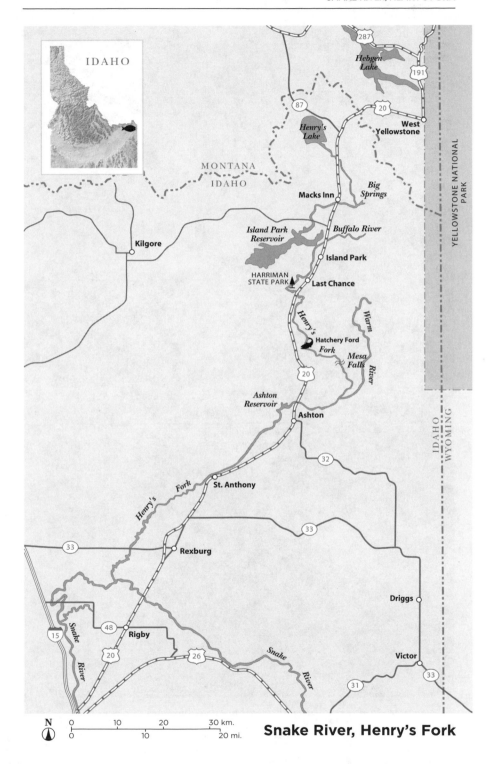

IDAHO

Hebgen
Lake

287

191

87

Henry's
Lake

West
Yellowstone

20

MONTANA
IDAHO

Big
Springs

Macks Inn

Island Park
Reservoir

Buffalo River

Kilgore

Island Park

HARRIMAN
STATE PARK

Last Chance

Henry's

Warm

Hatchery Ford

Fork

Mesa
Falls

River

20

YELLOWSTONE NATIONAL PARK

Ashton
Reservoir

Ashton

32

IDAHO
WYOMING

Henry's

Fork

St. Anthony

33

33

Rexburg

Driggs

Snake

15

48

20

Rigby

26

Snake

River

Victor

31

33

Snake River, Henry's Fork

N

| 0 | 10 | 20 | 30 km. |
| 0 | | 10 | 20 mi. |

Fishing a rise on Henry's Fork is something every trout angler needs to experience at least once in an angling career.

the Buffalo River. The Buffalo gives Henry's Fork a shot in the arm. For three miles, the river cuts down between a set of low basalt bluffs in mileage that's known as Box Canyon. Best access is by boat, though some paths lead from the old road that swings west of US 20 between Last Chance and Island Park. From July through August, the irrigation season, flows are heavy in the Box and wading can be treacherous. Floating is, then, the most productive way to cover the water. In June, after spring melt has surged through, and in September, wading allows thorough fishing of pockets behind angular boulders.

Rainbows of 20 inches plus are frequently hung in these stretches on big nymphs—Rubber Legs, Stones, Bitch Creek are all good—and once in a while on dries. This section is catch-and-release only, but it's open to spin fishermen, though very few hardware hurlers fish it. The angler who hurls a zero-sized Mepps or tiny Panther Martin won't be disappointed. You'll find more big fish in the Box than elsewhere on the river, but if stalking trout is your game, you'll have more fun on the 13-mile section that runs through Harriman State Park to Riverside Campground. Here is Henry's Fork at its most challenging. Above Last Chance—a wide spot in the road known for superb fly shops—the river gradient flattens and the stream takes on the characteristics of a spring creek. Aquatic grasses undulate with the current. Trout, some of them huge, lie and wait for just the right pattern and presentation. If you have the innate coordination that allows long and graceful and accurate casts, fire away. You're in fat city. But the angler who wades carefully will generally get close enough to deliver the pattern du jour with ample subtlety for the requisite drag-free float. Float tubes are also used on this stretch, and many outfitters run driftboats through as well. For me, there's nothing like spotting a fish, working it, and then getting the take.

Downstream from Osborne Bridge, the river begins to flex its muscle. The bed is increasingly rocky. Fish tend to be smaller than in the Box and Harriman sections, but they are more aggressive. Anglers traveling on shank's mare will find access at Pinehaven and from a woods road that runs west to the river from Osborne Springs. Launch ramps at Riverside and Hatchery Ford provide access. Park and hike a mile or so up or downstream before you wet a line. The four-mile float between these two launch sites is one of the prettiest and most productive on Henry's Fork. Nobody floats the next section—there are no other takeouts above Mesa Falls where the river charges over ledges of 65 feet and 115 feet, respectively. Trails lead down the cliffs to generally good and little-fished runs below the falls. If scenery and solitude soothe your soul—and you don't mind a bit of a climb (the section is called "Cardiac Canyon")—this may be the run for you.

Access eases at the bridge below the mouth of the Warm River, itself a pretty good stream. Along the north bank, the river is followed by a road, and on the south, an abandoned railroad grade. Best angling occurs here with the salmon fly hatch in late May, but it's consistently good throughout the season. Browns make their first appearance in Henry's Fork below Mesa Falls, though

rainbows outnumber them. Due east of Ashton, a dam by the same name impounds the river. The tailwater running from the base of the dam to Chester is
an increasingly ill-kept secret. Rainbows are fat, stream gradient is modest, the
bottom's cobbly and not hard to wade, and spring seeps like its course. Angling pressure picks up with the salmon fly hatch, but the savvy fly fisher plans
a visit in spring. Baetis variations begin coming off in mid-March, and caddis
begin to show up in late April. By mid-June, caddis hatches have become
prodigious. The river runs heavy with irrigation flows through much of the
summer but returns to normal in September.

That Henry's Fork continues to be an extremely productive fishery is due
in large measure to the labors and foresight of Mike Lawson, founder of
Henry's Fork Anglers, stellar guide, and author. Mike is prominent among
those who founded the Henry's Fork Foundation, a model public/private
partnership that has stewarded the river through tough times. Water flows
have always been an issue on Henry's Fork. For generations, only agriculture,
hydropower, mining, and manufacturing were considered important enough
to be legally entitled to place demands on stream flows. Since the 1980s with
the creation of the Henry's Fork Foundation, efforts have moved forward to
build a public-private partnership to re-establish healthy flows in this, Idaho's
most famous trout river. Trout Unlimited's Idaho Water Office is facilitating
cooperation among the Bureau of Reclamation, the Fremont-Madison Irrigation District, the Idaho Department of Fish and Game, and other stakeholders
to ensure that the ecology of the river is managed for a sustainable recreational
fishery. Policy leaders in Idaho, as elsewhere in the West, are coming to realize
that sport fishing is a rich and renewable economic resource, one that provides income and jobs to thousands of residents who live in the small towns
adjacent to the state's magnificent trout rivers.

RESOURCES

Gearing up: Henry's Fork Anglers, HC66, Box 491, Island Park, ID 83429-0491;
208-558-7525; www.henrysforkanglers.com.

Trout Hunter, 3327 N. Hwy. 20, Island Park, ID 83429; 208-558-9900;
wwww.trouthunt.com.

Conservation information: Henry's Fork Foundation, P.O. Box 550, Ashton, ID 83420;
208-652-3567; www.henrysfork.com.

Accommodations: Island Park Area Chamber of Commerce, P.O. Box 83, Island Park, ID
83429; 208-558-7755; www.islandparkchamber.org.

Books: *Flyfisher's Guide to Idaho* by Ken Retallic and Rocky Barker, Wilderness Adventure
Press.

Fly Fishing the Henry's Fork by Mike Lawson and Gary LaFontaine, Lyons Press.

Home Waters by Joseph Monninger, Broadway Books.

Idaho Blue-Ribbon Fly Fishing Guide by John Shewey, Frank Amato Publications.

River Journal: Henry's Fork by Larry Tullis, Frank Amato Publications.

53 SNAKE RIVER, SOUTH FORK

Location: Southwest Idaho.
Short take: A river of big cutts, big browns, and rainbows you can eat.
Type of stream: Tailwater.
Angling methods: Fly, spin.
Species: Cutthroat, brown, rainbow.
Access: Limited wading.
Season: Year-round.
Supporting services: Tackle shops, accommodations along river.
Handicapped access: Yes.
Closest TU chapter: Upper Snake.

BRAWLING OUT OF PALISADES DAM JUST WEST OF IDAHO'S BORDER
with Wyoming, the South Fork of the Snake has long been praised as a fine
tailwater for browns and eager-to-please large-spotted Yellowstone Cutthroat.
Rainbows, too, cruise the 60 miles of the South Fork below the dam. Among
the three, 18-inch fish are not at all rare. Big uglies—Woolly Buggers, Bead
Head Rubber Legs, and other garish streamers—fired tight against rocky
banks, undercut cliffs, and edges where grass overhangs the river produce excellent fish even in times of high flows.

Big news on the South Fork is this: keep all the rainbows you catch and eat
'em. They're delicious, and you'll be doing the river a favor. Introduced into
the South Fork off and on since the late 1890s, and stocked more heavily and
consistently in the 1970s and early 1980s, rainbows are out-competing the native Yellowstone cutts. Electroshocking over the past decade shows a dramatic
increase of rainbows and a corresponding decline in cutthroat. According to
Idaho fisheries managers, low winter releases from Palisades Dam favored
rainbows that spawn in the main river channel and inhibited propagation of
cutts that favor tributaries.

In one of the most enlightened bits of fish management policy ever to
grace a major watershed, a coalition of government and private organizations
including Trout Unlimited hatched a plan to restore the South Fork to promi-
nence as a native cutthroat river. The campaign rests on three legs: manage
flows to minimize rainbow spawning success, protect tributaries to maximize
propagation of cutts, and enlist anglers in the campaign to transform the fishery. Central to the campaign is the financial commitment of Mark Rockefeller,
owner of South Fork Lodge.

Traditionally, river managers would draw down Palisades Reservoir in
March and April so that it could absorb run-off from the Tetons and the upper
Snake watershed in Yellowstone National Park. But Idaho game and fish biologists found that high flows in May and June favored cutthroat. After extensive
negotiations with agricultural interests who own rights to the river's water,

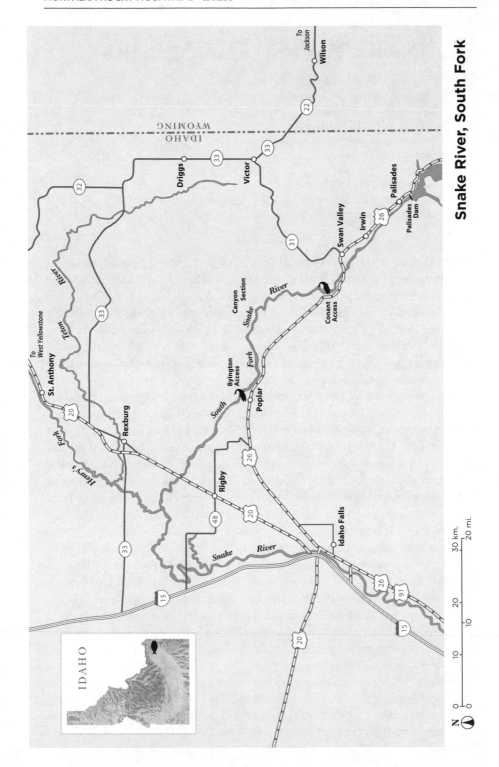

Snake River, South Fork

The South Fork is a great destination river—and the focus of an intense effort to restore native cutthroats. You'll find browns here, too.

flows were reduced in early spring and raised in May and June to flush fertile rainbow eggs from their redds. Weirs were established on primary cutthroat spawning streams to remove hybrid cuttbows and rainbows for transportation to lakes and ponds, and the tributaries were closed to angling until July 1. Anglers are now encouraged to keep all the rainbows they catch and required to release cutthroat unharmed. And the river was opened to fishing all year. Five tributary creeks—Prichard, Garden, Rainey, Trout, and Little Burns—are sites of conservation efforts as well. On Prichard, for instance, TU is working with a landowner to install stock-watering systems and fencing that replace impassable barriers, channel restoration, replacement of fish-blocking culverts, and habitat-enhancing plantings. Numerous county, state, and federal agencies—and scores of landowners—are collaborating in these efforts.

Angling on the South Fork in March and April can be awesome. Blue-Winged Olives and Midges can be productive on top, the best action is on streamers and big nymphs. The river is virtually empty of other anglers. During high flows of May and June, streamers continue to be most productive. But in late June and well into July, Salmon Flies, Golden Stones, and Yellow Sallies all offer dry-fly action. Terrestrials take over from here on out, along with Caddis, Mahogany Duns, and, again, Blue-Winged Olives as fall weather brings temperatures down.

For the first 14 miles from the dam to Conant, the river runs through the Swan Valley, an increasingly broad floodplain bounded by palisades of basalt. Eagles nest in the tops of cottonwoods; some trees have survived more than three centuries, making them among the oldest of the species in the country. Below Conant, the Snake enters the section called the "Canyon," but in reality this mileage passes a number of small 300-foot to 400-foot canyons—Dry, Ladder, Black, Bums—before emerging at Byington launch ramp near the town of Poplar. In the canyon, the river is narrower and water deeper. Yet, numerous islands divert the flow adding structure that holds fish. Below Byington, the river braids in a manner similar to the runs above Jackson in Wyoming. Channels fork to the left and right, and many lead to log jams impassable by driftboat—the preferred way to fish the river.

Most anglers think of the South Fork as a river for summer and fall—a tableau of deep, clear water flowing through a landscape of tawny yellows, dusty green cottonwoods, and dark lodgepole pine poking fingers up slopes of gray stone. In April, the Snake Valley blossoms with a verdance akin to Ireland. Fields kelly green with new barley and winter wheat cap the palisades, pods of yellow daisy-like flowers riot on sunny hillsides, and the sky shifts from bright and sunny to brooding cloud and back again in less time than it takes to tell. This is the Snake's second season, and it may be its best.

Much of the land along the river is privately owned. Opportunities for wading are limited to the waters near boat launches. Most productive is fishing the river from a driftboat, and a number of outfitters along its course provide that service. Some hostelries, such as South Fork Lodge at Conant, offer ample and interesting river frontage that can be waded. Were I planning the ideal weeklong angling vacation, I'd hole up in southeast Idaho. I'd divide my time between the South Fork's cutts and browns and rainbows on Henry's Fork, an hour or so north. Should I tire of either or both—which isn't at all likely—head for the Teton and Warm rivers, or hustle my bones to Flat Creek above Jackson, Wyoming—an hour and a half to the east—to be humbled by its finicky rainbows.

RESOURCES

Gearing up: South Fork Outfitters, P.O. Box 22, Swan Valley, ID 83449; 800-483-2110 or 208-483-7052; www.southforkanglers.com.

Accommodations: Idaho Falls Convention and Visitor's Bureau, P.O. Box 50498, 630 W. Broadway, Idaho Falls, ID 83405; 866-365-6943; www.visitidahofalls.com.

Books: *Flyfisher's Guide to Idaho* by Ken Retallic, Wilderness Adventures Press.

Guide to Fly Fishing in Idaho by Bill Mason, David Communications.

Idaho Blue-Ribbon Fly Fishing Guide by John Shewey, Frank Amato Publications.

Snake River Country Flies and Water by Bruce Staples, Frank Amato Publications.

Snake River Secrets by Lanny Hayward, Frank Amato Publications.

54 BIG HOLE RIVER

Location: Southwest Montana.
Short take: Marvelous river of many species, but subject to low flows.
Type of stream: Freestone.
Angling methods: Fly, spin.
Species: Brown, rainbow, cutthroat, brook, grayling.
Access: Moderate.
Season: Varies—generally late May through November.
Supporting services: Wisdom, Wise River, Twin Bridges.
Handicapped access: No.
Closest TU chapter: Lewis and Clark.

THOUGH ONE OF THE MOST POPULAR TROUT RIVERS IN THE WEST, the Big Hole is also among the most fragile. Irrigation demands and drought often leave it with little water—some sections become all but dry—adding stress to one of the few populations of fluvial grayling found in the United States. In 2004, the Montana Department of Fish, Wildlife and Parks was forced to close the upper river from the junction of the North Fork down to Rock Creek Road, a distance of about 19 miles. It was the fifth year in a row that sections of the river, some as long as 74 miles, had been shut down to angling. During periods of minimal flow, the river warms into the mid-70s and above. Trout hooked and played under such conditions may survive, but their chances are not good.

TU, in partnership with the Big Hole Watershed Committee and the Montana Department of Fish, Wildlife, and Parks and other state and federal agencies, developed a drought management plan that includes "flow triggers" to protect the river and its fish. The first trigger employs a phone tree to inform landowners throughout the basin of the current drought conditions and forecasts and asks that water use be reduced when necessary. The second sends out a notice to anglers and outfitters requesting angling activities to be limited to the morning hours, when angling pressure is least stressful to fish. The third and most serious causes a fishing closure for that reach.

Fluvial arctic grayling, known as much for their eager feeding as for their purple-hued, plume-like dorsal fin, were native to Michigan (as in grayling on the Au Sable) and Montana. The Michigan population is considered extinct. The largest remaining population is found in the Big Hole in the vicinity of Wisdom, but degradation of habitat, introduction of exotic species (brookies, browns, and rainbows), climatic change, and angling pressure are reducing their numbers. If caught, grayling must be promptly and safely released.

Rising in the Beaverhead Mountains above Jackson, the Big Hole flows in a broad arc north around the Pioneer Mountains before bending south and passing the town of Divide. At the village of Glen, the river bends back toward the northeast before joining the Beaverhead west of Twin Bridges. The course

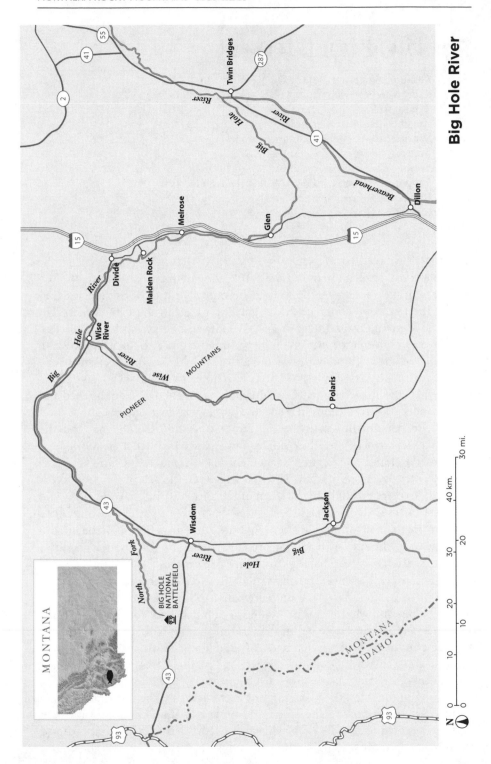

Big Hole River

The upper Big Hole supports a healthy population of rare and beautiful Montana grayling.

of the river covers 153 miles. Over the distance, the river grows from a tiny stream filled with brookies and cutthroat to a major river known for its browns. The wide and flat Big Hole Valley, green and tawny with its season, is among the most scenic in the West, rimmed as it is by deeply forested mountains that climb to rocky 10,000-foot peaks. This is Big Country.

It's also country of tragic history. As the North Fork of the Big Hole breaks out of the mountains and into the broad alluvial plain, its main channel runs through the camping place of Nez Perce Indians, who fled U.S. Army soldiers and homesteaders into Montana rather than be corralled on a reservation. With the dawn of August 9, 1877, troopers under Colonel John Gibbon attacked the sleeping village. Women and children fled their teepees and hid themselves in the waters of the North Fork as best they could beneath undercut banks that shelter brook trout today. As the battle surged up the slope of a nearby ridge, the women and children fled the stream. Surviving braves joined them later, and together they set off on a wandering, starving odyssey that would lead them through Yellowstone and into Canada before surrender.

At Big Hole National Battlefield, bones of the Nez Perce camp line the North Fork, and in their shadow, brookies and cutts and rainbows of a foot or so readily take dries, particularly the usual attractors. Better brook trout are found in the main fork of the river in the vicinity of Jackson. The two stems join at Wisdom, so named by Lewis and Clark for one of Thomas Jefferson's virtues. Below Wisdom, the broad valley narrows and the pace of the river quickens. The farther downstream one goes, the bigger the rainbows grow. Access is more than ample. Wading is easy. Prior to spring runoff, streamers lure healthy 'bows from pockets behind boulders and tree trunks washed into the river. After the surge passes, typically in late May, trout key on caddis. June brings salmon flies, and the word is that big nymphs in sizes 2 to 6 take more big fish than dries. Your choice.

A couple miles below Wise River, where the same-named river enters from the south, the Big Hole Valley tightens into a modest canyon. Many consider this the premier section of the river. Large browns dominate. The river breaks out of the canyon above Divide but pushes on through terrain of mixed boulder runs, gravel riffles, and long flats. Access varies as well. Much of the better water requires a hike of a mile or more up or downstream from designated access points. The salmon fly hatch in this section is prodigious as are, alas, the number of anglers who appear. Below Melrose, the valley widens and the river slows and warms. Access is more difficult for the foot-bound angler, and most tourists hire guides with driftboats. If truly large browns are your quarry, forget dries except in the heaviest hatches and toss big nymphs and streamers. Sink tip lines are useful here. From Glen down to Twin Bridges, the river loses too much water to irrigation and warms so significantly that it is best fished only in spring and fall. No longer shadowed by a highway, access is limited. Few outfitters float this section.

RESOURCES

Gearing up: Conover's General Store, Box 84, Hwy. 43, Wisdom, MT 59761; 406-689-3272.

Troutfitters, 62311 Hwy. 43, Wise River, MT 59762; 406-832-3212.

Frontier Anglers, 680 N. Montana, Dillon, MT 59725; 800-228-5263; www.frontier-anglers.com.

Accommodations: Beaverhead Chamber of Commerce, 125 S. Montana St., Dillon, MT 59725; 406-683-5511; www.bmt.net/~chamber/.

Books: *Fishing Montana* by Michael S. Sample, Falcon Press.

The Montana Angling Guide by Chuck Fothergill and Bob Sterling, Stream Stalker Publishing Co.

Montana Blue-Ribbon Fly Fishing Guide by Steve Probasco, Frank Amato Publications.

Montana Fly Fishing Guide West by John Holt, Lyons Press.

River Journal: Big Hole by Steve Probasco, Frank Amato Publications.

55 BIGHORN RIVER

Location: South-central Montana.
Short take: Classic western tailwater, sans solitude.
Type of stream: Tailwater.
Angling methods: Fly, spin.
Species: Rainbow, brown.
Access: Moderate.
Season: Year-round.
Supporting services: Fort Smith, Hardin.
Handicapped access: No.
Closest TU chapter: Magic City.

THOUGH IT GATHERS ITS WATERS FROM THE Wind River Range in Wyoming, the Bighorn is Montana's quintessential tailwater. Flows issuing from the base of Yellowtail Dam just south of Fort Smith are stabilized in an afterbay. They then feed into the gentle cobble-bottomed river that braids around islands and rushes past banks heavy with silvery-leaved Russian olive and shaded by cottonwood. The river runs clear and cold and is open to fishing year-round.

Quality water on the Bighorn is short. Only the first 13 miles from the afterbay to Bighorn access are considered truly excellent trout habitat. However, don't overlook the slower and less crowded run from Bighorn down to Two Leggins. Both browns and rainbows abound in the upper reach with typical fish averaging about 15 inches. The lower section contains a larger percentage of browns, though not nearly as many as the top water. Bounded by land of the Crow reservation, this run of the river is open to the public and can be fished without a special tribal permit.

Summer, of course, draws thousands of anglers to the Bighorn. They come to fish Blue-Winged Olives and Parachute Adamses and the usual nymphs—Hare's Ear, Pheasant Tail, and Prince. Little Yellow Stones appear in July when caddis patterns begin to produce as well. Caddis fishing swings into high gear in August when pale Morning Duns also get cranking. The Trico hatch in September is exceptional. As this is a tailwater, it's quite fishable in winter, and midge hatches bring good strikes from rainbows.

I'll have to admit that I have little stomach for crowds. But that's not the only reason my favorite time to float the Bighorn is early November. I know of no better river for decoying ducks and geese and jumping pheasants on grassy islands while nymphing for browns and rainbows in between. If you're of a mind and pocketbook to do so, book into one of the lodges along the river and arrange to hunt pheasants, chukar, huns, and sage grouse. Ducks with the dawn, ringnecks before lunch, an 18-inch brown on a 5-weight, and a brace of geese as dusk fades the Beartooths. Now that's my idea of a perfect day.

Bighorn River

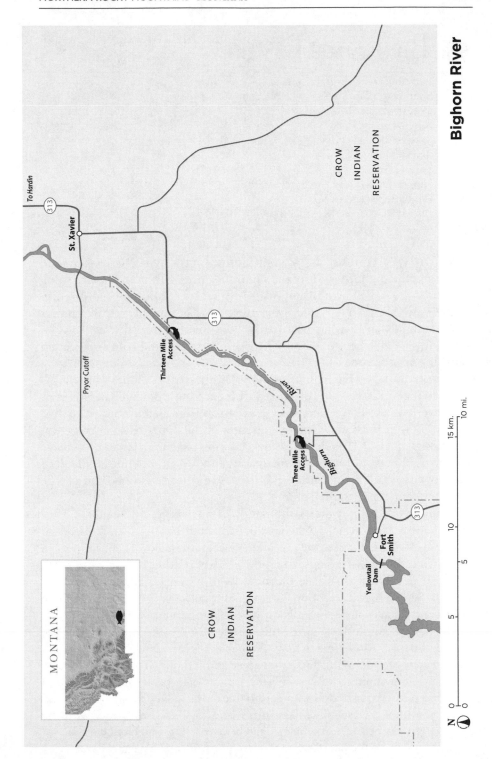

CROW INDIAN RESERVATION

To Hardin

St. Xavier

Pryor Cutoff

Thirteen Mile Access

River

Three Mile Access

Bighorn

Yellowtail Dam

Fort Smith

MONTANA

CROW INDIAN RESERVATION

N

15 km.

10 mi.

The Bighorn River below Fort Smith provides trophy trout for browns and rainbows throughout the year.

Headquarters for fishing the Bighorn are found at Fort Smith, an old and tiny town at the base of the dam at the end of Route 313, and downstream at Hardin where Interstate 90 crosses the river. The closest airport with commercial flights is Billings, about 55 miles west of Hardin. If you're in this region, and haven't yet done so, you owe yourself a drive to the Little Bighorn Battlefield National Monument—12 miles east of Hardin—and an early-morning walk among the white marble stones that mark where each of Custer's men died.

RESOURCES

Gearing up: Big Horn Fly and Tackle Shop, P.O. Box 7597, Fort Smith, MT 59035; 406-666-2253; www.bighornfly.com.

Accommodations: Hardin Area Chamber of Commerce, 15 Fourth St. E, Hardin, MT 59034-1826; 406-665-1672.

Books: *Fishing Montana* by Michael S. Sample, Falcon Press.

Flyfisher's Guide to Montana by Greg Thomas, Wilderness Adventure Press.

Montana Blue-Ribbon Fly Fishing Guide by Steve Probasco, Frank Amato Publications.

56 Blackfoot River

Location: Western Montana.
Short take: Upper reaches hold brookies and some of the last fluvial grayling in the United States.
Type of stream: Freestone.
Angling methods: Fly, spin.
Species: Browns, rainbow, cutthroat, bull.
Access: Easy.
Season: Varies—generally late May through November.
Supporting services: Missoula Lower waters, great browns.
Handicapped access: No.
Closest TU chapter: Big Blackfoot.

On the Big Blackfoot River above the mouth of Belmont Creek, the banks are fringed by large Ponderosa pines. In the slanting sun of late afternoon, the shadows of great branches reached from across the river, and the trees took the river in their arms. The shadows continued up the bank, until they included us.
—Norman Maclean, *A River Runs Through It and Other Stories,* 1976.

"It's a goddamned mess now, loaded with boats and people," he said. "To me, it's a piece of horror."—Norman Maclean on the Big Blackfoot as reported by Ginny Merriam from a 1987 interview in the *Missoulan.*

THE CURSE OF PUBLICITY PLAGUES SCORES OF FINE RIVERS (the most popular of which are included in this book, an irony with which I wrestle daily). There's no doubt that Norman Maclean's nostalgic novella drew hordes of anglers to the Big Blackfoot, stripping it of the solitude that he so valued. On the other hand, I can't help but wonder if the environmental community would have become as galvanized as they have to save the Big Blackfoot had the Mike Horse Mine debacle—100,000 tons of toxic, heavy metals–rich tailings washed into the upper Blackfoot when the company's waste-impounding dam failed in 1975—occurred on a river other the one made famous by Maclean's book and Robert Redford's movie adaptation.

For better or worse, the Big Blackfoot will ever be an icon. As this is being written, an informal coalition formed by the Big Blackfoot Chapter of TU; the U.S. Forest Service; Montana Fish, Parks and Wildlife (MFPW); The Nature Conservancy; and others continues to restore habitat—350 miles of streams, 2,500 acres of wetlands, 70,000 acres protected by conservation easement—and, at the same time, maintain ranching, public recreation, forestry, and wildlife habitat. This effort will persist as long as there are anglers who hold dear the vision of the river presented by Maclean.

For 132 miles, the Big Blackfoot flows from its headwaters near the continental divide to its confluence with the Bitterroot on the outskirts of Missoula.

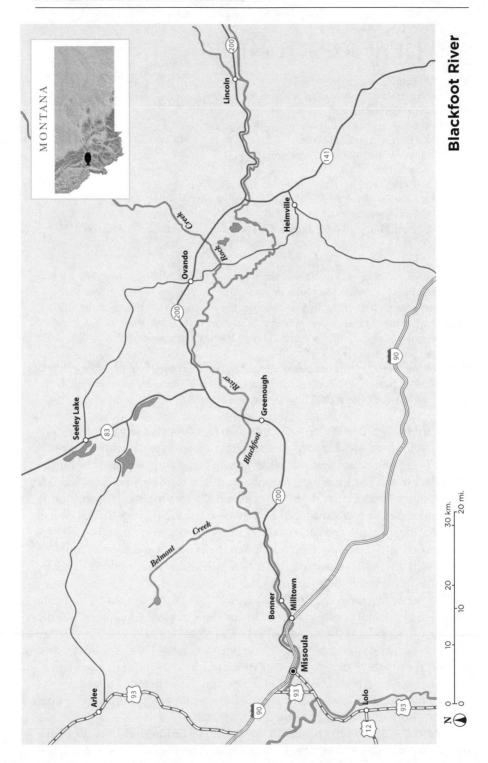

Blackfoot River

The fishable upper reaches, from Lincoln to Cedar Meadows, have pretty well recovered from the Mike Horse Mine disaster. Largish browns are occasionally caught in this relatively slow run of 43 miles. But numbers of fish are not as high as they are farther downstream.

In the 24 miles from Cedar Meadows to Clearwater, the river skirts first Green and then Bucktail mountains to the south and picks up speed. Rainbows make their appearance. Of special interest is a canyon section of about five miles with its increasingly rambunctious flows. From late April into early June runoff makes this mileage difficult to fish. Hardy anglers work it in March and return as soon as the color leaves the water.

Below Clearwater Crossing, the Big Blackfoot cuts through Ninemile Prairie, moving into a rollicking race of 14 miles or so of big boulders, heavy current, deep holes, and occasional long chutes. It is this section of the Big Blackfoot that Maclean, his father, and brother Paul so loved—particularly the water where Belmont Creek enters from the north. Scenic with rapids heavy enough to douse the angler riding a driftboat's bow, pockets in this water give up good rainbows to the usual array of nymphs and streamers. Montana State Route 200 crosses the river at Johnsrud Park, 11 miles east of Bonner. Good fishing continues on downstream, particularly larger streamers and big nymphs, to within a couple of miles from the confluence of Clark Fork at Bonner where the river is impounded.

Low flows, late in the summer of 2004, caused the Blackfoot Drought Response Committee—a partnership between TU, the Blackfoot Challenge, agricultural interests, and MFWP to request that anglers limit fishing to morning hours only and to not fish important bull-trout tributaries. Bull trout must be released as must cutthroat. At present, anglers may harvest rainbows and browns, though creel limits and allowable tackle vary within sections of the river. Check current MFWP regulations before wetting a line.

Toward late season's end or in the deepening gloaming when the air turns faintly lavender and the flotillas of Hydes and Clackacrafts have drifted round the bend, tranquility enfolds you. In this moment of solitude, so rare now but yours if you are patient, you can hear Maclean's cast whisper: "All existence fades to a being with my soul and memories and the sounds of the Big Blackfoot River and a four-count rhythm and the hope that a fish will rise."

RESOURCES

Gearing up: Kesel's Four Rivers, 1522 S. Reserve St., Missoula, MT 59801; 406-721-4796; www.fourrivers.net.

The Kingfisher Fly Shop, 926 E. Broadway, Missoula, MT 59802; 406-721-6141; www.kingfisherflyshop.com.

Accommodations: Missoula Chamber of Commerce, 825 E. Front St., P.O. Box 7577, Missoula, MT 59807; 406-543-6623; www.missoulachamber.com.

Books: *Fishing Montana* by Michael S. Sample, Falcon Press.

Flyfisher's Guide to Montana by Greg Thomas, Wilderness Adventure Press.

The Montana Angling Guide by Chuck Fothergill and Bob Sterling, Stream Stalker Publishing Co.

Montana Blue-Ribbon Fly Fishing Guide by Steve Probasco, Frank Amato Publications.

Montana Fly Fishing Guide West by John Holt, Lyons Press.

57 GALLATIN RIVER

Location: Southwest Montana.
Short take: The river for beginners.
Type of stream: Freestone.
Angling methods: Fly, spin.
Species: Rainbow, cutthroat, brown.
Access: Easy.
Season: Year-round.
Supporting services: Big Sky.
Handicapped access: No.
Closest TU chapter: Gallatin/Madison.

RISING IN A SMALL LAKE BENEATH THREE RIVERS PEAK in the northwest quadrant of Yellowstone National Park, the Gallatin drops about 1,400 feet in its first seven miles before entering a narrow valley where its gradient levels. For the next five miles it winds through a mostly open meadow. Browns, rainbows, and cutthroats, none of them huge but some to 16 inches, hide beneath grassy undercut banks. An easy pack trail running from U.S. Highway 191 over to the national park campground at the confluence of Obsidian and Indian creeks on the Yellowstone loop road rims the north bank. Anglers are more likely to find solitude in this section than on any other of the easily accessible streams in the park.

As it exits Yellowstone and crosses into Montana, the Gallatin enters a tight, narrow valley. Twisting around boulders, coursing down short chutes, swirling in little pools, the river is chased downstream by the highway and fishing pressure is fairly heavy. But, because of the easy access, anglers spread themselves out. Spring melt swells and discolors the Gallatin from mid-May until late June or early July. Fish before or after. For the next 50 miles, with the exceptions of a few short meadow sections, the river is characterized by open riffles, roaring canyon cataracts, and miles of miles of cobble-bedded runs, turns, and pools.

The river holds something for anglers of all skill levels: from the greenest novice who's yet to wet a wader to the grizzled pro who's been there and done that and plans to keep doing it forever. Roughly a third the size of the Yellowstone, and without a major entrance to the park at its headwaters, the valley of the Gallatin lacks the grandeur of its cousin to the east. While it's easy to reach fishable water, private holdings abound and the Gallatin is seeing more than its share of streamside development.

At Cinnamon Station, a one-time rail stop, the Gallatin enters a short canyon about three miles long. You'll find chutes and plunge pools here and some water that holds bigger fish. The canyon opens up into a valley called the Lower Basin and the tourist town of Big Sky—made famous by the late NBC

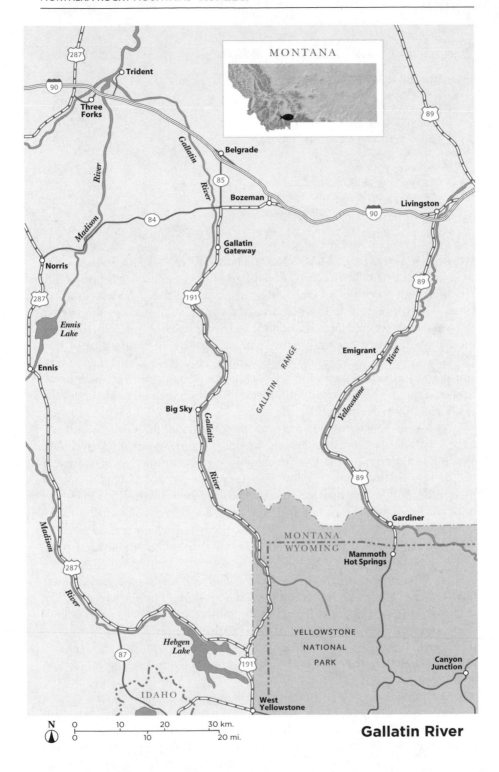

MONTANA

287
90
Trident
Three
Forks
Gallatin
River
Belgrade
85
River
Bozeman
90
Livingston
89
84
Madison
Gallatin
Gateway
Norris
191
89
287
Ennis
Lake
GALLATIN   RANGE
Emigrant
River
Ennis
Big Sky
Gallatin
Yellowstone
River
89
Gardiner
Madison
MONTANA
WYOMING
Mammoth
Hot Springs
287
River
YELLOWSTONE
87
Hebgen
Lake
NATIONAL
191
PARK
Canyon
Junction
IDAHO
West
Yellowstone

N
0   10   20   30 km.
0   10   20 mi.

Gallatin River

TV news anchor Chet Huntley who opened a resort here. The West Fork enters the basin at its northern end, and immediately the river gains volume and drops into a 22-mile canyon of turbulent runs and pools. As lovely as it looks, this water does not hold many large rainbows. The average is a foot or so. But every year a number of 18-inch fish are taken.

The canyon ends at Jack Creek where the Gallatin flows under US 191. From that point, five miles or so to the bridge over the river at Gallatin Gateway is considered best fishing on the river. The current has slowed; gravel runs lead to pools that undercut banks creating holds for larger rainbows and cuttbows (cutthroat-rainbow hybrids). An occasional brown will show up in this stretch, but they are rare. Rainbows, however, are larger than upstream. Downstream, dewatering the river to meet agricultural demands takes a toll on the fishery.

With the waters from the East Gallatin, the river gains the feel of some of the larger Western rivers. For ten miles, the river flows through an intricate riparian zone, heavily brushed, and loaded with wildlife, as well as with big browns under cutbanks and 'bows in the riffles. The best way to fish this water is from a driftboat—legal on this stretch—though the angler who's willing to walk a mile or two from access points such as the bridge at Nixon Gulch will find outstanding sport.

Not a river where matching the hatch is of utmost importance, Caddis and Blue-Winged Olives in spring and fall, with Pale Morning Duns and terrestrials in the height of summer and the usual nymphs and streamers will handle most chores. If runoff has abated (and sometimes it has), the salmon fly hatch in late June and early July can be marvelous. At this writing on the state-controlled waters, no special tackle restrictions are posted. But read the regs before you fish.

RESOURCES

Gearing up: East Slope Anglers, P.O. Box 160249, Big Sky, MT 59716; 406-995-4369; www.eastslopeanglers.com.

Wild Trout Outfitters and Guide Service, P.O. Box 160003, Big Sky, MT 59716; 406-995-2975; www.wildtroutoutfitters.com.

Accommodations: Big Sky Chamber of Commerce, P .O. Box 160100, Big Sky, MT 59716; 800-943-4111; www.bigskychamber.com.

Books: *Fishing Montana* by Michael S. Sample, Falcon Press.

Flyfisher's Guide to Montana by Greg Thomas, Wilderness Adventure Press.

The Montana Angling Guide by Chuck Fothergill and Bob Sterling, Stream Stalker Publishing Co.

Montana Blue-Ribbon Fly Fishing Guide by Steve Probasco, Frank Amato Publications.

58 THE MADISON RIVER IN MONTANA

Location: Southwest Montana.
Short take: The perennial favorite Western river.
Type of stream: Freestone (er . . . tailwater).
Angling methods: Fly, spin.
Species: Browns, rainbow.
Access: Moderate.
Season: Year-round.
Supporting services: Ennis, West Yellowstone.
Handicapped access: No.
Closest TU chapter: Gallatin/Madison.

THERE ARE TIMES I THINK OF THE TRIO of rivers that form and flow out of the volcanic zone that created the Yellowstone National Park caldera as a kind of piscatorial trilogy. The rivers—the Yellowstone, Henry's Fork, and the Madison—are each among the finest in the world. Yet, each is environmentally challenged. The Yellowstone lives with the specter of rainbows and lake trout out-competing native stocks of native cutthroat. Henry's Fork is ever susceptible to flows so low as to trigger fish kills. The Madison is recovering from bouts of whirling disease that greatly diminished its population of rainbows from the outflow of Hebgen Lake to Ennis.

Formed by the confluence of the Gibbon and Firehole rivers at Madison Junction in Yellowstone National Park, the river flows almost due west through the Madison Canyon for about 17 miles along U.S. Route 20 toward West Yellowstone, Montana. Opening on the Saturday of Memorial Day Weekend, the best fishing on park sections occurs with the salmon fly hatch in mid-June. Depending on snowpack depths, spring runoff may have coursed through this area. If so, angling for 'bows may be spectacular. Thereafter, this run settles down and produces average catches on caddis and mayfly patterns. With September's falling temperatures, browns begin to run up from Hegben Lake to spawn in the Madison, Firehole, and Gibbon Rivers. This is a marvelous time to be on the Madison and in Yellowstone.

In the less than two miles between Hebgen Dam and Quake Lake, the Madison gains vigor, plunging around boulders and swirling in dark eddies before hustling on again. Slowing through the lake caused by a landslide in 1959, the river regains its rambunctious character, brawling on for four more miles. For most anglers, this is not dry-fly water. Rather, streamers and big nymphs fished deep produce the best rainbows. Though closed to drift-boats from the lake to Lyon Bridge, fishing pressure is heavy because this

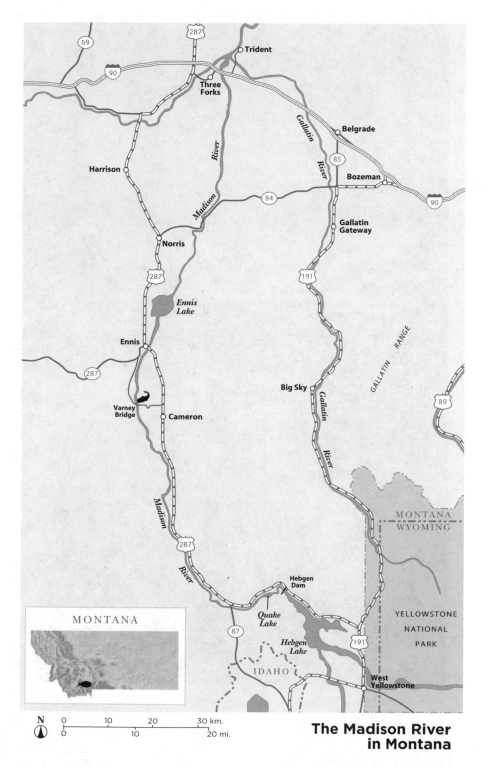

MONTANA

N
0   10   20   30 km.
0   10   20 mi.

**The Madison River
in Montana**

Think of a trout river chattering down a wide valley between fields of sage. That's the Madison.

mileage runs close to U.S. Route 287, and access is easy and ample. It's apt to be crowded.

Below Lyon Bridge, where Forest Service Route 8381 crosses the river, the Madison's gradient lessens and it dons a kinder, gentler persona. Though current is swift, this section of the river is homogenous. Flowing over a stable, cobbly bottom at about five miles per hour, the river bends slightly in its ancient channel but it never meanders. Where gradient is steeper, the water picks up steam. Then it slows and occasional gravel islands appear, but you wouldn't call the channel at all "braided." Patches of cottonwood and brush occasionally line the river, but you'll find little structure from submerged logs. The utter consistency of this stretch, easy wading, agreeable browns and rainbows, and more than a dozen points for public access make this wonderful water for a beginning angler.

From Lyon to Varney Bridge, only artificial lures may be used. Spin fishers will throw Mepps, Panther Martins, Roostertails, and minnow- or crayfish-pattern crankbaits. Anglers of the fly will open the season on those rare windless days in February when the sun feels good on your shoulders as it warms the riverbed just enough to trigger a midge hatch. Nymphing with the Hare's Ear, Prince, Pheasant Tail, and other similar ties begins in earnest in April. Stonefly Nymphs and black, brown, or olive Woolly Buggers pay off as well. After the surge of spring melt passes—usually but not always by the first of July—salmon flies hatch, triggering rapacious feeding by rainbows and browns and drawing hundreds of anglers from all over the world. That opens the summer season, and as water levels begin to drop, the first terrestrials—Hoppers—appear. Standard attractors also work well. In fall, bring out the streamers and large nymphs. Regulations on this section may vary. Read before fishing!

Downstream from Varney Bridge, the river slows further. In the eight miles from the bridge to Ennis, the channel braids. Gentler currents allow trout more time to inspect a fly, thus the demand that casts be precise and floats drag free. Brown trout begin to predominate.

RESOURCES

Gearing up: Blue Ribbon Flies, 305 Canyon St., W. Yellowstone, MT 59758; 406-646-7642; www.blueribbonflies.com.

The Tackle Shop Outfitters, 127 Main St., Box 625, Ennis, MT 59729; 406-682-4263; www.thetackleshop.com.

Madison River Outfitters, Inc. P.O. Box 398, 117 Canyon St., W. Yellowstone, MT 59758; 406-646-9644; www.madisonriveroutfitters.com.

Accommodations: Ennis Chamber of Commerce, Box 291, Ennis, MT 59729; 406-682-4388; www.ennischamber.com.

Books: *Fishing Montana* by Michael S. Sample, Falcon Press.

Fishing Yellowstone National Park by Richard Parks, Falcon Press.

Flyfisher's Guide to Montana by Greg Thomas, Wilderness Adventure Press.

Fly Fishing the Madison by Craig Mathews and Gary LaFontaine, Lyons Press.

The Montana Angling Guide by Chuck Fothergill and Bob Sterling, Stream Stalker Publishing Co.

Montana Blue-Ribbon Fly Fishing Guide by Steve Probasco, Frank Amato Publications.

Montana Fly Fishing Guide West by John Holt, Lyons Press.

River Journal: Madison River by John Holt, Frank Amato Publications.

Waters of Yellowstone with Rod and Fly by Howard Black, Lyons Press.

59 MISSOURI RIVER

Location: West-central Montana.
Short take: Big river, big tailwater, big trout.
Type of stream: Large tailwater.
Angling methods: Fly, spin.
Species: Rainbow, brown.
Access: Easy.
Season: Year-round.
Supporting services: Craig, Carter.
Handicapped access: No.
Closest TU chapter: Pat Barnes Missouri River.

ON JULY 25, 1805, LEWIS AND CLARK reached the confluence of three rivers that joined to form the Missouri. The easternmost of the trio they named for Albert Gallatin, secretary of the treasury in President Thomas Jefferson's cabinet. The middle was named in honor of James Madison, Jefferson's secretary of state and principal negotiator of the purchase of the Louisiana Territory from France. The western prong was named for Jefferson himself. At this junction, the Shoshone had made camp for generations, and it was here that the expedition's guide—Sacagawea—had been captured by the Mandans from whom Lewis and Clark had earlier rescued her.

The main corridor in the country's western expansion, the Missouri River runs for about 2,540 miles before joining the Mississippi north of St. Louis. It is the longest river system in the United States. The very top of it—the 100 miles from Three Forks to Cascade high in Montana's central arid steppe—carries stocks of trout. From the village of Trident just north of the confluence down to Toston Dam, a distance of about 20 miles, the river is subject to heavy sedimentation, fluctuations of spring runoff, warm summer temperatures, and low flows due to irrigation. This run is not much of a trout fishery. Below Toston Dam, an irrigation diversion structure that does little to cool the flows of the upper run of the river, the fishing picks up. From U.S. Route 287, turn east on the Toston Dam road. If you want to fish the west bank, cross the river at Toston and follow Lombard Road south. Some trout hold in this water year-round, but come fall, browns (along with a few rainbows) run up out of Canyon Ferry Lake and in the spring, rainbows do the same. Water levels are lower in the fall, and the fishing is generally best then throughout the reach down to the big lake.

As a lake, Canyon Ferry is wide and shallow and of scant interest to most trout anglers. But the short mile below it is known for big browns and rainbows, and, as a consequence, sees its share of pressure. Highway 284 heads northeast from US 287 at Clasoil, crosses the dam, and provides some access to its tailwater. The water below Hauser Dam flows through a canyon and can

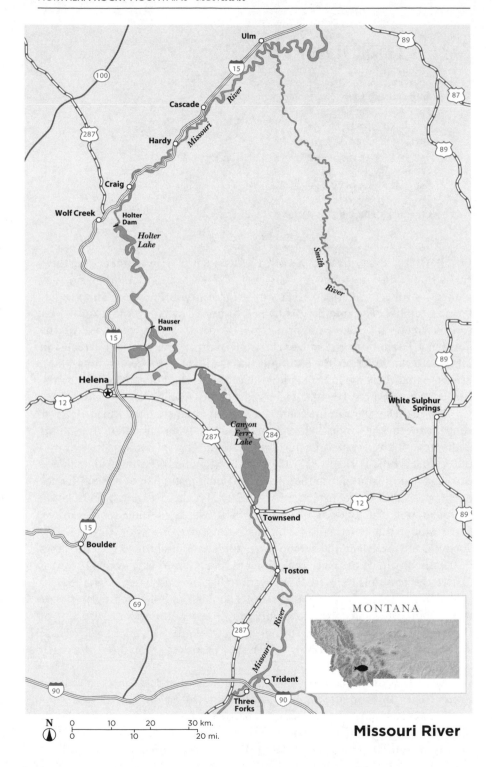

Missouri River

be reached on the construction road that heads north from Highway 453 on the north side of Lake Helena.

Below Holter Dam, the last of the impoundments, the river takes on the appearance of a massive spring creek. The 30 miles down to Cascade draw brigades of anglers. Blue-winged olive hatches in April attract the first battalions. Golden stones follow them in May. The second wave descends in June with the coming of pale morning duns. Caddis are also prevalent at this time. Tricos dominate morning hatches from July into September. Long, fine tippets and delicate presentations are the order of the day. Fish terrestrials in the afternoon. While the best of the Missouri's fly fishing tends to wrap up at Cascade, the slower water downstream holds its share of great brown trout and ought not to be overlooked.

RESOURCES

Gearing up: Missouri River Trout Shop and Lodge, 110 Bridge St., Craig, MT 59648; 800-337-8528; www.thetroutshop.com.

Accommodations: Helena Area Chamber of Commerce, 225 Cruse Ave., Helena, MT 59601; 406-442-4120; www.helenachamber.com.

Books: *Fishing Montana* by Michael S. Sample, Falcon Press.

Flyfisher's Guide to Montana by Greg Thomas, Wilderness Adventure Press.

The Montana Angling Guide by Chuck Fothergill and Bob Sterling, Stream Stalker Publishing Co.

Montana Blue-Ribbon Fly Fishing Guide by Steve Probasco, Frank Amato Publications.

Montana Fly Fishing Guide West by John Holt, Lyons Press.

60 YELLOWSTONE RIVER, MIDDLE

Location: South-central Montana.
Short take: Everybody's paradise, literally.
Type of stream: Freestone.
Angling methods: Fly, spin.
Species: Cutthroat, brown, rainbow.
Access: Moderate.
Season: Year-round.
Supporting services: Gardiner, Livingston.
Handicapped access: Best from driftboats.
Closest TU chapter: Joe Brooks.

ITS NAME DERIVED FROM THE MINNEATAREE INDIAN *mi tse a-da-zi* (yellow rock river), the Yellowstone, rising on the Two Ocean Plateau within spitting distance of the Pacific-bound Snake and then running for about 100 miles through an enchanting tableau of burbling paint pots, smoking fumaroles, and deep, isolated canyons banded in ochre and gold, charges out of the national park at Gardiner hell bent for Livingston, 60 miles downstream. Fully mature now, the Yellowstone gathers all of the snowmelt runoff from the west half of the park and funnels it through Yankee Jim Canyon and into Paradise Valley below. From mid-May into July, this otherwise lovely river carries the color of cappuccino and can be gritty to the touch. By the time it clears, hoppers dance in the grasslands.

Rainbows, cutthroats, hybrids of these two, and browns are jumbled together in the upper runs of the Montana section of the Yellowstone. The farther north the river flows, the greater the number of browns. Deep pools in the canyon section are known for its large fish and difficult access. Below Carbella launch ramp at the mouth of the canyon, gradient lessens and the river dons that persona of cobbly runs and broad pools that sustains it as far as Billings.

Just downstream from the bridge over Mill Creek at the Paradise access, the Yellowstone earns its reputation. The channel braids around small islands, here running deep against the bank, there swirling back on itself. Fame and crowds go hand in hand. Flotillas of driftboats bob along, and as long as their oarsmen mind their manners, they pose little problem for the wading angler.

Most anglers chuck fat, weighted streamers with 6-weight systems. You know the routine: big fly, big fish. Those intent on dry flies generally resort to caddis, midges, and BWOs before the melt and when September turns aspen to gold. Terrestrials are meat and potatoes (trout haven't heard about Atkins yet) for browns and 'bows.

More than a dozen sites maintained by Montana Fish, Wildlife and Parks provide access to much of the lower Yellowstone. Most are designed to launch

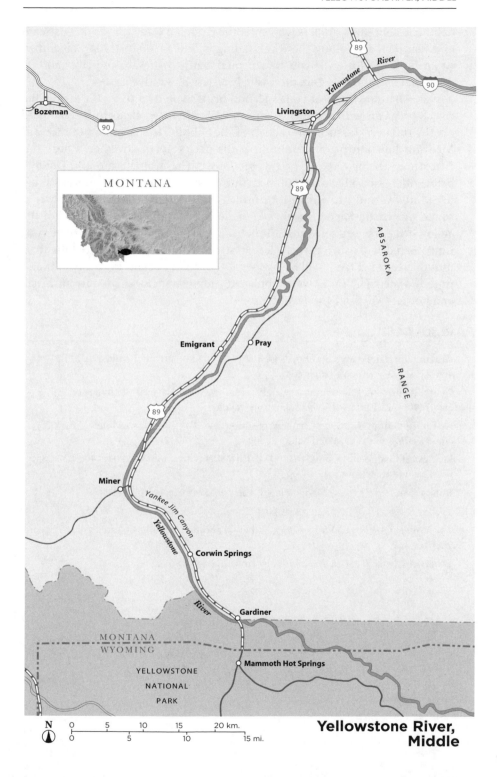

MONTANA

ABSAROKA

RANGE

89

90

Bozeman

90

Yellowstone River

Livingston

89

89

Emigrant   ○ **Pray**

Miner

Yankee Jim Canyon

Yellowstone

○ **Corwin Springs**

River

Gardiner

MONTANA
WYOMING

○ **Mammoth Hot Springs**

YELLOWSTONE

NATIONAL

PARK

N

0   5   10   15   20 km.

0   5   10   15 mi.

Yellowstone River, Middle

driftboats, but savvy anglers who enter the river can wade up- or downstream and fish the edges along the way. Wading is best in August and September, when flows are lower. If you wade, you'll want to stick to the river and its gravel bars. Landowners are increasingly restive about trespassers.

So what do you do if your vacation brings you into this valley while the river's pregnant with sediment? Your options are these: Beat it upstream and ply thy rod over the meadow section of the Gibbon, less than an hour toward Madison Junction from Mammoth at the park's north entrance. Check out Armstrong Spring Creek. The two sections O'Hair's at the top and DePuy's below offer—for a fee—a combined four miles-plus of quite technical fishing for rainbows and browns in the 16-inch class. Similar, but shorter water is found on Nelson Spring Creek, across the river on the east floodplain of the Yellowstone. There's one more thought. Though the main stem may be running turbid with spring melt, feeder streams may be clear and into their mouths really big trout will have moved. Nymph the seams between clear and muddy water. The same tactic applies to side channels where current is less and pockets will hold good trout.

RESOURCES

Gearing up: Dan Bailey's Fly Shop, P.O. Box 1019, 209 W. Park St., Livingston, MT 59047; 406-222-1673, www.dan-bailey.com.

George Anderson's Yellowstone Angler, P.O. Box 660, 5256 Hwy. 89, S. Livingston, MT 59047; 406-222-7130; www.yellowstoneangler.com.

Accommodations: Gardiner Chamber of Commerce, P.O. Box 81, Gardiner, MT 59030; 406-848-7971; www.gardinerchamber.com.

Livingston Chamber of Commerce, 303 E. Park St., Livingston, MT 59047; 406-222-0850; www.livingston.avicom.net.

Books: *The Angler's Guide to Montana* by Michael S. Sample, Falcon Press.

The Fly Fisher's Guide to Montana by Greg Thomas, Wilderness Adventure Press.

The Montana Angling Guide by Chuck Fothergill and Bob Sterling, Stream Stalker Publishing Co.

Waters of Yellowstone with Rod and Fly by Howard Back, Lyons Press.

61 FIREHOLE RIVER

Location: Northwestern Wyoming, Yellowstone National Park.
Short take: Amid geysers and fumaroles, rainbows and browns open Yellowstone's season.
Type of stream: Geothermal, freestone.
Angling methods: Fly.
Species: Rainbow, brown.
Access: Easy.
Season: Late May through mid-November.
Supporting services: West Yellowstone.
Handicapped access: Possible to fish, but no formal access.
Closest TU chapter: Jackson Hole.

WHEN THE DARK OF THE NIGHT COMES and sleep eludes me, I am sustained by visions of the terrain of trout. There are no vistas lovelier nor more soothing than those through which cold waters run. Enveloping them is a purity, a crispness like the first bite into a Jonathan or Winesap freshly picked from the tree. Each is so imbued with promise, not just of the rainbow that may rise to my Blue-Winged Olive but of a kind of consummate fulfillment that here, at last, at least for a moment, life is better than all right. It is very, very good.

I have told this story before, of my first trip to Yellowstone with friend Dale Smith. Though well into my forties, I was yet, and am still, a novice fly fisher. Having trimmed my tippet on tight streams of Eastern legend—Beaverkill, Letort, and Hazel Creek down in the Smokies—I was quite unprepared for the raw grandeur of Western waters. Dale and I started playing on Henry's Fork, and I'd lost a massive rainbow there. We casted for browns that late September beneath the falls of the Gibbon and found nary a fish. We drove that afternoon to Mule Shoe Bend on the Firehole and parked beneath the scrubby pines.

Sun and cloud played tag as they're wont to do that time of year. One moment the floor of Midway Geyser Basin glowed tawny in the late-day sun. From fumaroles, plumes of meteoric steam, virgin white in the sun, blew skyward. As dazzling as it was the first moment, cloud dulled it the next. Gone was the glistening gold of the grasses and platinum of the geysers. The tableau had turned pewter and dull bronze. A squall of snow drew a curtain across the low hills to the west.

The cloud triggered a hatch, Baetis. In the long, greasy run beneath the low bluff where aquatic grasses wreathed well below the surface, dimples appeared. Rising fish. We rigged our 5-weights with longish 6X tippets and began to intently work fish. Dale chose the middle of the run, and I, its tail. Though he was no more than 100 yards upstream, fog billowing from mud

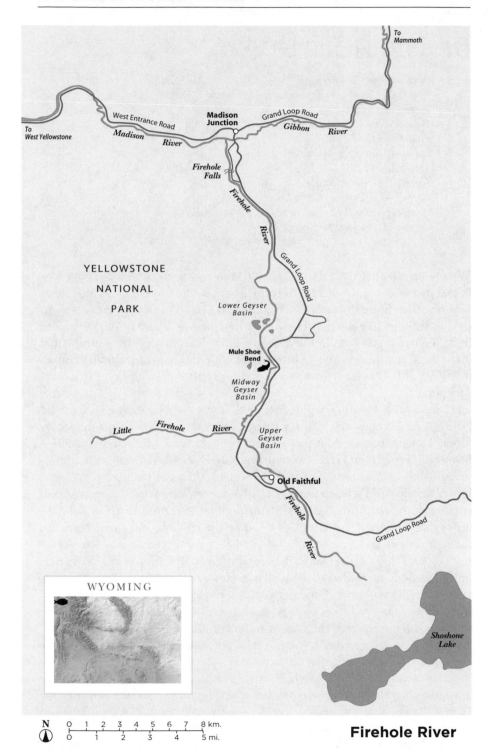

Firehole River

The most exotic free-flowing river in the country, the Firehole offers lovely vistas and trout to match.

pots and streams of the snow, which had moved up and enveloped us, hid him from view. In those moments, I was alone fishing a landscape that told of the formation of the earth.

Every angler owes him or herself a visit to Mule Shoe Bend. The Firehole is among the earliest of Yellowstone's storied streams to open, typically on the Saturday of Memorial Day Weekend. Even if your travels bring you here in July or August, time your first look at the Firehole for the cool airs of dawn. It is then that you will see the river in its most stunning attire. You can fish it later in the day.

Rising in Madison Lake, the Firehole is a very thin stream and not worth fishing above Old Faithful and closed to fishing immediately below. At Biscuit Basin, the Little Firehole comes in from the west, cooling the main stem and itself providing a fishery for browns, rainbows, and cutthroat. Below the basin, the Firehole opens into a broad meadow. Here in the Midway and Lower Geyser basins, its waters are really too warm to fish from late July into August. But like the Little Firehole, the tributaries of Sentinel, Fairy, and Nez Perce creeks hold good, if hard to take, fish that've moved in to escape the heat.

The gradient quickens below Nez Perce Creek and the flat, often weedy bed of the meadow stretch gives way to larger cobbles and boulders. The Grand Loop Road, which has been following the river, moves slightly east to a new route, but the old one turns off to the west at the top of Firehole Cascades. Here begins brawling water, frothing around goodly sized rock and creating deep eddies that are hard to fish well, but pay dividends in browns and rainbows of 14 inches and sometimes much better when you do. A falls punctuates the river about a mile upstream from the junction with the Gibbon where the two waters give birth to the Madison.

The Firehole is extremely popular, and its fish, very well educated. Small dry flies such as Hendrickson, Quill Gordons, Adams, Pale Morning Duns, Blue-Winged Olives, and Midges can be quite effective when presented with a drag-free float. Occasionally, terrestrials produce in the meadow stretches, and streamers do well in fall, which is considered by most the best time to fish this river. If you reach Yellowstone in late July or August of a drought year, you may find the Firehole, upper Madison, and lower Gibbon closed to angling due to high water temperatures. Then, if time presses, the quickest alternative is the meadow section of the Gibbon, known for its large and stubborn browns.

RESOURCES

Gearing up: Blue Ribbon Flies, 305 Canyon St., W. Yellowstone, MT 59758; 406-646-7642; www.blueribbonflies.com.

Bud Lilly's Trout Shop, P.O. Box 530, 39 Madison Ave., W. Yellowstone, MT 59758; 406-646-7801, www.budlillys.com.

Jacklin's Flyshop, P.O. Box 310, 105 Yellowstone Ave., W. Yellowstone, MT 59758; 406-646-7336; www.jacklinsflyshop.com.

Accommodations: West Yellowstone Chamber of Commerce and Visitors Center, P.O. Box 458, W. Yellowstone, MT 59758; 406-646-7701; www.westyellowstonechamber.com.

Books: *Fishing Yellowstone National Park* by Richard Parks, Falcon Press.

Flyfishers Guide to Wyoming (Including Grand Teton and Yellowstone National Parks) by Ken Retallic, Wilderness Adventure Press.

The Wyoming Angling Guide by Chuck Fothergill and Bob Sterling, Stream Stalker Publishing.

62 North Platte River

Location: Southeastern Wyoming.
Short take: Secluded, untamed river in the south, marvelous tailwaters below.
Type of stream: Freestone, then tailwater.
Angling methods: Fly, spin.
Species: Brown, rainbow.
Access: Moderate.
Season: Year-round.
Supporting services: Saratoga, Casper.
Handicapped access: Saratoga, but not formally.
Closest TU chapter: Platte Valley.

Two sections of the North Platte are especially worthy of note. First are the tailwater runs: the famed Miracle Mile—seven really—below Kortes Dam and the 30-mile stretch downstream from Grey Reef Dam. Then there's the 47 miles of river upstream from Saratoga, a charming town with a bevy of excellent fly shops, outfitters, and accommodations.

Anglers seeking a blue-ribbon Western trout river and solitude—generally an oxymoron under the Big Sky—should take a long look at the upper run of North Platte. Though flowing north from the Colorado border for more than 100 miles, little of it is shadowed by major or even secondary highways. Scores of private roads lead to the river, but Wyoming landowners are chary of their property rights and don't take kindly to trespassers. Keep in mind as well that streambeds in this state are considered private property and wading on them without permission is verboten. About 15 miles of the uppermost river flows along the Medicine Bow National Forest, which offers camping and access to anglers willing to walk in. Some of the best fishing on the river is found in this stretch of boulder gardens, riffles, and hustling pools.

The best way to fish the river upstream from Saratoga, however, is to float it. With populations estimated at 4,000 per mile and a 10- to 16-inch slot limit that restricts anglers to harvesting only one fish per day greater than 16 inches, odds of hooking 14- to 18-inch rainbows or browns are very good. Melt water generally has blown through this area by mid- to late June. Weighted streamers cast hard against the bank are extremely productive, as are terrestrials later on.

Below Interstate 80, the North Platte turns sluggish and slow, and it's of little interest. Angling picks up again with the outflow from Kortes Dam. Fishing very well all year, Miracle Mile is known for its midge hatches and finicky bug-sucking bruisers. May and June are favorite months with salmon flies, green drakes, and golden stones. Terrestrials begin to turn on trout in June and the renowned Trico hatch starts later that month and runs into September.

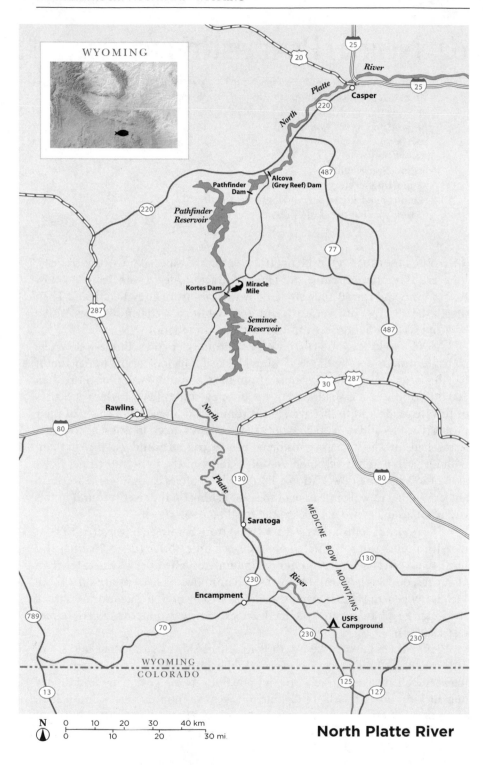

WYOMING

River

20

25

North Platte

25

Casper

220

487

Alcova
(Grey Reef) Dam

Pathfinder
Dam

220

Pathfinder
Reservoir

77

Kortes Dam

Miracle
Mile

Seminoe
Reservoir

487

30

287

287

Rawlins

80

North

130

Platte

130

Saratoga

MEDICINE

80

230

River

BOW

Encampment

MOUNTAINS

130

789

USFS
Campground

70

230

230

WYOMING
COLORADO

13

125

127

N   0   10   20   30   40 km
0   10   20   30 mi.

North Platte River

Given the size of the fish, a 6-weight is recommended. And overlining helps toss the weighted streamers needed to get down into deep holes.

Spring and fall spawners move up from Pathfinder Reservoir and collect in the river channel. Fall, with its lower flows and bigger browns, is the most popular time. Access is quite ample. This, however, is not a place to expect solitude. Yet, a spirit of camaraderie prevails on this stretch. While the Miracle Mile is known almost worldwide, the eight miles below Grey Reef (also known as Alcova) Dam may hold more trophy-sized fish. This is big, broad water, too deep to cross in waders. Fish nymphs and streamers and spinners and spoons in fall when flows are lowest and big browns on the prowl.

RESOURCES

Gearing up: Great Rocky Mountain Outfitters, Inc., 216 E. Walnut St., P.O. Box 1677, Saratoga, WY 82331; 307-326-8750; www.grmo.com.

North Platte River Fly Shop, 7400 Alcova Hwy. 220, Casper, WY 82604; 307-237-5997; www.wyomingflyfishing.com.

Accommodations: Platte River Chamber of Commerce, P.O. Box 1095, Saratoga, WY 82331; 307-326-8855; www.saratogachamber.info.

Books: *Fishing Wyoming* by Kenneth Graham, Falcon Press.

The Wyoming Angling Guide by Chuck Fothergill and Bob Sterling, Stream Stalker Publishing Co.

Wyoming Blue-Ribbon Fly Fishing Guide by Greg Thomas, Frank Amato Publications.

63 SLOUGH CREEK

Location: Northwestern Wyoming, Yellowstone National Park.
Short take: Famed for big cutthroat. Upper meadows require a healthy hike, which is why fishing is excellent.
Type of stream: Freestone.
Angling methods: Fly, spin.
Species: Cutthroat, rainbow.
Access: Easy to moderate.
Season: Saturday of Memorial Day weekend through first Sunday in November.
Supporting services: Silver Gate, Wyoming.
Handicapped access: No.
Closest TU chapter: Contact the state council of TU.

RISING IN THE BEARTOOTH-ABSAROKA WILDERNESS ACROSS THE BORDER in Montana, Slough Creek is regarded by many seasoned anglers as one of the last best trout streams in Yellowstone. Alas, Slough Creek was known for its gorgeous and pure Yellowstone cutthroat—and they still dominate the creek—but rainbows have worked their way into the system from the Lamar river system and are now found above the third meadow. The rap on this creek is straightforward: the farther you hike upstream, the better the fishing.

Essentially, the 16 miles of Slough Creek in the park are divided into five sections: the canyon of a mile or so above its junction with the Lamar, the three-mile lower meadow, and then the three upper meadows. The canyon above the confluence with the Lamar and the lower meadow generally produce the biggest fish. Filled with riffles punctuated by cascades, the lower canyon is not the kind of water favored by cutthroats. They prefer slower velocity with undercut banks, downed tree stumps, and gravel bar eddies for cover. If your heart's set on fishing Slough Creek and the parking lots are full, take the time to hike into the lower canyon. You'll find fish for sure, and far fewer anglers.

In the two and a half miles below Slough Creek Campground, the river runs relatively slowly, once the surge of spring melt water blows through by mid-July. Gravel runs separate flat pools. You'll see leviathan cutts cruising the banks. But they can see you too, and normally will not take a fly. Fishing pressure in the lower meadow is usually intense, but not always. And there is a way to beat the rush. Pack a picnic breakfast and lunch, a bird book, and a pair of binoculars. Arrive early, say sevenish. Hike down a mile or so to the pools you want to fish. Recline against the highwater bench and enjoy coffee, juice, and a muffin. Snooze a bit. By 10, the cutts will begin to work. Let them tell you when they're feeding. If you cast before you see them working, you'll put them down. Matching the hatch and presenting your fly with a drag-free float are essential if you want to score on this run. If you play this game right, you'll be rewarded by

Slough Creek

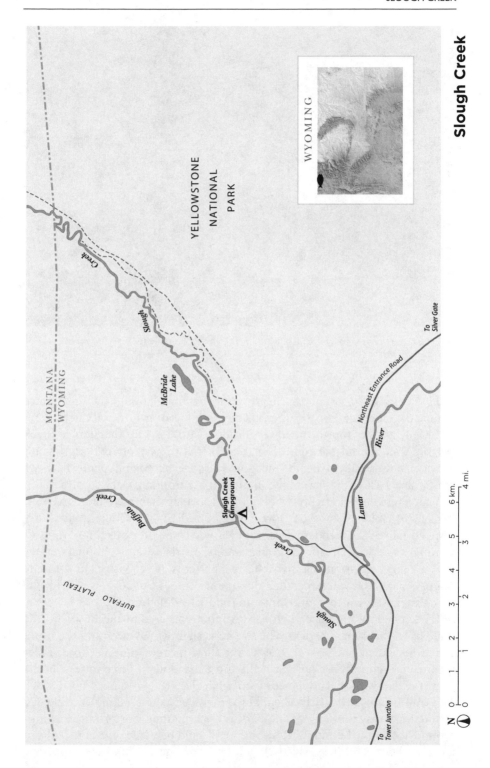

Slough Creek, famous for its cutthroat population, is regarded by many seasoned anglers as one of the best trout streams in Yellowstone.

fish in the 15- to 20-inch range. To give cutthroat populations a fighting chance against the more aggressive exotics, kill any rainbow or hybrid you catch.

Many anglers forego the lower meadow and head up the Slough Creek Wagon Trail behind the comfort station in the uppermost parking lot. It's about an hour's walk to the first meadow. Here the creek winds gently between grassy banks. Casts are never long, though these trout are wary. Accuracy and delicate presentation are probably more important than matching, precisely, the hatch. Golden Stones, Yellow Sallies, Caddis, Grey Drakes, and Blue-Winged Olives are standard fare. Tippets need not be exceedingly fine. As summer's sun dries streamside grasses and terrestrials mature, hoppers, crickets, and ants become increasingly effective patterns. If you visit in mid-to-late August, make sure you have a half dozen ants, sizes 14 to 20. You may hit the flying ant hatch, which sends trout into frantic feeding frenzies.

The primary difference between the first and second meadows are the three miles that separate them. The stream is slightly narrower, and the trout, somewhat easier. The same applies to the third meadow, another three miles upstream. A good hiker can reach the third meadow in three to four hours from the parking lot. Those of us whose hackles are sparse need more time. The trail is not particularly steep, but remember, you're hiking above 6,000 feet. Take it easy and enjoy. The park service maintains a primitive campground at the third meadow. Reservations should be made several months in advance. Local outfitters will pack you and your gear in and out, but for a price that's roughly the equivalent of a week at a better than good hotel.

RESOURCES

Gearing up: Parks' Fly Shop, P.O. Box 196, Gardiner, MT 59030; 406-848-7314; www.parksflyshop.com.

Accommodations: Cooke City/Silver Gate/Colter Pass Chamber of Commerce, P.O. Box 1071, Cooke City, MT 59020; 406-838-2495; www.cookecitychamber.com.

Books: *Fishing Yellowstone National Park* by Richard Parks, Falcon Press.

Flyfishers Guide to Wyoming (Including Grand Teton and Yellowstone National Parks) by Ken Retallic, Wilderness Adventure Press.

The Wyoming Angling Guide by Chuck Fothergill and Bob Sterling, Stream Stalker Publishing.

64 YELLOWSTONE RIVER, UPPER

Location: Northwestern Wyoming, Yellowstone National Park.
Short take: Riotous whitewater, deep pools, smoking springs.
Type of stream: Freestone.
Angling methods: Fly, spin.
Species: Cutthroat, rainbow, brown, brook.
Access: Moderate.
Season: July 15 through early November.
Supporting services: Gardiner.
Handicapped access: No.
Closest TU chapters: Joe Brooks, East Yellowstone.

THE YELLOWSTONE'S REPUTATION AS A TROUT RIVER stems not from its numbers and size of fish, but for the sheer and spectacular diversity of the environments through which it passes, from its headwaters on the Two Ocean Plateau to Livingston, Montana, where it exits the mountains, bends east, and starts the long valley run to its junction with the Missouri in North Dakota. Along its course, anglers witness the awesome forces that created the caldera memorialized by President Grant as America's first national park.

The Yellowstone Caldera—a varied terrain of plunging ridges, gentle highlands, tumultuous rivers, and broad valleys—was born of cataclysmic volcanic eruption. The latest, 600,000 years ago (the rocks of the Appalachians date back 600 million years), hurled 240 cubic miles of debris into the air, and collapsed the central cone into a basin of 28 by 47 miles. The violence of its geologic past lingers in geysers, fumaroles, bubbling mud pots, and steaming hot springs that burst forth along its course. You will see, too, the legacy of forest fire. Feathery stands of fresh green lodgepole and aspen stand where once old growth darkened the forest floor. And you'll learn of the tragedy of man's stocking of non-native species, particularly lake trout but also browns and rainbows and brook trout, that will likely, sadly, yet ultimately lead to the eradication of the genial native Yellowstone cutthroat in all but those few streams protected by natural barriers.

From its headwaters on the plateau to Yellowstone Lake is a distance of 30 utterly isolated miles. No roads and few trails probe this area. Native cutthroats of six inches or so ply these waters, except in the spring when bigger cutts enter the lower reaches that drain into the southeast arm of the lake. These runs occur in June, often before snow has melted from access trails and before the river opens in mid-July for fishing. You may find some of these larger cutts in the system in late July. If it's solitude you seek, and you don't mind a couple of days of strenuous hiking or parting with fees for a pack train, you'll find it up on this plateau.

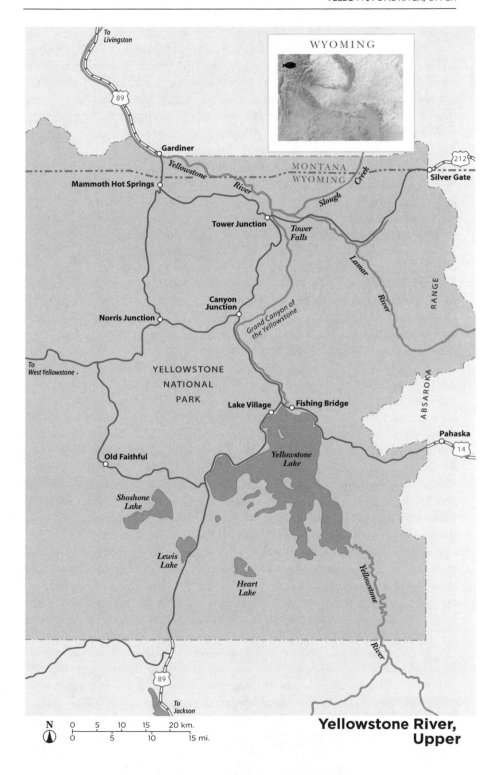

WYOMING

To Livingston

89

Gardiner

Yellowstone River

MONTANA
WYOMING

Slough Creek

212

Silver Gate

Mammoth Hot Springs

Tower Junction

Tower Falls

Lamar River

RANGE

Canyon Junction

Norris Junction

Grand Canyon of the Yellowstone

To West Yellowstone

YELLOWSTONE
NATIONAL
PARK

Lake Village

Fishing Bridge

ABSAROKA

Pahaska

14

Old Faithful

Yellowstone Lake

Shoshone Lake

Lewis Lake

Heart Lake

Yellowstone River

89

To Jackson

N

0   5   10   15   20 km.
0   5   10   15 mi.

Yellowstone River, Upper

In 1994, lake trout were discovered in Yellowstone Lake. Because lake trout are voracious feeders, they will eventually destroy native cutthroat populations that are threatened in the river below Upper and Lower falls by rainbows. Not only are cutthroat at risk. Their loss will disrupt the food supply for grizzly bears, bald eagles, loons, and a host of other species. Anglers are required to kill lake trout when they catch them. Harvesting by sport fishermen and the Park Service's valiant gill netting of lakers are the only hope to ensure the survival of a small stock of the park's namesake trout.

Below Yellowstone Lake, the river flows through a broad, gentle run before reaching Chittenden Bridge. Cutthroat spawn in the mile and a quarter immediately below the lake's outflow and the river here is closed to fishing. This area, below and above the fishing bridge are the sites of one of the greatest outbreaks of whirling disease as well. It's best to give this run a wide berth. Below Chittenden Bridge, the pace of the river quickens and then it plunges over the Upper Falls (108 feet) and then the Lower Falls (308 feet). The water between and below these falls is closed to fishing, and the first opportunity to fish the canyon is near the mouth of Sulphur Creek, about five miles down the Glacial Boulder trail from Inspiration Point. Sharp and steep, the lower quarter of the trail drops more than 1,200 feet in about a mile and a half. Cutthroats average about 14 inches in this section.

About mid-July, the salmon fly hatch reaches the mileage at Tower Falls. At the same time, melt is streaming out of the system and the river is becoming clear enough to fish. The falls are a barrier to cutthroat migrating upstream and fish in the runs downstream from the falls average about 13 inches or so. A relatively easy walk from the parking lot at Tower Store down to the river puts one on fishable water. A walk of a mile or so upstream will separate you from other, not so dedicated anglers. The last reach of the Yellowstone within the park is the Black Canyon run. The short take on this mileage says "make plans to camp overnight" if you fish it. Anglers will find reasonably easy access and fairly good fishing, however, in the run adjacent to the cluster of visitor services at Mammoth. Here, as elsewhere, the farther upstream you walk, the better the fishing. Rainbows are becoming more frequent in the Yellowstone system, as are hybrids called "cuttbows." Browns and stray brook trout also show up as well. Only artificial lures are permitted. Nymphs and streamers are most effective, but caddis attractors, such as the Wulff and Stimulator, and terrestrials all have their place, as do light spoons for the spinning crowd.

There's more than fishing on the Yellowstone. You'll see elk and white pelicans, most likely at least one bison, and maybe a bear. Bison are numerous, and despite their shaggy lumbering demeanor, they can be very aggressive. Walking through a meadow where bison are grazing may not be a really bright idea. Above all else, Yellowstone is a preserve, and angling here—when you're out of sight and earshot of others—is like fishing in a church.

RESOURCES

Gearing up: Parks' Fly Shop, P.O. Box 196, Gardiner, MT 59030; 406-848-7314; www.parksflyshop.com.

Accommodations: Gardiner Chamber of Commerce, P.O. Box 81, Gardiner, MT 59030; 406-848-7971; www.gardinerchamber.com.

Yellowstone Park hotels and campgrounds, P.O. Box 168, Yellowstone National Park, WY 82190–0168; 307-344-7381; www.nps.gov/yell/.

Books: *Fishing Yellowstone National Park* by Richard Parks, Falcon Press.

Flyfishers Guide to Wyoming (Including Grand Teton and Yellowstone National Parks) by Ken Retallic, Wilderness Adventure Press.

The Wyoming Angling Guide by Chuck Fothergill and Bob Sterling, Stream Stalker Publishing.

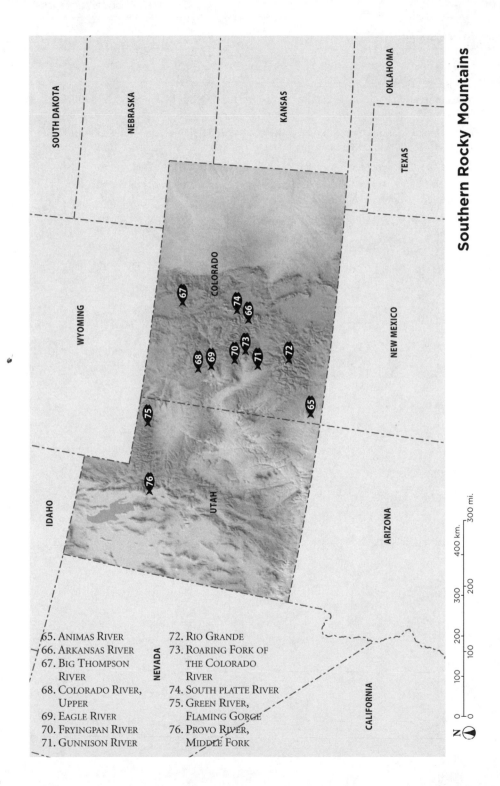

Southern Rocky Mountains

65. ANIMAS RIVER
66. ARKANSAS RIVER
67. BIG THOMPSON
    RIVER
68. COLORADO RIVER,
    UPPER
69. EAGLE RIVER
70. FRYINGPAN RIVER
71. GUNNISON RIVER

72. RIO GRANDE
73. ROARING FORK OF
    THE COLORADO
    RIVER
74. SOUTH PLATTE RIVER
75. GREEN RIVER,
    FLAMING GORGE
76. PROVO RIVER,
    MIDDLE FORK

SOUTHERN ROCKY MOUNTAINS

COLORADO

UTAH

65 ANIMAS RIVER

Location: Southwestern Colorado.
Short take: Ride the rails for wild rainbows.
Type of stream: Freestone.
Angling methods: Fly, spin, bait.
Species: Brown, cutthroat, rainbow.
Access: Moderate to difficult.
Season: Year-round.
Supporting services: Durango.
Handicapped access: Limited.
Closest TU chapter: Five Rivers.

IF CONVENIENCE IS YOUR KICK, the Animas is your river. Blow into Durango in the southwestern corner of the state, park your wheels at the visitor center downtown, rig your 5-weight, and beat it down to the river. For about three miles from the confluence of Lightner Creek to the Purple Cliffs just north of the Southern Ute Indian Reservation, the Animas wears the Gold Medal designation from the state. The first of Colorado's abundant trout streams to earn this tag, this run of the Animas is heavily stocked. Rainbows predominate, but you'll find large browns as well. Heavily favored by whitewater kayakers and rafters, this is big, lovely water. Heavy rapids swirl around massive boulders, then tail out into pools that give way to more fast runs. Most anglers choose to float this section to gain access to midstream pockets difficult to reach from shore. Highways follow the river, allowing easy access, but watch out for posted land. South of the Gold Medal stretch, the river enters the reservation where it continues to be managed as a trophy trout stream. A permit is required to fish reservation waters.

There's more to this river than the mileage below Durango. Fans of steam trains and rainbows will get a kick out of taking the Durango & Silverton narrow gauge up the stunningly beautiful Animas gorge to fish the river below Tenmile Creek. Along the route, the railroad crosses Ruby, Needle, and Noname creeks, all good fisheries for rainbows in the 8- to 12-inch range. The 8:15 a.m. from Durango will put you on the river about 10:00 p.m. On return, the 2:45 p.m. out of Silverton will reach your trestle about 3:30 p.m. or so. You'll need to make reservations a month or more in advance. And don't miss your return train. It's a long walk back to town.

With a drainage basin that's 85 miles long and bounded on both sides by more than a dozen 13,000-foot peaks, the Animas is a quintessential runoff stream. Warm and sunny days in February, March, and April provide good fishing, particularly with midges and streamers. In May, meltwater season starts, turning the river a chalky grayish brown. Surging current builds awesome haystacks—sheer delight for rafters and kayakers. Most consider the Animas

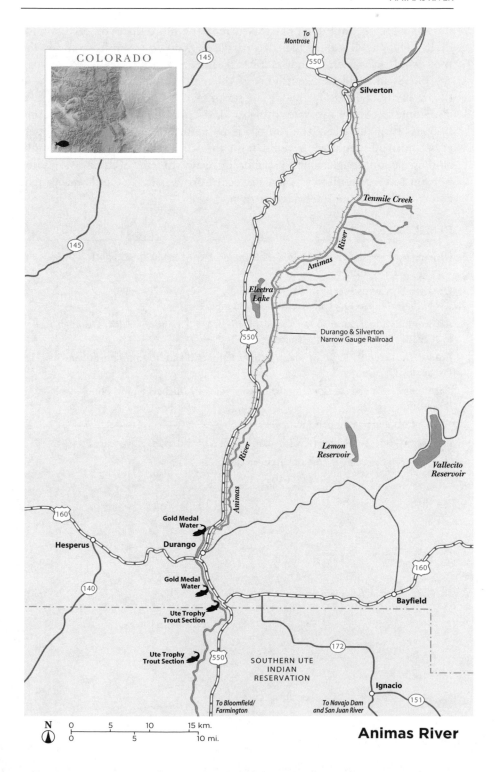

COLORADO

To Montrose

Silverton

Tenmile Creek

Animas River

Electra Lake

Durango & Silverton
Narrow Gauge Railroad

Lemon Reservoir

Vallecito Reservoir

Animas River

Gold Medal Water

Hesperus

Durango

Gold Medal Water

Ute Trophy Trout Section

Bayfield

Ute Trophy Trout Section

SOUTHERN UTE INDIAN RESERVATION

Ignacio

To Bloomfield/ Farmington

To Navajo Dam and San Juan River

N

| 0 | 5 | 10 | 15 km. |
| 0 | 5 | | 10 mi. |

Animas River

unfishable then; trout don't like the current any more than you do. Look for them in little eddies along the edge, particularly downstream from and in the mouths of clearwater tributaries. By early July, runoff has cleared the system.

Olives and midges take fish before the melt and, afterwards, anglers who throw anything other than caddis are staring fate in the eye. Golden stoneflies also come out when the water drops, and, as summer ages, ants, beetles, and hoppers turn the trick. The Animas is not a technical river, so fine tippets aren't normally required. Save them for the San Juan, an hour to the south. And, while some anglers may be put off by heavy stocking of rainbows, it's important to keep in mind a past state record brown of 23 pounds was caught below the U.S. Route 160 bridge in town.

RESOURCES

Gearing up: Duranglers, 923 Main Ave., Durango, CO 81301; 970-385-4081; www.duranglers.com.

Durango Fly Goods, 139 E. 5th St., Durango, CO 81301; 970-259-0999; www.southwestdirectory.com/business/DurangoFly/.

Accommodations: Durango Area Tourism Office, 111 S. Camino del Rio, Durango, CO 81302; 800-525-8855; www.durango.org.

Books: *The Colorado Angling Guide* by Chuck Fothergill and Bob Sterling, Stream Stalker Publishing Co.

The Complete Fly Fishing Guide for the Durango Area by Michael Shook, Shook Book Publishing.

Fishing Colorado by Ron Baird, Falcon Press.

Flyfisher's Guide to Colorado by Marty Bartholomew, Wilderness Adventure Press.

Fly Fishing in Colorado by Jackson Streit, Falcon Press.

66 ARKANSAS RIVER

Location: Central Colorado.
Short take: Big, rich water in a long, skinny park.
Type of stream: Freestone.
Angling methods: Fly, spin, bait.
Species: Brown, rainbow.
Access: Moderate to difficult.
Season: Year-round.
Supporting services: Salida, Canon City.
Handicapped access: Yes.
Closest TU chapter: Collegiate Peaks.

RISING IN THE SAN ISABEL NATIONAL FOREST north of Leadville, the Arkansas River flows for 148 miles before bursting into the high plains and emptying into Lake Pueblo just west of the city of the same name. For most of its length, the river flows through the Arkansas Headwaters Recreation Area, a model federal-state partnership joining the Colorado Parks Department and the Bureau of Land Management. A number of guides offer float trips on the river and access points abound.

The headwaters of the river—Tennessee Creek and the East Branch of the Arkansas—unite west of Leadville. Neither offers much in the way of fishing. And, thanks to mine drainage, the otherwise wildly beautiful run down to where Clear Creek enters downstream of Granite is not considered prime fishing water. From the hamlet of Princeton almost all the way to Pueblo, however, the Arkansas provides wonderful fishing for flingers of hardware as well as flies. From the top of the mileage on down to the lake, the river is big, bouldery, deep in many places, yet punctuated with riffles and pools often shaded by stands of fir and spruce.

East of Nathrop, the Arkansas cuts down through a monolith of pink granite, carving a stunningly gorgeous canyon that delights whitewater enthusiasts at times of high flows. The upper and, particularly, lower sections of the canyon fish well. But access is very difficult. Boaters who don't know the river are ill advised to run the canyon stretch without a licensed guide. Calming upon exiting the canyon, the river continues to drive through long stretches of pocket water as it bustles by Salida, headquarters of the fly-fishing community in these parts. Here too, it picks up flows from the South Arkansas River and then dives headlong into Big Sheep Canyon. The canyon gives way to a stretch with gravel bars and pools that anglers fish heavily.

There's gas in the river's tank yet, for it has yet to roughhouse its way through the Grand Canyon of the Arkansas, as it's called by locals, with rapids that carry names like Maytag, Lose-Your-Lunch, and Shark's Tooth. At the base of the canyon near Coaldale, the river enters a bed of large boulders,

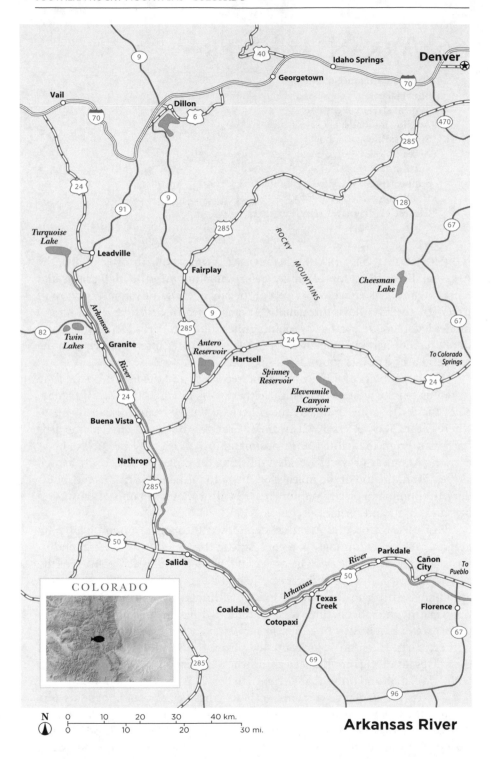

Vail

9

40

Idaho Springs

Georgetown

Denver

70

Dillon

70

6

470

285

24

91

128

285

67

Turquoise
Lake

Leadville

Fairplay

9

ROCKY
MOUNTAINS

Cheesman
Lake

67

82

Arkansas

Twin
Lakes

Granite

285

9

24

Antero
Reservoir

Hartsell

Spinney
Reservoir

To Colorado
Springs

67

24

River

24

Elevenmile
Canyon
Reservoir

Buena Vista

Nathrop

285

50

Salida

River

Parkdale

Cañon
City

To
Pueblo

COLORADO

Arkansas

50

Coaldale

Cotopaxi

Texas
Creek

Florence

67

285

69

96

N

0   10   20   30   40 km.

0   10   20   30 mi.

Arkansas River

providing ample and identifiable cover for trout—another section favored by anglers. A handicapped-access trail runs to the river at Lone Pine Recreation Site near Cotopaxi. For a while, the river takes on the cottonwood-bordered persona of the South Fork of the Snake below Palisades Dam, but the river's not done yet. Downstream of Parkdale, the river leaps into Royal Gorge with its thousand-foot walls of granite. Fishing is good all the way to Cañon City.

Though the state dumps tens of thousand of rainbows into the Arkansas, the main event is its populations of wild browns ranging up to 18 inches. Except for a few stretches around Salida, the river is 95 percent browns. Caddis proliferate as the water warms in April but by mid-May, the Arkansas is flowing too full to be much good for fishing. The river settles down again toward early July, but caddis hatches continue. The trout here are not particularly selective and most attractor patterns draw strikes. Heavier streamers will draw out browns when fished deep. The best time to fish the river is during the Mother's Day caddis hatch (mid-April to mid-May), and then in September when flows drop to the 400 fps range, temperatures fall, and browns warm up for their October to November spawn.

RESOURCES

Gearing up: ArkAnglers, 7500 W. Hwy. 50, Salida, CO 81201; 719-539-4223; www.arkanglers.com.

Arkansas River Fly Shop, 7500 W. Highway 50, Salida, CO 81201; 719-539-4223; www.arkanglers.com.

Royal Gorge Anglers, 1210 Royal Gorge Blvd., Cañon City, CO 81212; 719-269-3474; www.royalgorgeanglers.com.

Accommodations: Salida Area Chamber of Commerce, 406 W. Hwy. 50, Salida, CO 81201; www.salidachamber.org.

Books: *The Arkansas River Fishing Map and Guide* by Michael Shook, Shook Book Publishing.

The Colorado Angling Guide by Chuck Fothergill and Bob Sterling, Stream Stalker Publishing Co.

Fishing Colorado by Ron Baird, Falcon Press.

Flyfisher's Guide to Colorado by Marty Bartholomew, Wilderness Adventure Press.

Fly Fishing in Colorado by Jackson Streit, Falcon Press.

Fly Fishing the Arkansas: An Angler's Guide and Journal, by Bill Edrington.

67 BIG THOMPSON RIVER

Location: Central Colorado.
Short take: Two rivers at the feet of Rocky Mountain National Park.
Type of stream: Freestone, then tailwater.
Angling methods: Fly, spin, bait.
Species: Brown, rainbow, cutthroat, brook.
Access: Easy.
Season: Year-round.
Supporting services: Estes Park.
Handicapped access: No.
Closest TU chapter: Alpine Anglers.

IN REALITY, IF NOT IN FACT, THE BIG THOMPSON is two rivers separated by the gateway city for the Rocky Mountains, Estes Park. The Big "T" is fed, first, by a series of creeks that drain the northeast-facing flank of half-a-dozen 13,000-foot peaks that rise high above Forrest Valley. The course of the stream in the valley is dead straight flowing through chain of pools and little rapids; when the river is augmented by the flows of Spruce and Fern creeks, it makes an abrupt bend from the southeast to the northeast and is fed further by Mill Creek. The gradient of the river changes suddenly at Moraine Park and the stream braids through a grassy meadow, once the site of a thriving community.

The meadow is well worth fishing. Begin at the bridge that carries the Bear Creek Road over the stream and work your way upstream. Shortly the river forks. The right, rather than the left, is reportedly the better choice. Bends often contain deep turn holes, and undercut banks are frequent. In places, the river is no more than six inches deep; in others, it's over your head. Trout, browns, and rainbows, and maybe an occasional cutthroat or rare brook trout, are wary. Lack of tree cover exposes these fish to predators. And the ease of access makes this one of the most heavily fished sections of the park. Big uglies like Woolly Buggers and Bead Head Nymphs will draw strikes, especially when cast against the bank and let to dead-drift downstream. A strike indicator is not a bad idea. Greater numbers of fish, however, are taken on smallish dries—#16 to #18—often with a #20 or #22 nymph dropped beneath. A 4-weight rod is ideal for this game.

Leaving the meadow, the Big T enters Estes Park and then Lake Estes. Below Olympus Dam, which impounds the lake, the river has donned the cloak of a freestone mountain tailwater stream. Now, if the outflow of the river looks disproportionately large in comparison to the streams that feed the lake, remember that a 13-mile tunnel siphons water from Shadow Mountain Reservoir on the Upper Colorado, carries the flow beneath the park, and releases it in Lake Estes. This diverts water that would have eventually reached the Bay of

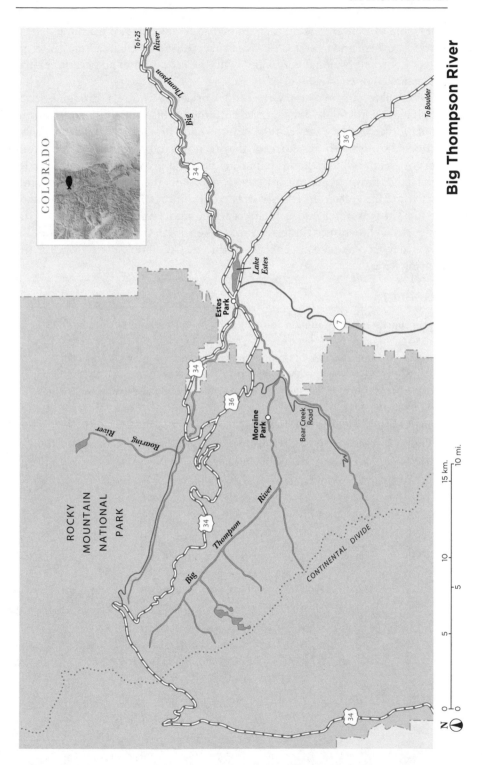

Big Thompson River

California to Denver. The mileage immediately downstream from the dam is privately owned and operated as a fee fishery. But in less than a mile, the river enters Roosevelt National Forest and, with the exception of an occasional private parcel, is open to fishing.

Typical of canyon country, the Big T works its way down through a series of plunges, into pools, long gravel-bottomed runs, and into pools again. Stoneflies seem to be a staple of the rainbows and browns in this heavily fished section. As most fish are stocked, they're none too skittish. Yet, like trout everywhere, they'll only stand so much clumsiness before running off to hide. The farther downstream toward Loveland you go, the more rapidly the river warms and the greater the fish are stressed in summer. I'll time my next trip to the Big Thompson for mid-September when nights turn crisp, fish are on the spawn, and elk whistles fill the air. And when I fish the meadow section, I'll save a day to play with greenback cutthroat, Colorado's State Fish, on the Roaring River.

RESOURCES

Gearing up: Estes Park Mountain Shop, 2050 Big Thompson Ave., P.O. Box 4079, Estes Park, CO 80517; 970-586-6548; www.estesparkmountainshop.com.

Accommodations: Chamber Of Commerce, 500 Big Thompson Ave., Estes Park, CO 80517; 970-586-4431; www.salidachamber.org.

Books: *The Colorado Angling Guide* by Chuck Fothergill and Bob Sterling, Stream Stalker Publishing Co.

Fishing Colorado by Ron Baird, Falcon Press.

Flyfisher's Guide to Colorado by Marty Bartholomew, Wilderness Adventure Press.

Fly Fishing in Colorado by Jackson Streit, Falcon Press.

68 COLORADO RIVER, UPPER

Location: Central Colorado.
Short take: The *Grand River* known as the Colorado.
Type of stream: Freestone.
Angling methods: Fly, spin, bait.
Species: Brown, rainbow, cutthroat, brook.
Access: Varies.
Season: Year-round.
Supporting services:
Glenwood Springs, Edwards, Eagle, Avon, Vail.
Handicapped access: No.
Closest TU chapter: Contact the state council of TU.

ANYONE WHO'S FISHED THE COLORADO AT LEES FERRY may wonder what it's like in the region where it begins. They'll find it on the back side of Rocky Mountain National Park where it rises above the old mining town of Lulu City. You could spit across it there, but by the time it leaves the state 200 miles to the west beyond Grand Junction at a wide spot in the road that maps call Utaline, it's drained most of the central part of the state and picked up water from a bevy of first-class trout rivers: Fraser, Blue, Eagle, Roaring Fork, and the Gunnison. *Grand* was the name French trappers affixed to the run of river from its headwaters to Moab, Utah. There it joined the Green and became the Colorado. In 1921, Colorado Governor Oliver H. Shoup convinced Congress to change the name of the Grand River to the Colorado, lest the state suffer chagrin by being named for a river that flowed nowhere in its borders.

Above Grand Lake, the Colorado flows through a bucolic glacial meadow—the Kawuneeche Valley—with abundant boggy braids and beaver ponds. Though the river here is seldom more than 10 to 30 feet wide, dark holes beneath undercut banks often hold browns of surprising size. In the main, this is brook trout water with a smattering of rainbows. Grand Lake is natural but next door is a man-made impoundment that produces the first tailwater on the Colorado. Rainbows, browns, and lake trout (called Mackinaws here) play in the frequently heavy outflow that runs for two miles before reaching the pool of Lake Granby. Due to its steep gradient, swirling currents, and boulder-strewn bottom, fishing this tailwater with fly gear can be a challenge. Check seasons and special regulations for this section.

Below Granby, gradient lessens and the river lopes through a broad valley before being held up yet again by Windy Gap Reservoir. A tunnel under the Continental Divide delivers diverted Colorado water to the Big Thompson for use in the burgeoning Interstate 25 corridor north of Denver. From Windy Gap to Byers Canyon the Colorado winds along in a rich agricultural valley. Access is very limited, and that which is open to the public is often crowded on

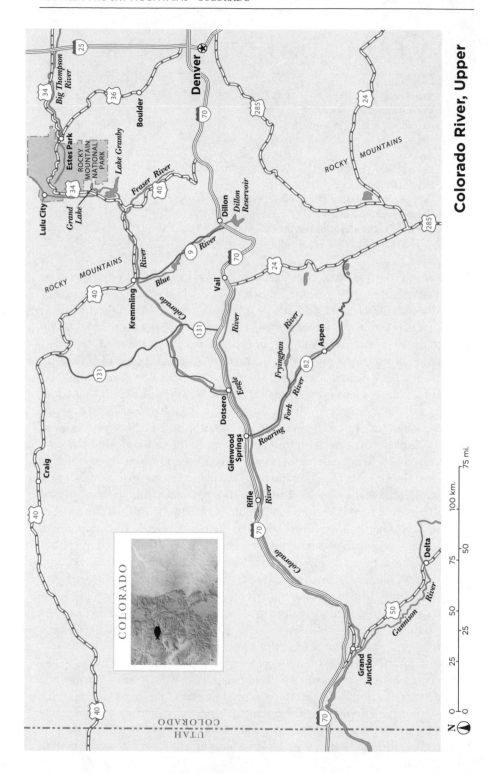

Colorado River, Upper

The Colorado above Lees Ferry is a stark world of red cliffs and green water rich with rainbows.

weekends. In the canyon, the river drops more than 200 feet in fewer than three miles. Sides of the canyon are steep and composed of loose gravels and boulders. Best access is from the parking areas at the downstream end.

Thanks to a number of parks, public access to the Colorado improves in the run from Byers Canyon to Kremmling. Though the valley is not wide—only half a mile or so—the river slows and braids in some places. Wading is easier. Anglers can spread out. Even during spring runoff, this section can be fished with success with heavily weighted streamers. Usually a good hatch of stoneflies comes off prior to the influx of higher water. And when the river returns to normal, Caddis become the pattern du jour. At Kremmling, the Blue River comes in from the south and the Colorado becomes an adult. Though several sections of the river west of Kremmling are wadable, most who fish this section float it. The current picks up as drop per mile increases. Class I through class III rapids occur in a number of places, and this run is a favorite with the watercraft crew. At Dotsero, the Eagle River adds to the flow.

The lower eight miles of Glenwood Canyon offer reasonably productive angling opportunities before and after runoff. A diversion dam in the canyon, however, nearly dewaters the bed immediately downstream during late summer. Ownership of land along this stretch is a combination of public and private. Check with local sources before venturing toward the river; Coloradans are justifiably protective of their property rights. Most fisher folk opt to float the mileage from Glenwood Springs to Rifle; covering more water creates better opportunity to fish water likely to hold good browns or 'bows. Much of this run, too, flows through privately held land. Quality angling generally declines below Rifle.

RESOURCES

Gearing up: Fly Fishing Outfitters, 1060 W. Beaver Creek Blvd., Avon, CO 81620; 970-845-8090; www.flyfishingoutfitters.net.

Roaring Fork Anglers, 2205 Grand Ave., Glenwood Springs, CO 81601; 970-945-0180; www.alpineangling.com.

Accommodations: Kremmling Area Chamber of Commerce, P.O. Box 471, Kremmling, CO 80459; 970-724-3472; www.kremmlingchamber.com.

Books: *The Colorado Angling Guide* by Chuck Fothergill and Bob Sterling, Stream Stalker Publishing Co.

Fishing Colorado by Ron Baird, Falcon Press.

The Fishing Map and Floater's Guide to the Colorado River by Michael Shook, Shook Book Publishing.

Flyfisher's Guide to Colorado by Marty Bartholomew, Wilderness Adventure Press.

Fly Fishing in Colorado by Jackson Streit, Falcon Press.

Fly Fishing the Colorado River: An Anglers Guide by Al Marlowe, Pruett.

69 EAGLE RIVER

Location: Central Colorado.
Short take: Born again, this river takes wing.
Type of stream: Freestone.
Angling methods: Fly, spin, bait.
Species: Brown, rainbow, cutthroat, brook.
Access: Varies.
Season: Year-round.
Supporting services: Vail.
Handicapped access: No.
Closest TU chapter: Ferdinand Hayden.

IN THE 1980S, SLUDGE FROM MINING OPERATIONS near the Eagle's headwaters beneath Tennessee Pass left the river foul and toxic. Now the mines are closed, and cleanup, championed by Colorado TU and others, is underway and the river runs clear and unfettered for nearly 70 miles to Dotsero, where it joins the Colorado. Along the way, at Dowd's Junction, it picks up the waters of Gore Creek, which flows through Vail. Above Gore Creek, the Eagle is a modest stream still suffering from a century of pollution. Though scenic, this mileage is purely a put-and-take fishery. The real action on the Eagle begins below Dowd's Junction.

From May through the middle of June, the Eagle runs dirty brown with spring melt. Its edges can be fished, and floats with an experienced river guide can be productive. Boulders that provide cover during lower flows in spring and fall drive the current into class III and class IV rapids, disaster in the making for driftboats and pontoon craft. The best months to fish the Eagle are March, April, and early May, and September into November. Brown trout are most prominent in the river above Avon, and rainbows dominate from Wolcott to the mouth at Dotsero. In late fall, big spawning browns enter the Eagle from the Colorado. Avoid their redds.

As is most central Colorado trout water, the Eagle is a caddis stream. Grannom is the signature hatch. These caddis begin coming off just as snowmelt enters the system, peak in June, but continue into the fall. Following is a good western sedge hatch. Smallish imitations of larvae fished as a trailing fly 18 inches behind a weighted nymph is the most productive way to hook trout when they're not taking on the surface. There's somewhat of a hatch of golden stoneflies during the peak of the grannom hatch and a run of salmon flies follows. Fall brings stunning hatches of blue-winged olives.

Skiers who venture to Vail to take advantage of deep powder should bring along their 4-weight systems and neoprenes. Daytime temperatures often flirt with the low 40s, the river is at its lowest flow, and radiant heat from noonday

Eagle River

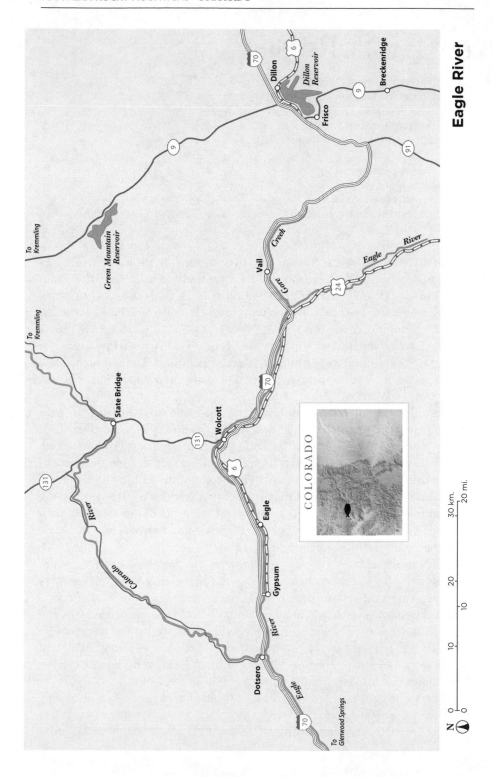

sun will trigger midge activity. Small nymphs fished with strike indicators are very effective.

If you've come to fish the Eagle, don't overlook Gore Creek. Though most streamside property is privately owned and flanked by high-priced vacation homes or hotels, the river itself is public water and can be accessed from bridges and parcels of parkland. Check with local fly shops for the most current information. Better yet, hire a guide for a day. Effluent from sewage-treatment facilities increases the fertility of the Gore above that normally associated with the Eagle's tributaries. That's a curse with a silver lining. The enhanced richness of the creek grows big trout, and they are finicky. With little of the classic dry-fly pool water, the Gore is essentially a long run of boulders and pockets. Most trout are caught with nymphs or streamers fished beneath strike indicators.

RESOURCES

Gearing up: Gore Creek Flyfisherman, 183–7 E. Gore Creek Dr., Vail, CO 81657; 970-476-3296; www.gorecreekflyfisherman.com.

Fly Fishing Outfitters, 1060 W. Beaver Creek Blvd., Avon, CO 81620; 970-845-8090; www.flyfishingoutfitters.net.

Accommodations: Vail Valley Chamber Tourism Bureau, 100 E. Meadow Dr., Suite 34, Vail, CO 81657; 970-476-1000; www.visitvailvalley.com.

Books: *The Colorado Angling Guide* by Chuck Fothergill and Bob Sterling, Stream Stalker Publishing Co.

The Complete Fly Fishing Guide for the Eagle Valley by Michael Shook, Shook Book Publishing.

Fishing Colorado by Ron Baird, Falcon Press.

The Fishing Map and Floater's Guide for the Eagle River and Gore Creek by Michael Shook, Shook Book Publishing.

Flyfisher's Guide to Colorado by Marty Bartholomew, Wilderness Adventure Press.

Fly Fishing in Colorado by Jackson Streit, Falcon Press.

Fly Fishing the Colorado River: An Anglers Guide by Al Marlowe, Pruett.

70 FRYINGPAN RIVER

Location: Central Colorado.
Short take: A favorite tailwater for huge rainbows. Crowded in summer, but much less so in spring and fall.
Type of stream: Tailwater.
Angling methods: Fly, spin.
Species: Rainbow, brown, brook.
Access: Easy to moderate.
Season: Year-round.
Supporting services: Basalt, Aspen, Carbondale, Glenwood Springs.
Handicapped access: Yes.
Closest TU chapter: Ferdinand Hayden.

WHIRLING DISEASE—CAUSED BY THE PARASITE *Myxobolus cerebralis* that enters the head and spinal cartilage of fingerling trout—has decimated populations of rainbows in many Colorado rivers. The Fryingpan, however, seems to have retained a significant rainbow trout fishery. Among the reasons appear to be the short length of the tailwater, continuing an extensive monitoring since 1995 when the disease was identified in Colorado, the institution of protective creel limits, and the identification and remediation of the primary source effluent carrying the parasite into the river. What this means for you and me, is that there's perhaps a better chance on the Fryingpan than on most other rivers in the state that a five-pound rainbow will suck in your imitation and make your reel's drag wail like a banshee.

Sixty years ago, fisheries biologists found that trout were reproducing in the Fryingpan from its junction with Roaring Fork of the Colorado clear up to its headwaters. The construction of Ruedi Dam and its closing in 1968 created a 14-mile tailwater that flows past Aspen to Roaring Fork. Shortly thereafter, the possum shrimp *Mysis relicta* was stocked in Ruedi Reservoir as forage for fish trapped in the impoundment. More than 15 years later, biologists discovered that shrimp were caught in the draw that feed the dam's outflow beneath the dam in what local anglers call with scatological respect, "the Toilet Bowl." Rainbow lie there, devouring shrimp like bluefish slashing in a chum line.

With the onset of whirling disease, the Colorado Department of Wildlife dramatically reduced is stocking of rainbows. Since 1996, the Fryingpan has received no legally stocked trout. Thus the bruising 'bows, bulldog browns, and occasional cutthroat (progeny of a 1993 stocking) or tributary-bred brookie are all wild fish. Gold Medal status—artificials only, minimum of 14 inches for up to two browns, and immediate release of rainbows—extends the entire length of the tailwater.

Below the dam, the river flows through a series of riffles and pools, coursing over a sandstone and shale bed that's littered in spots with large granite

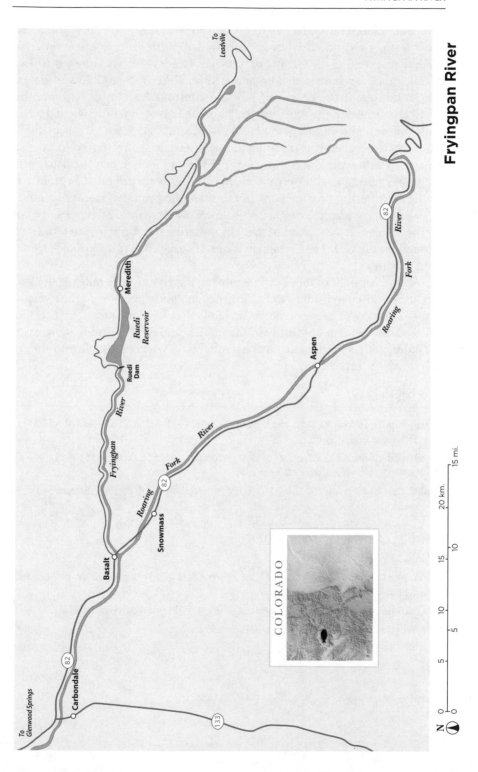

Fryingpan River

boulders. Seldom more than 40 feet wide and with flows averaging about 100 cubic feet per second, the river is easily waded. With little sediment entering the system, except in the vicinity of the Seven Castles, the river rarely discolors during rains. It's both a dry-fly and nymph fisher's dream. Green drakes, which start about the Fourth of July and continue for almost two months, might be considered the signature hatch on the Fryingpan. Blue-winged olives come off from mid-March through mid-May, and again from early September into early November. Pale morning duns abound from July deep into August. Imitations with a pinkish tint, such as the Melon Quill, match the hatch perfectly, says guide and author Michael Shook. Caddis are not quite as prolific as on the neighboring Roaring Fork, but they are the primary insect of summer. July and August also see hatches of little yellow stoneflies. Streamers are not overly popular on this river, but nymphs imitating the above insects work well throughout the year. The Fryingpan is one of Colorado's most popular winter trout fisheries.

Access throughout the river is a growing issue. About six miles of the Fryingpan are closed to fishing, and nearby Aspen's popularity—and the river's as well—is putting pressure on access on lands that are now open. The first two miles below the dam are firmly in the public domain. Beyond that, access is not contiguous. Fly shops sell maps that tell you which is which, and they're well worth the investment.

RESOURCES

Gearing up: Fryingpan Anglers, 132 Basalt Circle Center, Basalt, CO 81621; 970-927-3441; www.fryingpananglers.com.

Accommodations: Basalt Chamber of Commerce, P.O. Box 514, Basalt, CO 81621; 970-927-4031; www.basaltchamber.com.

Books: *The Colorado Angling Guide* by Chuck Fothergill and Bob Sterling, Stream Stalker Publishing Co.

The Complete Fly Fishing Guide for the Roaring Fork Valley by Michael Shook, Shook Book Publishing.

Fishing Colorado by Ron Baird, Falcon Press.

The Fishing Map and Floater's Guide for the Roaring Fork and Fryingpan Rivers by Michael Shook, Shook Book Publishing.

Flyfisher's Guide to Colorado by Marty Bartholomew, Wilderness Adventure Press.

Fly Fishing in Colorado by Jackson Streit, Falcon Press.

71 GUNNISON RIVER

Location: Western Colorado.
Short take: Browns dominate, but 'bows are rebounding.
Type of stream: Freestone, tailwater.
Angling methods: Fly, spin.
Species: Brown, rainbow, cutthroat, brook.
Access: Easy to extremely difficult.
Season: Year-round.
Supporting services: Cimarron, Gunnison, Montrose.
Handicapped access: None.
Closest TU chapters: Gunnison Gorge, Gunnison Angling Society.

WHEN YOU STEP OUT OF THE CAR at the visitor center on the south rim
and peer down into the Gunnison's Black Canyon, you can just imagine, as I
did, the seldom-fished behemoths that swim below. Here, the river carries
hues of blues and greens and turquoise normally reserved for marl flats in
Florida's Keys. So stark is the contrast between the dark gray walls of meta-
morphic schist and gneiss, that the Gunnison appears to glow from within.
The effect is heightened, to be sure, by foam from tortured currents frothing
in their harried dash downstream. Wrote U.S.G.S. geologist Wallace Hansen:
"Several western canyons exceed the Black Canyon in overall size. Some are
longer, some are deeper, some are narrower, and a few have walls as steep. But
no other canyon in North America combines the depth, narrowness, sheer-
ness, and somber countenance of the Black Canyon of the Gunnison." The
canyon section of the Gunnison runs from Crystal to the river's confluence
with the North Fork of the Gunnison.

High, arid semi-desert blankets the canyon's rims. If you did not know
that a river was there from maps, you would have little inkling of it. And once
you see it, you wonder how to reach its waters. In Black Canyon of the Gunnison National Park, formerly a national monument, three routes lead to the
river: the Tomichi with its loose rock, the Gunnison (80 feet of logging chain
about a third of the way down provides handholds for descents and ascents),
and the Warner Route, which with its vertical drop of 2,660 feet, is the longest
of the three. Fishermen also use SOB, Long, and Slide Draws from the North
Rim.

Joel Evans, president of TU's Gunnison Gorge Chapter, advises anglers to
plan twice as long as they'll think they'll need to climb down and then back up
one of these routes. "You'll need both hands free," he says. "Wear a daypack." A
school-sized, teardrop-shaped model won't cut it. Instead, invest in one with a
waist belt and pockets to hold water bottles. Prune your fishing vest of all but
the most essential flies and gear. Carry your waders, studded wading shoes,
raingear, lunch, etc. on your back. Two-piece rod tubes are an impediment.

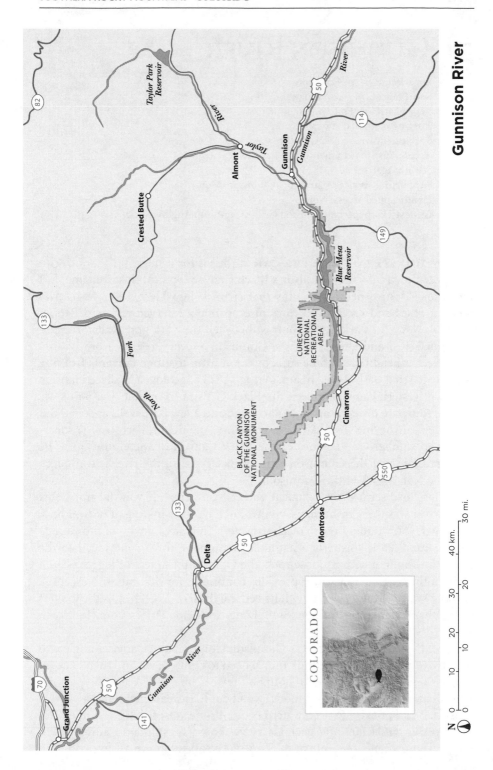

Gunnison River

Above Gunnison, the Gunnison River is a classic freestone stream with good access, but as it runs though the Black Canyon it turns into a wild tailwater and access is not for the faint of heart.

Use a four- or five-piece model that straps to the pack or fits inside. In addition, the rim of the canyon is well over 7,000 feet in elevation. Strenuous exertion can result in altitude sickness. If you contemplate hiking down into the canyon, consider spending a day on the upper river above the town of Gunnison or on the Taylor or East river upstream from Almont.

Backcountry permits are required to hike down into the canyon. At the base of each of the routes is anywhere from a half mile to a mile and a half of accessible river. You'll encounter browns up to 16 inches or so and a few rainbows, but not nearly as many as a decade ago. Whirling disease has wiped out virtually all of the native stocks, though the Colorado Department of Wildlife is rearing disease-free Gunnison-strain 'bows in its hatcheries and conducting experimental stockings to assess their mortality. For the past five years, to help restore a disease-free population of rainbows TU has been assisting in the stocking of five-inch rainbow fingerlings in the lower canyon downstream from the park. Any rainbows caught should be released immediately. Water flows in the canyon section are the subject of a bitter fight between conventional water users and the Department of Interior that want releases managed to meet the needs of agricultural interests and TU and other conservation groups that assert that maintaining habitat for fish and recreation is also important. TU won an important victory when its attorneys persuaded a proposed hydroelectric project to relinquish its rights to more than 1000 cfs of water from the Gunnison.

There is no float fishing through the Black Canyon section, but downstream, outfitters launch rafts at the base of the Chukkar Trail and take out where the North Fork comes in. Other access points along this run include the Duncan and Ute trails. Top to bottom elevation differential for these routes ranges between 600 and 1,200 feet. While it might be tempting to float this section solo, it's best not to. In places, the river piles up in class III and class IV rapids. Numerous outfitters offer three-day, two-night floats through the lower canyon. Others who want to fish this run hike up from the North Fork access. In the canyon, trout are not overly persnickety. Dropper rigs with a Caddis or attractor on top and a Bead Head Prince or Pheasant Tail below will usually draw strikes. More success is found, however, by fishing a double nymph rig with a small larvae pattern following a weighted streamer or Stonefly Nymph.

The upper stretch of the river above Gunnison is a classic sub-alpine freestone stream. From the top of its fishable runs to the town of Gunnison, the river flows across a high plateau along a cottonwood-lined route. Most of this property is private, but there is some public access, and it is a popular float. The upper section begins to fish well on those first sunny days of March with mid-day midge hatches. An initial spate of melt—snows up to 10,000 feet—blows through during the last two weeks of April, and then the river settles down and clears for two weeks. The main melt begins in late May, peaks about the tenth, and has cleared the system by the twentieth, about the same time as the first major hatch of stoneflies. Caddis begin then, too, and they're followed a month later by green drakes and gray drakes. After the grays come Baetis, which last into November. Nymphs are less often fished in this river because dry-fly action is relatively consistent, and because tributaries provide a plethora of dry-fly angling opportunities.

RESOURCES

Gearing up: Cimarron Creek, 317 E. Main St., Montrose, CO 81401; 970-249-0408; www.cimarroncreek.com.

High Mountain Drifter, 115 S. Wisconsin St., Gunnison, CO 81230; 970-641-4243.

Accommodations: Gunnison Area Chamber of Commerce, 500 E. Tomichi Ave., Box 36, Gunnison, CO 81230; 970-641-1501; www.gunnison-co.com.

Books: *The Colorado Angling Guide* by Chuck Fothergill and Bob Sterling, Stream Stalker Publishing Co.

The Complete Fly Fishing Guide for the Gunnison Drainage by Michael Shook, Shook Book Publishing.

Fishing Colorado by Ron Baird, Falcon Press.

The Fishing Map and Floater's Guide to the Gunnison and Lake Fork Rivers by Michael Shook, Shook Book Publishing.

Flyfisher's Guide to Colorado by Marty Bartholomew, Wilderness Adventure Press.

Fly Fishing in Colorado by Jackson Streit, Falcon Press.

72 Rio Grande

Location: South-central Colorado.
Short take: Headwaters of America's second longest river.
Type of stream: Freestone, tailwater.
Angling methods: Fly, spin, bait.
Species: Brown, rainbow, cutthroat, brook.
Access: Varies.
Season: Year-round
Supporting services: South Fork, Creede.
Handicapped access: No.
Closest TU chapter: Contact the state council of TU.

WHEN YOU CROSS THE DEWATERED DITCH that carries the Rio Grande between Cuidad Juarez and El Paso, the imagination strains to conceive the thought that this—at 1,885 miles—is the second longest river in the United States. Until I read Paul Horgan's Pulitzer and Bancroft–winning tome *Great River: The Rio Grande in North American History*, my sense of the westward exploration was limited to the way forged by Lewis and Clark up the Missouri. Horgan, like Francis Parkman of a century earlier, clothes the bones of Spanish exploration with purpose and sinew. Through his words, the human struggle to wrest sustenance from the arid mountains takes on life as rich and full as that of the Pilgrims at Plymouth Rock. Good fodder, this is, to ponder while drifting a nymph for browns sulking in Rio Grande gulches above Creede.

Like the Missouri, the Rio Grande heads up on the west flank of the Continental Divide. Beginning in a fine mountain stream, you can reach it via Lost Trail above the Rio Grande Reservoir. As you'd expect, the browns, brookies, and cutts here are smallish, up to 12 inches or so. But the trails are well maintained, and these opportunistic trout are eager to take virtually any #14 to #18 pattern that matches in color and size the hatch of the day. Pools and riffles are few, but pockets among angular boulders are abundant.

Below the reservoir, the river enters a narrow canyon six miles in length. The canyon can be difficult to access and offers good fishing only when releases from the dam are low. Beyond the canyon, the river breaks into a broad and open valley where it wanders to and fro. Too shallow to be floated, the Rio Grande here offers excellent fishing for those willing to walk in from limited access points and wade. The Colorado Department of Wildlife has placed the entire section from River Hill Campground downstream to the fence at Masonic Park, about 15 miles east of Creede, under special regulations. Anglers are allowed two browns per day of at least 12 inches, and must release all rainbows. Artificials-only rules apply.

From the Colorado Route 149 bridge at South Fork to the Rio Grande diversion canal at Del Norte, the Rio Grande has been designated a Gold Medal

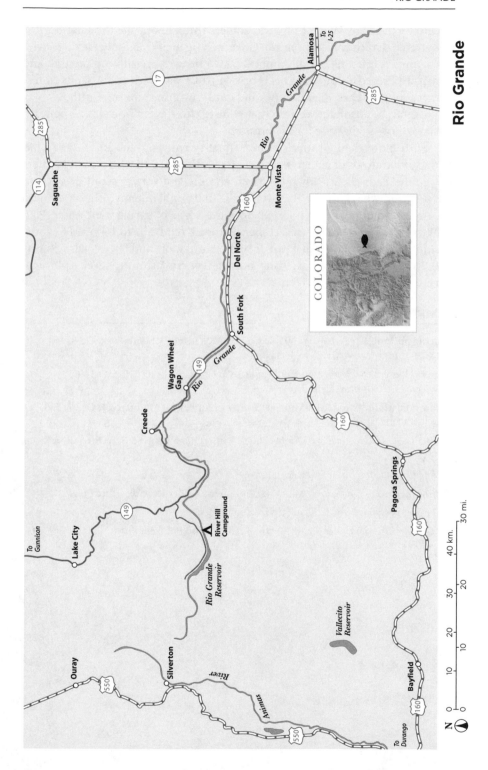

Rio Grande

COLORADO

stream by the state. When Colorado anglers think about the Rio Grande, it is this stretch that they have in mind. Governed by artificials-only tackle restrictions, anglers must release all rainbows. Two browns are allowed per day, and they must exceed 16 inches. This is brown trout water with thousands of fish in excess of 14 inches. Big rainbows and cuttbows also show up. Cuttbows may be kept, but be absolutely certain that you see those vermilion slashes beneath the jaw before saving one for the broiler.

With more than 70 miles of high-quality trouting, the Rio Grande has room for hundreds of anglers and can offer solitude to all who seek it. Numerous guides float clients down the river, an excellent way to scout new water. The only drawback to the Rio Grande is that, unlike many other Colorado streams, it generally fishes poorly before the surge of spring melt water. Plan your trips for late June into October. Patterns tend not to be overly exotic. Caddis, Adams, and the usual run of small stimulators and terrestrials will suffice. To tempt larger browns, bring along a few crayfish ties as well as brown, olive, and black Woolly Buggers.

RESOURCES

Gearing up: Wolf Creek Anglers, 001 Brown Dr., P.O. Box 263, South Fork, CO 81154; 719-873-1414; www.wolfcreekanglers.com.

Ramble House, 116 Creede Ave., P.O. Box 116, Creede, CO 81130; 719-658-2482; www.creede-co.com/ramblehouse.

Accommodations: Creede and Mineral County Chamber of Commerce, P. O. Box 580, Creede, CO 81130; 719-658-2374; www.creede.com.

Books: *The Colorado Angling Guide* by Chuck Fothergill and Bob Sterling, Stream Stalker Publishing Co.

Fishing Colorado by Ron Baird, Falcon Press.

Flyfisher's Guide to Colorado by Marty Bartholomew, Wilderness Adventure Press.

Fly Fishing in Colorado by Jackson Streit, Falcon Press.

Rio Grande: River Journal by Craig Martin, Frank Amato Publications.

73 Roaring Fork of the Colorado River

Location: Central Colorado, runs through Aspen.
Short take: Highways runs along it, but fish—some large—run in it. And don't overlook the tributaries.
Type of stream: Freestone.
Angling methods: Fly, spin.
Species: Brown, rainbow, brook, cutthroat.
Access: Moderate.
Season: Year-round.
Supporting services: Aspen, Basalt, Carbondale, Glenwood Springs.
Handicapped access: Yes.
Closest TU chapter: Ferdinand Hayden.

A NARROW FINGER OF THE WILLIAMS MOUNTAINS juts westward from the Continental Divide separating the Fryingpan and Roaring Fork watersheds. These rivers, though nearly twins, couldn't be more different. The "Pan" is at its best as a short tailwater from the outflow of Ruedi Dam to the village of Basalt where it surrenders its identity to the "Fork." Like the Pan, the Fork rises beneath 12,000-foot peaks, but it flows unfettered for more than 70 miles to its junction with the Colorado at Glenwood Springs. Unlike many Western rivers, this one doesn't wriggle back and forth in its valley, but makes a fairly straight shot of it to the northwest.

If you come west through the pass between Independence and Twining mountains on State Route 82, you'll cross a bridge over the uppermost run of Roaring Fork and then follow it down as it runs through the White River National Forest. For about 16 miles, access to the forest is open to the public, but that changes three miles upstream from Aspen, that winter and summer alpine tourist and think-tank mecca. Small rainbows, brook trout, and cutthroats make up the population as the river pushes down from cascade to pool to cascade again. Anglers are fewer and the terrain encourages solitude.

You won't discover much piece and quiet on the stretch below McFarlane Creek that enters the river four miles above Aspen. Spanning a dozen or so miles, the water from McFarlane Creek to upper Woody Creek Bridge, eight miles below the town, is designated a catch-and-release fishery. About half of this section is open to the public, and that which is and is not is less than well marked. Roaring Fork earns its name as it enters its first major canyon just below the mouth of Maroon Creek. Numerous boulders roil the water in this section, but an abandoned railbed turned hiking/biking path, eases access considerably. Artificial lures (nymphs work better than dries,

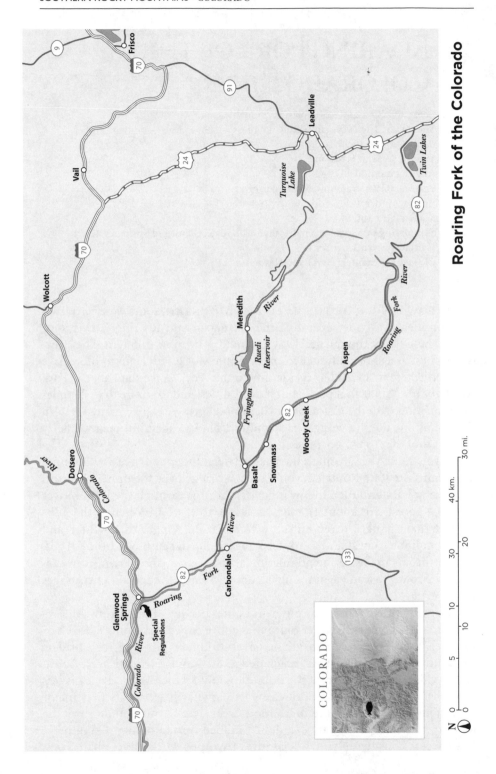

Roaring Fork of the Colorado

COLORADO

N

0   5   10   20   30 mi.

0   10   30   40 km.

with the exception of the early evenings of late summer) and catch-and-release are the rules here.

Roaring Fork exits the canyon at the upper Woody Creek (also known as True Smith) bridge. The river runs shallower, but is still quite swift. Wading will provide some interesting moments, even if you're wearing cleats and using a staff. Trout, browns mainly, are somewhat smaller than their siblings in the canyon above. The bottom in this run contains more gravel, and hatches are better. The river is still too small to require a driftboat, and most anglers fish it afoot, working Caddis, Green Drakes, Little Yellow Stones, or Pale Morning Duns. A dozen miles downstream from Woody Creek at Basalt, the Fryingpan enters from the north, and its heavy but clean waters change the nature of Roaring Fork.

No longer is it really wadable, and public land is mixed with private. Telling one from the other is difficult. Anglers fishing via shanks mare will find access to the river at Hooks Siding, Catherine, Carbondale, Westbank, and Sunlight Bridges. But better fishing will be from a driftboat, firing casts into pockets behind rocks within a foot or two of the bank. Gravel bars, so conducive to pullout and wade fishing on rivers like the South Fork of the Snake, are limited. You'll catch scores of trout—the largest will top 15 inches or so—and your casting arm will ache; all signs of a very good day.

Roaring Fork is a wild river and its flows are unimpeded by any dams. The river runs heavy with snowmelt from mid-May through June. Anglers, being sensible creatures, switch their affection to the Fryingpan tailwaters below Ruedi Dam when the Fork is unfishable. During pre-runoff, Blue-Winged Olives and little Buckskin Caddis will don the trick as will Mepps, Panther Martins, and small crankbaits with barbless hooks for spinning anglers. The green drake hatch is a local favorite and starts on the lower river in late June. This hatch heads upstream and reaches Aspen about a month later. A hatch of yellow stones brightens July and August.

Things slow a bit in August but pick up again toward the end of the month as waters cool. Best action in fall comes with BWOs and such streamers as a Black Flash-a-Bugger or Pearl Zonker. By the end of November, fish have become too lethargic for much activity, but even in midwinter skiers who happen to have a light rod, waders, and a box of Midges may have fun at high noon on a sunny day.

On Roaring Fork, TU's Ferdinand Hayden Chapter plays an important role. Over the years, members have established drop structures to aerate the flow, and the chapter was instrumental in securing the wild river and catch-and-release designations for the Fork. Underway is a project to restore wetlands in the Tree Farm section of the river. But what everybody loves are the annual Best of Trash Awards, where junk hauled from the river is arrayed in Basalt and prizes are presented for best in class.

RESOURCES

Gearing up: Alpine Angling, 981 Cowen Dr., Carbondale, CO 81623; 970-963-9245; www.alpineangling.com.

Fryingpan Anglers, 132 Basalt Center Circle, Basalt, CO 81621; 970-927-3441; www.fryingpananglers.com.

Roaring Fork Anglers, 2205 Grand Ave, Glenwood Springs, CO 81601; 970-945-0180; www.alpineangling.com.

Taylor Creek Flyshop, 183 Basalt Center Circle, Basalt, CO 81621; 970-927-4374; www.taylorcreek.com.

Accommodations: Aspen Chamber of Commerce, 425 Rio Grande Pl., Aspen, CO 81611; 970-925-1940; www.aspenchamber.org.

Basalt Chamber of Commerce, P.O. Box 514, Basalt, CO 81621; 970-927-4031; www.basaltchamber.com

Glenwood Springs Chamber of Commerce, 1102 Grand Ave., Glenwood Springs, CO 81601; 970-945-6589; www.glenwoodsprings.org

Books: *The Colorado Angling Guide* by Chuck Fothergill and Bob Sterling, Stream Stalker Publishing Co.

The Complete Fly Fishing Guide for the Roaring Fork Valley by Michael Shook, Shook Book Publishing.

Fishing Colorado by Ron Baird, Falcon Press.

The Fishing Map and Floater's Guide for the Roaring Fork and Fryingpan Rivers by Michael Shook, Shook Book Publishing.

Flyfisher's Guide to Colorado by Marty Bartholomew, Wilderness Adventure Press.

Fly Fishing in Colorado by Jackson Streit, Falcon Press.

74 SOUTH PLATTE RIVER

Location: Central Colorado, south of Denver.
Short take: Many miles, many fish, many anglers—but who cares?
Type of stream: Canyon tailwater.
Angling methods: Fly, spin.
Species: Rainbow, brown.
Access: Moderate.
Season: Year-round.
Supporting services: Denver.
Handicapped access: No.
Closest TU chapters: West Denver, Cheyenne Mountain.

THE MIDDLE AND LONGEST FORK OF THE SOUTH PLATTE RIVER gathers its waters from the east slope of the Continental Divide, curls around a trio of 13,500-foot mountains and then heads southeast through the little towns of Alma, Fairplay, and Garo. Below Hartsel, the main stem of the river joins the middle fork and together they enter Spinney Mountain Reservoir. While the tailwaters below Spinney, Eleven Mile Canyon, and Cheesman lakes attract most anglers who fish the South Platte, the headwaters should not be overlooked. Wild rainbows, cutthroat, and browns reside in these small mountain riffle/pool/chute streams, and during spawning seasons, fish of 20 inches and better move up out of Spinney Lake. From the Colorado Route 9 bridge 4.9 miles above Garo downstream to the lake's inlet, all trout between 12 and 20 inches must be immediately released and only artificial lures or flies are permitted. Within the Tomahawk Wildlife Management Area, fishing is closed from September 1 through January 31 to protect spawning trout.

Below Spinney Mountain Reservoir runs three miles of South Platte that are known for big trout. This open and wadable tailwater produces fish in the 14- to 18-inch range, and occasionally—again during spawning seasons—up to 24 inches or so. As much as I like catching big trout, I'm reluctant to intrude on their reproductive sessions. The reason is probably rooted in a combination of my puritanical upbringing with a dash of conservationist thrown in for good measure. Typical mayfly, caddis, and scud patterns are most effective, with golden stones coming off in May and terrestrials beginning to trigger strikes in July. The nine-mile section from Elevenmile Canyon dam to Lake George fishes similarly. Artificials-only and catch-and-release regs apply to the Spinney Lake tailwater and to the flows below Elevenmile Dam to Wagon Tongue Gulch.

North of the hamlet of Platte Springs, Tarryall Creek comes in from the northwest and it adds substantially to the South Platte. Good trout inhabit this

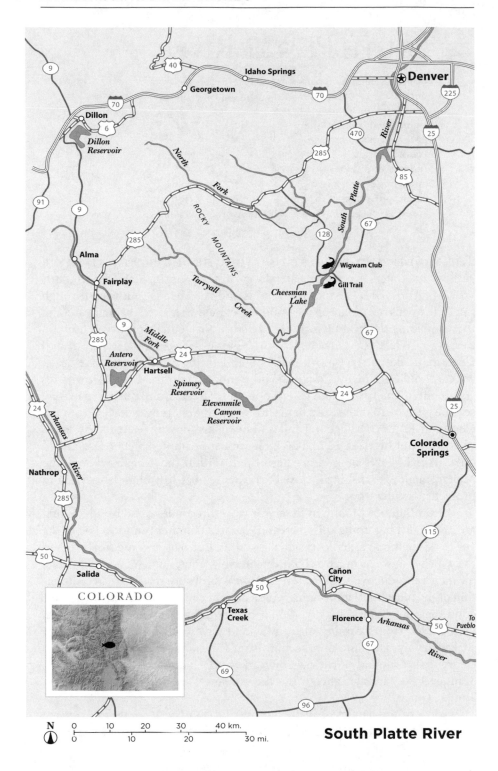

South Platte River

section, but better water is found below Cheesman Reservoir. This is the stretch that draws most fishers of this river. The river fishes best when flows are between 100 and 200 cubic feet per second. Twice that signals normal high water, but flows can reach 2,000 cfs. At 700 cfs the river becomes extremely dangerous. Call 303-831-7135, punch in 1, and then 40, followed by the # sign, to hear the most recent flow at Deckers just below the mouth of the canyon.

Good-sized browns and many rainbows inhabit this water. Nymphing is the most effective technique. Seven- to eight-foot leaders are the name of the game, with a second fly fished on an 18-inch dropper. Longer droppers make it difficult to feel the subtle take of these finicky trout. Your box should contain the Miracle Nymph, Brassie, Black Beauty, Pheasant Tail, and RS2. Sparse ties work better, generally speaking, than full-bodied versions. Sizes are tiny—18s to 22s. For dries, fish Blue-Winged Olives in spring and fall, Tricos in late summer, Caddis on summer evenings. Yellow Salleys and PMDs also produce in mid summer.

Thanks to the efforts of Sharon Lance, chair of the Colorado Council of Trout Unlimited, and scores of TU members from chapters in the Denver area, the Cheesman Trail Restoration project, which provides access via the Gill Trail to the tailwater below Cheesman Dam, has been completed. Lance led the charge to raise funds from a number of foundations and secure partnerships with the National Forest Foundation, Colorado State Parks, and the U.S. Forest Service. Volunteers worked for more than six years to repair washed-out sections of the trail and to create paths from the main trail down to the river, a steep drop of more than 100 feet in most places.

While the famous water on the South Platte is found in Cheesman Canyon, the trout fishery holds sport all the way to the Platte Canyon at Waterton, virtually in Denver's suburbs. Artificials-only and catch-and-release rules apply below Cheesman to the boundary of the private Wigwam. Below the clubs, property down to Scraggy View Picnic Ground, tackle restrictions still call for artificial lures, but anglers can keep two fish longer than 16 inches. Identical regs apply to the South Platte in Waterton Canyon, a brawling and beautiful section of river less than half an hour from downtown Denver. In the wake of forest fires in the South Platte watersheds, developers and others have been pressing to reduce water-quality standards on the river. Colorado Trout Unlimited was able to thwart these efforts, which would have resulted in increased pollution.

More than a decade ago, a coalition of conservation groups, including CTU, defeated proposals for Two Forks Dam on the South Platte, a project that would have inundated miles of gold-medal trout stream. In 2001, CTU worked side by side with former Two Forks proponent Denver Water to put together a new cooperative plan for protecting the South Platte future. The "South Platte Protection Plan" was developed by conservationists, local governments, and water providers as a means of protecting the unique values of the river, including both Elevenmile and Cheesman Canyons. The plan includes minimum streamflow commitments, sets habitat protection standards for the national forest, assures access for public recreational use to Denver Water's extensive landholdings along the river, and establishes a one million dollar endowment to support conservation projects along the river. CTU's efforts were made possible by support from the General Service Foundation and Compton Foundation.

RESOURCES

Gearing up: Denver and Colorado Springs boast a number of tackle shops, all of which can provide timely and accurate information about the South Platte.

Accommodations: Denver Metro Convention and Visitors Bureau, 1555 California St., Suite 300, Denver, CO 80202; 800-233-6837; www.denver.org.

Books: *The Colorado Angling Guide* by Chuck Fothergill and Bob Sterling, Stream Stalker Publishing Co.

Fishing Colorado by Ron Baird, Falcon Press.

Flyfisher's Guide to Colorado by Marty Bartholomew, Wilderness Adventure Press.

Fly Fishing in Colorado by Jackson Streit, Falcon Press.

The South Platte River Fishing Map and Guide by Michael Shook, Shook Book Publishing.

75 Green River, Flaming Gorge

Location: Northeast Utah.
Short take: Consistent, yes, but don't count your bugs before they're hatched.
Type of stream: Tailwater.
Angling methods: Fly, spin.
Species: Brown, rainbow, cutthroat.
Access: Easy.
Season: Year-round.
Supporting services: Dutch John.
Handicapped access: Yes, at Little Hole.
Closest TU chapter: Contact the state council of TU.

THE ARCH OF FLAMING GORGE DAM is thrust against the walls of Red Canyon by the pressure of 100 miles of impounded water from the Green River. The lake is famous for huge browns and kokanee salmon, but the tailwater below is known among anglers throughout the world for its river-run browns, cutthroats, and rainbows. Unlike the big tailwater on the Colorado between Glen Canyon Dam and Lees Ferry, the Green below Flaming Gorge is accessible by foot. For 11 miles, a well-maintained trail follows the north bank of the river and leads anglers to a dozen rapids and flats. Even in periods of low flow, crossing the river is very difficult. But wading and casting along the edge will yield very nice fish (browns averaging 16 inches and 'bows and cutthroats of 15 inches or so).

Most who fish the river float it, launching just below the dam and floating the 7.2 miles to Little Hole, a takeout and picnic ground maintained by the U.S. Forest Service. This is the most famous section of the river, and the most heavily fished. A second float of 9 miles from Little Hole to Indian Creek Crossing is also popular and productive. Red Creek comes in from the north about halfway down. In spate, Red Creek pumps fine, orange sediment into the river. The last stretch of the best water flows from Indian Creek and Browns Park (one-time hangout of Butch Cassidy's Wild Bunch) for 15 miles to Swinging Bridge (just shy of the Colorado/Utah boarder) and reportedly contains some large browns. Yet, after a heavy thunderstorm, fine sediment from Red Creek hangs in the slower-moving lower section. Sometimes days are required before it clears.

Another plus for the Green are reasonably predictable and constant flows. The river runs between 2,500 and 3,000 cubic feet per second during the winter, rising to about 4,600 cfs in May. This burst is designed to complement natural runoff from the Yampa, 100 river miles downstream, providing an environmental flood to recharge wetlands so that endangered species may

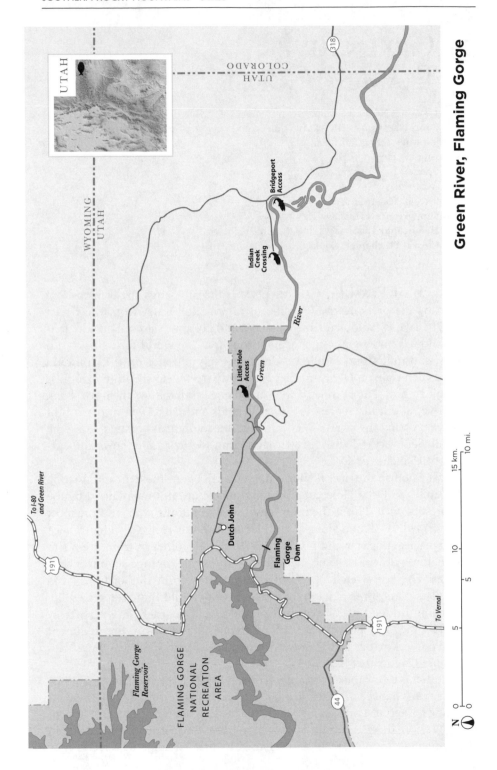

Green River, Flaming Gorge

UTAH

WYOMING
UTAH

COLORADO
UTAH

318

Bridgeport
Access

Indian
Creek
Crossing

Green River

Little Hole
Access

To I-80
and Green River

191

Dutch John

Flaming
Gorge
Dam

FLAMING GORGE
NATIONAL
RECREATION
AREA

Flaming Gorge
Reservoir

191

To Vernal

44

N

15 km.

10

5

10 mi.

5

thrive. In late June or early July, flows drop back to about 1,800 cfs, where they are maintained through the fall.

The 19,000-acre fire of July 2002 seems to have altered the cycle of hatches from Little Hole downstream, says Dennis Breer of Trout Creek Flies, which opened in 2001. A plume of silt was deposited at mile marker six, resulting in a decline of the Baetis hatches, but increased numbers of PMDs and yellow sallies. As on most rivers, it is imprudent to time a trip to fish a specific hatch that only lasts a week or so. You may be on time, but the hatch may not. If your destination happens to be Flaming Gorge, and the vagaries of weather intrude on your plans, you'll always find great fish taking other bugs. Generally speaking, however, the season begins with midges in February and March, shifts to blue-winged olives from March into May, big cicadas in May, and then terrestrials—hoppers, crickets, ants. Hatches of pale morning duns and Tricos come off in July and August. And later, coinciding with spawning runs of browns in the fall, is an excellent hatch of blue-winged olives. Nymphs and scuds, particularly when fished below a big dry that serves as a strike indicator, can be very effective. Sizes tend to be small—#16 to #26.

RESOURCES

Gearing up: Flaming Gorge Lodge, 155 Greendale, US 191, Dutch John, UT 84023; 435-889-3773; www.fglodge.com.

Trout Creek Flies, P.O. Box 247, Dutch John, UT, 84023; 435-885-3338; www.fishgreenriver.com.

Accommodations: Flaming Gorge Chamber of Commerce, P.O. Box 122, Manila, UT 84046; 435-784-3154 or 435-784-3445; www.flaminggorgecountry.com.

Books: *The Green River* by Larry Tullis, River Journal Series, Frank Amato Publications.

The Green River Fishing Map and Floater's Guide by Michael Shook, Shook Book Publishing.

76 PROVO RIVER, MIDDLE FORK

Location: Northeast Utah.
Short take: Trout see so many patterns they ought to know better than to suck in yours.
Type of stream: Tailwater.
Angling methods: Fly, spin.
Species: Brown, cutthroat, rainbow.
Access: Easy.
Season: Year-round.
Supporting services: Park City, Heber City.
Handicapped access: Not exactly.
Closest TU chapter: Contact the state council of TU.

NOT MUCH MORE THAN AN HOUR AND A HALF FROM Salt Lake City and less than 30 minutes from the university city of Provo, this river handles heavy angling pressure with aplomb. No matter how crowded, you can always find a spot where trout are willing, and some of them are big enough to know better. But they don't. Often, anglers whose interest is spring skiing beat a path to the middle section of the Provo, pound the water with but few casts, hook and land a brown of 14 to 18 inches, say "been there, done that," and go light a self-congratulatory cigar. The Provo has a way of fish'n' easy. And for that, I love it.

Best known for its tailwater sections below Jordanelle and Deer Creek reservoirs, the Provo begins, as all rivers do, as a trickly mountain stream rising in the Uintah Range at Trail Lake. During the next 36 miles it matures, growing lovely wild browns of a foot or so as well as 'bows, brookies, and cutts. The country with its high meadows and stands of black pine is achingly beautiful, and the river is well away from the crowded sections downstream. Access is difficult because most of the mileage is private. Fly shops in Heber City and Park City can steer you in the right direction.

The Middle Fork is the water that resonates with me. The outflow from Jordanelle Dam is less than 30 feet wide and not very deep. With shaded riffles and runs in the channel above the U.S. Route 40 bridge, this tailwater produces trout all year. Anglers willing to fish small nymphs below strike indicators can take fish every 10 minutes or so. Catch one, wait a few minutes, and another will move into the feeding station. On this run, every angler is an expert.

Below the bridge, the Middle Fork is receiving a makeover, thanks to the ambitious 30-million-dollar Provo River Restoration Project. Forced into a fairly straight channel in a misguided effort at flood control years ago, the Utah Reclamation Mitigation and Conservation Commission began returning the Provo to its heritage channel. Begun in 1999 and expected to be completed in 2006, the plan is providing a natural floodplain 800 to 2,000 feet in width so

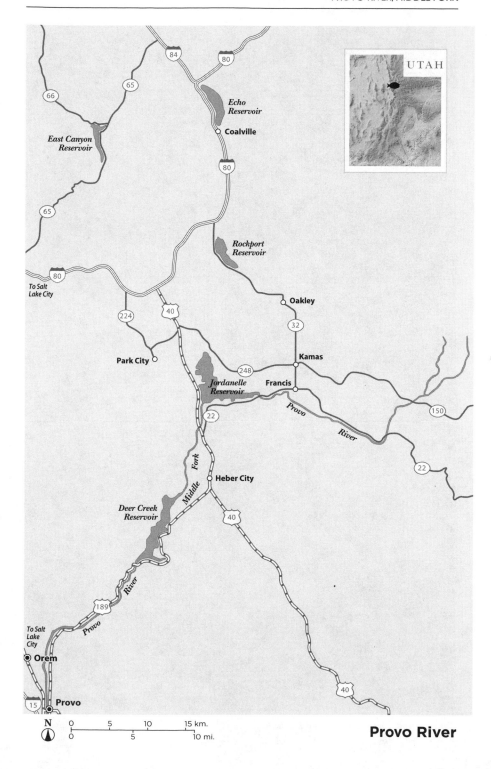

UTAH

84
80
65
66
Echo Reservoir
Coalville
East Canyon Reservoir
80
65
Rockport Reservoir
To Salt Lake City
80
40
224
Oakley
32
Park City
Kamas
248
Jordanelle Reservoir
Francis
Provo River
150
22
Heber City
Middle Fork
22
Deer Creek Reservoir
40
189
River
To Salt Lake City
Provo River
Orem
40
15
Provo

N

| 0 | 5 | 10 | 15 km. |
| 0 | | 5 | 10 mi. |

Provo River

On the Provo River, no matter how crowded, you can always find a spot where trout are willing takers of your fly.

the river can meander more or less naturally. Wetlands to filter runoff and provide riparian habitat are being created, and plantings of native streamside vegetation will create shade and cover for trout. Stiles are being erected at fence crossings and a public-access corridor will run the length of the 10 miles down to the inlet of Deer Creek Lake. Studies have shown the lower two and a half miles of the middle run to be overpopulated with smaller trout, so the Utah Division of Wildlife has opened angling to use of bait and increased creel limits. You'll want to check current regs when you buy your license.

As it comes out of Deer Creek Dam, the Provo runs hard by U.S. Route 189 and drops some 600 feet in the nine miles down to Orem. Considered by many to be "Blue Ribbon" water, what this section lacks in ambience it makes up for with its 4,500 trout per mile. You'll find all the usual Western flies hatching on the Provo, but the most effective patterns are small, typically in the #18 to #22 range, with the exception of the green drake hatch in June and early July. If you hate crowds and want quality fish, plan your trip for late winter.

RESOURCES

Gearing up: Trout Bum 2, 343 N. Hwy. 224, Suite 101, Park City, UT 84060; 435-658-1166; 877-878-2862; www.troutbum2.com.

Four Seasons Fly Fishers; 44 W. 100 St., Heber City, UT 84032; 435-657-2010; www.utahflyfish.com.

Accommodations: Heber Valley Chamber of Commerce and Visitor Center, 475 N. Main St., Heber City, UT 84060; 435-654-3666; www.hebervalleycc.org.

Park City Chamber Of Commerce-Convention and Visitors Bureau, 528 Main St., Park City, UT 84060; 435-649-6104; www.parkcityinfo.com.

Books: *Flyfishers Guide to Utah* by James B. DeMoux, Wilderness Adventure Press.

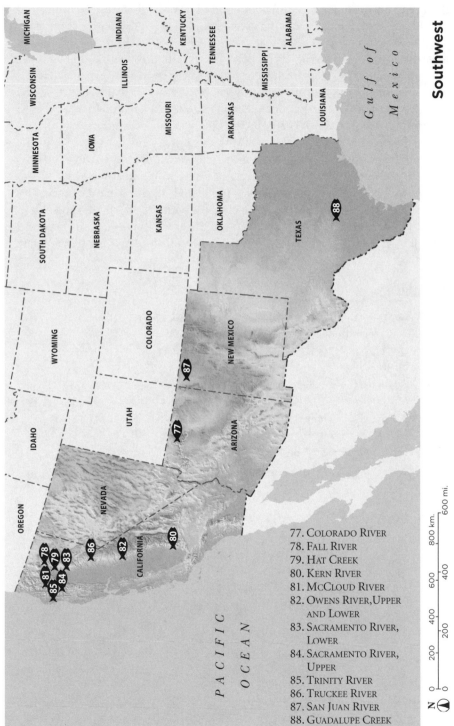

Southwest

77. Colorado River
78. Fall River
79. Hat Creek
80. Kern River
81. McCloud River
82. Owens River, Upper
    and Lower
83. Sacramento River,
    Lower
84. Sacramento River,
    Upper
85. Trinity River
86. Truckee River
87. San Juan River
88. Guadalupe Creek

SOUTHWEST

ARIZONA

CALIFORNIA

NEVADA

NEW MEXICO

TEXAS

77 COLORADO RIVER

Location: Northern Arizona.
Short take: Lots and Lots of 'bows, and some of 'em are huge.
Type of stream: Tailwater.
Angling methods: Fly, spin.
Species: Rainbow.
Access: Limited.
Season: Year-round.
Supporting services: Marble Canyon.
Handicapped access: Yes.
Closest TU chapter: Lees Ferry.

DURING THE 1990S, THE COLORADO RIVER below Glen Canyon Dam upstream from the top of the Grand Canyon was the place where aficionados of tiny flies could tussle with rainbows of occasionally gargantuan size. Still can, but regulations governing the 15.5 miles from the dam to Lees Ferry encourage anglers to keep four trout per day with a possession limit of eight. Tackle is still restricted to artificial flies and lures with barbless hooks, and all trout longer than 12 inches must be released. The reason: officials with Arizona Game and Fish cite burgeoning populations of smaller trout.

Low river flows, high levels of reproduction, and excellent fry survival rates all contributed to the doubling of two-year-old trout in the river. Persistent drought and resulting minimal releases seem to have reduced fish habitat and food sources. It's hoped that the harvesting of smaller fish, while mandating catch-and-release for all larger trout, will reduce pressure on the food base and provide anglers with more big bruisers. At the head of the walk-in section at Paria Riffle, where the river of the same name enters from the northwest, anglers can use any tackle they wish and keep as many as six trout per day.

Though big trout may not be as plentiful as they once were, the Colorado River above Lees Ferry is one of the most stunning places to fish in the United States. Sinuous, cold, and very dark green from deep and life-giving beds of aquatic mosses, the Colorado flows past 1,000-foot cliffs of rugged red sandstone. Eagles and condors soar on thermals rising along the canyon's vertical walls. But the slick river is, itself, eerily quiet. The river environment is wholly artificial—a long, frigid tailwater—in a hot and dry canyon where cloudbursts once turned the river into a churning brown slurry in a heartbeat.

With the exception of the Paria Riffle, there's little access for foot-bound anglers. Most rent boats or hire guides and motor upstream to anchor at gravel bars and wade. Midge hatches, black, grey, or olive, in early spring draw legions of anglers. Look for rises in calm water. But day in and day out, scuds and nymphs are most productive because crustaceans constitute the primary food source here. Grey or tan in sizes #10 to #16 are most effective. Frequently

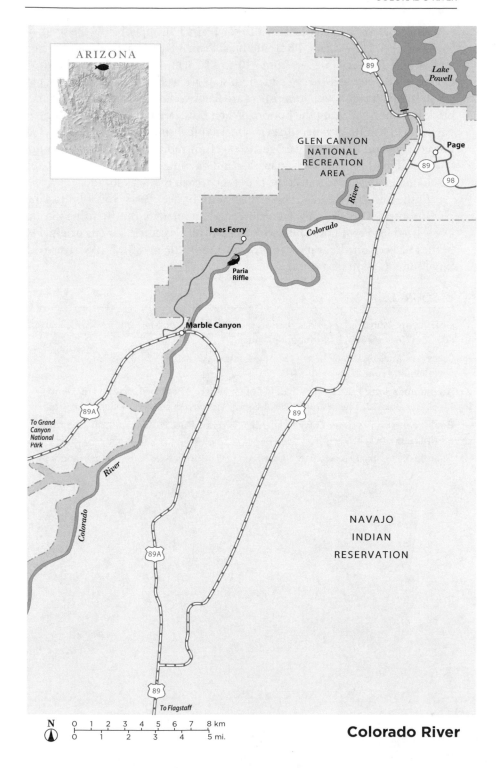

ARIZONA

Lake Powell

89

GLEN CANYON
NATIONAL
RECREATION
AREA

Page

89

98

Lees Ferry

Colorado River

Paria
Riffle

Marble Canyon

89A

To Grand
Canyon
National
Park

Colorado River

89

NAVAJO

INDIAN

RESERVATION

89A

89

To Flagstaff

N

| 0 | 1 | 2 | 3 | 4 | 5 | 6 | 7 | 8 km |
| 0 | 1 | 2 | 3 | 4 | 5 mi. |

Colorado River

a Brassie in #16 to #24 is fished on a 10- or 12-inch dropper below the scud. As you'd suspect, Hare's Ears, Pheasant Tails, Prince Nymphs, San Juan Worms, and Woolly Buggers in sizes from #10 to #16 will occasionally do the trick. During midwinter spawn, egg patterns also work well. During high flows, terrestrials attract rainbows. Spin fishers are likely to find success with brown or black jigs bounced along the bottom. When flows are below 14,000 cubic feet per second, fishing is generally best. On a typical summer's day, due to peak power demands, flows can average 20,000 cfs or more. Winter flows are much lower, and that, coupled with spawning and daytime highs in the 40s and 50s, make this an ideal time to fish the Lees Ferry reach of the Colorado.

In the town of Marble Canyon, just south of Lees Ferry, you'll find a couple of motels, a service station, a store, and an airstrip. But fly fishers in the know head for Vermilion Cliffs, with its rustically eccentric bar (its original 99 bottles of beer on the wall have grown to more than 180), funky river-rock motel, and fly shop next door.

RESOURCES

Gearing up: Ambassador Guides Services Inc., P.O. Box 6229, Marble Canyon, AZ 86036; 800-256-7596; www.ambassadorguides.com.

Lees Ferry Anglers, HC-67 Box 30, Marble Canyon, AZ 86036; 928-355-2261; www.leesferry.com.

Accommodations: Lake Powell Chamber of Commerce, 644 North Navajo Dr., Dam Plaza, P.O. Box 727, Page, AZ 86040; 928-645-2741; www.pagelakepowellchamber.org.

Books: *Dave Foster's Guide to Fly Fishing Lee's Ferry* by Dave Foster, California Bills Automotive Handbook.

Guide to Fly Fishing in Arizona by Glenn Tinnin, California Bill's Automotive Handbooks.

78 FALL RIVER

Location: North-central California.
Short take: A Hex of a river for 'bows.
Type of stream: Spring Creek.
Angling methods: Fly, spin.
Species: Rainbow.
Access: Difficult.
Season: Late April to mid-November.
Supporting services: Fall River Mills.
Handicapped access: Via boat.
Closest TU chapter: Contact the state council of TU.

NORTHERN CALIFORNIA IS RICH WITH SPRING CREEKS, but none so fertile as the Fall River. Rising in the Thousand Springs area of northern California, the Fall River meanders through a broad valley of tawny grasslands and pine. Gradient on the Fall River is not steep; it seems to belie its name except at its junction with the Pit at the town of Fall River Mills about 20 miles downstream. Green as the glass in an old Coke bottle, the upper third of the Fall River picks its way through a sparse woodland before breaking into the open at Spring Creek Bridge. The upper mileage includes riffles and occasional pockets, but below the bridge it flows over tufts of aquatic grasses rooted in clayish mud. Wading, alas, is not an option. Not only is the bottom unsuitable, but banks are also owned privately. Access requires payment of a rod fee, booking at a lodge, or hiring a guide. Cal Trout maintains a launching ramp with limited parking at the Island Road Bridge, and California Fish and Game has a launch site on Pacific Gas & Electric property where McArthur Road crosses Fall River a couple miles below its confluence with the Tule.

That said, the gentle current and lack of obstructions make this a boater's dream. Launch a pram or other raft powered by electric motor and ease your way upstream to anchor. You'll need two anchors to keep the boat from swinging in the steady, cold current. Among the more effective presentations is to cast a tiny dry downstream, so that it drifts into a pod of rising trout.

When the river opens in late April, pale morning duns begin to hatch. The hatch improves into late June and then fades only to rise again in late September. Green drakes are plentiful as well. July brings Tricos that continue into October. You can find little blue-winged olives most any time on the upper section. On the lower section of the river, downstream from Island Road to the Tule River, you'll find more tan caddis hatches than on the upper section. Anglers fishing caddis dries or pupae are almost guaranteed a fish during those gentle evenings of high summer.

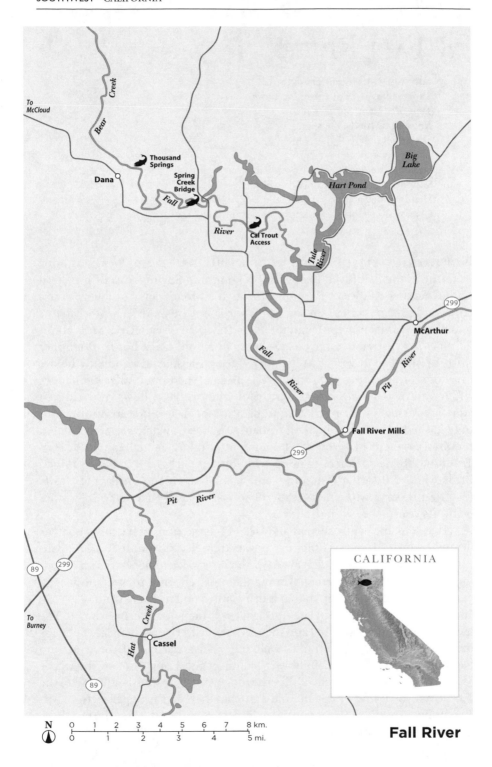

Fall River

CALIFORNIA

N

| 0 | 1 | 2 | 3 | 4 | 5 | 6 | 7 | 8 km. |
| 0 | 1 | 2 | 3 | 4 | 5 mi. |

From the Tule River to McArthur Road Bridge, *Hexagenia limbata* begins in mid-June. That's the hatch everybody lives for. Water temperature may trigger these huge mayflies, because the hatch begins at the junction with the Pit and daily works its way upstream. Predicting the date the hatch begins is akin to guessing the year's first frost. In July, the Hex hatch thickens to blizzard proportions before fading by the end of the month. Fished in gathering night, Hex patterns—first nymphs, then dries—attract fish by size, not color. Rainbows feed with utter abandon, continuing long after the hour ending legal angling is past.

Fall River is rainbow water that holds some browns. Average fish run in the 12- to 14-inch range. Water clarity demands long, fine leaders of 5X or 6X and #14 to #20 flies. The valley is apt to be windy, so shun rigs lighter than a 5-weight, no matter how tempting. From its origin at Thousand Springs downstream to the mouth of the Tule, anglers must release all trout larger than 14 inches. And barbless-hooked artificial lures are required.

RESOURCES

Gearing up: The Fly Shop, 4140 Churn Creek Rd., Redding, CA 96002; 530-222-3555; web: www.flyshop.com.

Accommodations: Fall River Valley Chamber of Commerce, P.O. Box 475, Fall River Mills, CA 96028; 530-336-5840.

Books: *California Blue-Ribbon Trout Streams* by Bill Sunderland and Dale Lackey, Frank Amato Publications.

Flyfisher's Guide to Northern California by Seth Norman, Wilderness Adventures Press.

Guide to Fishing in Northern California by Ken Hanley, David Communications.

Trout Fishing in California by Ron Kovach, Marketscope Hourglass Books.

79 HAT CREEK

Location: Northern California.
Short take: Wild trophy trout waters are both highly technical and suited for the novice. Upper reaches offer good put-and-take fishing.
Type of stream: Freestone, then tailwater spring creek.
Angling methods: Fly, spin.
Species: Rainbow, brown.
Access: Easy.
Season: Late April through mid-November.
Supporting services: Cassel.
Handicapped access: Yes.
Closest TU chapter: Contact the state council of TU.

THOUGH HAT CREEK FLOWS NORTHWARD FOR MORE THAN 20 miles from its headwaters on Badger Mountain to where it meets the waters of the Pit River in Lake Britton, only the 3.2-mile Wild Trout section from the outflow of Powerhouse No. 2 below Cassel is of compelling interest to masochistic fly fishers who love to be humbled by prima donna rainbows. The first two miles-plus of this stretch is the ultimate spring creek look-alike, save the heavily fished Powerhouse Riffle. Below, Hat Creek slows and broadens. The surface, here, reminds me of old poured window glass. Tiny seams separate microcurrents, the presence of which are only evident by the way the water seems to bulge slightly. There is naught but one way to fish this kind of stuff: slowly. Forget long casts, but stealth your way close enough so you can place your fly with delicate precision.

If such discipline is found in your nature as seldom as it appears in mine, push down to the lower third of this run and fish the pockets and pools in the stretch above Lake Britton. Fewer trout inhabit this run, but those that lurk in these crannies are larger and much more opportunistic feeders.

Hatches of midges and mayflies are prolific. So are the anglers who rise to the hatch du jour in a manner not dissimilar from trout. (Okay, I'll play this out for you. Curled in the seats of our SUVs, we resemble larvae. Pupating, we uncurl and stretch as we navigate the ether between car door and trunk. In our emerger stage, we're donning all the trappings of an adult angler—though my spouse might quarrel with the "adult" bit. To the river, we take wing. After mating with Piscator or Piscatoria as is our wont, we fall back to our vehicles, spent.)

Along with mayflies, salmon flies open the season in April and extend into late May. May brings little sister sedges as well as green drakes. The drakes hang around well into June and favor cloudy days and spitting rain. Sedges persist into July. As summer advances, smaller mayflies—pale morning and evening duns—draw trout. Tricos reach their peak in midsummer; anglers

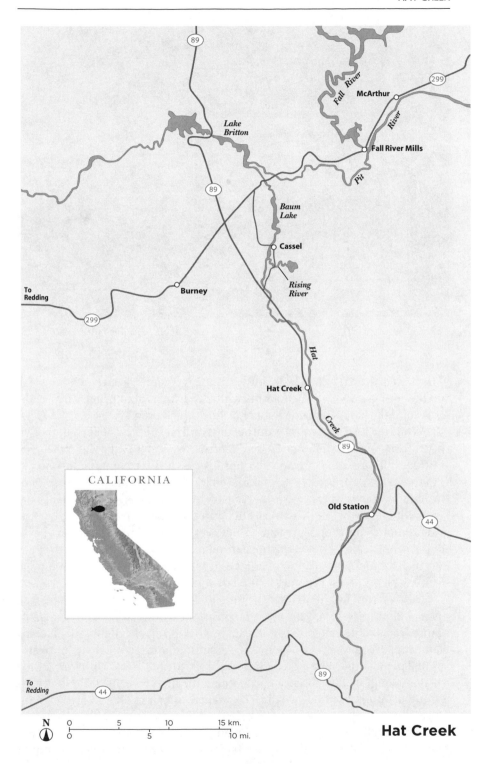

CALIFORNIA

Hat Creek

The alkaline waters of Hat Creek support prolific insect populations—and the trout that eat them.

who master the Trico hatch do so with long, gossamer leaders. Cooling fall weather brings caddis in such numbers that they're hard to believe. Especially glorious is the hatch of giant October caddis, which even I can see.

While the lower 3.2 miles is the big deal on Hat Creek, that ain't all there is to it. Rising on the slopes of Lassen Volcanic National Park, Hat Creek is a bustling little freestone stream that hustles down the mountain and breaks into the valley floor below Old Station. There it slows and begins to meander through meadows where livestock—fenced from the creek—graze. Banks are laden with heavy brush that sweeps the water and provides cover for browns and rainbows. In the upper reaches, Hat Creek is a put-and-take stream, heavily stocked. There is, however, some natural reproduction. Mileage in the park and the abutting national forest is open to public angling but once bounded by private land, access becomes limited to guests at lodges along its course.

Inflows from bubbling springs of the Rising River, which joins Hat Creek just south of Cassel, cool the river to consistent temperatures and change its nature from a freestone meadow stream to a spring creek. Highly alkaline, the water supports a wealth of aquatic life, resulting in myriad hatches and substantial populations of crustacea. Cassel sits astride the creek. Upstream of the town is a long, shallow forebay impounding the intake for the Hat No. 1 generating plant for Pacific Gas & Electric. Open to bait as well as artificial angling, the forebay and Baum Lake below exhibit many of the characteristics of the famed three-mile stretch upstream from Lake Britton. Bait (crickets, nightcrawlers, salmon eggs) and lure (small minnowlike crankbaits, spinners, and spoons) anglers are very successful on the forebay and Baum Lake , and fly anglers who are willing to launch a flat-bottomed boat or raft can do quite well.

Three years of coalition-building and aggressive advocacy work by TU attorneys finally paid off when Pacific Gas & Electric agreed to a bankruptcy settlement that preserves 140,000 acres in California's Sierra Nevada region. Spread among nearly 1,000 parcels in 22 counties from Mount Shasta to Bakersfield, the lands comprise hallowed angling destinations like Hat Creek, as well PG&E's vast network of dams, reservoirs and powerhouses. The settlement agreement ensures that the lands will be donated to parks or wildlife agencies or protected through easements, and it provides $100 million to manage the acreage over the next decade. All told, the deal represents the country's largest-ever conservation agreement for hydro lands.

RESOURCES

Gearing up: Vaughn's Sporting Goods, 37307 Main St., Burney, CA 96013; 530-335-2381; www.vaughnfly.com.

Accommodations: Burney Chamber of Commerce, 37088 Main St., P.O. Box 36, Burney, CA 96013; 530-335-2111; www.burneychamber.com.

Books: *California Blue-Ribbon Trout Streams* by Bill Sunderland and Dale Lackey, Frank Amato Publications.

Flyfisher's Guide to Northern California by Seth Norman, Wilderness Adventures Press.

Guide to Fly Fishing in Northern California by Ken Hanley, David Communications.

Trout Fishing in Northern California by Ron Kovach, Marketscope Hourglass Books.

80 KERN RIVER

Location: Central California.
Short take: Where anglers come to prospect for wild gold.
Type of stream: Freestone.
Angling methods: Fly, spin.
Species: Rainbow, brown.
Access: Easy.
Season: Late April through mid-November.
Supporting services: Kernville.
Handicapped access: No.
Closest TU chapter: Contact the state council of TU.

THE GOLD IN THE MOUNTAINS OF THE UPPER KERN RIVER watershed above Kernville refers to three subspecies of golden rainbows: South Fork Kern Golden Trout, Golden Trout Creek Golden Trout, and Little Kern River Golden Trout. In choosing "Golden Trout" for its state fish, California has created an alloy of the three subspecies. In addition, a fourth subspecies—the Kern River Rainbow Trout—resides in the higher reaches of the river's main stem.

There are no rainbows colored more vividly than these three golden trout. A burst of orange-crimson, the way the horizon flames on a clear and bitter cold morning the instant before sunrise, streaks through parr marks of deep purple along the lateral line. In the main, wild golden trout are not yellow like their hatchery cousins, but a burnished brass that's darker on the back and then brightens to orange and then deepens to brilliant crimson, yet not so red as the flash on the lateral line. Few are the dark spots on the back of the Golden Creek subspecies, extending no farther forward than the front of the dorsal fin. On the South Fork Kern golden, the spots trickle back from the nose. They are tiny at first and grow larger toward the tail. The Little Kern River golden bears more spots than the other two and they extend below the lateral line. By comparison, the Kern River rainbow's back is greener and darker, the red lateral line not so bright, the parr marks—which all carry through adulthood—less distinct, and the spots smaller and much more profuse.

The drainage of these exquisite natives is a wildly beautiful wilderness of 12,000-foot peaks, forests of Ponderosa pine and giant sequoia and sugar pine, open meadows like Hole in the Ground and Grasshopper Flat, and rivers that tumble through chute to pool and into gardens of pocket water. All carry trout. Populations of the three goldens are pretty well restricted to their respective watersheds. Their size seldom, but occasionally, extends beyond 12 inches. Browns are, however, foraging inroads, and there are those that were up to 25 inches when caught.

The golden trout's population has been dropping for more than 30 years, prompting the U.S. Fish and Wildlife Service to rule two years ago that the

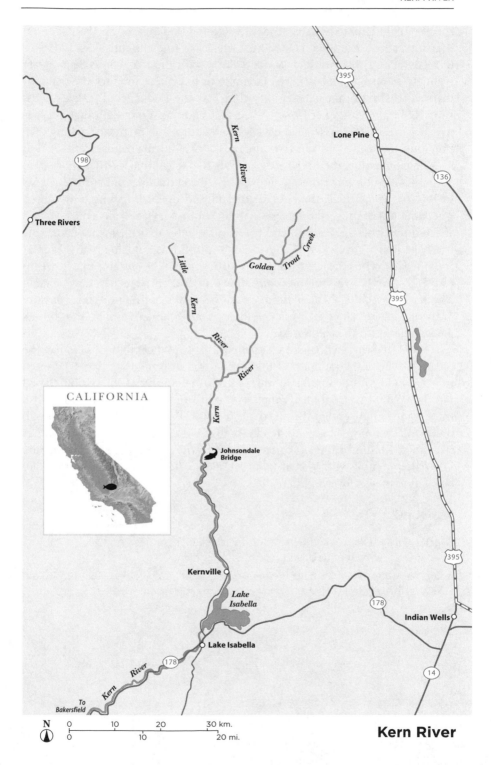

CALIFORNIA

Three Rivers

Kern River

Little Kern River

Golden Trout Creek

River

Kern River

Johnsondale Bridge

Lone Pine

Indian Wells

Kernville

Lake Isabella

Lake Isabella

Kern River

To Bakersfield

N

0   10   20   30 km.

0   10   20 mi.

Kern River

species might have to be listed under the federal Endangered Species Act. That decision came a year after TU sued the agency to force its consideration. Now the federal and state wildlife services, along with the U.S. Forest Service, are trying to avoid a formal listing by taking steps to protect and increase the population. That's an unusual step and comes as the Endangered Species Act is subjected to increasing criticism. TU is willing to go along with that alternative, because this recovery plan has more substance and financial backing than previous proposals, said Chuck Bonham, TU's California counsel.

Taken together, the upper Kern and its major tributaries offer more than 100 miles of wilderness angling. From Kernville at the inlet of Lake Isabella up to Johnsondale Bridge, the river is stocked and open to fishing year-round. The four miles above the bridge to U.S. Forest Service Trail 33E30 are restricted to barbless artificials, and two trout greater than 14 inches constitute the creel limit. This water becomes catch-and-release outside of the regular season, which runs the last Saturday in April through November 15. Upstream of this trail, only two rainbows, and none longer than 10 inches, may be kept. The barbless artificial rule continues in effect, but there's no winter season. Trails shadow much of the Kern and its tributaries, and a number of outfitters pack anglers into the wilderness.

Had I the wherewithal, I'd set up an old-time tent camp high in one of the meadows above the junction of the Little Kern with the main river. I'd pitch my canvas in mid-September and stay until the closing of the season chased me out. With a seven-foot, six-inch 4-weight rod of cane, I'd cast Caddis on the bright happy waters. I'd meander as do the Kern's tributaries through meadows, probing grassy undercut banks with small buggers and other streamers. Each morning, as coffee steeped in the pot on the rock by the fire, I'd write my notes with pencil in an engineer's field book. Stream notes are best left to mature overnight.

RESOURCES

Gearing up: Kern River Troutfitters, 11301 Kernville Rd., Kernville, CA 93238; 760-376-2040; www.kernriverflyfish.com.

Accommodations: KRV Chamber of Commerce, P.O. Box 567, 6117 Lake Isabella Blvd., Lake Isabella, CA 93240; 760-379-5236; www. kernrivervalley.com.

81 McCloud River

Location: North-central California.
Short take: Black rocks, brooding pines, and bruising 'bows and browns.
Type of stream: Freestone above the dam, tailwater below.
Angling methods: Fly, spin, bait.
Species: Rainbow, brown.
Access: Moderate.
Season: Late April through mid-November.
Supporting services: Dunsmuir, Redding.
Handicapped access: Yes.
Closest TU chapter: Contact the state council of TU.

FOR MOST OF A CENTURY, THE McCLOUD RIVER harbored the healthiest and wiliest of California's wild rainbow population. It was from this river that eggs were shipped East in 1874 to grow big trout for anglers of Atlantic watersheds. In exchange, browns sired by imports from Germany and England took the train west where they happily found water to their liking. You'll find remnants of native rainbow populations and a burgeoning population of browns in this river that many Californians claim as home water.

Rising in Dead Horse Canyon, the McCloud flows for about 56 miles before reaching Shasta Lake. In the 1960s, a reservoir impounded the river about 30 miles downstream from its headwaters. As is typical of dams, this one is both blessing and curse. The blessing is that it provides cool, clear, and stable flows for about 20 miles of glorious water—the mileage that everyone dreams about when they think of McCloud River trout. The impoundment traps much of the glacial sediment from Mud and Ash creeks, which would otherwise silt the river when the snows of 14,000-foot Mount Shasta begin to melt in June. And it provides a haven for big browns and rainbows, which enter the upper river to spawn in winter and spring. Unfortunately, the dam diverts much of the flow into the Pit River in the next watershed to the east and the result has been low flows that have brought to virtual extinction one of the southernmost populations of Dolly Varden in the United States.

For 30 miles above McCloud Reservoir, the river is a classic freestone stream. The McCloud Loop Road shadows much of the river and Highway 89 generally runs along its course. At Alonga, the upstream-most access, the river is not much wider than a healthy hop. Fishing pressure is heavy, as it is on sections immediately below—Four-Mile Flat and Skunk Hollow. The eastern terminus of the Loop Road begins at Cattle Camp. The large pool here marks the start of the some of the best public fishing on the upper river. Below 40-foot Middle Falls, and at the plunge pool below Lower Falls, 8- to 14-inch rainbows are released. Here, the Loop Road circles back to Route 89, and downstream,

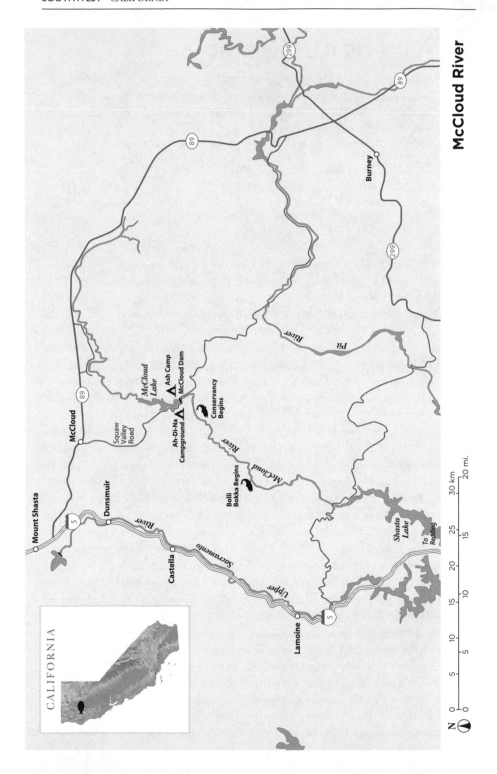

McCloud River

CALIFORNIA

299

89

89

Burney

299

McCloud Lake

Ash Camp

McCloud Dam

Conservancy Begins

Squaw Valley Road

Ah-Di-Na Campground

Pit River

McCloud River

Bolli Bokka Begins

89

McCloud

Mount Shasta

Dunsmuir

5

Sacramento River

Castella

Upper

Shasta Lake

To Redding

5

Lamoine

N

0   5   10   15   20   25   30 km
0   5   10   15   20 mi.

the river soon enters the Hearst estate, which is closed to the public, angling all the way to the reservoir.

The dam on the reservoir spills water into the lower river at a rate of 150 to 220 cubic feet per second. Heavily shaded, the river works through hefty boulders of basalt, creating deep pockets and runs that hold trout. From the dam downstream about five miles to Ladybug Creek, the river runs through Shasta National Forest and the road to Ah-Di-Na Campground puts you in the middle of this fine stretch of public water. Below are six miles of Nature Conservancy water. The upper two-and-a-half miles are open only to 10 rods per day. Because of restricted access, this is arguably the best public section of the river. Below a section of a few miles where no fishing is permitted, the stream is in private hands of the McCloud River Club and Bolli Bokka Club. The latter rents a few lavish, yet rustic furnished camps and provides guide service on the river upstream from Shasta Lake.

The McCloud is most productively fished with nymphs, and angling is quite technical. The most effective strategy is to dead-drift nymphs through three zones in the flow: the upper zone to seduce trout that may come up aggressively, a mid-zone for those not so eager, and then the bottom where most of the biggest trout lie. Among the most effective nymph patterns are Black Rubber Legs, Golden Stones, October Caddis, Prince, and PTs. Also recommended are Woolly Buggers, Marabou Leeches, and Woolhead Sculpins. Dry flies take a backseat here, but May brings good hatches of golden stone and salmon flies. The Little Yellow Stone is consistent from June through September when October caddis come in. You'll also encounter PMDs and green drakes early in the season and blue-winged olives in the fall. Midges hatch throughout the season. Kris Kennedy of The Fly Shop in Redding recommends fluorocarbon tippets. These trout see lots of flies once the opening month of dumbness passes.

Something of a seasonal river, the McCloud fishes well in May and June, before being discolored by glacial melt. (Some anglers believe that when the river runs a chalky green, trout are less wary and more apt to take artificials and indeed such has proven to be the case.) But the best action occurs in October and November, when large lake-run browns move into the river to spawn. Fishing pressure picks up then, as well, but the public water in the canyons of the McCloud is not easily fished and to reach the best water one must clamber over rocks, ever cautious of rattlesnakes. Needless to say, the number of anglers declines rapidly as distance from parking lots increases.

RESOURCES

Gearing up: Ted Fay Fly Shop, 4310 Dunsmuir Ave. Dunsmuir, CA 96025; 530-235-2969; www.tedfay.com.

The Fly Shop, 4140 Churn Creek Rd., Redding, CA 96002; 530-222-3555; www.theflyshop.com.

Accommodations: McCloud Chamber of Commerce, P.O. Box 372, McCloud, CA 96057; 530-964-3113; www.mccloudchamber.com.

Books: *California Blue Ribbon Trout Streams* by Bill Sunderland and Dale Lackey, Frank Amato Publications.

Flyfisher's Guide to Northern California by Seth Norman, Wilderness Adventure Press.

Shasta's Headwaters: An Angler's Guide to the Upper Sacramento and McCloud Rivers by Craig Ballenger, Frank Amato Publications.

82 OWENS RIVER, UPPER AND LOWER

Location: East-central California.
Short take: Excellent browns and 'bows—those fat orange guys'll put a real bend in your rod.
Type of stream: Spring creek, tailwater.
Angling methods: Fly, spin.
Species: Brown, rainbow, carp.
Access: Moderate.
Season: Late April through mid-November.
Supporting services: Mammoth Lakes, Bishop.
Handicapped Access: Yes.
Closest TU chapter: Contact the state council of TU.

HIGH-STICKING IT, YOU DRIFTED YOUR Gold-Ribbed Hare's Ear perfectly. You could see the guy, nose down, nymphing. You led the fly perfectly. The sharp point pricked his lip, and your reel shrieked and the fish rocketed downstream. Your line melted, you fumbled to tighten the drag. Finally he stopped. And you began hustling down the gorge, picking up line as you went. It was a cinch you couldn't pull him upstream, not even with a minimal flow. You kept saying, "Wow! What a trout!" Your guide laughed and laughed, 'cause he knew better. So did you when you saw the dime-sized scales and fat orange lips of the carp. Must have gone 10 pounds. What the heck. What a fight.

The Owens's tailwaters are similar, yet different. The first issues from the base of Crowley Lake and flows for about 20 miles though a dry and narrow gorge of pocket water. Walls are steep, arid, and home to rattlers and other desert-dwelling critters. This section fishes well for smallish browns—a 12-inch fish is considered good—and occasional carp. Plunging from one pocket to another down a very steep gradient with a flow of something less than 90 cubic feet per second, the gorge section is little, but good, water. Trout feed on steady hatches of mayflies and caddis with some midge and Baetis activity in later months.

At the end of the gorge, the Owens slides into Pleasant Valley Lake and then reemerges as a cold-spring, creeklike tailwater, offering 3.3 miles of wild trout water. Open year-round, the best fishing occurs in spring and fall when electricity needs are lowest. But trout gotta eat during periods of high flows. Look for them bunched up in eddies. Where you find one, you'll find three dozen, and none of them shy about nailing your fly. Caddis is the go-to pattern here, but mayflies and stoneflies come off as well.

Above Crowley Lake, the Owens meanders through a wide and shallow glacial valley between mountains that brush 9,000 feet or more. Above Benton

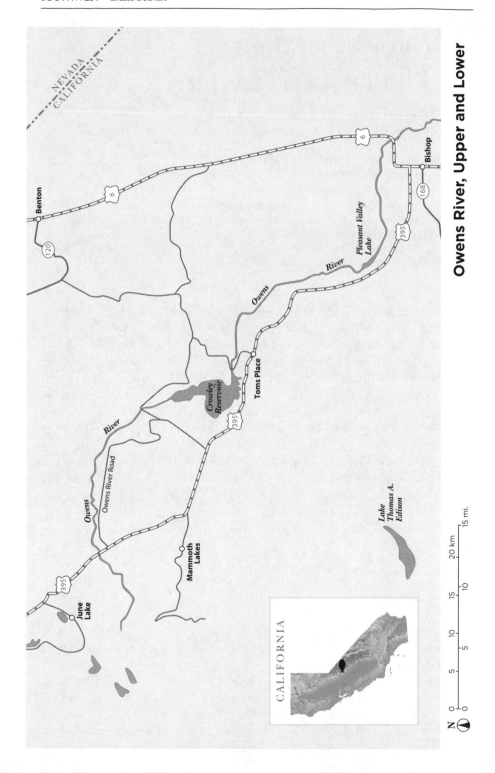

Owens River, Upper and Lower

Bridge, at least as I write this, the river is managed for wild trout. It's artificials-only water and no fish larger than 16 inches may be kept. Check regulations, though, before you fish. About two thirds of this 15-mile section is open to public angling. Additional stretches can be accessed for a fee.

Before start of the fishing season in late April, spawning rainbows run up from Crowley into the upper Owens, and spawning rainbows and browns come up in the fall. You can see them on their redds. Some of the veteran anglers who've worked this water for decades are content to give spawning fish a pass. Others for whom sight-fishing to trout of 14 inches or more is a novelty have at it. Spring fishing is largely a matter of working nymphs—Gold-Ribbed Hare's Ears and Pheasant Tails are favorites—and streamers such as a peacock and black Woolly Buggers. Toward the end of May or early June, spawners have begun to move back down the river to the lake. Dry-fly action—largely caddis with some mayflies—heats up in early July, but fish tend to be much smaller, averaging 10 to 12 inches during the height of summer. Terrestrials are very effective in the meadow section. When autumn comes brood fish return to the river. Fish big Matukas and Woolly Buggers, and tighten your Gore-Tex against blowing drizzle and snow. Winter comes early to this valley in the High Sierras.

RESOURCES

Gearing up: The Troutfiller Trout Fly, P.O. Box 7819, Shell Mall Center, Mammoth Lakes, CA 93546; 760-934-2517; www.thetroutfly.com.

Accommodations: Mammoth Lakes Visitors Bureau, P.O. Box 48, Mammoth Lakes, CA 93546; 760-934-2712; www.visitmammoth.com.

Books: *California Blue-Ribbon Trout Streams* by Bill Sunderland and Dale Lackey, Frank Amato Publications.

The Fly Fishing Guide to Northern California by Seth Norman, Wilderness Adventure Press.

83 SACRAMENTO RIVER, LOWER

Location: Northern California, below Shasta Dam.
Short take: Will 40-pound salmon unfurl your fly line?
Type of stream: Tailwater.
Angling methods: Fly, spin, bait.
Species: Rainbow, chinook, steelhead.
Access: Float or work park waters.
Season: Year-round.
Supporting services: Redding.
Handicapped access: No.
Closest TU chapter: Contact the state council of TU.

LIKE AN EXCELLENTLY BLENDED WHISKEY, the Sacramento as it flows from beneath Shasta Dam north of Redding contains waters from the McCloud, Pit, and Upper Sacramento, all first-class coldwater fisheries. Below Shasta Dam, the Lower Sacramento immediately enters Keswick Reservoir, which functions much like a 10-mile long afterbay in stabilizing flows downstream. In addition, the reservoir serves as a catchment basin for migrating steelhead and salmon. There, California Game and Fish biologists strip eggs for transport to and rearing in Coleman Hatchery. Not particularly good for anadromous species, Keswick has a solid, though local, reputation as a fishery for rainbows and browns that are, in the main, wild fish.

As it issues from beneath Keswick Dam, the Lower Sacramento ripples with power. For 25 miles, until warming too much to hold trout, this huge tailwater courses among banks of gravel and cobble, cutting against rock outcroppings here and there, surging over bars that reveal themselves when flows drop, and cantering down straight stretches as if eager to reach the sea. A number of public parks can be found in the 16-mile run from Redding to Anderson, and they provide access to the river, which is otherwise banked by private land. Flows peak in the summer during maximum power demand. In winter, electricity needs fall as do stream levels. Thus a greater amount of the river's channel is suitable for wading. This, however, is also the region's rainy season. Most anglers who fish the river float it in crafts ranging from flat-bottomed skiffs with twin outboards to driftboats to canoes and kayaks. The river is open all year from 650 feet below Keswick Dam (river is closed above that line) to the Deschutes Road bridge east of Anderson. This mileage is closed to the taking of salmon and steelhead, and only one trout, no longer than 16 inches, may be kept. Barbless hooks are required, but oddly bait—as of this writing in late 2004—is permitted.

Salmon move into the river in late September and reach their largest population in October and November. As they spawn, rainbows dine on salmon eggs. So guess which patterns are most productive? At the same time, there's a

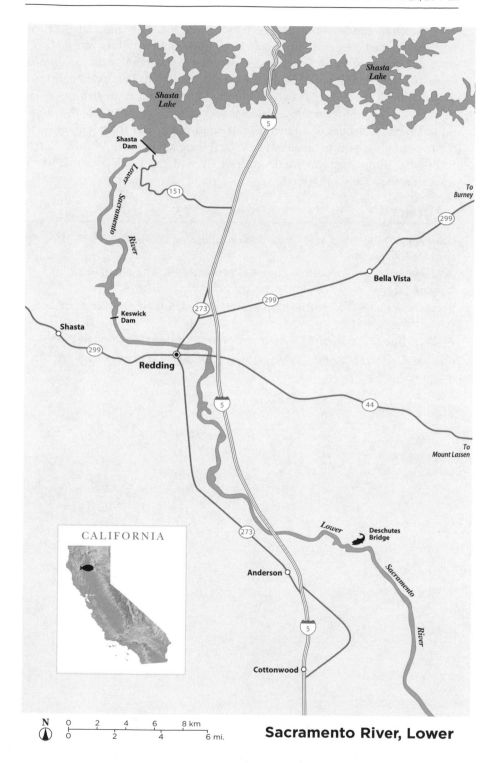

Shasta Lake

Shasta Lake

5

Shasta
Dam

Lower

Sacramento

151

River

To
Burney

299

Bella Vista

Keswick
Dam

273

299

Shasta

299

Redding

5

44

To
Mount Lassen

CALIFORNIA

273

Lower

Deschutes
Bridge

Anderson

Sacramento

5

River

Cottonwood

N

| 0 | 2 | 4 | 6 | 8 km |
| 0 | | 2 | | 4 | 6 mi. |

Sacramento River, Lower

good hatch of caddis which brings 'bows to the top. Still, most anglers fish with submerged ties, and strike indicators are required unless you feel, as I once did, that they spook fish. I've since learned better, thanks to a long lesson from TUer James Pelland down on the Guadalupe. Baetis hatch during winter months. Small Blue-Winged Olives (#16 to #18) generally draw strikes.

Is the Lower Sacramento a destination stream? I'm not sure. But if 40-pound salmon, steelies of a third that size and more, and abundant 'bows in the two- to three-pound range unfurl your fly line, then factor it into a fall trip to fish the Upper Sac, McCloud, and Fall rivers. I can think of much worse ways to waste a week in October.

RESOURCES

Gearing up: The Fly Shop, 4140 Churn Creek Rd., Redding, CA 96002; 530-222-3555; www.theflyshop.com.

Accommodations: Greater Redding Chamber of Commerce, 747 Auditorium Dr., Redding, CA 96001; 530-225-4433; www.reddingchamber.com.

Books: *California Blue-Ribbon Trout Streams* by Bill Sunderland and Dale Lackey, Frank Amato Publications.

Flyfisher's Guide to Northern California by Seth Norman, Wilderness Adventure Press.

Guide to Fly Fishing in Northern California by Ken Hanley, David Communications.

84 SACRAMENTO RIVER, UPPER

Location: Northern California, at the head of Shasta Lake.
Short take: Once you see it, you'll dream of it forever.
Type of stream: Freestone.
Angling methods: Fly, spin, bait.
Species: Rainbow.
Access: Easy and ample.
Season: Year-round
Supporting services: Dunsmuir.
Handicapped access: No.
Closest TU chapter: Contact the state council of TU.

RAILROADS FOLLOW THE RIVER. SO IT IS WITH the 35-mile stretch of the Upper Sacramento between Lakehead and Cantara. Here, the Upper Sac tumbles through a canyon and down a boulder-strewn course, ever widening and smoothing into riffles and runs as it gathers strength from numerous creeks: Soda, Castle, Flume, Shotgun, Slate, and Dog. The Union Pacific's main north–south line runs along the river's course, as does Interstate 5, yet the pounding of train and truck traffic is muted by aspen, pine, and spruce along the river's course.

The Sacramento drains Mount Shasta and neighboring peaks. Early in the season, from April into May, the river is fishable with conventional fly and spinning tackle. But in mid- to late May the river begins to rise with snowmelt from the mountains and it is generally difficult to fish into June. But then levels lower and the river becomes a paradise. During the warmer months of July and early August, fishing slows with rising water temperatures. It is best then from Mossbrae Falls—a veil of spring seeps that plunge into the river a mile and a half upstream from the bridge at Shasta Retreat—to Cantara. Most fish run between 9 and 14 inches, but 20-inch rainbows are not uncommon. Revered for their scorching runs, these rainbows, it is believed, are genetically linked to steelhead what ran this river system before the construction of Shasta Dam in the late 1930s and early 1940s.

From Box Canyon Dam down to Scarlett Way Bridge, near but not at Exit 733, requires barbless artificial lures and is catch-and-release throughout the season. Below Scarlett Way Bridge to the county bridge at Sweetbriar, the river is stocked and anglers may retain fish and no restrictions apply. But from Sweetbriar on to Shasta Lake, the Upper Sac reverts to barbless, artificials-only lures and the limit falls from five trout per day to two. From the close of the regular season on November 15 until the regular season opening on the last Saturday in April, the river is open to fishing, but all that are caught must be immediately released.

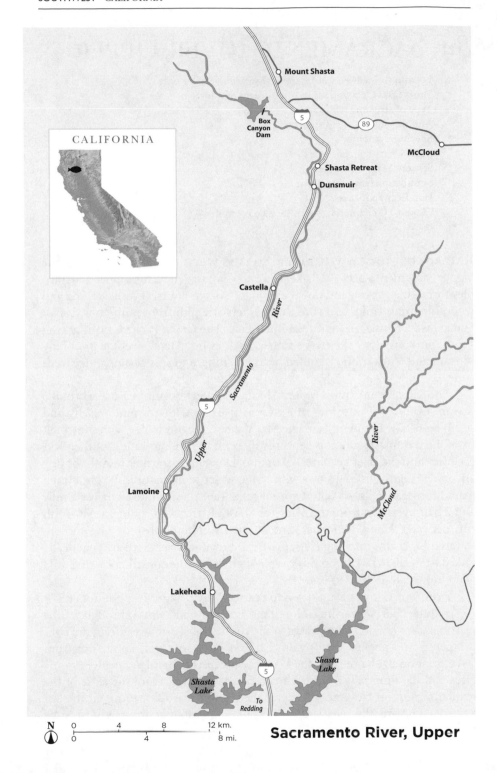

CALIFORNIA

Mount Shasta

Box Canyon Dam

McCloud

Shasta Retreat

Dunsmuir

Castella

Sacramento River

Upper

Lamoine

River

McCloud

Lakehead

Shasta Lake

Shasta Lake

To Redding

N
0   4   8   12 km.
0   4   8 mi.

Sacramento River, Upper

Fly fishers tend to use weighted Stonefly Nymphs, fished with strike indicators, early in the season. Also Bird's Nest, Hare's Ear, Prince, Pheasant Tail, and variations of Bead Head Caddis Pupae and Larvae bring success. Caddis is the primary fly in this system. When water is warm, fish morning and evening with black or elk-hair patterns in sizes from 16 to 22. June sees hatches of green drakes and salmon flies as well as some pink cahills. Blue-winged olives come off when the water cools off in September and you'll find midges all season. While fishing slows during the middle of the day, Stimulators and similar patterns can draw strikes when fished blindly in the riffles of the lower section, and don't overlook terrestrials—hoppers, ants, crickets, and similar fodder. A 4- or 5-weight rod with weight-forward floating line is ample for the Upper Sac. And in the narrow-water Soda Creek, an ability to roll cast will aid anglers confronted with brushy banks.

Access to the river is more than ample. Every two or three miles along I-5 from Lakehead to Azalea, a hamlet near Lake Siskiyou above Dunsmuir, there's an exit. Side roads either cross the railroad, leading to private retreat developments, or stop at the tracks. Anglers park outside gates (they may be open when you arrive, but padlocked when you're ready to leave) and walk in. A stroll of half a mile or so from the parking area will take you away from most other anglers. Campers will enjoy sites at Castle Crag State Park and at Sims Road about eight miles downstream. Fly and tackle shops as well as motels, restaurants, banks, and retail stores are all handy in Dunsmuir.

RESOURCES

Gearing up: Ted Fay Fly Shop, 4310 Dunsmuir Ave., Dunsmuir, CA 96025; 530-235-2969; www.tedfay.com.

Accommodations: Dunsmuir Chamber of Commerce, 4118 Pine St., P.O. Box 17, Dunsmuir, CA 96025; 530-235-2177; www.dunsmuir.com.

Books: *California Blue-Ribbon Trout Streams* by Bill Sunderland and Dale Lackey, Frank Amato Publications.

Flyfisher's Guide to Northern California by Seth Norman, Wilderness Adventure Press.

Shasta's Headwaters: An Angler's Guide to the Upper Sacramento and McCloud Rivers by Craig Ballenger, Frank Amato Publications.

85 TRINITY RIVER

Location: Central California.
Short take: Too many rising fish results in Angler ADD.
Type of stream: Tailwater with alpine headwaters.
Angling methods: Fly, spin.
Species: Rainbow, brown, salmon, steelhead.
Access: Easy.
Season: Late April through mid-November.
Supporting services: Truckee.
Handicapped access: No.
Closest TU chapter: Contact the state council of TU.

FEW SIGHTS ARE MORE INSPIRING TO AN ANGLER than seeing 'bows and browns in the 20-inch class cruising the surface of slack water as they gulp clusters of midges or Baetis drifting on the surface. My tendency is to cast everywhere at once, first here, then there, then off to my left where that monster rose. Every new wake kicks my eagerness up a notch. And in the end, of course, I've achieved nothing more than a bunch of sloppy casts that have scared the spots off these foraging trout. Best to play the game. When you spot a pod of trout feeding in a tight area, cast to where you expect a fish to rise, tighten oh-so-slowly any slack in your line or leader, and let the fly sit. If you manage its drift well, more than likely you'll get a strike and a hookup.

The upper third of Lewiston Lake on the Trinity River is one place where strategies such as this work wonderfully well. Emerging from the base of Trinity Dam, which impounds California's third largest lake, the Trinity is almost immediately backed up by another dam. Before Lewiston's waters deepen, the shallows take on the characteristics of a broad spring creek. Aquatic grasses wave in laminar flows. Browns and rainbows lie in quiet seams beneath the strands of riverweed. They'll move slowly to intercept a drifting midge or mayfly larvae, then ease back to their station. Only one thing changes this sedate behavior: when there's a hatch or a stocking of fingerlings. Radiant heat from the sun triggers the daily Baetis hatch, typically about midmorning. As the hatch progresses, trout become more aggressive and reach a state where they're feeding with abandon. Midges typically follow the Baetis and, in both cases, nymph patterns or emergers fished just under the film are most effective.

The most popular trout water on the Trinity begins at the base of Lewiston Dam and extends 20 miles down to Junction City where Canyon Creek enters. At one time, two miles of this from the base of the dam to the Old Lewiston Bridge was managed as fly-fishing-only water. No more, apparently. As this is being written, anglers may keep five trout per day, with 10 in possession, and use any legal tackle. You should, however, check current fishing regulations.

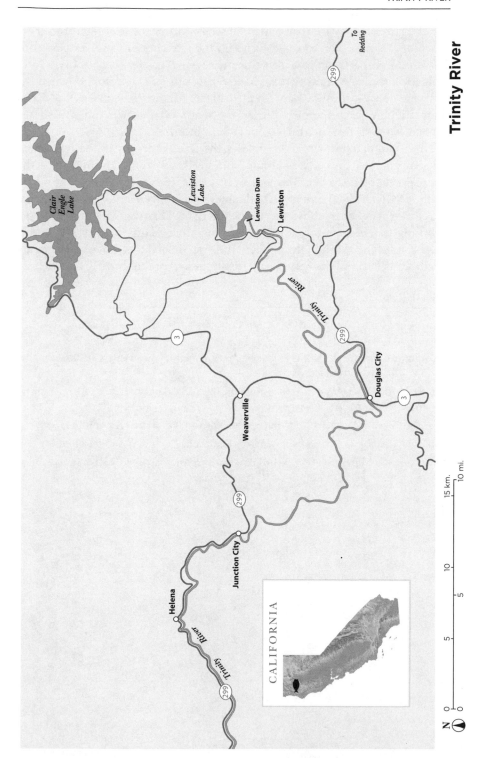

Trinity River

On the last Saturday in April when the season opens, little golden stones are hatching. Salmon flies, too, are found on the stretches of the river closest to Lewiston Dam early in the season. Streamers—that usual array of Buggers and Golden Stonefly Nymphs that we hate to use, but quickly resort to when the chips are down—are always apt to entice bigger fish on this mileage. Caddis do their thing in heavy numbers during the shank of summer, and terrestrials, particularly ants, produce throughout warm months.

In addition to browns and rainbows, the Trinity sees strong spring and fall runs of chinook and silver salmon and steelhead trout. Though once the river's strain of Loch Level browns went to sea, Iron Gate Dam on the Klamath, of which the Trinity is a tributary, and Trinity Dam dramatically reduced the viability of those species in the river. That said, angling for these lightning-fast behemoths adds an exciting dimension to the river below Lewiston. Chinook and silvers enter the system in June. They're joined by steelhead in fall, and the best month for all three is probably early October.

RESOURCES

Gearing up: Trinity Fly Shop, P.O. Box 176, Lewiston, CA 96052; 530-623-6757; www.trinityflyshop.com

Accommodations: Trinity County Chamber of Commerce, Weaverville, CA 96093; 530-623-6101; www.trinitycounty.com.

Books: *California Blue-Ribbon Trout Streams* by Bill Sunderland and Dale Lackey, Frank Amato Publications.

Flyfisher's Guide to Northern California by Seth Norman, Wilderness Adventure Press.

Guide to Fly Fishing in Northern California by Ken Hanley, David Communications.

Trout Fishing in Northern California by Ron Kovach, Marketscope Hourglass Books.

86 TRUCKEE RIVER

Location: Central California.
Short take: The river to fish between skiing and your second divorce.
Type of stream: Freestone.
Angling methods: Fly, spin.
Species: Rainbow, brown.
Access: Easy.
Season: Late April through mid-November.
Supporting services: Truckee.
Handicapped access: No.
Closest TU chapter: Contact the state council of TU.

THE TRUCKEE RIVER BEGINS AT THE OUTLET OF LAKE TAHOE, crashes through a 12-mile gorge-like valley beneath the Sierra Nevadas, slows, and breaks east as it enters the Donner Pass and the village of Truckee, and then makes a run for the Nevada state line. The entire route covers nearly 30 miles and much of it is open to public fishing. Those who know it divide the river into three sections: Lake Tahoe to Truckee, Truckee to the outflow from Boca Reservoir, and the mileage below Boca outflow.

With steeply forested mountains looming on either side, the run from the dam to the confluence with Donner Creek west of Truckee is classic freestone trout water. Fishing is prohibited for 1,000 yards below the outlet proper, but the rest of this section provides excellent fishing for stocked trout. Runoff from the high Sierras shoots through this section in May and June, turning most of the river the color of dirty chalk. The exception is the 4.2-mile stretch from the outlet to the junction of Bear Creek at Alpine Meadows. This section seldom discolors, and, while higher than normal, fishes well with streamers and hardware. Nymphing is the most effective tactic, here, though Baetis and midges hatch sporadically. Caddis provide the best bet for dry-fly fishers.

As it nears Donner Pass, the gradient lessens and the river broadens. Fishing deteriorates through the cluster of highways, railroads, interstates, and assembled businesses, but picks up again where Trout Creek comes in from the north. That marks the beginning of 14 miles of wild trout water that's governed by artificials-only, two-trout-of-at-least-15-inches regs. The first four miles of this section winds through sagebrush, and secondary roads shadow its course. Access is ample from numerous pulloffs. Add generally easy wading and reasonable hatches of caddis and mayflies throughout the season, and you'll know why lots of fly fishers work this water for rainbows and, occasionally, lunker browns. Fishing tapers off in July and August with the warming of the high desert sun.

Perhaps the best of the wild trout Truckee starts with the inflow of Prosser Creek. The river becomes faster and deeper. Access becomes limited to those

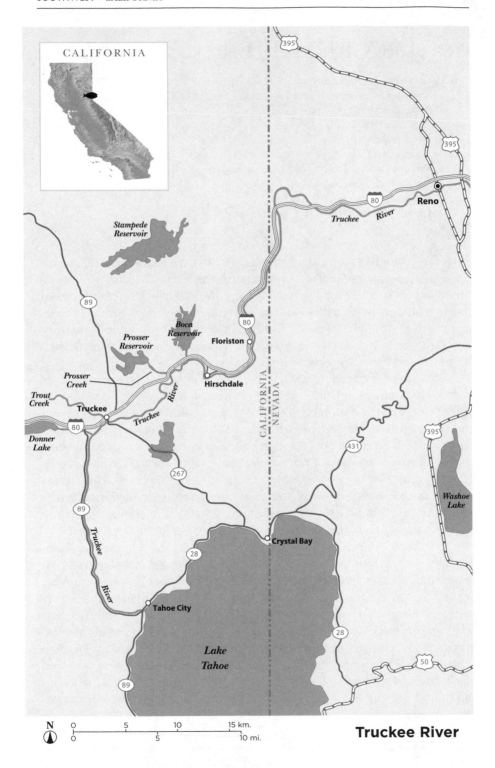

CALIFORNIA

Stampede
Reservoir

Boca
Reservoir

Prosser
Reservoir

Floriston

Prosser
Creek

Hirschdale

Truckee   River

Trout
Creek

Truckee

Truckee

Donner
Lake

CALIFORNIA
NEVADA

Crystal Bay

Washoe
Lake

Truckee

River

Tahoe City

Lake
Tahoe

Reno

Truckee   River

N

0   5   10   15 km.
0   5   10 mi.

Truckee River

willing to hike canyon trails or float. Wading can be challenging. But the benefits are there. Trout are less wary and will chase big streamers. The specially regulated section of the Truckee ends at Boca Bridge. Below, the 10 miles of river are heavy with good trout and increasing populations of smallmouth. On its sprint to the Nevada state line, the Truckee runs through a number of small canyons. Best access is found in the upper part of this section, from Hirschdale to Floriston.

RESOURCES

Gearing up: Truckee River Outfitters, 10200 Donner Pass Rd., Truckee, CA 96161; 530-582-0900; www.renoflyshop.com.

Reno Fly Shop, 294, East Moana Lane, #14, Reno, NV 89502; 775-825-3474; www.renoflyshop.com.

Accommodations: Truckee-Donner Chamber of Commerce, 10065 Donner Pass Rd., Truckee, CA 96161; 530-587-2757; www.truckee.com.

Books: *California Blue-Ribbon Trout Streams* by Bill Sunderland and Dale Lackey, Frank Amato Publications.

Fly Fishing the Sierra Nevada by Bill Sunderland, Aguabonita.

Fly Fishing the Tahoe Region by Stephen Rider Haggard, Aguabonita.

Sierra Trout Guide by Ralph Cutter, Frank Amato Publications.

87 SAN JUAN RIVER

Location: Northern New Mexico.
Short take: Zillions of midges with 'bows to match.
Type of stream: Tailwater.
Angling methods: Fly, spin.
Species: Rainbow.
Access: Easy.
Season: Year-round.
Supporting services: Navajo Dam.
Handicapped access: Yes, at Texas Hole.
Closest TU chapter: Rio Grande.

NOT BEING OVERLY BRIGHT AND TOO DUMB TO ASK, the first time I saw one I had no idea what'n hell a San Juan Worm was supposed to imitate. Ubiquitous as they are in fly fisher's boxes on Western and winter waters, I figured that the red was an attractor, and fish went for them because they look like half-inch mini-worms. Well, sort of. Actually, "worms" in fly-fisher's parlance generally refers to the larval stage of insects of the genus *Chironomidae*. Ranging in color from red to pinkish white, they cling to bottoms until dislodged by increased stream flow, an angler's boot, or the urge to evolve into the bug that buzzes up our noses and behind our specs. The cold, constant flows of the San Juan couldn't be better midge habitat. It's the go-to fly on this New Mexico tailwater. Don't let me mislead you. On the San Juan, you'll find caddis and mayflies, too, as well as leeches.

Though rainbows, browns, and a few cutts are found for a couple dozen miles below Navajo Dam, it's the first 10 miles that attract nearly all anglers. And of that, the first quarter mile below the dam is reserved strictly for catch-and-release angling with an artificial fly or lure with a barbless hook. The next 3.5 miles, known as the "Trophy Water" along State Route 511, gets most of the attention. From the base of the dam, the channel braids among numerous willow-capped islands in the Upper and Lower Flats sections. During low flows of winter and early spring, you'll find dry-fly fishing with midge patterns. When runoff swells the river in May and June, the water spreads out into high-water channels in the willows. As long as it is clear enough to fish—and it often is—you can work each of these little runs as if it were a tiny creek. Short, accurate casts are a must, as is stealth. Later, as the water falls, the riffles and pools in the main stem become accessible to wading anglers. The gradient of the San Juan is not as steep as many other Western tailwaters, thus currents are slower and trout have more time to inspect a fly before taking. Anglers adept at managing the drift of their flies so that drag is imperceptible will achieve consistent

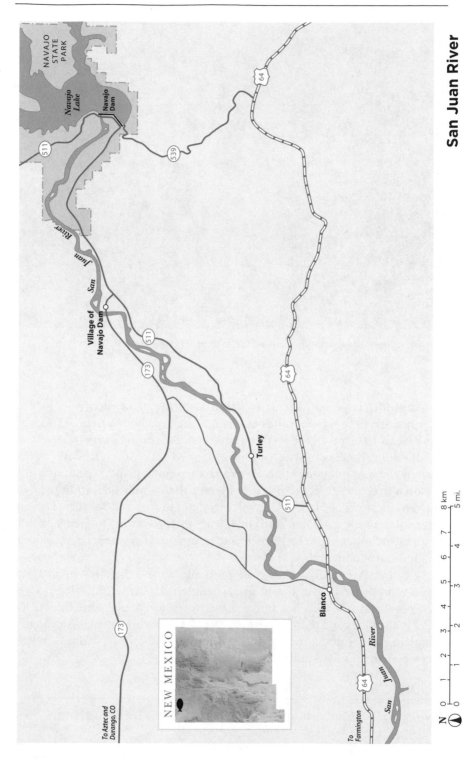

San Juan River

NAVAJO
STATE
PARK

Navajo Lake

Navajo Dam

511

539

64

San Juan River

Village of
Navajo Dam

511

173

64

Turley

511

173

Blanco

64

San Juan River

To Aztec and
Durango, CO

NEW MEXICO

To
Farmington

N

0   1   2   3   4   5   6   7   8 km
0   1   2   3   4   5 mi.

The cold, constant flows of the San Juan couldn't be better midge habitat.

hookups with large fish. The flats section is apt to get crowded, even in winter when daytime temperatures can reach the 50s. But somehow there always seems to be room for everyone, and the fish couldn't care less.

If wading is not your style, or you've planned a stay of several days (a good idea, by the way—nobody but a writer like me should plan to spend only one day on a river and expect to fish it well), take the 14-mile float from the dam down to the town of Blanco. This will carry you to flats and bars generally inaccessible to wading anglers. And you'll have an opportunity to dredge Woolly Buggers and other big wet streamers and nymphs down where large, seldom-caught browns and rainbows hide.

Nearby Aztec and Bloomfield offer nice motels and chain restaurants. But if you want the real flavor of this place, hang out at Abe's, Chuck Rizuto's, or the Sportsman Inn. This is a funky desert town where everyone carries rod tubes in their cars and more waders than work clothes are hung outside to dry. Durango is the closest airport with good commercial service, and if you fly in there, plan to visit the Animas River as well.

RESOURCES

Gearing up: Abe's Motel and Fly Shop, 1793, Hwy. 173, Navajo Dam, NM 87419; 505-632-2194; www.sanjuanriver.com.

Rizuto's Fly Shop and San Juan River Lodge, 1796 Hwy. 173, Navajo Dam, NM 87419; 505-632-3893; www.rizutos.net.

Books: *Flyfisher's Guide to New Mexico* by Van Beacham, Wilderness Adventure Press.

Fly Fishing in Northern New Mexico by Craig Martin, Ed., U. of New Mexico Press.

88 GUADALUPE RIVER

Location: Central Texas.
Short take: Texas trout? No kidding!
Type of stream: Tailwater.
Angling methods: Fly, spin.
Species: Rainbow.
Access: Easy.
Season: Year-round.
Supporting services: Gruene.
Handicapped access: No.
Closest TU chapter: Guadalupe River.

THE GUADALUPE RIVER WAS GREEN AS CHINESE TEA WITH A HINT of milk when TUer and guide James Pelland and I stepped into it gingerly on an early April morning. Murky and deep, the water dashed along the base of a cliff draped in the flora—laurel blooms amid tufts of juniper and creamy yucca flowers—of this arid Texas jungle midway between Austin and San Antonio. On the water, an occasional caddis and Baetis struggled free of surface film. A smattering of brown drakes surfed down the current. A rainbow of Rubenesque physique shouldered her way out of the jade flow and nabbed the fly. Catching sight of the double-hand span of her back, I suddenly understood that Texas trout wasn't an oxymoron. In the next few days, we'd see more, many more, of these big 'bows in this funky tailwater.

Were it not for James and the 4,000-plus members of the Guadalupe River Chapter, the chances of jousting with these beauties would be next to nil. Since 1974, GRTU and Texas Parks and Wildlife have planted more than two million fingerlings and catchable trout (rainbows and some browns) in the river. Their efforts have been so successful that the TU members rated this 10-mile tailwater the top trout stream in the Southwest. Even more remarkable, the Guadalupe has a darn good shot at producing wild trout populations one day.

The closing of Canyon Dam on the Guadalupe in 1964 created a river with flows as cold as the Hiwassee in east Tennessee or the San Juan in New Mexico. Cold water dramatically changed the river environment, opening the possibility of creating the first year-round trout fishery in Texas. Texas TU members began to congregate at this river, the only game in town, though a few wild rainbows are found in Kitterick Canyon in the far northwest corner of the state. GRTU was formed in 1968, and ever since the chapter has been a very savvy steward of the river.

As is the case everywhere, water is an economic commodity. In the late 1990s, the Guadalupe Blanco Water Authority (GBWA) wanted to restrict guaranteed summer releases to maintain relatively high pool levels in Canyon Lake and store enough capacity to sell water to meet the needs of agricultural

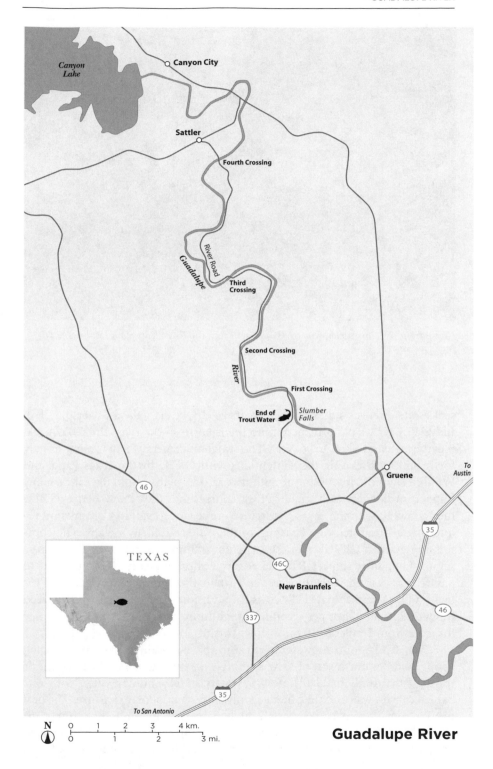

Canyon Lake

Canyon City

Sattler

Fourth Crossing

River Road

Guadalupe

Third Crossing

Second Crossing

River

First Crossing

End of Trout Water

Slumber Falls

Gruene

To Austin

46

35

TEXAS

46C

New Braunfels

337

46

35

To San Antonio

N

0   1   2   3   4 km.
0   1   2   3 mi.

Guadalupe River

"Texas trout" isn't an oxymoron on the Guadalupe River; you'll see plenty of big rainbows in this funky tailwater.

real estate interests suffering from years of dry spells. Like a poker player in Judge Roy Bean's old jurisdiction up the road from the river, the GBWA was playing its hand close to its vest. The water managers weren't being exactly forthright in disclosing their intentions with GRTU or the Texas Parks and Wildlife Division. In public, the authority said its plans would have little if any impact on flow levels. Turned out, of course, that they knew better. GRTU filed a lawsuit with the Texas Natural Resource Conservation Commission requesting a "contested case hearing" of the water authority's plans. The commission granted GRTU's request. (There's nothing Texans love better than a scrap.) Long story short, GRTU raised a war chest of nearly 100,000 dollars to pay fees associated with the case, and when the commission ruled in TU's favor, GBWA had to pay TU's costs. In addition, the settlement guaranteed flows of 200 cubic feet per second, enough to extend the summer-over range for trout from 5 miles to 10 miles downstream.

The 10 miles of trout water begin at the base of Canyon Dam near Sattler, about 20 miles northwest of New Braunfels on Interstate 35. The river winds through the thinly bedded limestones of the Hill Country, often with one bank a canyon wall and the other a gently sloping floodplain pasture. The best fishing comes from November through February. As air temperatures increase, fish become more concentrated in the top four miles of the tailwater, and in spring holes along the river's course. GRTU members tend to wade wet when they can. Chest waders are de rigueur, however; hippers and trouser-length waders are too short. In places, the riverbed is gravel, but in others it's composed of grooved ledges two feet or more in depth. This is one place where a wading staff is well worth the annoyance. So too is a good net. Bring one with an 18-inch opening. At least one of your fish will be that long.

Public access to the river is scant, but five dollars will buy you a parking spot at any of a dozen canoe liveries along the route. Or you can log onto GRTU's Web site and make arrangements to buy an annual parking pass (about $100) or find a new friend who'll take you fishing. You'll need a non-resident Texas fishing license and trout stamp. Licenses can be bought at a K-Mart or Wal-Mart on your drive to the river. Be warned that Texas Hill Country is extremely sensitive to heavy rainfall, and it receives more than its share. One storm dumped 36 inches of rain in a day! Because the river is so sensitive to high water, check NOAA.gov or other weather services for three-day forecasts. Anything longer is just a guess. Scheduled releases from Canyon Dam can be found at GRTU.org.

RESOURCES

Gearing up: Action Angler & Outdoor Center, 9751 River Rd., New Braunfels, TX 78132; 830-964-3166; www.actionangler.net.

Gruene Outfitters, 1629 Hunter Rd., New Braunfels, TX 78130; 830-625-4440; www.grueneoutfitters.com.

Accommodations: New Braunfels Chamber of Commerce, P.O. Box 311417, New Braunfels, TX 78131-1417; 800-572-2626; www.nbcham.org.

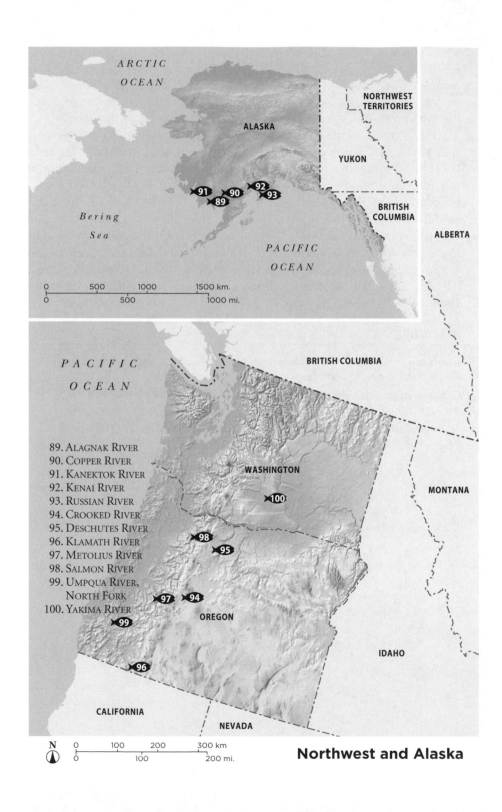

ARCTIC
OCEAN

ALASKA

NORTHWEST
TERRITORIES

YUKON

BRITISH
COLUMBIA

ALBERTA

Bering
Sea

91 90 92
89 93

PACIFIC
OCEAN

0   500   1000   1500 km.
0   500   1000 mi.

PACIFIC
OCEAN

BRITISH COLUMBIA

WASHINGTON

MONTANA

100

89. ALAGNAK RIVER
90. COPPER RIVER
91. KANEKTOK RIVER
92. KENAI RIVER
93. RUSSIAN RIVER
94. CROOKED RIVER
95. DESCHUTES RIVER
96. KLAMATH RIVER
97. METOLIUS RIVER
98. SALMON RIVER
99. UMPQUA RIVER,
    NORTH FORK
100. YAKIMA RIVER

98
95

97 94

99

OREGON

IDAHO

96

CALIFORNIA

NEVADA

N
0   100   200   300 km
0   100   200 mi.

Northwest and Alaska

NORTHWEST

ALASKA

OREGON

WASHINGTON

89 ALAGNAK RIVER

Location: Southwest Alaska.
Short take: Isolated, expensive, and well worth the second mortgage.
Type of stream: Freestone.
Angling methods: Fly, spin.
Species: King, red, silver, pink, and chum salmon; rainbow, grayling, Dolly Varden trout.
Access: Remote—floatplane required.
Season: June through April.
Supporting services: King Salmon.
Handicapped access: No.
Closest TU chapter: Contact the state council of TU.

"WILD AND SCENIC" IS THE NATIONAL PARK SERVICE DESIGNATION for the Alagnak River. It flows for some 56 miles from a pair of lakes through a string of class II and III rapids beneath towering cliffs and stands of dark forest. Other sections meander through 20 miles of braided channel, passing boggy meadows as they scoot down gravel runs over sandbars and into pools. At its mouth, the Alagnak feeds Bristol Bay, the mother lode of Alaskan salmon. And the bay reciprocates, charging the river with fish.

Tens of thousands of all five species of Pacific salmon spawn in this river. Kings (20 to 60 pounds) are present from late June through August. You'll find silvers (8 to 17 pounds) from late July into September, and sockeyes (4 to 9 pounds) from mid-June through mid-July. Chum salmon (8 to 17 pounds) and pinks (2 to 8 pounds) arrive in mid-July and are catchable into late August. Rainbows up to 10 pounds and grayling to 4 pounds run from the second week in June through September. Add Arctic char and Dolly Varden, and you've got yourself a river. There's no bad time on this river, and the best time to be there is probably either early June when rainbows are ravenous or in September when they are gorging on salmon flesh and spawn. Count on cool, but not cold temperatures. Count too, on drizzle and a bit of breeze—but you won't mind. You'll be too busy hooking fish. A 6- or 7-weight is ideal.

Alas, there is no cheap way to access this river. Most who fish it arrive via floatplane from King Salmon, a community of about 400 on Bristol Bay. The normal drill is to fly in Saturday night from Anchorage and be collected by your outfitter on Sunday for the trip into the lodge or tent camp, a number of which are permitted on the river. Excluding airfare and lodging in Anchorage, a week (and it's foolish to do less) on the Alagnak will set you back at least $3,500 and some packages top $6,000. Last-minute supplies can be purchased in King Salmon.

Alagnak River

RESOURCES

Gearing up and accommodations: Through your outfitter.

Books: *The Angler's Guide to Alaska* by Evan and Margaret Swenson, Falcon Press.

Fly Fisher's Guide to Alaska by Scott Haugen, Dan Busch, and Will Ricek, Wilderness Adventure Press.

Fly-Fishing Alaska's Wild Rivers by Dan Heiner, Stackpole Books.

90 COPPER RIVER

Location: South-central Alaska.
Short take: Alaska has two Copper Rivers. Glacier-fed, the first carries some steelhead and rainbows in its tributaries. The second is the one everybody raves about.
Type of stream: Freestone.
Angling methods: Fly.
Species: Rainbow trout, Pacific salmon.
Access: Restricted.
Season: June through September.
Supporting services: Private lodges.
Handicapped access: Fishing from a boat is possible, but otherwise no.
Closest TU chapter: Contact the state council of TU.

WHILE ALASKA BOASTS AT LEAST TWO "COPPER RIVERS," the one everyone points to is the one down on the south side of Lake Iliamna. Stair-stepping down a chain of lakes, first Meadow, then Upper and Lower Copper, Mack Minnard once called it a "beautiful piece of water with all the attributes of a first class rainbow river." He should know. An Alaska Fish and Game biologist, he worked in the drainage for 18 years. The Copper is one of the few Alaskan rivers that sees hatches of mayflies, stoneflies, and caddis. Stoneflies—mahogany in #6 and #8 and lime greens in #16s and #18s—begin to come off in mid-June. They're followed by yellow sallies (#14s and #16s) toward the end of the month. Caddis appear in the full range of colors and sizes. By early July, mayflies and stoneflies have faded, but there's caddis activity into the end of the month.

By the third week of July, top water action virtually ceases. Sockeye are the first of Alaska's five salmon species to spawn in the river, and their eggs, maturing in gravelly redds, have attracted the interest of rainbows. Soon they're feeding on the bottom like hogs at a trough. So guess which patterns are most effective? Eggs. In virtually any color. And flesh flies—combed-out strips of orange yarn tied on a hook. You may also stir up some action with mouse patterns, big Matukas, and Muddlers. Most rainbows run in the 12-inch to 20-inch range, but the number of 24-inch fish is large enough so most anglers play one or two while they're on the river. The further the season goes, the fatter the fish. July and August are peak months for salmon on the river, but that too begins to pale as the weeks slide into September when the 'bows are at their largest.

Thirteen miles of the Copper, from its mouth on Intricate Bay up to a set of 50-foot falls, are navigable. The drill here is to jetboat upstream and then drift down, fishing runs around gravel bars, banks undercutting sluices, and the heads and tails of slick pools. Anyone can boat up the river. The banks,

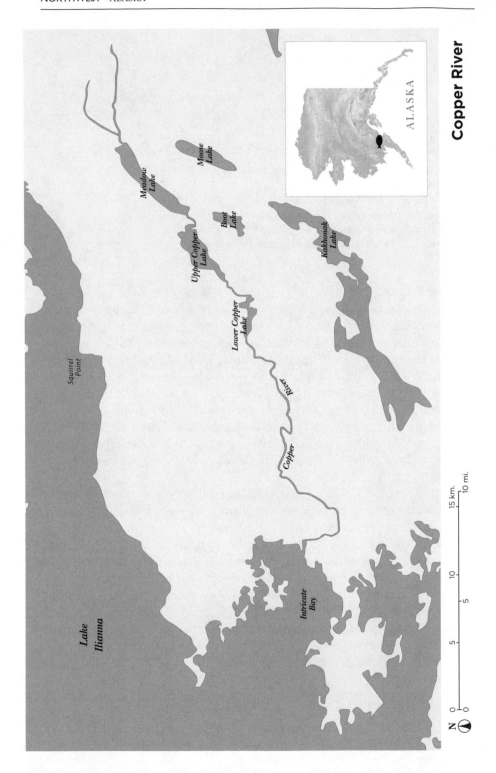

Copper River

ALASKA

Meadow Lake

Moose Lake

Boot Lake

Kakhonak Lake

Upper Copper Lake

Lower Copper Lake

Squirrel Point

Copper River

Lake Iliamna

Intricate Bay

N

Rainbows of 24 inches are the draw on the Copper River in the Iliamna region of Alaska.

however, are private property and trespassing is prohibited, except within the normal high-water marks that define the river's main corridor. Wading is okay, but a trip into the bush is not.

You won't find much freelance activity on this river. Flown or boated in from the plethora of lodges around Lake Iliamna, most anglers fish with guides. In the last two decades, fishing pressure on the river has more than trebled. Some guides, like the late Ted Gerkin, believe that the Copper suffers from overfishing and declining runs of the salmon that bring trout into the system. His argument was that the increasing commercial salmon catch is limiting the numbers of salmon that come into the Copper, thus causing decreases in the amount of food—eggs and decaying flesh—on which rainbows feed.

Subject, of course, to vagaries of weather, the river should continue to fish well. With no limit on the number of anglers, the number of days of solitude on the river will be few indeed. Does that make a difference in the quality of your angling experience? That's up to you. The story is the same on most of the established rainbow and salmon fisheries in the forty-ninth state and elsewhere as well. Big fish draw crowds, and if they get to be too much for you, head up above the falls and play with the grayling (12 inches to 20 inches) for a while.

RESOURCES

Gearing up: Lodges carry local flies and lures, but otherwise, fill your tackle boxes before you come. Numerous lodges and outfitters guide in the area.

Accommodations: King Salmon Visitors Center, P.O. Box 298, King Salmon, AK 99613; 907-246-4250; www.alaskanha.org/king-salmon-visitor-center.htm.

Books: *The Angler's Guide to Alaska* by Evan and Margaret Swenson, Falcon Press.

Fly Fisher's Guide to Alaska by Scott Haugen, Dan Busch, and Will Ricek, Wilderness Adventure Press.

Fly-Fishing Alaska's Wild Rivers by Dan Heiner, Stackpole Books.

91 KANEKTOK RIVER

Location: Western Alaska.
Short take: Amazing hatches for an Alaskan river.
Type of stream: Freestone.
Angling methods: Fly, spin.
Species: King, red, silver, pink, chum, rainbow, grayling, Dolly Varden.
Access: Remote—floatplane required.
Season: June through September.
Supporting services: King Salmon.
Handicapped access: No.
Closest TU chapter: Contact the state council of TU.

NO BETTER WAY IS THERE TO KNOW A RIVER than to float the entirety of its course. It is as if you have watched it grow from childhood. You see it take its first steps, there where it flows from its womb of a lake. Each tributary, rivulet, or foaming feeder stream adds to its age and broadens its experience. You can read a river's history written on its terraced banks, in the strand lines cutting its beaches, in flotsam tossed head high in the trees. The genealogy of the Kanektok is plain to see, and worth a look.

Many outfitters offer weeklong floats down the Kanektok, one of a dozen major rivers found in the Togiak National Wildlife Refuge, well north of the famed Bristol Bay/King Salmon region of famous Alaskan salmon and rainbow streams. If you are not opposed to roughing it in tents, eating good grub, and smelling of whatever potion you believe will hold mosquitoes at bay (it won't), then by all means arrange a journey down this almost pristine river.

Your air charter service will deposit you on Pegati Lake, which, with its sibling Kagati, forms the headwaters of the Kanektok. While no major whitewater impedes your raft, the river hustles right along through a broad bowl among the mountains before entering a valley sharply defined by mountains that close in from all sides. Peaks rise 1,500 to 2,000 feet above the river. At the mouth of each tributary, in pools below riffles, in eddies along the bank and behind boulders in the main stream, you'll find fish.

Bring two rods: a 5-weight and a 7 or soft 8. The upper third of the river is wonderful for grayling—called the "sailfish of the north" because of its high fan-shaped dorsal fin—and char. Rainbows and all five species of salmon (though pinks return only on even years) enter the river in June and July. August is the best month for targeting all five. Or you may want to hold off until rainbows begin to fatten on salmon eggs and flesh. Time your trip for late August, and you'll have silver salmon take your flies as well. About 45 miles downstream from Pegati, the river emerges from the Aklum Mountains and meanders through taiga forests of black spruce, cottonwood, and birch. Braids in the channel are more frequent than in the mountain run. Guides know which

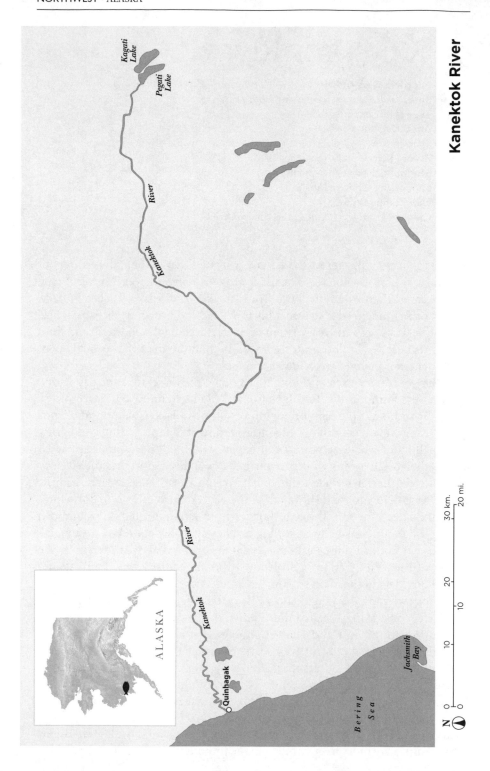

Kagati
Lake

Pegati
Lake

River

Kanektok

River

Kanektok

Quinhagak

ALASKA

Bering
Sea

Jacksmith
Bay

Kanektok River

N

0
0

10
10

20
20

30 km.
20 mi.

to follow. At the end of a week, you'll have reached Quinhagak and will hop a plane back to Dillingham for the connection to Anchorage.

The trouble, of course, with writing a profile like this is that more anglers will be encouraged to make the trip. Increased number of rafters, vegetation beaten down by campers, bank and gravel bed erosion from jetboats blasting up, are all are taking a toll on this river. The answer lies, I suppose, in some sort of a permitting system similar to that used to control commercial use on other famed rivers in the Lower 48.

RESOURCES

Gearing up and accommodations: Through your outfitter.

Books: *The Angler's Guide to Alaska* by Evan and Margaret Swenson, Falcon Press.

Fly Fisher's Guide to Alaska by Scott Haugen, Dan Busch, and Will Ricek, Wilderness Adventure Press.

Fly-Fishing Alaska's Wild Rivers by Dan Heiner, Stackpole Books.

92 Kenai River

Location: South-central Alaska.
Short take: Most heavily fished river in Alaska . . . with good reason.
Type of stream: Freestone.
Angling methods: Fly, spin.
Species: King, red, silver, and pink salmon; rainbow, steelhead, and Dolly Varden trout.
Access: Easy.
Season: Varies by species and location.
Supporting services: Kenai, Soldotna.
Handicapped access: No.
Closest TU chapter: Contact the state council of TU.

FOR MORE THAN 68 MILES, FROM THE OUTLET OF KENAI LAKE to its mouth near the village of Kenai on Cook Inlet, the Kenai River draws more anglers than any other river in Alaska. (And its banks face serious degradation because of the pressure.) The fact that the river lies about 100 miles from Anchorage—and is connected and then paralleled by good road—tells part of the story. The other half is that the Kenai, according to Alaska Department of Fish and Game, "hosts the largest freshwater king salmon fishery in the state." No one is sure how many kings use the river, but they begin traveling upstream in May. The early run crests in June, but is followed immediately with a run of larger fish that peaks in late July.

Kenai kings are big. The current world-record rod/reel king—a 97-pound, 4-ounce battleship of a fish—was taken here in 1985. Yet, size varies widely. Those that have spent only a year at sea before returning to spawn weigh only a few pounds. Two years of ocean life returns kings in the 10- to 20-pound range. The largest percentage of returning kings, however, has been feeding in the ocean for three years and tips the scales between 25 and 60 pounds. Weight versus years at sea comparisons vary with river drainage. Most anglers targeting kings fish from boats. The trick is to get your lure or fly down to the bottom before a king's nose. Easy access draws thousands of anglers, so if it's solitude you're seeking—or the opportunity to challenge king salmon on light fly tackle—you'll be happier elsewhere. Courtesy and patience pay huge dividends on the Kenai.

In early July, a brief but intense run of sockeye, or red salmon, enters the Kenai. They're bound for the Russian River and a number of headwater tributaries. ADFG sonar has reported more than 20,000 reds streaming up the Kenai per day, but the run lasts only a week or so. Biologists report that 16 percent of those make the turn into the Russian, and at the confluence of the two rivers, more than 1,000 anglers gather during the height of the run. Look for sockeyes in pools at the base of riffles or near shore.

Kenai River

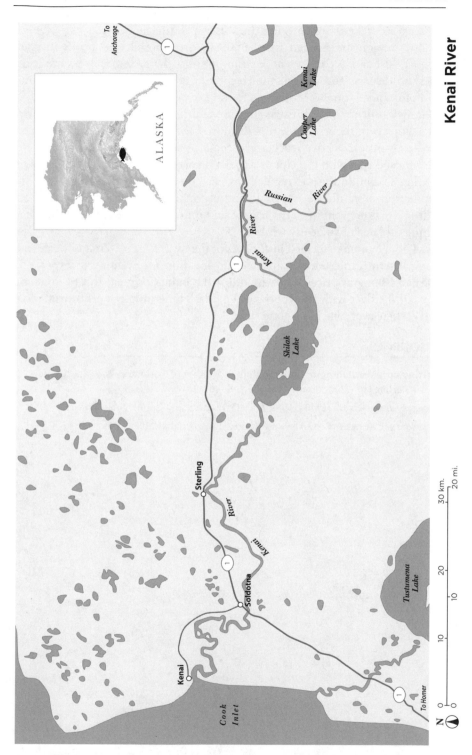

Just as sockeye are entering the Russian drainage, the first run of silver (coho) salmon are headed up the Kenai. That population peaks in mid-August, just as a second wave is steaming into the system. Silvers are more likely to disperse throughout the river seeking deeper pools as holds. You'll find pinks here, too. Best fishing is found near the river's mouth. The flesh of these fish is firm and reddish as they come in from the ocean, but it deteriorates quickly in their journey upstream to spawn. Rainbows live in the Kenai all year. Most productive reaches are found upstream from the confluence of the Moose River, with the Upper Kenai a favored destination. Regulations regarding season and tackle regulations vary by section of the river since the population of rainbows is being carefully managed. Anglers serious about fishing for 'bows wait until the frantic salmon season has passed, timing their fishing for late fall and early winter.

Though often described by flingers of the fly as a "zoo," "circus," or in scatological terms, the Kenai is an excellent location for a family to experience Alaskan fishing at prices that won't bust the bank. It's great fun to float sections of the river with an experienced guide. Think of it as a piscatorial block party where everyone has a good time.

RESOURCES

Gearing up and accommodations: Soldotna Chamber of Commerce & Visitor Center, 44790 Sterling Hwy., Soldotna, AK 99669; 907-262-9814.

Books: *Fishing Alaska's Kenai Peninsula* by Dave Atcheson, Countryman Press.

River Journal: Kenai River by Anthony Route, Frank Amato Publications.

93 RUSSIAN RIVER

Location: South-central Alaska.
Short take: A fine fall fishery for 'bows. Great for sockeyes during the summer.
Type of stream: Freestone.
Angling methods: Fly, spin.
Species: Red, silver, rainbow, steelhead, Dolly Varden.
Access: Easy.
Season: Varies by species and location.
Supporting services: Kenai, Soldotna.
Handicapped access: No.
Closest TU chapter: Contact the state council of TU.

ONLY A FEW FOLKS I KNOW, AND I'M SURE not one of 'em, are well-heeled enough to afford to hire a Beaver to fly into premier Alaskan rainbow water like Lower Talarik that drains into Lake Illiamna. Yet we dream of six-pound 'bows that have never known a hatchery. The Russian River is one place where you can catch them without taking a second mortgage. I think of the Russian as a tributary to the Kenai, which, indeed, it is. It is short—with only 11 miles separating its headwaters at Upper Russian Lake from its mouth on the Kenai. A trail follows most of its length. Time your trip so you arrive in September, after the waves of sockeye have reached the head of the system. You'll avoid, then, the shoulder-to-shoulder fishing for which the Russian is appropriately famed. Or come in the fly-fishing-only season, which runs from June 15 to August 20. And if, perchance, your travels bring you to this neck of the woods in April, invest a day on the Russian.

Sockeye up to six pounds or so and, to a much lesser degree, silver salmon are the draw. The first run enters the Russian in mid-June and the second surge kicks in about mid-July. Easily caught on rod and reel, these species make great table fare. My favorite recipe comes from the old April Point Lodge at Campbell River, British Columbia. Leaving the skin attached, fillet the fish. Drizzle it with olive oil, grated ginger, and a little crushed garlic. Sear it flesh-side down over charcoal, then flip it on its skin side, cover with aluminum foil, and cook for five minutes longer. Yum.

A private ferry will carry you across the Kenai to the trail along the river. Walk up as far as you want, heeding any special-regulations signs posted by Alaska Fish and Game.

Because this river and the Kenai are so popular, their banks have been trampled in a manner that puts me in mind of cows in a spring creek. ADFG is deeply engaged in bank habitat restoration. Anglers are urged to stay on established paths that lead from the trail to the stream. Once on the river, wading is preferred over trying to fish from the bank. Streamside vegetation is to be

Russian River

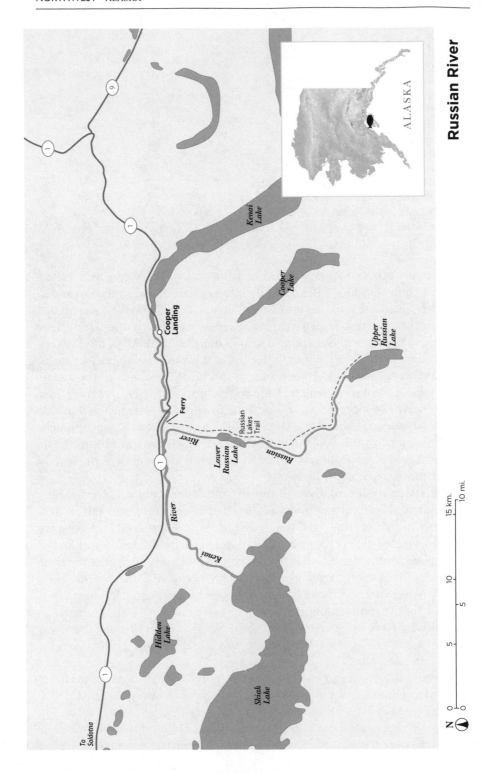

ALASKA

To Soldotna

Hidden Lake

Skilak Lake

Kenai River

Lower Russian Lake

Russian River

Russian Lakes Trail

Ferry

Upper Russian Lake

Cooper Lake

Cooper Landing

Kenai Lake

N

0   5   10   15 km.
0   5   10 mi.

protected. The growing season here on Alaska's balmy south coast is still pretty short. Carry a trash bag with you and pick up streamside litter.

RESOURCES

Gearing up and accommodations: Soldotna Chamber of Commerce & Visitor Center, 44790 Sterling Hwy., Soldotna, AK 99669; 907-262-9814.

Books: *Fishing Alaska's Kenai Peninsula* by Dave Atcheson, Countryman Press.

River Journal: Kenai River by Anthony Route, Frank Amato Publications.

94 CROOKED RIVER

Location: Central Oregon.
Short take: Kick back on this laid-back river.
Type of stream: Tailwater.
Angling methods: Fly, spin.
Species: Redband rainbow.
Access: Easy.
Season: Year-round.
Supporting services: Prineville.
Handicapped access: No.
Closest TU chapter: Contact the state council of TU.

OREGON IS A STATE FULL OF BIG RIVERS. And they're the main attraction for out-of-state anglers. Wide water, heavy flows, runs of large fish, plenty of elbowroom for flotillas of driftboats, that's the rap on destinations like the Deschutes. But tucked away in isolated corners of the state are little gems like the Crooked River tailwater. From beneath the 245-foot-tall, earth-fill Bowman Dam, consistent and cold flows offer about five miles of fine fishing for wild redband rainbows.

Over mossy boulders, the river trips its way through a narrow canyon. Sheer walls of dark tan basalt rise 700 feet above the streambed. Fingers of juniper, dusty gray-green the way they always look in arid climes, poke out onto narrow floodplains. But they seldom get close to the water, giving way instead to grasses and low brush not high enough to snag a backcast. Few stretches of the river are more than 50 yards wide, and not often are its runs too deep to wade. Here and there, boulders protrude from the surface, but in the main they're submerged and covered with slick mosses. Studded wading shoes are a must. Few anglers fish from boats: they're not needed because access from the riverside highway is ample and easy.

Guiding on the river since 1986, fish carver and sculptor Rodger Carbone (carbonesflyfishing.com) thinks of this river as a sort of safety valve. To the Crooked River, he likes to bring novice anglers and parents who want to teach their kids to fish. Some days on this river are difficult, and anglers are often put off by the discolored flows, a result of fine clay particles suspended in the water. Trout—generally in the 6-inch to 10-inch range—don't seem to mind the turbid water. Usually the Crooked's 'bows are eager. They'll feed readily on midges and mayflies from fall through late spring. In the coldest months, the river becomes a mid-day fishery. This is a river where you can tie on a #18 Parachute Adams, fish for a couple of hours, and let your mind wander.

About halfway between the dam and Prineville, the nearest community, the river frees itself from the canyon and slows. You'll still find trout here, but gone is the scenic isolation of the canyon stretch. Well above the lake, the

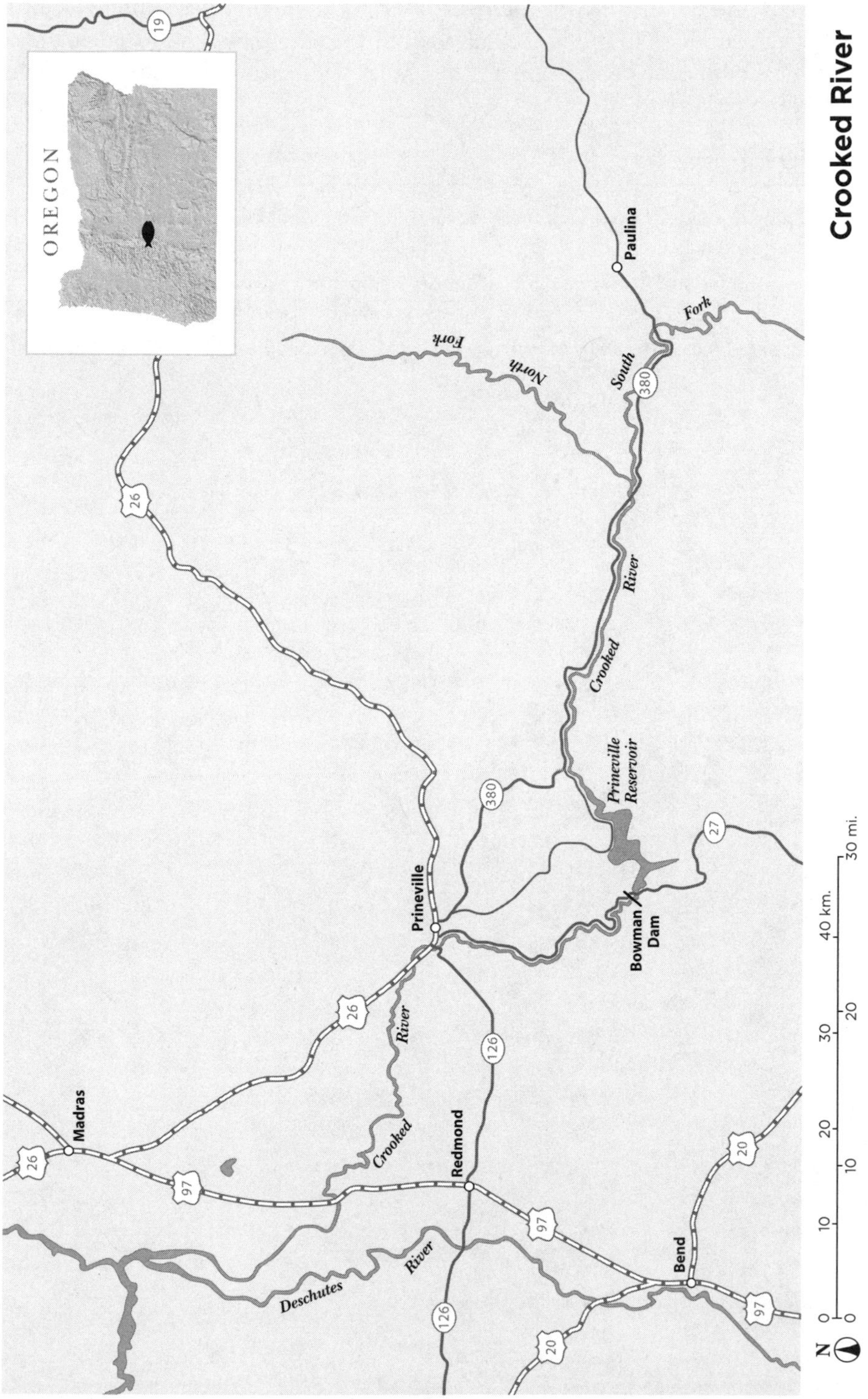

Crooked River

OREGON

Paulina

South Fork

North Fork

Crooked River

380

26

19

Prineville Reservoir

Bowman Dam

27

Prineville

380

126

26

Crooked River

Madras

26

97

Redmond

126

20

Bend

20

97

Deschutes River

N

0
0

10
10

20
20

30
30

20

40 km.

30 mi.

North and South forks of the river offer good angling for rainbows a little larger than those found in the tailwater. But reaching these waters demands a vehicle with good suspension and an angler willing to walk a couple of miles beyond road's end.

RESOURCES

Gearing up: Several fly shops in Bend, Redmond, Sisters, and Prineville can provide tackle and information.

Accommodations: Prineville-Crook County Chamber of Commerce, 390 NE Fairview, Prineville, OR 97754; 541-447-6304; www.prineville-cookcounty.org.

Books: *Fishing in Oregon* by Madelynne Diness Sheehan and Dan Casali, Flying Pencil Publications.

95 DESCHUTES RIVER

Location: North-central Oregon.
Short take: Redband 'bows, steelhead, and salmon itch to bust up your gear.
Type of stream: Freestone, tailwater.
Angling methods: Fly, spin.
Species: Steelhead, rainbow, salmon.
Access: Moderate.
Season: Year-round in some sections, but check regulations.
Supporting services: Maupin.
Handicapped access: Yes, below Maupin.
Closest TU chapter: Deschutes River.

LIKE A SOMEWHAT SQUIGGLY ARROW, THE DESCHUTES HEADS virtually due north from Pelton Dam and Lake Simtustus. For more than 100 miles to its confluence with the Columbia, the river saws its way through a layered landscape of basalt flows and beds of volcanic ash that take on subtle hues of khaki and rose depending on the play of sun and cloud. Draining the eastern slope of the Cascades, the Deschutes watershed sees scant precipitation. Snow and rain melt into the fine soils, percolate through fractured basalts, and seep into the river, providing thousands of little springs that cool the river. Minerals leached from the basalts and other igneous rocks create a fishery incredibly rich in invertebrates. Hatches of caddis, mayflies, and stoneflies are massive. For eons, they've feed trout and juvenile salmon headed seaward for the first time.

Rainbows indigenous to the Deschutes are called "redsides" by natives who claim that these are hybrids of cutthroat and rainbows. Robert Behnke asserts that the Deschutes' native 'bows are redband trout (*Oncorhyncus mykiss gairdneri*). During spawn, the gill plates, lateral line, and bellies of males turn deep burnished red. Beneath their jaws is an angry slash of vermilion, often cited as evidence of the relationship to cutthroat. Steelhead are of the same species. The difference is that steelhead, once they've left their spawning streams, seldom return. Dams on the Columbia, which interdict the migration of coho and chinook salmon as well, are the primary barrier. Though the Deschutes is managed for natural reproduction, supplemental stockings of steelhead and salmon are regularly scheduled.

Big and brawny, the Deschutes crashes across horizontal ledge rock, shoulders aside angular boulders, races through long pools that tail out in riffles. Anglers seeking steelhead (and show me one that isn't!) swing their favorite streamers downstream, mending the line so that the fly slows and rubs the nose of steelhead lying near the bottom. Others, yours truly included, prefer to skate bombers and other bushy drys on top, provoking, I devoutly hope, that Poseidon-like strike and searing run that strips me to backing instantly.

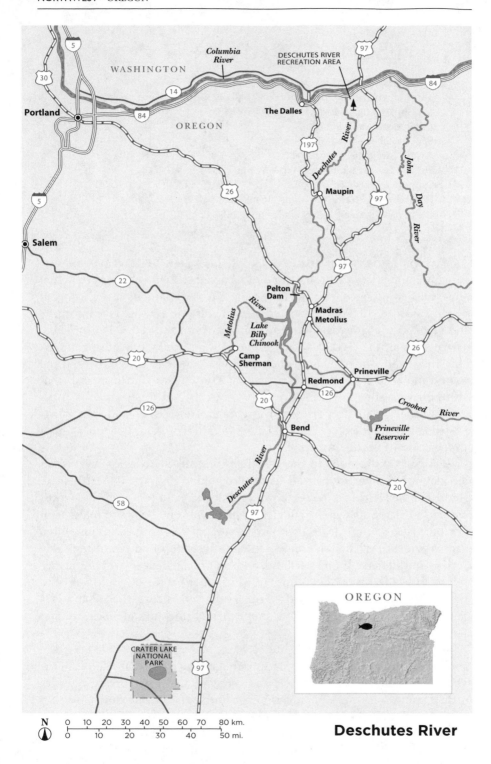

WASHINGTON

Columbia River

DESCHUTES RIVER
RECREATION AREA

Portland

OREGON

The Dalles

Deschutes River

John Day River

Maupin

26

97

Salem

22

Pelton Dam

Metolius River

Madras Metolius

Lake Billy Chinook

Camp Sherman

26

20

Redmond

Prineville

126

Crooked River

Prineville Reservoir

126

Bend

Deschutes River

20

58

97

CRATER LAKE NATIONAL PARK

OREGON

N

| 0 | 10 | 20 | 30 | 40 | 50 | 60 | 70 | 80 km. |
| 0 | 10 | 20 | 30 | 40 | 50 mi. |

Deschutes River

The odds of taking steelhead in the Deschutes are probably better than in the Umpqua simply because anglers can work more productive water in a day. Float the river through the canyon below Maupin and look for ideal runs, then beach the boat, climb out, and cast. Wear your waders, because fishing from boats is illegal.

If you want to know this river, drive up past Bend to its headwaters. The main stem of the Deschutes has its origins in Little Lava Lake and it flows through a pair of lakes—Crane Prairie and Wickiup—before tumbling over Pringle Falls and meeting the Little Deschutes at near Sun River west of U.S. Route 97. The upper waters offer reasonable angling for brooks, browns, and rainbows, and might be worth a look. The middle section of the river begins at Bend and beats a course north-northeast into Lake Billy Chinook. Aggressive agricultural usage all but waters the middle section in summer. You'll find some winter fishing here.

The largest town in this neck of the woods is Maupin, about midway between the dam and the river's mouth. Here, a few tackle shops and bed and breakfasts cater to anglers. You'll find motels and restaurants as well. What you won't find is an airport with commercial flights. Best bet is to fly to Portland, rent a car, and plan to fish the Deschutes for a week.

RESOURCES

Gearing up: Deschutes Canyon Fly Shop, 599 S. Hwy. 197, P.O. Box 334, Maupin, OR 97044; 541-395-2565; www.flyfishingdeschutes.com.

Accommodations: Maupin Chamber of Commerce, P.O. Box 220, Maupin, OR 97037; 541-395-2599; www.maupinoregon.com.

Books: *Fishing in Oregon* by Madelynne Sheehan and Dan Casali, Flying Pencil Publications.

Fishing in Oregon's Best Fly Waters by Scott Richmond, Flying Pencil Publications.

Fishing Oregon's Deschutes River by Scott Richmond, Frank Amato Publications.

Fly Fisher's Guide to Oregon by John Huber, Wilderness Adventure Press.

River Journal: Crane Prairie and Upper Deschutes by Scott Richmond, Frank Amato Publications.

96 KLAMATH RIVER

Location: Southwest Oregon.
Short take: Where rainbows rise all day long.
Type of stream: Tailwater.
Angling methods: Fly, spin.
Species: Rainbow.
Access: Easy.
Season: Year-round.
Supporting services: Ashland.
Handicapped access: No.
Closest TU chapter: Contact the state council of TU.

A TAILWATER, THE KLAMATH IS, BUT THE KIND OF CLEAR, cold, full-of-scuds tailwater that you and I are used to, the Klamath ain't. The river heads in Klamath Lake, which is fed by those wonderfully technical trout rivers, the Wood and Williamson. But though huge, Klamath Lake never gets much deeper than 12 feet or so. It warms quickly in spring, driving 'bows up into its tributaries. No sooner has its waters left the lake on their journey to the Pacific, more than 200 miles away, than the river is impounded in 16-mile-long Lake Ewana by the dam at Keno.

Often turbid and not nearly as cold as one might expect, the six miles downstream from Keno Dam offer excellent fishing for large rainbows, very good fish in the four- to six-pound category. Hatches are scant and fish feed primarily on sculpins, minnows, and crayfish. Charles Gehr, who works the fishing department in the Ashland Outdoor Store, fishes the Klamath year-round. For the stretch below Keno Dam, he recommends a dead-drifted Woolly Bugger, cast out in to the brown water and left to ride the current. When you're ready, strip it back, fast and as close to the bank as you can. Strip it all the way to your rod tip, he advises. Because of the clouded water, trout will strike that close. Charles will often cast dead downstream to work his fly tight to the bank. Average fish here run 14 to 16 inches with a solid shot at a 20- to 24-inch 'bow. Because water temperatures reach levels dangerous to fish in summer, this section of the Klamath is closed from June 16 to October 1.

About three miles below Keno Dam, the Klamath again begins to back up, impounded in J. C. Boyle Reservoir. The outflow at the base of Boyle dam splits. A minimum level of water is maintained in the river channel, but the bulk of it is diverted to the powerhouse about four miles downstream. The mileage between the dam and the powerhouse is chock-full of tame wild rainbows. Though you'll not often see a rise to a natural, pitch a #14 or #16 attractor, say a Royal Wulff, upstream, and it'll be inhaled by a 10- to 14-inch rainbow. Charles says 'bows take this way "all day, every day." The angler equipped with a 3-weight will have a ball. Sounds to me like a great place to regain confidence

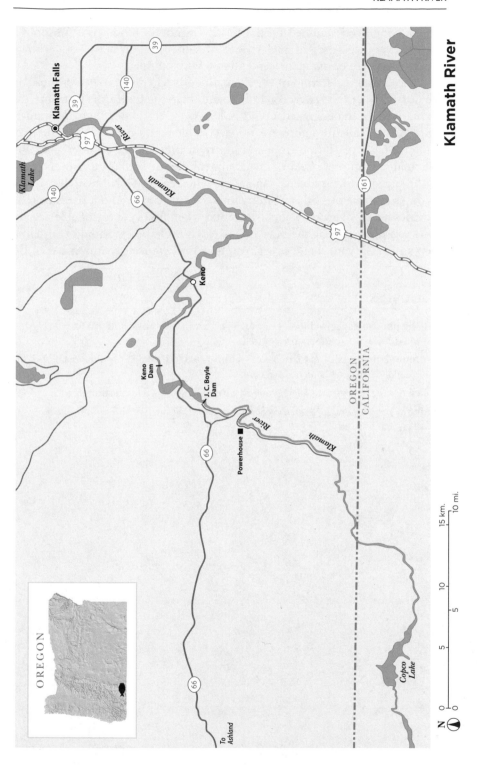

Klamath River

after having been shunned by the finicky rainbows of the Williamson. Of course, every well-dressed angler wears waders, but you need not get them wet. Banks are open and grassy and littered with boulders.

The dewatered section of the Klamath ends where at the powerhouse on the north bank of the river. For 11 miles down to the California state line, the Klamath has been designated a Wild and Scenic River. Flows fluctuate dramatically, due to calls for and curbs on electric generation. If you hit the river when it's high, you'll find trout—bigger than those in the dewatered section but smaller than those below Keno Dam—along the bank. You may get lucky and find generators off when you arrive. When the water's down, this stretch becomes a marvelous fishery throughout the entire year. And a riverside road provides plenty of access. Should you enter when flows are reasonable, try not to be too distracted by the bevy of 14- to 16-inch 'bows. Should you fail to keep an eye on your marker rock, you may find yourself swimming with the fishes.

RESOURCES

Gearing up: The Ashland Outdoor Store, 75 N. Third St., Ashland, OR 97520; 541-488-1202; www.outdoorstore.com.

Accommodations: Ashland Chamber of Commerce, 110 E. Main St., Ashland, OR 97520; 541-482-3486; www.ashlandchamber.com.

Books: *Fishing in Oregon* by Madelynne Sheehan, Flying Pencil Publications.

Fishing in Oregon's Best Fly Waters by Scott Richmond, Frank Amato Publications.

97 METOLIUS RIVER

Location: North-central Oregon.
Short take: Fast and technical, perhaps Oregon's best spring river.
Type of stream: Freestone spring creek.
Angling methods: Fly, spin.
Species: Bull, rainbow, brown, brook, Kokanee, mountain whitefish.
Access: Easy.
Season: Year-round.
Supporting services: Sisters.
Handicapped access: No.
Closest TU chapter: Contact the state council of TU.

ISSUING FROM SPRINGS BURBLING UP FROM THE base of a volcanic stock that rises 3,400 feet above the river valley, the Metolius flows nearly due north for about 18 miles before hanging a right and running another 10 miles into the west arm of Lake Billy Chinook. Along the way it gathers water from scores of springs and feeder creeks. Dropping about 1,000 feet, the velocity of the stream is fairly high for a spring creek, making wading somewhat challenging. Though exposed to the sun for all of its run, water temperatures seldom exceed 50 degrees Fahrenheit.

Because basalts make up most of the country rock in the drainage, the Metolius is quite rich and supports fine populations of mayflies, stoneflies, and caddis. According to Steve Erickson who guides out of The Fly Fisher's Place in nearby Sisters, the green drakes of late May and June probably constitute the signature hatch on this river, but caddis are the mainstay of summer.

Once heavily stocked, plantings of fish stopped in the late 1980s or early 1990s. Today the Metolius is managed as wild trout water. Rainbows dominate and you'll find some browns and brookies. Many anglers target bull trout, which come up from Billy Chinook to spawn in the fall and remain in the river for the winter. Also present are mountain whitefish, the salmonoid that nobody loves but which takes dries and fights well anyway. Kokanee salmon arrive with the bull trout, and you'll see them easily, bright vermilion against the dark green of aquatic vegetation waving in the strong current. The surface of the river seems to seethe with boils, seams, and a million microcurrents. Tippets must be long and fairly fine, and flies, on the smallish #18 to #20 size. Short, precise casts are more easily managed than long, lovely tight-looped works of art!

Catch-and-release rules apply to all species, including bull trout, for the full length of the river. From its origins down to Bridge 99, angling is restricted to fly fishing only with barbless hooks. From the bridge down to the lake, only artificial lures may be used. The main stem is closed to all angling above Allingham Bridge from November 1 through May 21.

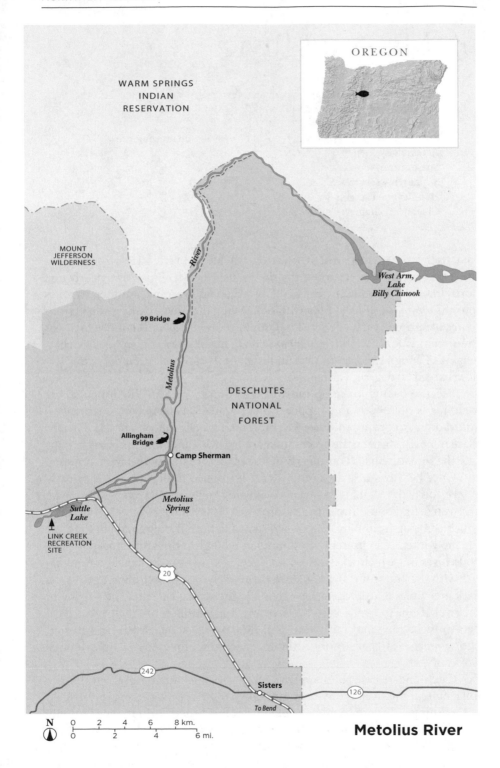

WARM SPRINGS
INDIAN
RESERVATION

OREGON

MOUNT
JEFFERSON
WILDERNESS

River

West Arm,
Lake
Billy Chinook

99 Bridge

Metolius

DESCHUTES

NATIONAL

FOREST

**Allingham
Bridge**

○ **Camp Sherman**

*Suttle
Lake*

*Metolius
Spring*

LINK CREEK
RECREATION
SITE

20

242

Sisters

126

To Bend

N

0 2 4 6 8 km.
0 2 4 6 mi.

Metolius River

Along the east bank, a forest service road follows the river to Bridge 99. Beyond the bridge, the roadbed continues and eventually degrades into a trail. Campsites are numerous, and opportunities for solitude increase with each step downstream. Because of the stiff flows and lack of fish-holding structure, trout tend to lie along the edges. I'd carve out a section of the river I'd like to fish, start at the downstream end, wade out a bit, and cast back to the bank as I worked my way upstream.

RESOURCES

Gearing up: The Fly Fisher's Place, 151 W. Main St., Sisters, OR 97759; 541-549-3474; www.theflyfishersplace.com.

Accommodations: Bend Chamber of Commerce, 777 NW Wall St., Bend, OR 97701; 541-382-3221; www.bendchamber.org.

Books: *Fishing in Oregon* by Madelynne Diness Sheehan and Dan Casali, Flying Pencil Publications.

Fishing in Oregon's Best Fly Waters by Scott Richmond, Flying Pencil Publications.

98 SALMON RIVER

Location: Northwest Oregon.
Short take: Superior steelheading and trout not an hour from Portland.
Type of stream: Freestone.
Angling methods: Fly, spin.
Species: Steelhead, rainbow, cutthroat, brook.
Access: Moderate.
Season: Late May through October 31.
Supporting services: Welches.
Handicapped access: No.
Closest TU chapter: Contact the state council of TU.

SWOLLEN WITH MELT WATER AND CARRYING TONS of rock flour, braids of the Salmon River trickle from fingers of the Zigzag Glacier on Mount Hood's southwest slopes and coalesce near the junction of U.S. Route 26 and Oregon Route 35, just west of Tom, Dick and Harry Mountain. Designated a Wild and Scenic River in 1988, the Salmon is the only river in Oregon to carry the designation for its entire length, from headwaters to mouth, in this case at the confluence with the Sandy River, 33.5 miles downstream. Typically, glacially fed streams run chalky gray with fine sediments, but just below the road junction, the Salmon enters a broad alpine meadow where it slows dramatically. Here the fines settle to the bottom. At the base of the meadow, Mud Creek enters—itself cleansed of sediment by a small lake midway down the mountain—and together they plunge into an increasingly steep valley

For almost 20 miles, the Salmon works its way down through the Huckleberry-Salmon Wilderness, a forest heavy with Douglas and other firs, and western red cedar and hemlock that have never faced a logger's saw. Along the way it plunges over a number of waterfalls, some more than 100 feet high. Above the falls, native wild cutthroat predominate, interspersed with a few brookies stocked before we knew better. A few rainbows, also wild fish but a mixture of stocked and native strains, are found in plunge pools beneath the falls.

Steelhead ply the Salmon from Sandy River up as far as Final Falls. You'll find steelies in this river all year long, says Mark Bachmann, author of a book on the Sandy and owner of the Fly Fishing Shop in Welches. And he should know—the Salmon flows through his backyard. The winter run brings the most and biggest fish and the summer run is smaller. And after the summer steelies have come and gone, a third, or fall, group makes its way up river. Maps show the Salmon River National Recreation Trail following the river for much of its course. It does, but what it doesn't tell you is that it runs along the mountainside a few hundred feet above the bank. Be prepared to climb down and climb up.

Salmon River

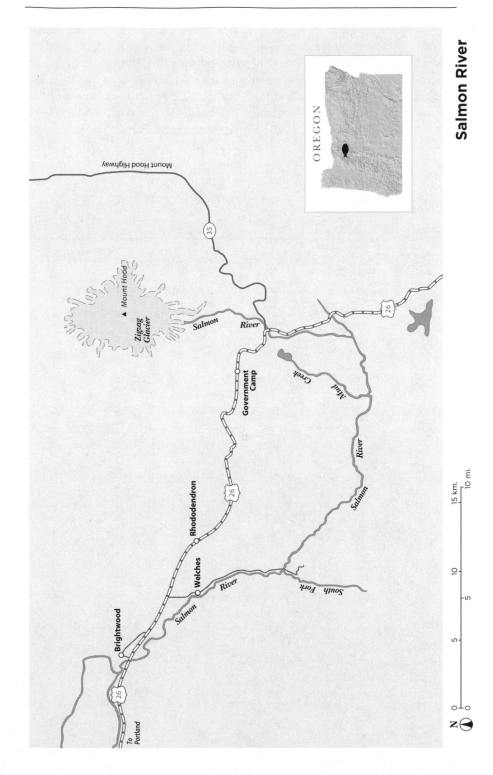

Mark believes that there's no river as beautiful as the Salmon, and he may be right. Despite stringent regulations governing the harvesting of steelhead and salmon (check before you fish!), fish populations seemed to have been declining, however. The reason: heavy poaching. "The river is having a very difficult time," he said. The best time to fish the Salmon is in June and July. Streamers fished downstream work on steelhead. Trout above the falls take the usual assembly of Green Drakes, Pale Morning Duns, Caddis, Stoneflies, and worms and ants that tumble from streamside vegetation. If you fish this river, and it's really worth a visit, bring your raingear. Welches is on the western side of the Cascades and receives upwards of 100 inches of rain per year. In case your math is rusty, that's about an inch of rain every three days.

RESOURCES

Gearing up: The Fly Fishing Shop, P.O. Box 368, 67296 E. Hwy. 26, Welches, OR 97067; 503-622-4607; www.flyfishusa.

Accommodations: Mt. Hood Area Chamber of Commerce, P.O. Box 819, 65000 E. Hwy. 26, Welches, OR 97067; 503-622-3017l; www.mthood.org.

99 UMPQUA RIVER, NORTH FORK

Location: Southwest Oregon.
Short take: Zane Grey's favorite river is still the best.
Type of stream: Freestone.
Angling methods: Fly, spin.
Species: Steelhead.
Access: Moderate.
Season: Year-round.
Supporting services: Roseburg.
Handicapped access: Yes.
Closest TU chapter: Middle Rogue Steelhead.

ON HIS WAY TO CAMPBELL RIVER TO FISH for Tyee, Zane Grey paused at the confluence of Canton and Steamboat Creeks, in the then unspoiled watershed of the North Fork of the Umpqua. The year was 1932. Logging had yet to strip towering firs from the high Cascades to the northwest of Crater Lake. Grey and his entourage returned annually, drawn by heavy runs of summer steelhead, the best then as now in the continental United States. His camps were spotless and well organized and often equipped with a makeshift fighting chair, where he worked out, practicing for his battles with marlin. It was in his camp on this river that he suffered his fatal stroke in 1937.

Umpqua has changed from the days when Grey fished it. Though lakes have been impounded in its headwaters, the river still flows cold and as green as jade through the black rock canyon where he fished it. Steelhead, fewer now, but still many, make annual runs. Summer fish start in June and are in the system until October. The winter run begins in January and reaches its peak in February before tailing off in March. The 32 miles from Rock Creek upstream to Soda Springs Dam is fly-fishing-only, catch-and-release water. Below Rock Creek general rules apply.

The river is narrow in the mileage upstream from Rock Creek. You might say it flows through a gorge of slab rock, chutes, occasional gravel bars, and runs so deep that, though the water is very clear, you'll never see the bottom. It is good water, ideal for an 8-weight. Most of the year water levels are stable, but in spring and fall, rains on late or early snow can raise the river precipitously. Most of the pressure on the river comes in summer when the steelhead are a little smaller. In summer, approximately 2,400 wild fish and twice that number of stockers are found in the river. But the best fishing is in winter, when gray skies and blustery days drive snow in your eyes as you cast. The steelhead of winter run larger, and anglers are many times fewer. Purists on the river use floating lines with non-weighted flies. Others depend on sinking lines and heavy flies to get down to where big steelhead lie. The patterns that produce fish on the North Fork of the Umpqua are larger by a size or two than

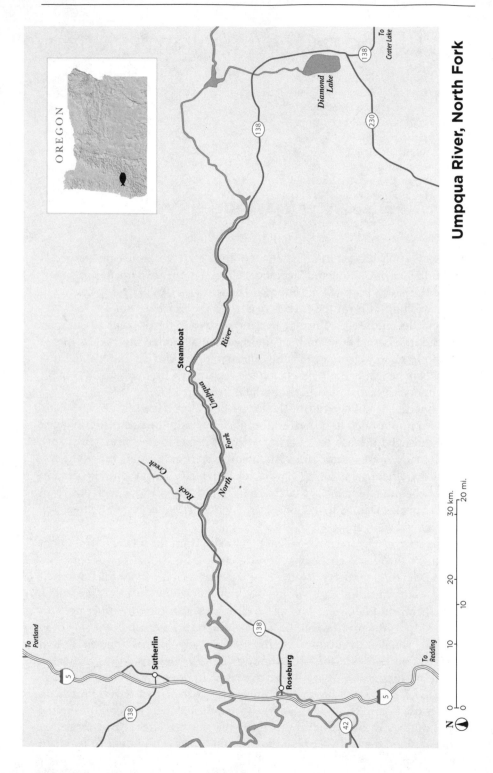

Umpqua River, North Fork

Steamboat Creek was the first tributary of the North Umpqua to capture Zane Grey's imagination.

those used on other steelhead rivers. Among favorites are streamers in black, gray, brown, and purple: Green Butt Skunk, Muddlers, and the Buck-Tailed Caddis. The best time of the angling day is early morning, after the fish have had a night's rest.

If you fish for summer steelhead, there's a chance that you'll hook a sea-run cutthroat. These must be released immediately. The river is closed to taking of any kind of trout, a situation that's likely to prevail for the next few years.

Accommodations abound in the valley downstream around Roseburg, a small city a few miles south of the Interstate 5 bridge over the river. And up in the river valley, on the spot where Zane Grey spent his last summer, sits the charming Steamboat Inn. This is the quintessential streamside fishing lodge—gourmet meals, well-appointed rooms with porches overlooking the river, an extensive fishing library, and an excellent tackle shop. The lodge is the focal point for efforts to protect the watershed, and owners Jim and Sharon Van-Loan spearhead a worldwide network of activists.

RESOURCES

Gearing up: Blue Heron, 109 Hargis Rd., Idleyld, OR 97447; 541-496-0488.

Accommodations: Roseburg Chamber of Commerce, 4105 S. E. Spruce St., Roseburg, OR 97470; 541-672-2648.

Books: *Fishing in Oregon's Best Fly Waters* by Scott Richmond, Flying Pencil Publications.

100 YAKIMA RIVER

Location: Central Washington.
Short take: Best bet for spring and fall.
Type of stream: Top-draw tailwater.
Angling methods: Fly, spin.
Species: Rainbow, cutthroat, chinook.
Access: Easy to moderate.
Season: Year-round.
Supporting services: Yakima, Ellensberg.
Handicapped access: No.
Closest TU chapter: Contact the state council of TU.

A BACKWARD RIVER, THE YAKIMA IS. When other Western rivers flow high, wide, and muddy with snowpack melt, the Yak runs low and clear. Summer brings falling water to most rivers, but not this one. As irrigation needs build with summer's temperatures, the Yakima's channels fill. Spring flows rarely exceed a few hundred cubic feet per second. You'll have ten times as much in August. With the growing season done, the three reservoirs—Keechelus, Kachess, and Cle Elum—at the river's head end close their gates to gather water for the next season's discharge.

While the Yakima's tributaries poke up the sides of Mount Rainier, fishing in the river doesn't really begin upstream of the top-release outflow of Lake Easton. The exception is the bottom-draw tailwater from Keechelus down to the town of Cle Elum. In the fall, after levels have returned to minimum, eager 8- to 12-inch trout will take almost any dry. This run is unfishable in summer. At Cle Elum, waters from that system are added to that from Lake Easton. For the next 40 miles down to Ellensburg, the river flows, sometimes in braids, through a broad and arid valley. Pools separate gravel bars. Much of this run is forested. Access varies with public launching ramps separating parcels of private land. There's another four miles of river below Ellensburg, but it sees little pressure because everybody's headed for the canyon section that begins at Thrall.

Rainbows are the mainstay, but you'll find a goodly number of cutts. In addition, an effort is underway to restore chinook salmon, once native to the river. Reared at the Yakima/Klickitat Fisheries Project research hatchery at Cle Elum, juvenile chinook are being stocked to supplement populations of wild Naches River chinook. Wild salmon (those with adipose fin intact) must be released immediately. Check regulations for creel limits on hatchery stocks.

Rather than the river vanishing into a canyon the way the Colorado does below Lees Ferry, a high plateau followed by an elevated series of ridges rise more than 2,000 feet above the water. Through the gorge runs Washington Route 821 and, on the other side of the river, a railroad grade. Access is easy

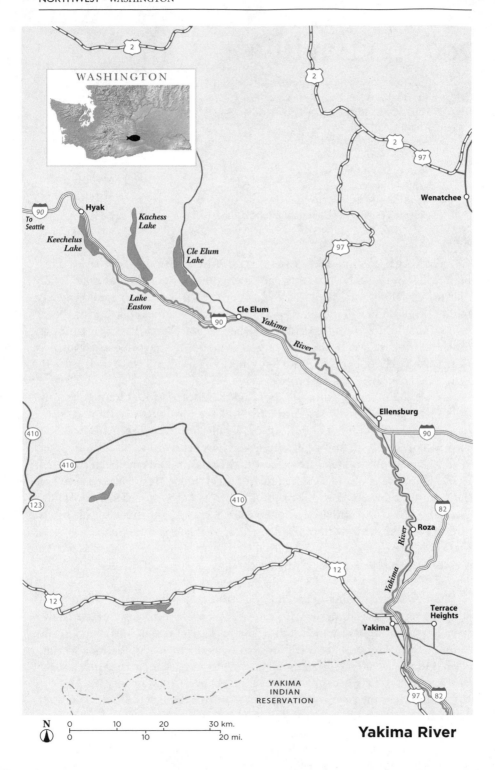

WASHINGTON

2

2

2

97

Wenatchee

90
To
Seattle

Hyak

Keechelus
Lake

Kachess
Lake

Cle Elum
Lake

97

97

Lake
Easton

Cle Elum

90

Yakima

River

Ellensburg

90

410

410

123

410

410

82

Yakima River

Roza

12

12

Yakima River

12

Terrace
Heights

Yakima

YAKIMA
INDIAN
RESERVATION

97   82

N
0   10   20   30 km.
0   10   20 mi.

Yakima River

and ample. In this steep valley, the river retains its primary character, though pocket water and large boulders are more prevalent. This is the premier run of the Yakima. And it's an invertebrate factory. The skwala hatch gets things started in late February, lasting into early April. March browns pick up in the midst of their namesake month and terminate when flows begin to rise in June. You'll also find some green drakes in May and June. Caddis are steady on the river from March on to November. Pale morning duns are prevalent from mid-May into mid-July, overlapping with the salmon fly hatch, which comes into its own in June. Baetis are available spring and fall. In the early part of the year, use #18 to #20, and plan to go one size smaller in the fall. In addition, terrestrials and normal streamers—the Woolly Bugger, for instance—work quite well. And, midges continue to hatch throughout the winter.

RESOURCES

Gearing up: The Evening Hatch, P.O. Box 1295, 2308 Yakima River Canyon Rd., Ellensburg, WA 98926; 866-482-4480; www.theeveninghatch.com.

Red's Flyshop, P.O. Box 186, Ellensburg, WA 98926; 509-929-1802; www.redsflyshop.com

Worley Bugger Fly Co., 306 S. Main #3, Ellensburg, WA 98926; 509-962-2033; www.worleybuggerflyco.com.

Accommodations: Yakima Chamber of Commerce, 10 N. Ninth St., Yakima, WA 98901; 509-248-2021; www.yakima.org.

Books: *Yakima River Journal* by Steve Probasco, Frank Amato Publications.

INDEX